THE POWER OF VISUAL BASIC

Mark Goodwin

First edition—1992
ISBN 1-55828-183-5

Printed in the United States of America
10 9 8 7 6 5 4 3 2 1

MIS:Press books are available at special discounts for sales promotions, premiums, fund-raising, or educational use.
Special editions or book excerpts can also be created to specifications.

For details contact: Special Sales Director
MIS:Press
a subsidiary of Henry Holt and Company, Inc.
115 West 18th Street
New York, NY 10011

TRADEMARKS

IBM is a trademark of IBM Corporation
Microsoft, MS, MS-DOS, Visual Basic, and Windows are trademarks of Microsoft Corporation

Dedication

To one of the coolest dudes around: Ryan.

Acknowledgment

I would like to express my most sincere thanks to the people at Microsoft Corporation. Their generous contribution greatly eased the writing of this book.

Contents

PART III: THE VISUAL BASIC STATEMENTS AND FUNCTIONS 461

xviii ■ *The Power of Visual Basic*

Introduction

Long before the IBM PC was introduced, Microsoft was the world leader in Basic programming languages. Indeed, Microsoft Corporation was built on its excellent line of Basic interpreters. Since the PC's introduction, Microsoft Basic has continued to grow into a very diverse collection of interpreters and compilers. Without a doubt, one of Microsoft's most revolutionary Basic language products is its excellent QuickBasic compiler. QuickBasic was responsible for turning the Basic programming language from its spaghetti code origins into a modern structured programming language. Recently, Microsoft's new QBasic interpreter has done for Basic interpreters what QuickBasic did for Basic compilers. Simply put, Microsoft has turned the Basic programming language into a robust language that's not only easy for the beginner to understand but powerful enough for even the professional programmer to utilize.

Besides its line of Basic language products, one of Microsoft's most successful products is Microsoft Windows. Although Windows was a slow starter, the introduction of Windows 3.0 saw Windows take off like a rocket. Consequently, Windows development has soared in the past few years. Unfortunately, Windows development has been hampered by the need to use heavy duty programming languages like C to write even a simple Windows program. Furthermore, writing a Windows application required the Windows Software Development Kit and a lot of time spent overcoming the very steep learning curve that faces all beginning Windows programmers. Although many larger companies could afford to invest the time and money into developing Windows applications in such a manner, smaller firms and individual programmers could rarely devote the time and money that was required to develop Window applications.

Recognizing that Windows development could be further enhanced by somehow simplifying the development process, Microsoft decided to produce a language just for building Windows applications. Because the Basic programming language has proven through the years that it is the ideal language for programmers who can't devote a lot of time learning the ins and outs of the language itself, Microsoft decided that its Windows programming language would be a Basic compiler. The result of Microsoft's efforts is Visual Basic. Essentially, Visual Basic is a Quick Basic-like compiler just for developing Windows programs. Unlike more traditional programming languages, Visual Basic is a true Windows application itself. Therefore, Visual Basic programs can be created, run, and debugged right in the Windows environment. Additionally, Visual Basic allows the programmer to create windows and controls simply by drawing them on the screen. Once a program's windows and controls are in order, the programmer need only add little snippets of code here and there to make them interact correctly. Thus, Visual Basic automatically takes care of the nitty-gritty that used to be required to write Windows applications.

To better understand how you can put "the power of Visual Basic" to work for you, this book presents a tutorial and reference guide for the Visual Basic programming language. The tutorial will get the experienced programmer up to speed with the Visual Basic programming language in short order. In addition, the reference guide provides all of the nuts-and-bolts details about the Visual Basic programming language's many built in statements, functions, methods, properties, and events. In order for you to understand the Visual Basic programming language more fully, *The Power of Visual Basic* offers many short example programs and illustrations to reinforce the textual material.

What You Need To Use This Book

To use this book, you will need an IBM-compatible machine with an 80286 processor or better, Microsoft Windows 3.0, and Microsoft Visual Basic. You should note that Visual Basic requires a hard drive, a mouse, MS-DOS 3.1 or higher, and one megabyte of memory. Furthermore, Microsoft recommends an EGA or higher-resolution monitor. Although the tutorial section of this book is written for someone with at least a working knowledge of computer programming and the Windows environment, even the novice programmer should find the book's reference section an invaluable tool. As with any programming language, you will need a great deal of patience while you are learning the ins and outs of Visual Basic. If you are familiar with QuickBasic or QBasic, you will feel right at home with Visual Basic. If you've done any Windows development with more traditional programming languages, you're in for a real treat. Visual Basic's way of doing things is a far cry from the more traditional Microsoft C and SDK torturous approach to developing windows applications.

Style Conventions

This book uses the following style conventions to more clearly illustrate the components of the Visual Basic programming language:

Style	*Description*
Keyword	A word printed in bold type is a Visual Basic keyword. Any bold punctuation marks are required to make the program statement syntactically correct.
user supplied	An italicized word indicates the position for information that the programmer must supply.
[optional]	Items surrounded by brackets are optional.
{choice1 | choice2}	Two or more items surrounded by braces and separated by a vertical bar are items the programmer is required to choose between.
Repeating...	An item followed by three dots may be repeated in the statement.
Program . . . Fragment	A column of three dots indicates a program fragment.

PART I

A Visual Basic Tutorial

This section of *The Power of Visual Basic* presents a tutorial for learning the Visual Basic programming language. It covers such topics as predefined data types, operators, program flow, subroutines, procedures, arrays, records, text file input/output, and binary file input/output.

Chapter 1

A Simple First Program

T he first step in understanding the Visual Basic programming language is to become familiar with the components of a Visual Basic program. Accordingly, this chapter starts by acquainting you with all of the Visual Basic programming language's basic and essential components. The chapter concludes with a simple first program, which serves to illustrate how all of Visual Basic's components are brought together to form an actual working program.

Keywords

All programming languages use a special set of words to perform certain functions. These special words are called **keywords**. Note that some programmers like to refer to keywords as **reserved words**. These two terms are interchangeable and either is acceptable. Figure 1-1 presents a complete list of the Visual Basic programming language's keywords. Because a

Abs	EndDoc	Len	Randomize
AddItem	Environ$	Let	ReDim
And	Eof	Line	Refresh
AppActivate	Eqv	Line Input	Rem
As	Erase	LinkExecute	RemoveItem
Asc	Erl	LinkPoke	Reset
Atn	Err	LinkRequest	Resume Return
Beep	Error	LinkSend	RGB
ByVal	Error$	Load	Right$
Call	Exit	LoadPicture	RmDir
CCur	Exp	Loc	Rnd
CDbl	FileAttr	Lock	RSet
ChDir	Fix	Lof	RTrim$
ChDrive	For	Log	SavePicture
Chr$	Form	Long	Scale
CInt	Format$	Loop	Second
Circle	FreeFile	LSet	Seek
CLng	Function	LTrim$	Select Case
Clear	Get	Mid$	SendKeys
Close	GetData	Minute	SetData
Cls	GetFormat	MkDir	SetFocus
Command$	GetText	Mod	SetText
Const	Global	Month	Sgn
Control	GoSub	Move	Shell
Cos	GoTo	MsgBox	Show
CSng	Hex$	Name	Sin
CurDir$	Hide	NewPage	Single
Date$	Hour	Not	Space$
DateSerial	If	Now	Spc
DateValue	Imp	Oct$	Sqr
Day	Input #	On	Static
Declare	Input$	Open	Step
Deftype	InputBox$	Option Base	Stop
Dim	InStr	Or	Str$
Dir$	Int	Point	String$
Do	Integer	PrintForm	String
DoEvents	Is	Print #	Type
Double	Kill	Print	Sub
Drag	LBound	PSet	Tab
Else	LCase$	Put	Tan
End	Left$	QBColor	TextHeight

Figure 1-1 The Visual Basic reserved words.

TextWidth	TimeValue	Unload	While
Then	To	Unlock	Width #
Time$	Type	Val	Write #
Timer	UBound	Weekday	Xor
TimeSerial	UCase$	Wend	Year

Figure 1-1 The Visual Basic reserved words (continued).

programming language's keywords all serve a specific purpose, they can never be used in a program for anything other than their intended purpose.

Identifiers

As their name implies, identifiers are used to identify something in a Visual Basic program. For example, program variables, constants, statements, and functions all require a name. Consequently, each of them is assigned a unique identifier. When constructing an identifier, you must keep four rules in mind:

1. An identifier can be up to 40 characters in length.
2. An identifier can be composed of letters, numbers, the decimal point, and the type declaration characters (%, &, !, #, @, and $).
3. The first character of an identifier must be a letter.
4. Type declaration characters must be the last character of the identifier name.

The following are some examples of valid identifiers:

```
NUMBER
count
NAME$
RECORDNUMBER&
First
```

You should note that case isn't significant with Visual Basic identifier names. Thus, the identifiers **FIRST**, **first**, and **First** are all equivalent and would refer to the same thing.

Below are some examples of invalid identifiers. Next to each identifier is an explanation of how the identifier violates the Visual Basic identifier rules.

Identifier	Reason for Being Invalid
4square	Starts with a digit.
number count	Space between **number** and **count**.
cnt*four	* is an invalid identifier character.
nam$e	$ is a type identifier and must be the identifier's last character.

Constants

As with all other programming languages, any data found in a Visual Basic program that never changes its value is called a constant. Constants come in many types (e.g., string, integer, long integer, single-precision, double-precision, etc.).

The following are examples of Visual Basic constants:

Constant	Type
"Hello"	String constant
3.14	Single or double precision constant
12345	Integer constant
"Another"	String constant
"b"	String constant
-5	Integer constant

The Visual Basic programming language also permits you to name a constant. Once you assign this name, you can substitute it freely for the constant's value. The following are two examples of named constants:

```
CONST PI = 3.14
GLOBAL CONST AUTHOR$ = "Mark Goodwin"
```

Variables

Although constants are a handy tool for the Visual Basic programmer, variables are even more useful. As its name implies, a variable is a type of data that has a value that can be changed throughout the life of a Visual Basic program. Unlike constants that can be referred to by their literal values, a variable must always have an identifier name.

Operators

The Visual Basic operators are a collection of symbols and keywords that are used to build expressions. Figure 1-2 presents a list of the Visual Basic operators. With these operators at the programmer's disposal, a wide variety of expressions can be built.

Some examples built from the Visual Basic operators follow:

```
4 <> 6
44.3 * 66 / 2
33 <= 44
33 / 2.25
```

Visual Basic Program Lines

A Visual Basic program is made up of one or more **program lines**. Figure 1-3 illustrates the format for a Visual Basic program line. As this figure illustrates, a Visual Basic program line is constructed from an optional line identifier and one or more program statements. You should note that multistatement lines must have a colon (:) separating the individual statements.

Operator	Class
^ (Exponentiation)	Arithmetic
- (Negation)	Arithmetic
* (Multiplication)	Arithmetic
/ (Division)	Arithmetic
\ (Integer Division)	Arithmetic
Mod (Modulo Arithmetic)	Arithmetic
+ (Addition)	Arithmetic
- (Subtraction)	Arithmetic
+ (Concatenation)	String
= (Equal To)	Relational
> (Greater Than)	Relational
< (Less Than)	Relational
<> (Not Equal To)	Relational
<= (Less Than or Equal To)	Relational
>= (Greater Than or Equal To)	Relational
Not (Logical Complement)	Logical
AND (Conjunction)	Logical
OR (Disjunction)	Logical
XOR (Exclusive OR)	Logical
EQV (Equivalence)	Logical
IMP (Implication)	Logical

Figure 1-2 The Visual Basic operators.

If you are familiar with other forms of the Basic programming language, you may be surprised that, with Visual Basic, line identifiers are an optional part of the language. Additionally, a Visual Basic line identifier need not be a number as most other forms of Basic require. Indeed, you may use either a series

```
[line identifier] statement
```

or

```
[line identifier] statement [: statement]...
```

Where:

`line identifier`   is a valid Visual Basic line identifier.

`statement`   is a valid Visual Basic program
                       statement.

Figure 1-3 A Visual Basic program line.

of digits from 0 to 65529 to form a line identifier or a combination of up to 40 letters and digits. Furthermore, alphanumeric line identifiers must start with a letter and end with a colon (:). As with other Visual Basic identifiers, line identifiers are not case significant. The following are some examples of valid Visual Basic program lines:

```
10 Print "This is line 10!"
Print "This is a line without a line identifier!"
ALPHANUMERIC: Print "This is a line with an
alphanumeric line identifier"
```

Visual Basic Program Comments

A Visual Basic program comment is exactly what its name implies. It is simply a comment for the programmer's benefit and serves no function as far as the program's execution is concerned. Although they don't affect the program's execution, program comments are a valuable tool for documenting a program. Strategically placed comments can greatly illuminate a program's inner workings. Many times a program will require modification at a future date. While a program's implementation (how the program is written) can seem quite clear when it was originally created, it won't be anywhere near as clear even just a week or two down the road. Consequently, program comments are one of the Visual Basic programmer's most valuable tools. You can create a Visual Basic comment by

Rem *comment*

or

' comment

Where:

comment   is the desired comment.

Figure 1-4 A Visual Basic program comment.

starting the comment with either a **Rem** keyword or an apostrophe ('). Figure 1-4 more clearly illustrates how a Visual Basic program comment is formed. You should note that once a comment has started, the Visual Basic compiler will ignore the rest of the line and program execution will continue with the start of the next program line when the program is executed.

Some examples of valid Visual Basic comments appear below:

```
Rem This is a comment
Print "Hello" : ' This comment is part of a
multistatement line
' This too is a valid comment
100 Rem I'm a comment too!!!
```

Visual Basic Program Statements

We've already learned that a Visual Basic program is constructed from one or more program lines and these program lines are constructed from one or more program statements. Visual Basic program statements come in two distinct forms: executable statements and nonexecutable statements. An executable statement performs a certain specific task. For example, a **Print** statement tells Visual Basic to display something in the current form. A nonexecutable program statement is a statement that doesn't perform a specific task. Nonexecutable program statements are used for such tasks as declaring variables, defining new variable types, defining constants, and so on. We've already studied one of the most important nonexecutable Visual Basic program statements: the program comment.

Although a program comment is part of the Visual Basic program and does perform a very useful and important task, it doesn't actually perform a task during the execution of the Visual Basic program.

Visual Basic Procedures

Unlike older forms of Basic, Visual Basic supports two different procedure types: the **Sub** procedure and the **Function** procedure. Essentially, a procedure is a collection of program lines that has been given a name. A **Sub** procedure is a procedure that doesn't return a value and a **Function** procedure defines a procedure that does return a value. Basically, a procedure is nothing more than a miniature program that is defined in a much larger program. Whenever a procedure name is encountered in a Visual Basic program, the program branches away from the part of the program it is currently executing and executes the procedure's associated statements. If the called procedure is a **Function** procedure, it will return a value to be used as part of a Visual Basic expression. Another nice feature that Visual Basic procedures offer is the ability to define their own variables.

The Three Major Components

Visual Basic programs all have three major components: a global module, one or more modules, and one or more forms. You should note that all three of these major components are optional, but all Visual Basic programs need at least one of the components to be a program. Each of these three major components plays an essential role in constructing a Visual Basic program.

The Global Module

The global module is used to define and declare data items that are part of the whole Visual Basic application program. The definitions and declarations that a global module can hold are global variable declarations, global constant definitions, default variable type declarations, and user-defined record type definitions.

Forms

A Visual Basic's forms are what makes a Visual Basic program a Windows program. Essentially, each form is a Windows window. It holds all of the information that the Visual Basic program needs to create the desired window's appearance on the display screen. A form is able to provide all this information through the use of object-oriented programming techniques. A Visual Basic form is nothing more than an instance of a **Form's** object class. Each instance of the object class has both properties (data items) and methods (**Sub** and **Function** procedures). A form's properties are used to control many aspects of its appearance: the client window's size, whether or not the window can be minimized, and so forth. A form's methods are procedures that are called when an event occurs. Some of the many events that can happen to a form include painting, resizing, loading, unloading, mouse button up, mouse button down, and so on. Figure 1-5 illustrates how a Visual Basic form appears at design time, and Figure 1-6 how the same form appears at run time.

You will note from Figures 1-5 and 1-6 that the example form has a command button labeled **Command1** and a text box with **Text1** for its contents. Both the command button and the text box are Visual Basic control objects. As forms are objects that define a Visual Basic program's windows, control objects are used to define a window's controls. Moreover, Visual Basic control objects have both properties and methods just like Visual Basic forms. Visual Basic comes equipped with a wide variety of controls: check boxes, command buttons, scroll bars, text boxes, and so on.

Modules

Many Visual Basic applications will make use of multiple forms. In these multiform application programs, there will be a number of procedures that are common to two or more of the

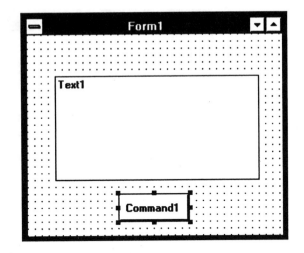

Figure 1-5 A Visual Basic form at design time.

application program's forms. Instead of redundantly redefining the common procedures in all of the forms that require them, Visual Basic allows programmers to create modules that hold the code for these common procedures. Essentially, then, a Visual Basic module is a library of routines that are used by one or more of the application program's forms.

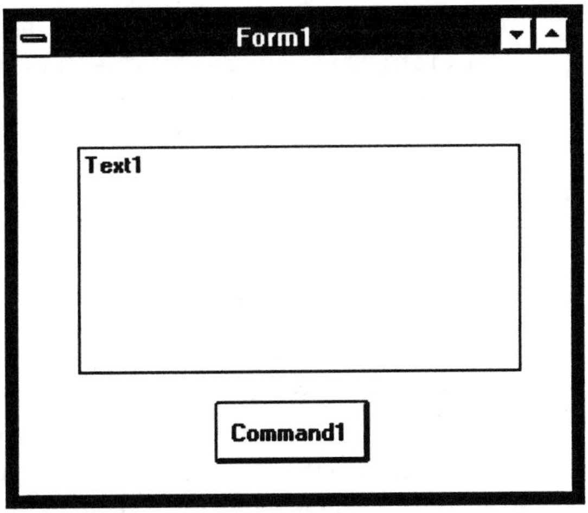

Figure 1-6 A Visual Basic form at run time.

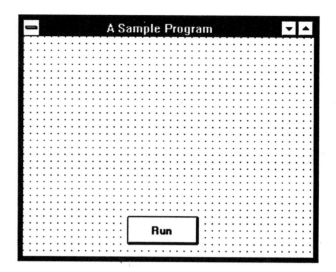

Figure 1-7 Sample program form.

A First Visual Basic Program

Now that you know the essential components in a Visual Basic program, you are ready to write your first Visual Basic program. Figure 1-7 presents the form for this first Visual Basic program and Figure 1-8 illustrates how the form's control is configured.

Listing 1-1 presents the global module for this first sample program. Although a global module isn't really necessary for a program as simple as this one, it is included to illustrate how all of the three major components are joined together to form a complete Visual Basic program.

Listing 1-1:

```
DefInt A-Z

Global Const number = 2
```

Listing 1-2 presents a module for the sample program. As with the global module, this module isn't really necessary for a program as simple as the one we are creating. The module's function procedure could have easily been included as part of the form's code.

Control	CtlName Property	Caption Property
Command Button	RunButton	Run

Figure 1-8 The command button's properties.

Listing 1-2:

```
Function multiply (n1 As Integer, n2 As Integer) As
Integer
    multiply = n1 * n2
End Function
```

Finally, Listing 1-3 presents the form's code. This code defines a procedure that Visual Basic will call each time the user clicks the **Run** button.

Listing 1-3:

```
Sub RunButton_Click ()
    count% = 2
    result = count% * number
    Print result
    result = multiply(count%, number)
    Print result
End Sub
```

Although this first sample program is fairly simple, it serves a very important purpose by illustrating how the Visual Basic programming language's essential components are brought together in unison to form a complete program. To better understand the basic structure of a Visual Basic program, let's go through the program's code a line at a time.

`DefInt A-Z` sets the default data type for all variables that start with the letters **A** through **Z** in the global module to integer variables.

`Global Const number = 2` assigns the constant **2** to **number**.

`Function multiply (n1 As Integer, n2 As Integer) As Integer` defines a **Function** procedure called **multiply**. The function expects two integer arguments, **n1** and **n2**, and returns an integer result.

`multiply = n1 * n2` multiplies the **Function** procedure's arguments and assigns the result as the return value.

`End Function` defines the end of the **multiply Function** procedure's body.

`Sub RunButton_Click ()` defines a **Sub** procedure called **RunButton_Click**. This procedure is called whenever the **RunButton** control is clicked.

`count% = 2` declares an integer variable named **count** and assigns it a value of **2**. You should note that Visual Basic and Basic in general don't require you to specifically declare a variable at the start of a program or procedure. This is unlike most other high-level programming languages that do require that all variables be declared before they are used in a program.

`result = count% * number` declares the variable **result** and assigns it the result of the expression **count% * number**.

`Print result` displays **result**'s contents in the window's client area.

`result = multiply(count%, number)` calls the **Function** procedure **multiply** and assigns the result to **result**.

`Print result` displays **result**'s contents in the window's client area.

`End Sub` defines the end of the **RunButton_Click Sub** procedure's body.

Figure 1-9 illustrates what the sample program's window will look like after the **Run** button has been clicked a few times.

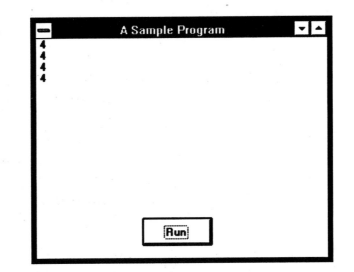

Figure 1-9 The sample program.

Summary

You are now familiar with some of the essential components of the Visual Basic programming language and have examined a simple Visual Basic program. Although all of this may seem a bit hazy at this point, don't worry. The rest of this book is devoted to unwrapping the many remaining mysteries of the Visual Basic programming language.

Chapter 2

Predefined Data Types

S ince a Visual Basic program is called upon to handle many different types of data, the Visual Basic programming language comes equipped with a variety of data types. This chapter takes a detailed look at all of these data types, showing how Visual Basic can meet the needs of almost any data handling requirements. The data types covered in this chapter are integers, floating point numbers, fixed point numbers, and strings.

Integers

Integers are the most basic of the Visual Basic data types. Simply put, an integer data type can represent whole numbers. The following are examples of integer constants:

```
32457
-5303
0
```

```
999
5678910
&o123
&h2f
```

You may be wondering what the constants &o123 and &h2f in the above example mean. The integer constant &o123 is the way the number 83 is represented using the octal numbering system and the integer constant &h2f is the way the number 47 is represented using the hexadecimal number system. The octal number system is base 8 and is represented by the digits **0..7**. Figure 2-1 illustrates how numbers are represented using the octal number system's 8 distinct digits. To define an octal constant in a Visual Basic program, you must prefix the constant with either **&**, **&O**, or **&o**. Failure to use the proper prefix will result in Visual Basic compiling the constant as a regular old decimal number. Because the octal number system is base 8, &o123's value is easily determined as follows:

$$1 * 64 + 2 * 8 + 3 = 83$$

The hexadecimal number system is base 16 and is represented by the digits **0..9** and the letters **A..F** or **a..f**. Figure 2-2 illustrates how numbers are represented using the hexadecimal number system's 16 distinct digits. To define a hexadecimal constant in a Visual Basic program, you must prefix the

Digit	*Represents*
0	0
1	1
2	2
3	3
4	4
5	5
6	6
7	7

Figure 2-1 The octal number system (base 8).

Digit	Represents
0	0
1	1
2	2
3	3
4	4
5	5
6	6
7	7
8	8
9	9
A	10
B	11
C	12
D	13
E	14
F	15

Figure 2-2   The hexadecimal number system (base 16).

constant with either **&H** or **&h**. Failure to use the proper prefix will result in Visual Basic interpreting the constant as a variable name for constants that start with a letter or as a decimal number for constants that are all digits. Unprefixed hexadecimal constants that start with a numeric digit and have one or more letters will result in a syntax error. Because the hexadecimal number system is base 16, &h2f's value can be easily determined as follows:

2 * 16 + 15 = 47

Because a small whole number, such as number 4, doesn't require as much of the computer's memory to store as a larger whole number, such as 5566677, Visual Basic offers two different integer data types: the **Integer** and the **Long**. Figure 2-3

Data	Range of Values	Size in Bytes
Integer	-32,768 to 32,767	2
Long	-2,147,483,648 to 2,147,483,647	4

Figure 2-3 The Visual Basic integer types.

shows the range of numbers these two integer data types can represent. Additionally, the figure illustrates that a **Long** takes twice as much of the computer's memory to store as an **Integer** does. An efficient Visual Basic programmer will always strive to use the smallest possible data type. For example, an integer variable that will never hold a value less than -32,768 or greater than 32,767 should be stored as an **Integer** instead of a **Long**. Not only does the smaller data type require a great deal less memory than its larger counterpart, but the computer can perform operations, such as addition and subtraction, on the smaller data type at much greater speeds.

As the previous chapter mentioned, you do not have to specifically declare a Visual Basic variable. You simply use an appropriate identifier name at the desired spot in your program. However, Visual Basic must have a way to determine a variable's data type. That is where Visual Basic's type declaration characters come into play. Figure 2-4 illustrates the syntax for declaring an **Integer** variable name with an **Integer** type declaration character (%) and Figure 2-5 illustrates the syntax for declaring a **Long** variable name with a **Long** declaration character (&).

```
identifier%
```

Where:

`identifier`   is a valid Visual Basic variable
                           identifier.

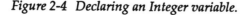

Figure 2-4 Declaring an Integer variable.

---

identifier&

Where:

identifier	is a valid Visual Basic variable identifier.

Figure 2-5   Declaring a Long variable.

Some examples of valid **Integer** and **Long** variable names follow:

```
count%
RecordNumber&
RecordOffset&
i%
j%
```

Besides declaring **Integer** and **Long** variables with type declaration characters, they can be declared without their proper type declaration characters if Visual Basic's default identifier types are set with the **DefInt** or **DefLng** statements. Figure 2-6 illustrates the syntax for using the **DefInt** statement, and Figure 2-7 the syntax for using the **DefLng** statement. At the start of a program, Visual Basic sets the default data type for all variable names to **Single** (single-precision numbers will be discussed next). Consequently, any variables that don't have a specific type declaration character at the end of their names will be treated as a **Single** variable. If a **DefInt** or **DefLng** is used to override any or all of the Visual Basic defaults, the new data type will be assumed for any variable names that start

---

DefInt *range[,range]* ...

Where:

range	is a single letter or a range of letters separated by a hyphen (-).

Figure 2-6   The DefInt statement.

```
DefLng range[,range]...
```

Where:

range   is a single letter or a range of letters
                                separated by a hyphen (-).

Figure 2-7 The DefLng statement.

with the letters that have been overridden. You should note that the **DefInt** and **DefLng** statements are placed in the declarations section of a form or module and only apply to the form or module they appear in.

The following are some examples of valid **DefInt** and **DefLng** statements:

```
DefInt A-Z
DefLng A-C,D,G-H,Z
DefInt I
DefLng M-O
```

Although it isn't strictly necessary to declare a variable before it can be used in a program, Visual Basic does allow the programmer to predeclare a variable in a program. One of the advantages to predeclaring a variable is that it isn't necessary to use a type declaration character for the variable even if the Visual Basic variable name defaults are set for another data type. Figure 2-8 illustrates how an **Integer** variable can be predeclared in a Visual Basic program, and Figure 2-9 how a **Long** can be predeclared in a Visual Basic program.

Although a variable declaration can be preformed in **Dim**, **Global**, **ReDim**, and **Static** statements, declaring them in a **Dim** statement is the most commonly used method. Some examples of variable declarations using the **Dim** statement appear below:

```
Dim I As Integer
Dim AccountNumber As Long
Dim Offset As Long
Dim Account As Integer
```

```
declare identifier As Integer
```

Where:

declare	is either **Dim, Global, ReDim,** or **Static.**
identifier	is a valid Visual Basic variable name.

Figure 2-8 Declaring an Integer variable.

Program 2-1 illustrates the use of Visual Basic's integer data types. Essentially, this program is the same program that appeared in the first chapter except this new version doesn't have either a global module or an extra program module. Listing 2-1-1 presents the code for the form's declaration section and Listing 2-1-2 presents the code for the program's **RunButton_Click** procedure. Figure 2-10 shows how the program's window will appear after the program has been run. (Unless otherwise indicated, the remainder of this book's example programs will continue to redefine the form for the "sample" program to simplify presenting example programs. Although the "sample" program is an extremely simple Visual Basic program, it serves the purpose of illustrating Visual Basic's many features quite well.)

Listing 2-1-1:

```
DefInt A-Z
```

```
declare identifier As Long
```

Where:

declare	is either **Dim, Global, ReDim,** or **Static.**
identifier	is a valid Visual Basic variable name.

Figure 2-9 Declaring a Long variable.

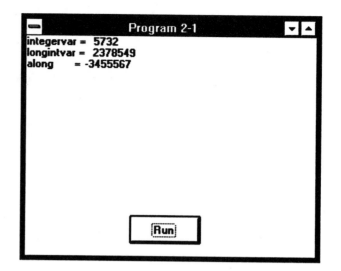

Figure 2-10 The Visual Basic integers.

Listing 2-1-2:

```
Sub RunButton_Click ()

    Dim along As Long
    integervar = 5732
    longintvar& = 2378549
    along = -3455567
    Print "integervar = "; integervar
    Print "longintvar = "; longintvar&
    Print "along      = "; along

End Sub
```

Floating Point Numbers

Although Visual Basic's integer types are quite useful and can meet the needs of a wide variety of numeric data, many types of numeric data require a fractional part to maintain a high degree of accuracy. Visual Basic provides two basic number types to fulfill this requirement. These number types are floating point numbers and fixed point numbers. This section describes the Visual Basic floating point number types and how

Data Type	Range of Values	Size in Bytes	Significant Data
Single	-3.37E+38 to 3.37E+38	4	7
Double	-1.67D+308 to 1.67D+308	8	15–16

Figure 2-11   The Visual Basic floating point number types.

they are used in a Visual Basic program. The following are some examples of floating point numbers:

```
3.14
-2.305E-06
29.33
99.67899D-05
-53.23
```

In order to represent floating point numbers efficiently, Visual Basic offers two different floating point number types: the **Single** and the **Double**. Figure 2-11 illustrates the range of numbers that Visual Basic's two floating point number types can represent.

As with the integer types, Visual Basic's floating point number types take a varying amount of memory to store. Consequently, you should always try to use the smallest floating point number type possible for a given task. Like their integer counterparts, calculations are performed much faster for **Single** numbers than on **Double** numbers.

As you have already learned, the Visual Basic programmer doesn't have to specifically declare a Visual Basic floating point variable. As with the integer data types, you can use a type declaration character to specify a floating point variable. Figure 2-12 illustrates the syntax for declaring a **Single** variable name with a **Single** declaration character (!); Figure 2-13 illustrates the syntax for declaring a **Double** variable name with a **Double** declaration character (#).

```
identifier!
```

Where:

identifier   is a valid Visual Basic variable
                               identifier.

Figure 2-12 Declaring a Single variable.

The following are some examples of valid **Single** and **Double** variable names:

    balance#
    result!
    NetIncome#
    Debits!
    Credits#

Besides declaring **Single** and **Double** variables with type declaration characters, they can be defined without their proper type declaration characters if Visual Basic's default identifier types haven't been changed for **Single** variables or the defaults have been overridden with a **DefDbl** statement. You should note that once Visual Basic's variable type defaults have been overridden, they can be changed back to **Single** by using the **DefSng** statement. Figure 2-14 illustrates the syntax for using the **DefSng** statement, and Figure 2-15 the syntax for the **DefDbl** statement. After the defaults have been changed with a **DefSng** or **DefDbl**, the new data type will be assumed for any variable names that start with letters that have been overridden and do not contain a type declaration character at the end of their names. You should note that the **DefSng** and **DefDbl** statements are placed in the declarations section of a

```
identifier#
```

Where:

identifier   is a valid Visual Basic identifier.

Figure 2-13 Declaring a Double variable.

```
DefSng range[,range]...
```

Where:

range   is a single letter or a range of letters
                                   separated by a hyphen (-).

Figure 2-14 The DefSng statement.

form or module and only apply to the form or module they
appear in.

   Some examples of valid **DefSng** and **DefDbl** statements
follow:

```
DefDbl A,B
DefSng O-Z
DefDbl Q-R,T-V
DefSng V
```

   As with Visual Basic's integer variables, Visual Basic's
floating point variables can be predeclared in a program before
they are actually used. Figure 2-16 illustrates how a **Single**
variable can be predeclared in a Visual Basic program, and
Figure 2-17 how a **Double** variable can be predeclared in a
Visual Basic program.

   The following are some examples of variable declarations
using the **Dim** statement:

```
Dim Balance As Single
Dim Account As Double
Dim RecordNumber As Single
Dim A As Double
```

```
DefDbl range[,range]...
```

Where:

range   is a single letter or a range of letters
                                   separated by a hyphen (-).

Figure 2-15 The DefDbl statement.

```
declare identifier As Single
```

Where:

declare	is either **Dim, Global, ReDim,** or **Static.**
identifier	is a valid Visual Basic variable name.

Figure 2-16 Declaring a Single variable.

Program 2-2 illustrates the use of Visual Basic's floating point number types. Listing 2-2 presents the code for the program's **RunButton_Click** procedure. Figure 2-18 illustrates how the program's window will appear after the program has been run.

Listing 2-2:

```
Sub RunButton_Click ()

    Dim adouble As Double

    singlevar = 33.23567
    doublevar = -5678.02
    adouble = 45.67
    Print "singlevar = "; singlevar
    Print "doublevar = "; doublevar
    Print "adouble   = "; adouble

End Sub
```

```
declare identifier As Double
```

Where:

declare	is either **Dim, Global, ReDim,** or **Static.**
identifier	is a valid Visual Basic variable name.

Figure 2-17 Declaring a Double variable.

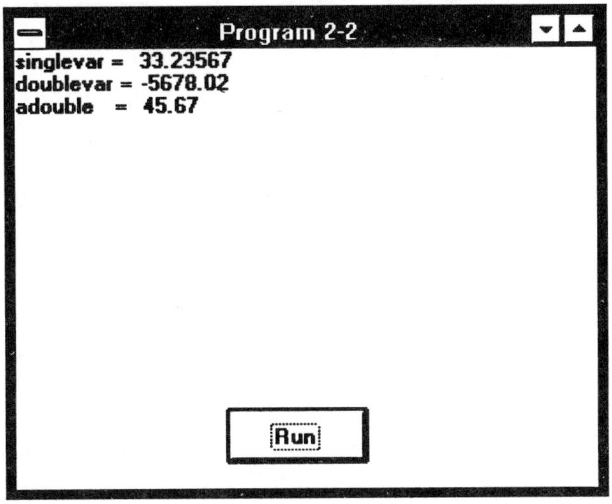

Figure 2-18   The Visual Basic floating point numbers.

Fixed Point Numbers

Although Visual Basic's floating point number types are very well suited for a number of applications that require numbers with fractional parts, they aren't exactly ideal for business programs that require data to be stored to the exact amount. Because Visual Basic stores floating point numbers as their binary equivalents, there's always a certain amount of inaccuracy caused by the conversion of the numbers from base 2 to base 10 and vice versa. To better represent data that symbolizes monetary amounts, Visual Basic provides a fixed point number type called **Currency**. The **Currency** number type can accurately represent numbers with up to 4 digits to the right of the decimal point and 14 digits to the left of the decimal point. The following are some examples of fixed point numbers that the **Currency** number type could represent:

```
-22.36
1000567.38
-55.333
-200.91
```

Figure 2-19 illustrates the range of numbers that Visual Basic's **Currency** number type can represent.

Data Type	Range of Values	Size in Bytes
Currency	-9.22E+14 to 9.22E+14	8

Figure 2-19 The Visual Basic Currency number type.

As with Visual Basic's other number types, the Visual Basic programmer doesn't have to specifically declare a Visual Basic **Currency** variable. As with the other data types, you can use a type declaration character to specify a **Currency** variable. Figure 2-20 illustrates the syntax for declaring a **Currency** variable name with a declaration character (@).

Some examples of valid **Currency** variable names are

Balance@
NetIncome@
credits@
debits@
Sales@

Besides declaring **Currency** variables with type declaration characters, they can be defined without their proper type declaration characters if Visual Basic's defaults have been overridden. The Visual Basic variable type defaults can be changed to **Currency** variables with the **DefCur** statement. Figure 2-21 illustrates the syntax for the **DefCur** statement. After the defaults have been changed with a **DefCur** statement, a **Currency** data type will be assumed for any variable names that start

---

```
identifier@
```

Where:

```
identifier
```
                              is a valid Visual Basic variable
                              identifier.

Figure 2-20 Declaring a Currency variable.

```
DefCur range[,range]...
```

Where:

range   is a single letter or a range of letters
                             separated by a hyphen (-).

Figure 2-21 The DefCur statement.

with the letters that have been overridden and do not contain
a type declaration character at the end of their names. You
should note that **DefCur** statements are placed in the declarations section of a form or module and only apply to the form
or module they appear in.

The following are some examples of valid **DefCur** statements:

DefCur C-D
DefCur A
DefCur Q,M,L,Z
DefCur A-C,Q-S

As with Visual Basic's other data types, **Currency** variables can be predeclared in a program before they are actually
used. Figure 2-22 illustrates how **Currency** variables can be
predeclared in a Visual Basic program.

```
declare identifier As Currency
```

Where:

declare   is either **Dim, Global, ReDim,** or
                             Static.

identifier   is a valid Visual Basic variable
                             name.

Figure 2-22 Declaring a Currency variable.

The following are some examples of variable declarations using the **Dim** statement:

Dim AccountBalance As Currency
Dim NetIncome As Currency
Dim Debits As Currency
Dim Credits As Currency

Program 2-3 illustrates the use of Visual Basic's **Currency** type. Listing 2-3 presents the code for the program's **RunButton_Click** procedure. Figure 2-23 illustrates how the program's window will appear after the program has been run.

Listing 2-3:

```
Sub RunButton_Click ()

    Dim acurrency As Currency
    currencyvar@ = 33.45
    acurrency = -23.66
    Print "currencyvar = "; currencyvar@
    Print "acurrency   = "; acurrency

End Sub
```

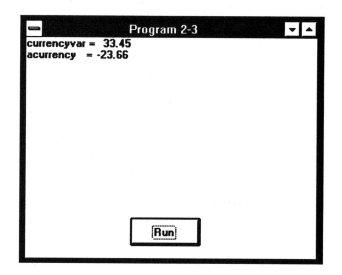

Figure 2-23 The Visual Basic Currency data type.

Strings

Although all of the previously described Visual Basic data types are important, string data is perhaps the most important data a Visual Basic program handles. From text editing programs to simple utility programs, strings are by far the most prevalent type of computer data. Visual Basic offers both variable-length strings and fixed-length strings to meet the needs that string handling imposes upon a computer language. Examples of string data appear below:

> "This is a sample string"
> "This is another sample string"
> "I'm a string too!"

As with all of the other previously mentioned Visual Basic data types, the Visual Basic programmer doesn't have to specifically declare a variable-length **String** variable. As with the other data types, the Visual Basic programmer can use a type declaration character to specify a variable-length **String**. Figure 2-24 illustrates the syntax for declaring a variable-length **String** variable with the **String** declaration character ($).

The following are some examples of valid variable-length **String** variable names:

> NAME$
> City$
> state$
> Zip$

As with Visual Basic's numeric data types, a **String** variable can be declared without a type declaration character if Visual Basic's defaults have been overridden. The Visual Basic

---

identifier$

Where:

identifier	is a valid Visual Basic variable identifier.

Figure 2-24 Declaring a string variable.

DefStr *range[,range]* . . .

Where:

range   is a single letter or a range of letters
                                        separated by a hyphen (-).

Figure 2-25   The DefStr statement.

variable type defaults can be changed to **String** with a **DefStr** statement. Figure 2-25 illustrates the syntax for using the **DefStr** statement. After the defaults have been changed with a **DefStr** statement, a **String** data type will be assumed for any variable names that start with the letters that have been over-ridden and do not contain a type declaration character at the end of their names. You should note that **DefStr** statements are placed in the declarations section of a form or module and only apply to the form or module they appear in.

Some examples of valid **DefStr** statements are

DefStr A–Z
DefStr A
DefStr B,D,F,K–Z
DefStr Q–S,V

Like the Visual Basic numeric data types, Visual Basic **String** variables can be predeclared in a program before they are actually used. Additionally, Visual Basic will allow the programmer to specify a fixed length for the **String** variable. Normally, a Visual Basic **String** variable's contents can vary in length from 0 to 65,535 characters. However, a Visual Basic fixed-length **String** variable has a predefined length and the string will always be that length throughout the life of the variable. If a fixed-length **String** variable is assigned a string that is shorter than the variable's predefined length, the string will be stored in the variable as a left-justified string and padded with enough spaces to fill in the variable's predefined length. If a fixed-length **String** variable is assigned a string that is longer than the variable's predefined length, the string will be truncated (chopped off at the right) to eliminate the un-

---

```
declare identifier As String
```

Where:

declare	is either **Dim, Global, ReDim,** or **Static.**
identifier	is a valid Visual Basic variable name.

Figure 2-26 Declaring a variable-length String variable.

wanted characters. Figure 2-26 illustrates how a variable-length **String** is predeclared in a Visual Basic program, and Figure 2-27 how a fixed-length **String** is predeclared in a Visual Basic program.

The following are some examples of string variable declarations using the **Dim** statement:

```
Dim Name As String * 30
Dim City As String
Dim State As String * 2
Dim zip As String * 5
```

Program 2-4 illustrates the use of Visual Basic's variable-length and fixed-length **String** data type. Listing 2-4 presents the code for the program's **RunButton_Click** procedure. Figure 2-28 illustrates how the program's window will appear after the program has been run.

```
declare identifier As String * length
```

Where:

declare	is either **Dim, Global, ReDim,** or **Static.**
identifier	is a valid Visual Basic variable name.

Figure 2-27 Declaring a fixed-length String variable.

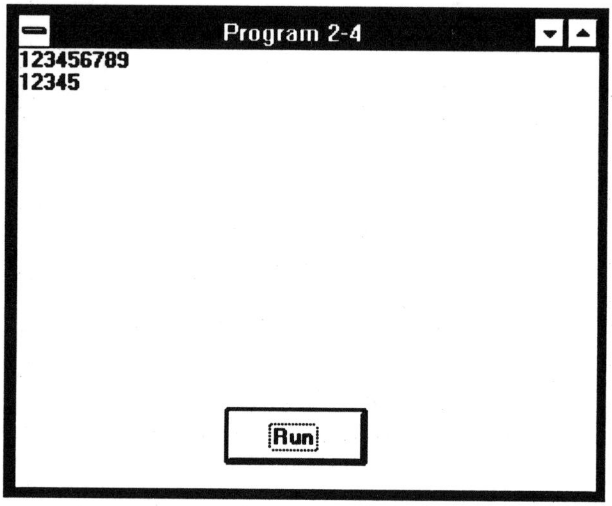

Figure 2-28 The Visual Basic String data type.

Listing 2-4:

```
Sub RunButton_Click ()

    Dim fstring As String * 5
    vstring$ = "123456789"
    fstring = "123456789"
    Print vstring$
    Print fstring

End Sub
```

Summary

This chapter presented Visual Basic's predefined data types: **Integer, Long, Single, Double, Currency,** and **String.** Chapter 3 discusses how you can use the Visual Basic operators to build expressions to manipulate the data these data types can represent.

Chapter 3

The Visual Basic Operators

This chapter shows you how to use the Visual Basic operators to manipulate data. When combined with other variables and constants, the Visual Basic operators can be used to build powerful and useful expressions. This chapter concludes with a discussion of operator precedence.

The Assignment Statement

As its name implies, a Visual Basic assignment statement assigns the result of an expression to a variable. Because of its extensive use in the programs listed in Chapter 2, you should already be familiar with the Visual Basic assignment statement. Figure 3-1 defines the syntax for a Visual Basic assignment statement.

The following examples illustrate the proper use of the Visual Basic assignment statement:

```
Count = Count + 1
Name$ = FirstName$ + " " + MiddleInitial$ + " " +
   LastName$
PI = 22 / 7
Key$ = C$
```

Program 3-1 demonstrates how the Visual Basic assignment statement is used in an actual program that assigns values to a wide variety of variables. Listing 3-1-1 presents the code for the form's declarations section and Listing 3-1-2 presents the code for the program's **RunButton_Click** procedure. Figure 3-2 illustrates how the program's window would appear after the program has been run.

Listing 3-1-1:

```
DefInt A-Z
```

```
[LET] identifier = expression
```

Where:

LET	is an optional Visual Basic keyword. Although **LET** is required with some very old versions of Basic, most modern forms of Basic no longer require it and it is very rarely seen in today's programs.
identifier	is a valid Visual Basic variable name.
expression	is a valid Visual Basic expression. Note that the result of the expression must have the same data type as does the identifier.

Figure 3-1 The Visual Basic assignment statement.

```
┌────────────────────────────────────────────┐
│ ─              Program 3-1              ▼ ▲ │
├────────────────────────────────────────────┤
│ Count = 2                                  │
│ FName$ = John Q. Public                    │
│                                            │
│                                            │
│                                            │
│                                            │
│                                            │
│                                            │
│                 ┌─────────┐                │
│                 │  Run    │                │
│                 └─────────┘                │
└────────────────────────────────────────────┘
```

Figure 3-2 The Visual Basic assignment statement.

Listing 3-1-2:

```
Sub RunButton_Click ()

    Count = 1
    Count = Count + 1
    FName$ = "John" + " " + "Q. " + "Public"
    Print "Count  = "; Count
    Print "FName$ = "; FName$

End Sub
```

The Negation Operator

The Visual Basic negation operator (-) negates the value of an expression. If the expression is negative, the negation operator makes it positive. If the expression is positive, the negation operator makes it negative. Figure 3-3 defines the syntax for the negation operator.

The following examples illustrate the proper use of the negation operator:

    -N1
    -2.345678
    -Count

```
-expression
```

Where:

```
expression                    is a numeric expression.
```

Figure 3-3 The Visual Basic negation operator.

Program 3-2 demonstrates how the Visual Basic negation operator is used in an actual program. Listing 3-2-1 presents the code for the form's declaration section, and Listing 3-2-2 the code for the program's **RunButton_Click** procedure. Figure 3-4 shows how the program's window would appear after the program has been run.

Listing 3-2-1:

```
DefInt A-Z
```

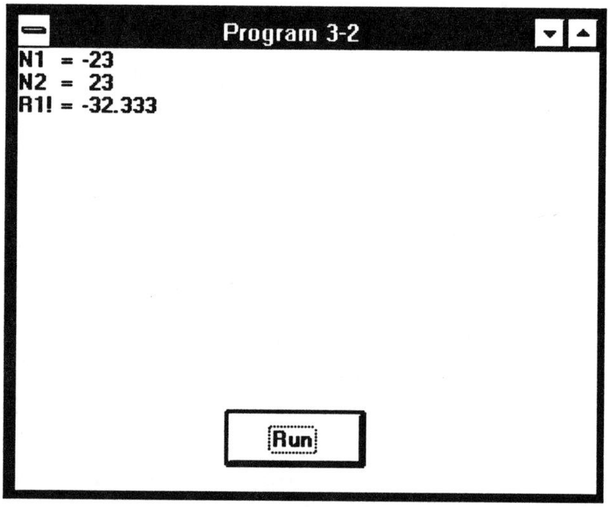

Figure 3-4 The Visual Basic negation operator.

Listing 3-2-2:

```
Sub RunButton_Click ()

    R1! = -32.333
    N1 = -23
    N2 = -N1
    Print "N1  = "; N1
    Print "N2  = "; N2
    Print "R1! = "; R1!

End Sub
```

The Addition Operator

The Visual Basic addition operator (+) adds together two expressions. Figure 3-5 defines the syntax for the addition operator.

Examples that illustrate the proper use of the addition operator follow:

```
1 + 1
N1 + 3
33.3333 + 500
22 + N2
I + J
```

Program 3-3 shows how the Visual Basic addition operator is used in an actual program. Listing 3-3-1 presents the code for the form's declaration section and Listing 3-3-2 presents the code for the program's **RunButton_Click** procedure. Figure 3-6 illustrates how the program's window would appear after the program has been run.

---

expression + *expression*

Where:

expression   is a numeric expression.

Figure 3-5 The Visual Basic addition operator.

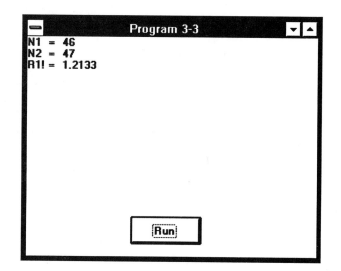

Figure 3-6 A sample addition operator program.

Listing 3-3-1:

```
DefInt A-Z
```

Listing 3-3-2:

```
Sub RunButton_Click ()

    R1! = -32.4567 + 33 + .67
    N1 = 1 + 45
    N2 = N1 + 1
    Print "N1  = "; N1
    Print "N2  = "; N2
    Print "R1! = "; R1!

End Sub
```

The Subtraction Operator

The Visual Basic subtraction operator (-) subtracts the result of one expression from the result of another expression. Figure 3-7 defines the syntax for the subtraction operator.

```
expression - expression
```

Where:

```
expression
```
is a numeric expression.

Figure 3-7 The Visual Basic subtraction operator.

The following examples illustrate the proper use of the subtraction operator:

$2 - 3$
$33.456 - 1.325$
$N1 - G - C$
$55 - N1 - 3$
$6 - 1$

Program 3-4 demonstrates how the Visual Basic subtraction operator is used in an actual program. Listing 3-4-1 presents the code for the program's declaration section, and Listing 3-4-2 the code for the form's **RunButton_Click** procedure. Figure 3-8 shows how the program's window would appear after the program has been run.

Listing 3-4-1:

```
DefInt A-Z
```

Listing 3-4-2:

```
Sub RunButton_Click ()

    R1! = -32.4567 - 33 - .67
    N1 = 1 - 45
    N2 = N1 - 1
    Print "N1  = "; N1
    Print "N2  = "; N2
    Print "R1! = "; R1!

End Sub
```

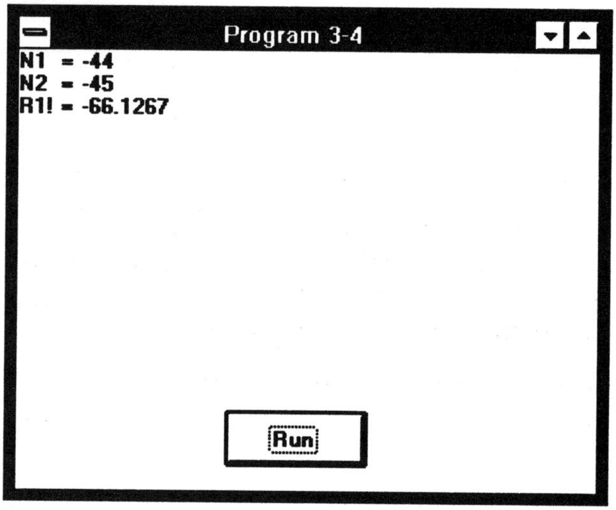

```
┌────────────────────────────────────────────┐
│ ▬              Program 3-4            ▼ ▲   │
│ N1 = -44                                    │
│ N2 = -45                                    │
│ R1! = -66.1267                              │
│                                             │
│                                             │
│                                             │
│                                             │
│                       ┌─────────┐           │
│                       │  Run    │           │
│                       └─────────┘           │
└────────────────────────────────────────────┘
```

Figure 3-8 A sample subtraction operator program.

The Multiplication Operator

The Visual Basic multiplication operator (*) multiplies the result of one expression by the result of another expression. Figure 3-9 defines the syntax for the multiplication operator.

Examples of proper use of the multiplication operator are shown below:

3 * 4
N * PI
3.43 * .5
99 * 6
X * Y * Z

---

expression * *expression*

Where:

expression   is a numeric expression.

Figure 3-9 The Visual Basic multiplication operator.

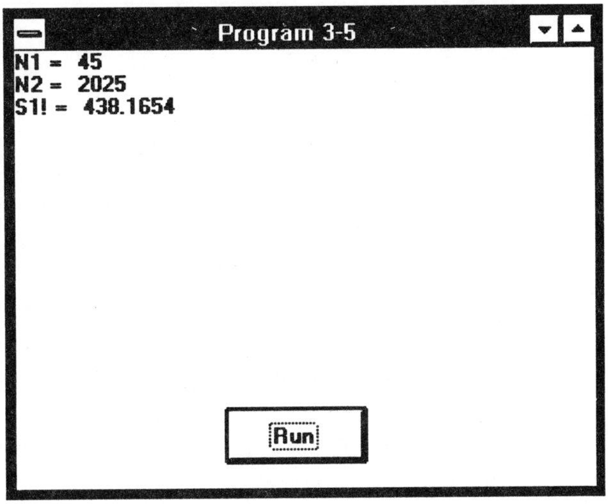

Figure 3-10 A sample multiplication operator program.

Program 3-5 shows how the Visual Basic multiplication operator is used in an actual program. Listing 3-5-1 presents the code for the form's declaration section and Listing 3-5-2 presents the code for the program's **RunButton_Click** procedure. Figure 3-10 illustrates how the program's window would appear after the program has been run.

Listing 3-5-1:

```
DefInt A-Z
```

Listing 3-5-2:

```
Sub RunButton_Click ()

    S1! = 32.4567 * 27 * .5
    N1 = 1 * 45
    N2 = N1 * N1
    Print "N1 = "; N1
    Print "N2 = "; N2
    Print "S1! = "; S1!

End Sub
```

```
expression / expression
```

Where:

```
expression
```
                         is a numeric expression.

Figure 3-11 The Visual Basic floating point division operator.

The Floating Point Division Operator

The Visual Basic floating point division operator (/) divides the result of one expression by another expression and returns a floating point result. Figure 3-11 defines the syntax for the floating point division operator.

The following examples illustrate the proper use of the floating point division operator:

```
22 / 7
15 / N1
X / Z / Y
Count / 2
15.333 / 2.1023
```

Program 3-6 demonstrates how the Visual Basic floating point division operator is used in an actual program. Listing 3-6-1 presents the code for the program's **RunButton_Click** procedure. Figure 3-12 illustrates how the program's window would appear after the program has been run.

Listing 3-6-1:

```
Sub RunButton_Click ()

    S1 = 32.4567 / 27 / .5
    Print "S1 = "; S1

End Sub
```

The Integer Division Operator

The Visual Basic integer division operator (\) divides the result of one expression by the result of another expression. The

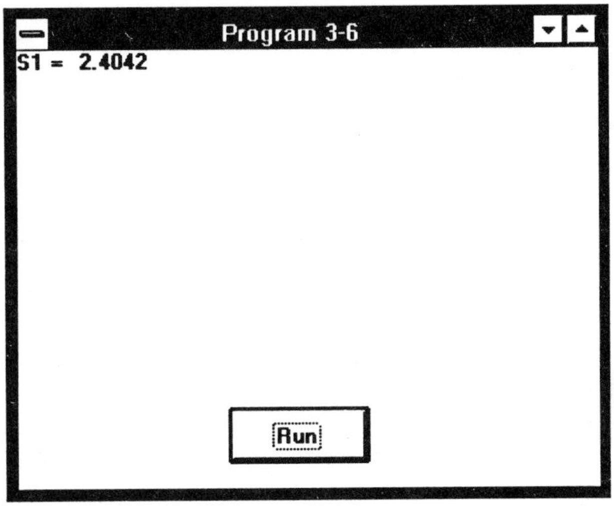

Figure 3-12 A sample floating point division operator program.

integer division operator always returns an integer result. Figure 3-13 defines the syntax for the integer division operator.

The following examples illustrate the proper use of the integer division operator:

    22 \ 7
    N \ 3
    X \ Y \ 2
    16 \ 8
    6666 \ N1

Program 3-7 demonstrates how the Visual Basic multiplication operator is used in an actual program. Listing 3-7-1 presents the code for the form's declaration section and Listing 3-7-2 presents the code for the program's **RunButton_Click**

---

expression \ *expression*

Where:

expression   is a numeric expression.

Figure 3-13 The Visual Basic integer division operator.

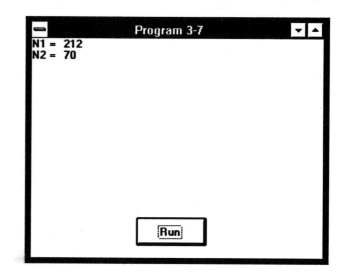

Figure 3-14 A sample integer division operator program.

procedure. Figure 3-14 shows how the program's window would appear after the program has been run.

Listing 3-7-1:

```
DefInt A-Z
```

Listing 3-7-2:

```
Sub RunButton_Click ()

    N1 = 3400 \ 16
    N2 = N1 \ 3
    Print "N1 = "; N1
    Print "N2 = "; N2

End Sub
```

The Modulo Operator

The Visual Basic modulo operator (**Mod**) calculates the remainder of dividing the result of one expression by the result of another expression. The modulo operator always returns an

---

```
expression Mod expression
```

Where:

```
expression
```
is a numeric expression.

Figure 3-15 The Visual Basic modulo operator.

integer result. Figure 3-15 defines the syntax for the modulo operator.

Examples of proper use of the modulo operator follow:

Count Mod 5
33 Mod 2
45 Mod N
X Mod Y Mod Z
N1 Mod N2

Program 3-8 demonstrates how the Visual Basic modulo operator is used in an actual program. Listing 3-8-1 presents the code for the form's declaration section, and Listing 3-8-2 the code for the program's **RunButton_Click** procedure. Figure 3-16 illustrates how the program's window would appear after the program has been run.

Listing 3-8-1:

```
DefInt A-Z
```

Listing 3-8-2:

```
Sub RunButton_Click ()

    N1 = 3400 Mod 16
    N2 = N1 Mod 3
    Print "N1 = "; N1
    Print "N2 = "; N2

End Sub
```

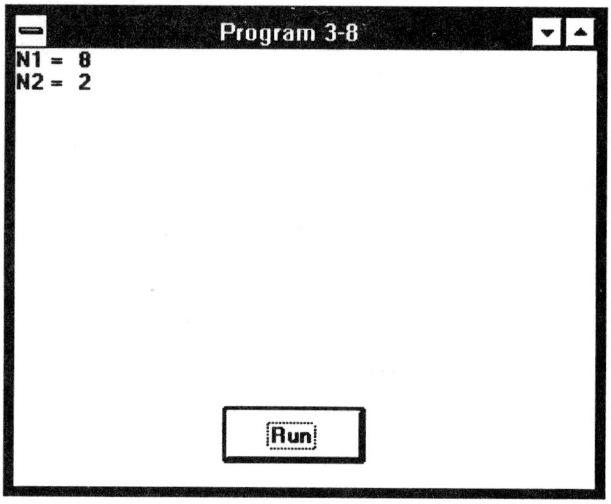

Figure 3-16 A sample modulo operator program.

The Exponentiation Operator

The Visual Basic exponentiation operator (^) raises the result of one expression to the power of the result of a second expression. Figure 3-17 defines the syntax for the exponentiation operator.

The following examples illustrate the proper use of the exponentiation operator:

```
2 ^ 2
X ^ 3
X ^ Y
3 ^ Y
```

---

expression ^ *expression*

Where:

expression   is a numeric expression.

Figure 3-17 The Visual Basic exponentiation operator.

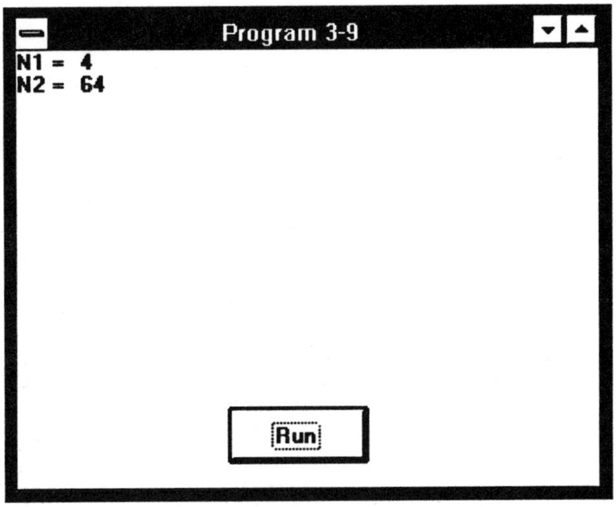

Figure 3-18 A sample exponentiation operator program.

Program 3-9 demonstrates how the Visual Basic exponentiation operator is used in an actual program. Listing 3-9-1 presents the code for the form's declaration section and Listing 3-9-2 presents the code for the program's **RunButton_Click** procedure. Figure 3-18 illustrates how the program's window would appear after the program has been run.

Listing 3-9-1:

```
DefInt A-Z
```

Listing 3-9-2:

```
Sub RunButton_Click ()

    N1 = 2 ^ 2
    N2 = N1 ^ 3
    Print "N1 = "; N1
    Print "N2 = "; N2

End Sub
```

X	Not X
True	False
False	True

Figure 3-19 A logical complement truth table.

The Logical Complement Operator

The Visual Basic logical complement operator (**Not**) negates the result of a logical expression. If the logical expression is equal to True (any nonzero value, but Visual Basic uses -1 internally as True), the logical complement operator makes it False (0). If the logical expression is equal to False, the logical complement operator makes it True. Figure 3-19 presents a truth table that illustrates how the logical complement operator performs its function. Figure 3-20 defines the syntax for the logical complement operator.

The following examples illustrate the proper use of the logical complement operator:

```
Not Flag
Not FALSE
Not ErrorFlag
```

Program 3-10 demonstrates how the Visual Basic logical complement operator is used in an actual program. Listing 3-10-1 presents the code for the form's declaration section, and Listing 3-10-2 the code for the program's **RunButton_Click**

Not *expression*

Where:

expression   is a logical expression.

Figure 3-20 The Visual Basic logical complement operator.

procedure. Figure 3-21 shows how the program's window would appear after the program has been run.

Listing 3-10-1:

```
DefInt A-Z

Const True = -1
Const False = 0
```

Listing 3-10-2:

```
Sub RunButton_Click ()

    Form1.FontName = "Courier"
    Form1.FontSize = 8
    Print "Logical Complement Truth Table"
    Print "=============================="
    Print "Value      Value      Result"
    Print "X                      Not X"
    Print "------------------------------"
    Print "-1                    "; Not True
    Print " 0                    "; Not False
    Print "=============================="

End Sub
```

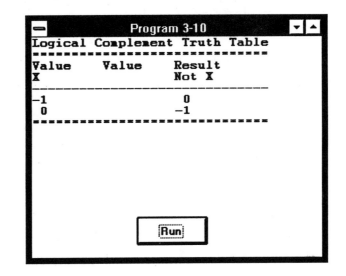

Figure 3-21 A sample logical complement operator program.

X	Y	X And Y
True	True	True
True	False	False
False	True	False
False	False	False

Figure 3-22 A logical and truth table.

The Logical And Operator

The Visual Basic logical and operator (**And**) compares two logical expressions and returns a True result only if both of the logical expressions are equal to True. Otherwise, the logical and operator returns a False result. Figure 3-22 presents a truth table that illustrates how the logical and operator performs its function. Figure 3-23 defines the syntax for the logical and operator.

Examples of proper use of the logical and operator follow:

Flag And True
ErrorFlag And Test
KeyPressed and Flag

Program 3-11 demonstrates how the Visual Basic logical and operator is used in an actual program. Listing 3-11-1 presents the code for the form's declaration section and Listing 3-11-2 presents the code for the program's **RunButton_Click** procedure. Figure 3-24 illustrates how the program's window would appear after the program has been run.

```
expression And expression
```

Where:

```
expression
```
        is a logical expression.

Figure 3-23 The Visual Basic logical and operator.

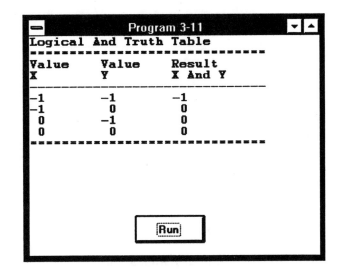

Figure 3-24 A sample logical and operator program.

Listing 3-11-1:

```
DefInt A-Z

Const True = -1
Const False = 0
```

Listing 3-11-2:

```
Sub RunButton_Click ()

    Form1.FontName = "Courier"
    Form1.FontSize = 8
    Print "Logical And Truth Table"
    Print "=============================="
    Print "Value    Value    Result"
    Print "X        Y        X And Y"
    Print "------------------------------"
    Print "-1       -1       "; True And True
    Print "-1        0       "; True And False
    Print " 0       -1       "; False And True
    Print " 0        0       "; False And False
    Print "=============================="

End Sub
```

X	Y	X Or Y
True	True	True
True	False	True
False	True	True
False	False	False

Figure 3-25 A logical or truth table.

The Logical Or Operator

The Visual Basic logical or operator (**Or**) compares two logical expressions and returns a True result if either of the logical expressions is equal to True. The logical or operator returns a False result only if both logical expressions are equal to False. Figure 3-25 presents a truth table that illustrates how the logical or operator performs its function. Figure 3-26 defines the syntax for the logical or operator.

The following examples illustrate the proper use of the logical or operator:

```
Flag Or True
ErrorFlag Or FileError
KeyPressed Or MouseClicked
```

Program 3-12 demonstrates how the Visual Basic logical or operator is used in an actual program. Listing 3-12-1 presents the code for the form's declaration section and Listing 3-12-2 presents the code for the program's **RunButton_Click** procedure. Figure 3-27 shows how the program's window would appear after the program has been run.

```
expression Or expression
```

Where:

```
expression
```
                is a logical expression.

Figure 3-26 The Visual Basic logical or operator.

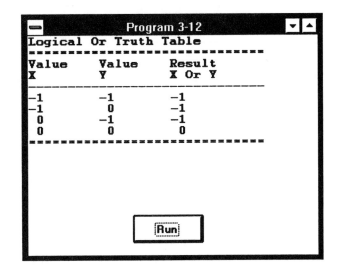

Figure 3-27   A sample logical or operator program.

Listing 3-12-1:

```
DefInt A-Z

Const True = -1
Const False = 0
```

Listing 3-12-2:

```
Sub RunButton_Click ()

    Form1.FontName = "Courier"
    Form1.FontSize = 8
    Print "Logical Or Truth Table"
    Print "==============================="
    Print "Value     Value     Result"
    Print "X         Y         X Or Y"
    Print "------------------------------"
    Print "-1        -1        "; True Or True
    Print "-1         0        "; True Or False
    Print " 0        -1        "; False Or True
    Print " 0         0        "; False Or False
    Print "==============================="

End Sub
```

X	Y	X Xor Y
True	True	False
True	False	True
False	True	True
False	False	False

Figure 3-28 A logical exclusive or truth table.

The Logical Exclusive Or Operator

The Visual Basic logical exclusive or operator (**Xor**) compares two logical expressions and returns a True if both of the logical expressions are different. Otherwise, the logical exclusive or operator returns a False result. Figure 3-28 presents a truth table that illustrates how the logical exclusive or operator performs its function. Figure 3-29 defines the syntax for the logical exclusive or operator.

The following examples illustrate the proper use of the logical exclusive or operator:

Flag Xor True
ErrorFlag Xor False
KeyPressed Xor MouseClicked

Program 3-13 demonstrates how the Visual Basic logical exclusive or operator is used in an actual program. Listing 3-13-1 presents the code for the form's declaration section, and Listing 3-13-2 the code for the program's **RunButton_Click** procedure. Figure 3-30 illustrates how the program's window would appear after the program has been run.

```
expression Xor expression
```

Where:

expression   is a logical expression.

Figure 3-29 The Visual Basic logical exclusive or operator.

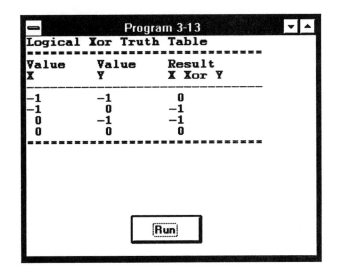

Figure 3-30 A sample logical exclusive or operator program.

Listing 3-13-1:

```
DefInt A-Z

Const True = -1
Const False = 0
```

Listing 3-13-2:

```
Sub RunButton_Click ()

    Form1.FontName = "Courier"
    Form1.FontSize = 8
    Print "Logical Xor Truth Table"
    Print "================================"
    Print "Value     Value     Result"
    Print "X         Y         X Xor Y"
    Print "-------------------------------"
    Print "-1        -1        "; True Xor True
    Print "-1         0        "; True Xor False
    Print " 0        -1        "; False Xor True
    Print " 0         0        "; False Xor False
    Print "================================"

End Sub
```

X	Y	X Eqv Y
True	True	True
True	False	False
False	True	False
False	False	True

Figure 3-31 A logical equivalence truth table.

The Logical Equivalence Operator

The Visual Basic logical equivalence operator (**Eqv**) compares two logical expressions and returns a True if both of the expressions are equal. Otherwise, the logical equivalence operator returns a False result. Figure 3-31 presents a truth table that illustrates how the logical equivalence operator performs its function. Figure 3-32 defines the syntax for the logical equivalence operator.

The examples that follow illustrate the proper use of the logical equivalence operator:

```
Flag Eqv True
ErrorFlag Eqv False
KeyPressed Eqv MouseClicked
```

Program 3-14 demonstrates how the Visual Basic logical equivalence operator is used in an actual program. Listing 3-14-1 presents the code for the form's declaration section and Listing 3-14-2 presents the code for the program's **RunButton_Click** procedure. Figure 3-33 shows how the program's window would appear after the program has been run.

```
expression Eqv expression
```

Where:

expression   is a logical expression.

Figure 3-32 The Visual Basic logical equivalence operator.

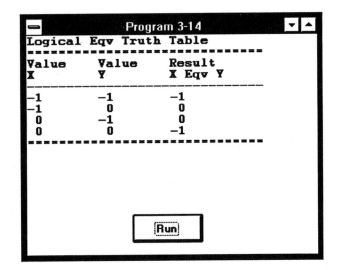

Figure 3-33 A sample logical equivalence operator program.

Listing 3-14-1:

```
DefInt A-Z

Const True = -1
Const False = 0
```

Listing 3-14-2:

```
Sub RunButton_Click ()

    Form1.FontName = "Courier"
    Form1.FontSize = 8
    Print "Logical Eqv Truth Table"
    Print "==============================="
    Print "Value     Value     Result"
    Print "X         Y         X Eqv Y"
    Print "-----------------------------"
    Print "-1        -1        "; True Eqv True
    Print "-1         0        "; True Eqv False
    Print " 0        -1        "; False Eqv True
    Print " 0         0        "; False Eqv False
    Print "==============================="

End Sub
```

X	Y	X Imp Y
True	True	True
True	False	False
False	True	True
False	False	True

Figure 3-34 A logical implication truth table.

The Logical Implication Operator

The Visual Basic logical implication operator (**Imp**) compares two logical expressions and returns a False result if the first logical expression is True and the second logical expression is False. Otherwise, the logical implication operator returns a True result. Figure 3-34 presents a truth table that illustrates how the logical implication operator performs its function. Figure 3-35 defines the syntax for the logical implication operator.

The following examples illustrate the proper use of the logical implication operator:

```
Flag Imp True
ErrorFlag Imp False
KeyPressed Imp MouseClicked
```

Program 3-15 demonstrates how the Visual Basic logical implication operator is used in an actual program. Listing 3-15-1 presents the code for the form's declaration section and Listing 3-15-2 presents the code for the program's **RunButton_Click** procedure. Figure 3-36 shows how the program's window would appear after the program has been run.

```
expression Imp expression
```

Where:

```
expression
```
                                    is a logical expression.

Figure 3-35 The Visual Basic logical implication operator.

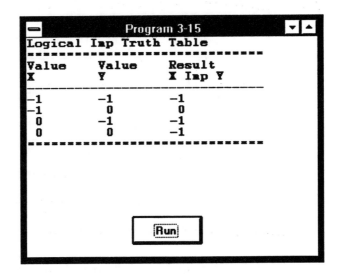

Figure 3-36 A sample logical implication operator program.

Listing 3-15-1:

```
DefInt A-Z

Const True = -1
Const False = 0
```

Listing 3-15-2:

```
Sub RunButton_Click ()

    Form1.FontName = "Courier"
    Form1.FontSize = 8
    Print "Logical Imp Truth Table"
    Print "=============================="
    Print "Value     Value     Result"
    Print "X         Y         X Imp Y"
    Print "------------------------------"
    Print "-1        -1        "; True Imp True
    Print "-1         0        "; True Imp False
    Print " 0        -1        "; False Imp True
    Print " 0         0        "; False Imp False
    Print "=============================="

End Sub
```

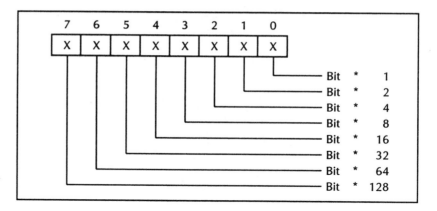

Figure 3-37 A byte of bits.

The Bitwise Complement Operator

The Visual Basic bitwise complement operator (**Not**) negates the result of an integer expression. The bitwise complement operator performs its intended function by inverting the value of each of the integer's **bits**. If you are unfamiliar with the term bit, Figure 3-37 should be of assistance. As this figure illustrates, each byte of memory (one character of memory) is comprised of eight bits. Each bit holds the value of either 1 or 0. By simply inverting each of the integer expression's bits, the bitwise complement operator effectively negates the expression.

Figure 3-38 presents a truth table that illustrates how the bitwise complement operator performs its function. Figure 3-39 defines the syntax for the bitwise complement operator.

The examples below show the proper use of the bitwise complement operator:

    Not Mask
    Not Pixels
    Not BitMask

Program 3-16 shows how the Visual Basic bitwise complement operator is used in an actual program. Listing 3-16-1 presents the code for the form's declarations section and Listing 3-16-2 presents the code for the program's **RunButton_Click** procedure. Figure 3-40 illustrates how the

	Bit X	*Not X*
	1	0
	0	1

Figure 3-38 A bitwise complement truth table.

program's window would appear after the program has been run.

Listing 3-16-1:

```
DefInt A-Z

Const One = Not 0
Const Zero = Not 1
```

Listing 3-16-2:

```
Sub RunButton_Click ()

    Form1.FontName = "Courier"
    Form1.FontSize = 8
    Print "Bitwise Complement Truth Table"
    Print "=============================="
    Print "Value     Value     Result"
    Print "X                   Not X"
    Print "----------------------------"
    Print "1                   "; Not One
    Print "0                   "; Not Zero
    Print "=============================="

End Sub
```

Not *expression*

Where:

expression   is a numeric expression.

Figure 3-39 The Visual Basic bitwise complement operator.

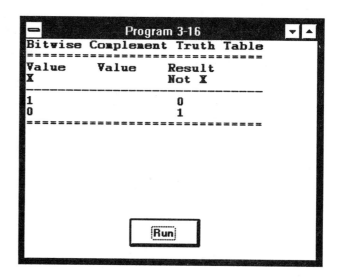

Figure 3-40 A sample bitwise complement operator program.

The Bitwise And Operator

The Visual Basic bitwise and operator (**And**) compares two integer expressions and returns the result of performing **And** operations on them bit-by-bit. Figure 3-41 presents a truth table that illustrates how the bitwise and operator performs its function. Figure 3-42 defines the syntax for the bitwise and operator.

Examples illustrating the proper use of the bitwise and operator follow:

    Value And BitMask
    ShiftPressed And 1
    Pixels And &HF0

Program 3-17 demonstrates how the Visual Basic bitwise and operator is used in an actual program. Listing 3-17-1 presents the code for the form's declaration section, and Listing 3-17-2 the code for the program's **RunButton_Click** procedure. Figure 3-43 shows how the program's window would appear after the program has been run.

Bit X	Bit Y	X And Y
1	1	1
1	0	0
0	1	0
0	0	0

Figure 3-41 A bitwise and truth table.

Listing 3-17-1:

```
DefInt A-Z
```

Listing 3-17-2:

```
Sub RunButton_Click ()

    Form1.FontName = "Courier"
    Form1.FontSize = 8
    Print "Bitwise And Truth Table"
    Print "=============================="
    Print "Value     Value     Result"
    Print "X         Y         X And"
    Print "----------------------------"
    Print "1         1         "; 1 And 1
    Print "1         0         "; 1 And 0
    Print "0         1         "; 0 And 1
    Print "0         0         "; 0 And 0
    Print "=============================="

End Sub
```

expression **And** *expression*

Where:

expression   is a numeric expression.

Figure 3-42 The Visual Basic bitwise and operator.

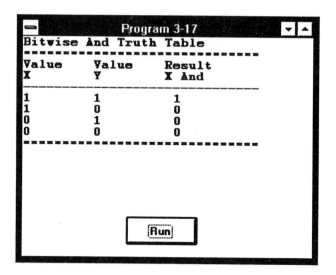

Figure 3-43 A sample bitwise and operator program.

The Bitwise Or Operator

The Visual Basic bitwise or operator (**Or**) compares two expressions and returns the result of performing **Or** operations on them bit-by-bit. Figure 3-44 presents a truth table that illustrates how the bitwise or operator performs its function. Figure 3-45 defines the syntax for the bitwise or operator.

The following examples illustrate the proper use of the bitwise or operator.

    Pixel Or 1
    Flags Or Mask
    ShiftMask Or 2

Program 3-18 demonstrates how the Visual Basic bitwise or operator is used in an actual program. Listing 3-18-1 presents the code for the form's declarations section and Listing 3-18-2 presents the code for the program's **RunButton_Click** procedure. Figure 3-46 shows how the program's window would appear after the program has been run.

Bit X	Bit Y	X Or Y
1	1	1
1	0	1
0	1	1
0	0	0

Figure 3-44 A bitwise or truth table.

Listing 3-18-1:

```
DefInt A-Z
```

Listing 3-18-2:

```
Sub RunButton_Click ()

    Form1.FontName = "Courier"
    Form1.FontSize = 8
    Print "Bitwise Or Truth Table"
    Print "==============================="
    Print "Value    Value     Result"
    Print "X        Y         X Or Y"
    Print "-----------------------------"
    Print "1        1         "; 1 Or 1
    Print "1        0         "; 1 Or 0
    Print "0        1         "; 0 Or 1
    Print "0        0         "; 0 Or 0
    Print "==============================="

End Sub
```

expression **Or** *expression*

Where:

expression   is a numeric expression.

Figure 3-45 The Visual Basic bitwise or operator.

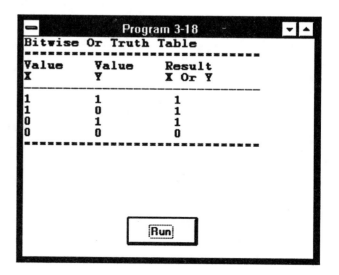

Figure 3-46 A sample bitwise or operator program.

The Bitwise Exclusive Or Operator

The Visual Basic exclusive or operator (**Xor**) compares two integer expressions and returns the result of performing **Xor** functions on them bit-by-bit. Figure 3-47 presents a truth table that illustrates how the bitwise exclusive or operator performs its function. Figure 3-48 defines the syntax for the bitwise exclusive or operator.

The following examples illustrate the proper use of the bitwise exclusive or operator:

Pixels Xor &HFF
ErrorFlag Xor Mask
ShiftFlag Xor 1

Program 3-19 demonstrates how the Visual Basic bitwise exclusive or operator is used in an actual program. Listing 3-19-1 presents the code for the form's declarations section, and Listing 3-19-2 the code for the program's **RunButton_Click** procedure. Figure 3-49 shows how the program's window would appear after the program has been run.

Bit X	*Bit Y*	*X Xor Y*
1	1	0
1	0	1
0	1	1
0	0	0

Figure 3-47 A bitwise exclusive or truth table.

Listing 3-19-1:

```
DefInt A-Z
```

Listing 3-19-2:

```
Sub RunButton_Click ()

    Form1.FontName = "Courier"
    Form1.FontSize = 8
    Print "Bitwise Xor Truth Table"
    Print "=============================="
    Print "Value     Value      Result"
    Print "X         Y          X Xor Y"
    Print "------------------------------"
    Print "1         1         "; 1 Xor 1
    Print "1         0         "; 1 Xor 0
    Print "0         1         "; 0 Xor 1
    Print "0         0         "; 0 Xor 0
    Print "=============================="

End Sub
```

expression **Xor** *expression*

Where:

expression is a numeric expression.

Figure 3-48 The Visual Basic bitwise exclusive or operator.

```
 ⊟            Program 3-19              ▼ ▲
Bitwise Xor Truth Table
■■■■■■■■■■■■■■■■■■■■■■■■■■■■■■■■■■■
Value        Value        Result
X            Y            X Xor Y
─────────────────────────────────
1            1            0
1            0            1
0            1            1
0            0            0
■■■■■■■■■■■■■■■■■■■■■■■■■■■■■■■■■■■



              ┌─────────┐
              │  Run    │
              └─────────┘
```

Figure 3-49   A sample bitwise exclusive or operator program.

The Bitwise Equivalence Operator

The Visual Basic bitwise equivalence operator (**Eqv**) compares two integer expressions and returns the result of performing Eqv functions on them bit-by-bit. Figure 3-50 presents a truth table that illustrates how the bitwise equivalence operator performs its function. Figure 3-51 defines the syntax for the bitwise equivalence operator.

The following examples illustrate the proper use of the bitwise equivalence operator:

Pixels Eqv &HFF
ErrorFlag Eqv Mask
ShiftFlag Eqv 1

Program 3-20 demonstrates how the Visual Basic bitwise equivalence operator is used in an actual program. Listing 3-20-1 presents the code for the form's declarations section and Listing 3-20-2 presents the code for the program's **RunButton_Click** procedure. Figure 3-52 illustrates how the program's window would appear after the program has been run.

Bit X	*Bit Y*	*X Eqv Y*
1	1	1
1	0	0
0	1	0
0	0	1

Figure 3-50 A bitwise equivalence truth table.

Listing 3-20-1:

```
DefInt A-Z

Const One = -1
```

Listing 3-20-2:

```
Sub RunButton_Click ()

    Form1.FontName = "Courier"
    Form1.FontSize = 8
    Print "Bitwise Eqv Truth Table"
    Print "=============================="
    Print "Value     Value      Result"
    Print "X         Y          X Eqv Y"
    Print "------------------------------"
    Print "1         1          "; Abs(One Eqv One)
    Print "1         0          "; Abs(One Eqv 0)
    Print "0         1          "; Abs(0 Eqv One)
    Print "0         0          "; Abs(0 Eqv 0)
    Print "=============================="

End Sub
```

expression **Eqv** *expression*

Where:

expression   is a numeric expression.

Figure 3-51 The Visual Basic bitwise equivalence operator.

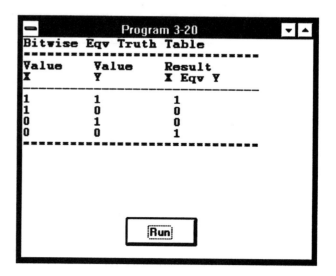

Figure 3-52   A sample bitwise equivalence operator program.

The Bitwise Implication Operator

The Visual Basic bitwise implication operator **(Imp)** compares two integer expressions and returns the result of performing **Imp** functions on them bit-by-bit. Figure 3-53 presents a truth table that illustrates how the bitwise implication operator performs its function. Figure 3-54 defines the syntax for the bitwise implication operator.

The following are examples illustrating the proper use of the bitwise implication operator:

```
Pixels Imp &HFF
ErrorFlag Imp Mask
ShiftFlag Imp 4
```

Program 3-21 demonstrates how the Visual Basic bitwise implication operator is used in an actual program. Listing 3-21-1 presents the code for the form's declarations section, and Listing 3-21-2 the code for the program's **RunButton_Click** procedure. Figure 3-55 shows how the program's window would appear after the program has been run.

Bit X	Bit Y	X Imp Y
1	1	1
1	0	0
0	1	1
0	0	1

Figure 3-53 The bitwise implication truth table.

Listing 3-21-1:

```
DefInt A-Z

Const One = -1
```

Listing 3-21-2:

```
Sub RunButton_Click ()

    Form1.FontName = "Courier"
    Form1.FontSize = 8
    Print "Bitwise Imp Truth Table"
    Print "=============================="
    Print "Value      Value      Result"
    Print "X          Y          X Imp Y"
    Print "------------------------------"
    Print "1          1          "; Abs(One Imp One)
    Print "1          0          "; Abs(One Imp 0)
    Print "0          1          "; Abs(0 Imp One)
    Print "0          0          "; Abs(0 Imp 0)
    Print "=============================="

End Sub
```

expression **Imp** *expression*

Where:

expression   is a numeric expression.

Figure 3-54 The Visual Basic bitwise implication operator.

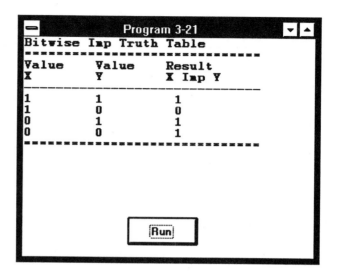

Figure 3-55 A sample bitwise implication operator program.

The String Concatenation Operator

The Visual Basic string concatenation operator (+) is used to combine two string expressions to form an even larger string. Figure 3-56 defines the syntax for the string concatenation operator.

Examples illustrating the proper use of the string concatenation operator are:

> "Washington" + "D.C."
> "A String" + CHR$(33)
> FirstName$ + MiddleInitial$ + LastName$

---

expression + expression

Where:

expression   is a string expression.

Figure 3-56 The Visual Basic string concatenation operator.

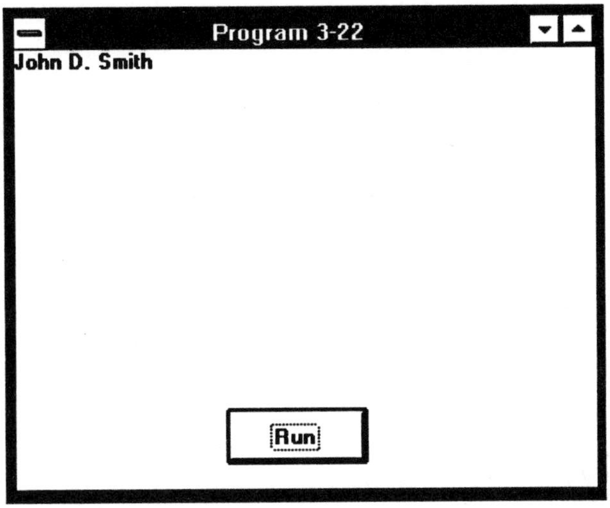

Figure 3-57 A sample string concatenation operator program.

Program 3-22 demonstrates how the Visual Basic string concatenation operator is used in an actual program. Listing 3-22 presents the code for the program's **RunButton_Click** procedure. Figure 3-57 shows how the program's window would appear after the program has been run.

Listing 3-22:

```
Sub RunButton_Click ()

    FirstName$ = "John"
    MiddleInitial$ = "D"
    LastName$ = "Smith"
    FullName$ = FirstName$ + " " + MiddleInitial$ +
". " + LastName$
    Print FullName$

End Sub
```

The Equal To Operator

The Visual Basic equal to operator (=) compares two expressions to see if they are equal in value. If they are, the equal to operator returns a value of True. If the two expressions aren't

---

```
expression = expression
```

Where:

```
expression
```
 is a valid Visual Basic expression.

Figure 3-58 The Visual Basic equal to operator.

equal, the equal to operator returns a value of False. Figure 3-58 defines the syntax for the equal to operator.

The following examples illustrate the proper use of the equal to operator:

Flag = True
N = 1
15.0 = Diameter

Program 3-23 demonstrates how the Visual Basic equal to operator is used in an actual program. Listing 3-23 presents the code for the program's **RunButton_Click** procedure. Figure 3-59 shows how the program's window would appear after the program has been run.

Listing 3-23:

```
Sub RunButton_Click ()

    Print "1 = 1 is "; 1 = 1
    Print "2 = 1 is "; 2 = 1
    Print "1 = 2 is "; 1 = 2

End Sub
```

The Not Equal To Operator

The Visual Basic not equal to operator (<>) compares two expressions to see if they are unequal in value. If the two expressions are unequal, the not equal to operator returns a value of True. If the two expressions are equal, the not equal to operator returns a value of False. Figure 3-60 defines the syntax for the not equal to operator.

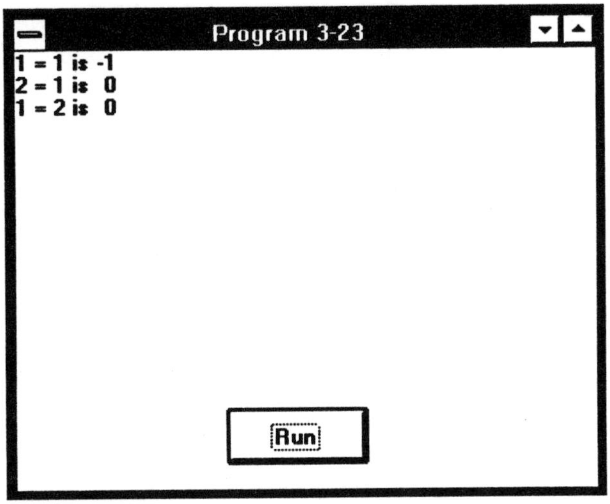

Figure 3-59 A sample equal to operator program.

The following examples illustrate the proper use of the not equal to operator:

    Flag <> True
    Count <> 2
    MouseButton <> Clicked

Program 3-24 demonstrates how the Visual Basic not equal to operator is used in an actual program. Listing 3-24 presents the code for the program's **RunButton_Click** procedure. Figure 3-61 illustrates how the program's window would appear after the program has been run.

```
expression <> expression
```

Where:

`expression`   is a valid Visual Basic expression.

Figure 3-60 The Visual Basic not equal to operator.

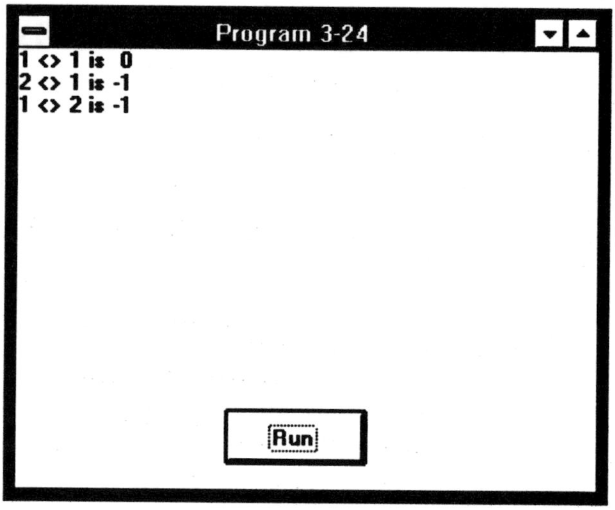

Figure 3-61 A sample not equal to operator program.

Listing 3-24:

```
Sub RunButton_Click ()

    Print "1 <> 1 is "; 1 <> 1
    Print "2 <> 1 is "; 2 <> 1
    Print "1 <> 2 is "; 1 <> 2

End Sub
```

The Greater Than Operator

The Visual Basic greater than operator (>) compares two expressions to see if the first expression is greater than the second. If it is, the greater than operator returns a value of True. If the first expression is less than or equal to the second expression, the greater than operator returns a value of False. Figure 3-62 defines the syntax for the greater than operator.

The following examples illustrate the proper use of the greater than operator:

N > 1
Count > Maximum
MouseColumn > 80

expression > *expression*

Where:

expression   is a valid Visual Basic expression.

Figure 3-62   The Visual Basic greater than operator.

Program 3-25 demonstrates how the Visual Basic greater than operator is used in an actual program. Listing 3-25 presents the code for the program's **RunButton_Click** procedure. Figure 3-63 illustrates how the program's window would appear after the program has been run.

Listing 3-25:

```
Sub RunButton_Click ()

    Print "1 > 1 is "; 1 > 1
    Print "2 > 1 is "; 2 > 1
    Print "1 > 2 is "; 1 > 2

End Sub
```

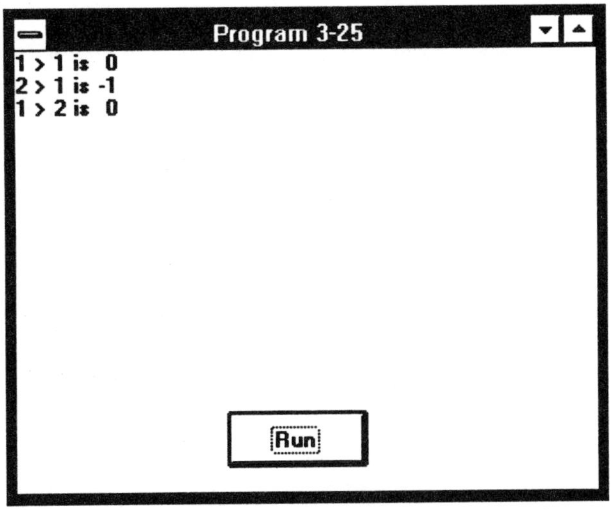

Figure 3-63   A sample greater than operator program.

The Greater Than Or Equal To Operator

The Visual Basic greater than or equal to operator (>=) compares two expressions to see if the first expression is greater than or equal to the second. If it is, the greater than or equal to operator returns a value of True. If the first expression is less than the second expression, the greater than or equal to operator returns a value of False. Figure 3-64 defines the syntax for the greater than or equal to operator.

Examples illustrating the proper use of the greater than or equal to operator follow:

```
Count >= 55
DisplayRow >= 23
N >= 5
```

Program 3-26 demonstrates how the Visual Basic greater than or equal to operator is used in an actual program. Listing 3-26 presents the code for the program's **RunButton_Click** procedure. Figure 3-65 illustrates how the program's window would appear after the program has been run.

Listing 3-26:

```
Sub RunButton_Click ()

    Print "1 >= 1 is "; 1 >= 1
    Print "2 >= 1 is "; 2 >= 1
    Print "1 >= 2 is "; 1 >= 2

End Sub
```

---

expression >= *expression*

Where:

expression   is a valid Visual Basic expression.

Figure 3-64 The Visual Basic greater than or equal to operator.

```
┌─────────────────────────────────────────────┐
│ ▄    Program 3-26             ▼ ▲ │
│ 1 >= 1 is -1                                  │
│ 2 >= 1 is -1                                  │
│ 1 >= 2 is  0                                  │
│                                               │
│                                               │
│                                               │
│                                               │
│                                               │
│                                               │
│              ┌──────────┐                     │
│              │  Run    │                     │
│              └──────────┘                     │
└─────────────────────────────────────────────┘
```

Figure 3-65 A sample greater than or equal to operator program.

The Less Than Operator

The Visual Basic less than operator (<) compares two expressions to see if the first expression is less than the second. If it is, the less than operator returns a value of True. If the first expression is greater than or equal to the second expression, the less than operator returns a value of False. Figure 3-66 defines the syntax for the less than operator.

The following examples illustrate the proper use of the less than operator:

```
N < 3
MouseRow < 0
Counter < 55
```

---

expression **<** *expression*

Where:

expression   is a valid Visual Basic expression.

Figure 3-66 The Visual Basic less than operator.

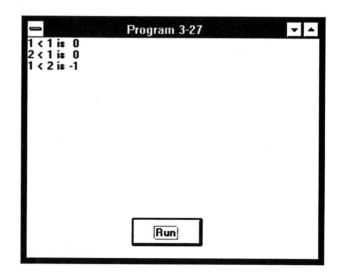

Figure 3-67 A sample less than operator program.

Program 3-27 demonstrates how the Visual Basic less than operator is used in an actual program. Listing 3-27 presents the code for the program's **RunButton_Click** procedure. Figure 3-67 shows how the program's window would appear after the program has been run.

Listing 3-27:

```
Sub RunButton_Click ()

    Print "1 << 1 is "; 1 < 1
    Print "2 < 1 is "; 2 < 1
    Print "1 < 2 is "; 1 < 2

End Sub
```

The Less Than Or Equal To Operator

The Visual Basic less than or equal to operator (**<=**) compares two expressions to see if the first expression is less than or equal to the second. If it is, the less than or equal to operator returns a value of True. If the first expression is greater than the second expression, the less than or equal to operator returns a value of

---

expression <= *expression*

Where:

expression   is a valid Visual Basic expression.

Figure 3-68 The Visual Basic less than or equal to operator.

False. Figure 3-68 defines the syntax for the less than or equal to operator.

The following examples illustrate the proper use of the less than or equal to operator:

Count <= 5
DisplayColumn <= 78
N <= 3

Program 3-28 demonstrates how the Visual Basic less than or equal to operator is used in an actual program. Listing 3-28 presents the code for the program's **RunButton_Click** procedure. Figure 3-69 illustrates how the program's window would appear after the program has been run.

Listing 3-28:

```
Sub RunButton_Click ()

    Print "1 <<= 1 is "; 1 <= 1
    Print "2 <= 1 is "; 2 <= 1
    Print "1 <= 2 is "; 1 <= 2

End Sub
```

Operator Precedence

Evaluating an expression with only one operator type is a fairly straightforward task. For example, the expression **2 + 3 + 6** is evaluated in two steps: 1) the expression **2 + 3** is figured and a result of **5** is returned and 2) the **6** is added to the previous result. Accordingly, the expression returns a value of **11**.

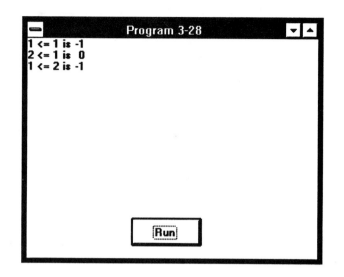

Figure 3-69 A sample less than or equal to operator program.

When expressions have the same operator type, Visual Basic simply evaluates them from left to right. But how does Visual Basic evaluate expressions that have more than one operator type? How, for instance, does Visual Basic evaluate the expression **2 + 3 * 6**?

If Visual Basic was to evaluate the **2 + 3** portion of the expression first, the result would be determined as follows:

```
2 + 3 * 6
  5   * 6 = 30
```

But if Visual Basic was to evaluate the **3 * 6** portion of the expression first, the result would be determined as follows:

```
2 + 3 * 6
2 +  18  = 20
```

It's rather obvious that the two different methods for evaluating the same expression return two vastly different results. The Visual Basic programming language uses a set of rules called operator precedence to evaluate expressions in order to overcome these types of conflicts. Essentially, Visual Basic assigns a precedence level for each of its operators. When an expression is evaluated, the subexpression (one of the individual expressions that make up a more complex expression) that contains the operator with the highest precedence is evaluated first, the subexpression that contains the operator with the next highest precedence is evaluated second, and so on. This method continues until the portion of the expression with the lowest precedence has been evaluated.

Figure 3-70 defines the precedence levels that Visual Basic assigns to its wide range of operators. As the figure shows, some of the operators have equal levels of precedence. Whenever Visual Basic encounters two or more subexpressions with operators of equal precedence, they are evaluated on a strictly left-to-right basis.

It is possible to override the Visual Basic precedence rules by simply surrounding a subexpression with parentheses. Surrounding a subexpression with parentheses tells Visual Basic

Level	*Operators*
13	^
12	– (Negation)
11	*,/
10	\
9	Mod
8	+,– (Subtraction)
7	=,>,<,<>,<=,>=
6	Not
5	And
4	Or
3	Xor
2	Eqv
1	Imp

Figure 3-70 The Visual Basic operator precedence levels.

to evaluate the subexpression first. For example, the expression **5 * 3 - 2** would be evaluated as follows:

$$5 * 3 - 2$$
$$15 \;\; - 2 = 13$$

On the other hand, the expression **5 * (3 - 2)** would be evaluated as follows:

$$5 * (3 - 2)$$
$$5 * \;\;\; 1 \;\; = 5$$

What if you had an expression, such as **150 \\ ((4 - 2) * 3)**, with nested (one inside the other) parentheses? Visual Basic would interpret such an expression by evaluating the inner-most subexpression first. Thus, the expression **150 \\ ((4 - 2) * 3)** would be evaluated as follows:

$$150 \backslash ((4 - 2) * 3)$$
$$150 \backslash (\;\;\; 2 \;\;\; * 3)$$
$$150 \backslash \;\;\;\;\; 6 \;\;\;\;\; = 25$$

Program 3-29 demonstrates how Visual Basic evaluates a variety of expressions. Listing 3-29 presents the code for the program's **RunButton_Click** procedure. Figure 3-71 illustrates how the program's window would appear after the program has been run.

Listing 3-29:

```
Sub RunButton_Click ()

    Print "1 + 3 * 4 = ?"
    Print "1 + "; 3 * 4; " ="; 1 + 3 * 4
    Print "150 \ ((4 - 2) * 3 = ?"
    Print "150 \ ( "; 4 - 2; " * 3) = ?"
    Print "150 \        "; 2 * 3; "    ="; 150 \ ((4 -
2) * 3)

End Sub
```

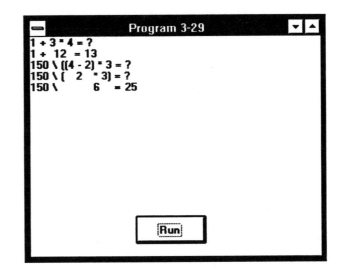

Figure 3-71 A sample operator precedence program.

Summary

You now know how to use the Visual Basic operators to manipulate data. Furthermore, you are also familiar with the Visual Basic precedence rules and how they can be overridden through the use of parentheses. Chapter 4 describes Visual Basic's program flow.

Chapter 4

Program Flow

This chapter describes Visual Basic's program flow, which can be summarized as follows. Essentially, a Visual Basic program is comprised of a collection of procedures. These procedures are called by Windows whenever an appropriate event has occurred. When an event does occur, Windows calls the related event's procedure. The event procedure is executed from the top of the procedure to the bottom until it either reaches the end of the procedure or is prematurely halted by either an **Exit** or an **End** statement. In addition to examining this basic structure, this chapter introduces you to the program flow statements and shows how they are used in actual programs.

If...Then Statements

Many times a program will have to do different things depending on a certain condition. To meet these conditional demands, Visual Basic is equipped with a variety of decision-making statements. The simplest Visual Basic decision-making statement is the **If...Then** statement. Visual Basic supports two

93

```
If expression Then statement[: statement]...
```

Where:

expression   is a logical expression.

statement   is a valid Visual Basic statement.

Figure 4-1   A single-line If...Then statement.

distinct forms of the **If...Then** statement: single-line **If...Then** statements and block **If...Then** statements. Figure 4-1 defines the syntax for Visual Basic's single-line **If...Then** statements. Figure 4-2 defines the syntax for block **If...Then** statements. Although single-line **If...Then** statements are useful, their restriction to a single program line greatly hampers the amount of code that can be executed by the **If...Then** statement. Conversely, block **If...Then** statements allow for an almost unlimited number of statements inside of their conditional block. Accordingly, the block **If...Then** statement is usually the superior method for implementing a decision-making statement.

The logic behind the Visual Basic **If...Then** statement is extremely simple. **If** the logical expression following the **If** keyword is equal to True, **Then** the program statement or statements following the **Then** keyword will be executed.

```
If expression Then
    statement
    .
    .
    .
    statement
End If
```

Where:

expression   is a logical expression.

statement   is a valid Visual Basic statement.

Figure 4-2   A block If...Then statement.

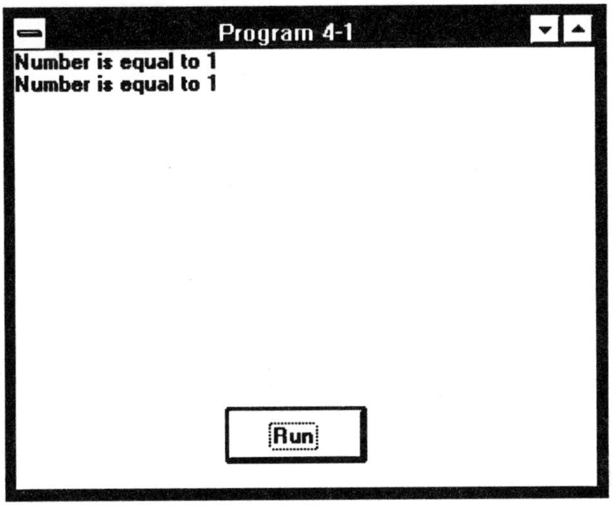

Figure 4-3 A sample If...Then program.

Program 4-1 demonstrates how both single-line and block **If...Then** statements are used in an actual Visual Basic program. Listing 4-1-1 presents the code for the form's declarations section and Listing 4-1-2 presents the code for the program's **RunButton_Click** procedure. Figure 4-3 illustrates how the program's window would appear after the program has been run.

Listing 4-1-1:

```
DefInt A-Z
```

Listing 4-1-2:

```
Sub RunButton_Click ()

    Number = 1
    If Number = 1 Then Print "Number is equal to 1"
    If Number = 0 Then Print "Number is equal to 0"
    If Number = 1 Then
        Print "Number is equal to 1"
    End If
    If Number = 0 Then
        Print "Number is equal to 0"
    End If

End Sub
```

```
If expression Then statement[: statement]... Else
statement[:statement]...
```

Where:

expression   is a logical expression.

statement   is a valid Visual Basic statement.

Figure 4-4   A single-line If...Then...Else statement.

If...Then...Else Statements

Besides being able to perform an action if a condition is True, an **If...Then** statement can be extended with an **Else** clause to perform an action if the condition is False. This new type of decision-making statement is known as the **If...Then...Else** statement. Figure 4-4 illustrates how a single-line **If...Then...Else** statement is constructed. Figure 4-5 shows how a block **If...Then...Else** statement is constructed.

```
If expression Then
    statement
    .
    .
    .
    statement Else
    statement
    .
    .
    .
    statement
End If
```

Where:

expression   is a logical expression.

statement   is a valid Visual Basic statement.

Figure 4-5   A block If...Then...Else statement.

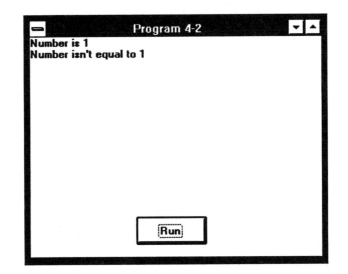

Figure 4-6 A sample If...Then...Else program.

The logic behind an **If...Then...Else** statement is easy to understand. **If** the condition is True, **Then** the program statement or statements following the **Then** keyword are executed, **Else** the statement or statements following the **Else** keyword are executed.

Program 4-2 shows how both single-line and block **If...Then...Else** statements are used in an actual Visual Basic program. Listing 4-2-1 presents the code for the form's declarations section, and Listing 4-2-2 the code for the program's **RunButton_Click** procedure. Figure 4-6 illustrates how the program's window would appear after the program has been run.

Listing 4-2-1:

```
DefInt A-Z
```

Listing 4-2-2:

```
Sub RunButton_Click ()

    Number = 1
    If Number = 1 Then Print "Number is 1" Else Print
"Number isn't 1"
```

```
        Number = 0
        If Number = 1 Then
            Print "Number is equal to 1"
        Else
            Print "Number isn't equal to 1"
        End If

End Sub
```

Many times a decision-making statement will need to make more than one decision in the statement. For example, the following **If...Then...Else** statement checks for a second condition in the **Else** clause:

```
If Number > 0 Then
    Print "Number is greater than 0"
Else
    If Number < 0 Then
        Print "Number is less than 0"
    End If
End IF
```

To simplify decision-making statements like the above, Visual Basic allows programmers to use the **ElseIf** clause. Simply put, the **ElseIf** clause tests for a second condition. If the **ElseIf** condition is True, Visual Basic will execute the **ElseIf** clause's associated statement or statements. Unlike **Else** clauses, an **ElseIf** clause can't be used in a single-line statement. Figure 4-7 illustrates how an **If...Then...ElseIf** statement is constructed. You should note from this illustration that Visual Basic allows you to use an optional **Else** clause in an **If...Then...ElseIf** statement. Furthermore, multiple **ElseIf** clauses in a single statement are permissible.

Program 4-3 demonstrates how the **If...Then...ElseIf** statement is used in an actual Visual Basic program. Listing 4-3-1 presents the code for the form's declarations section and Listing 4-3-2 presents the code for the program's **RunButton_Click** procedure. Figure 4-8 illustrates how the program's window would appear after the program has been run.

Listing 4-3-1:

```
DefInt A-Z
```

```
If expression Then
    statement
    .
    .
    .
    statement
ElseIf expression Then
    statement
    .
    .
    .
    statement
Else
    statement
    .
    .
    .
    statement
End If
```

Where:

expression   is a logical expression.

statement   is a valid Visual Basic expression.

Figure 4-7   An If...Then...ElseIf statement.

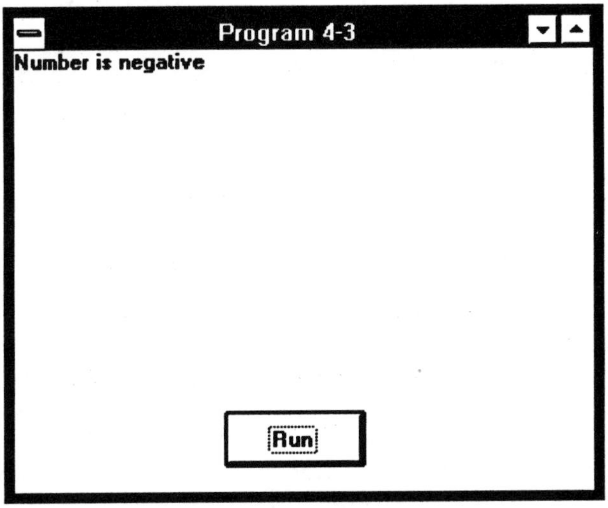

Figure 4-8   A sample If...Then...ElseIf program.

Listing 4-3-2:

```
Sub RunButton_Click ()

    Number = -1
    If Number = 0 Then
        Print "Number is equal to 0"
    ElseIf Number < 0 Then
        Print "Number is negative"
    Else
        Print "Number is positive"
    End If

End Sub
```

Select Case Statements

Although **If...Then** and **If...Then...Else** statements are useful for performing actions depending on a condition being either True or False, many situations arise in a program that require a variety of actions to be performed depending on an expression's value. To meet this requirement, Visual Basic provides the **Select Case** statement. Figure 4-9 defines how a Visual Basic **Select Case** statement is constructed. As this figure illustrates, the **Case** expression lists can either be a single expression or a group of expressions. The individual expressions in a **Case** expression list are separated with commas. **Case** expressions can either be a single value, a range of values, or a relational check. The following are some examples of single-value **Case** expression lists:

> Case 1
> Case 33, 44, 55, 66
> Case "Match"
> Case "Y", "y"

Case expressions that specify a range of values use the **To** keyword to separate the range's lower limit and the range's upper limit. Some examples of **Case** expression lists that use a range of values follow:

Case -5 To 55
Case 1 To 3, 5 To 7
Case 33 To 1000
Case 99 To 100

Case expressions that perform a relational check with the **Select Case** expression use the **Is** keyword and a relational operator. Below are some examples of **Case** statements that perform a relational check:

Case Is < 3
Case Is > 1000
Case Is >= 32
Case Is <> 55

Of course, Visual Basic allows you to put all three types of expressions in a single **Case** statement. The following are some examples of a variety of valid **Case** statements:

Case 22, 30 To 40, Is > 100
Case 33, 29
Case Is < 100
Case -100 To 0, 100 to 200

The illustration also shows that Visual Basic supports a **Case Else** clause in a **Select Case** statement. The statements following a **Case Else** clause will only be executed if none of the **Case** statements match the **Select Case** expression. Although a **Case Else** clause is strictly optional, Visual Basic will generate a run time error if the **Select Case** expression doesn't match any of the expressions in the **Case** statements. Therefore, a **Case Else** clause should be used at all times. If the **Case Else** clause isn't really necessary in the **Select Case** statement, simply put in the **Case Else** clause without any statements. That way, Visual Basic will simply do nothing if a match isn't found in the **Case** statements.

Program 4-4 demonstrates how the **Select Case** statement is used in an actual Visual Basic program. Listing 4-4-1 presents the code for the form's declarations section and Listing 4-4-2 presents the code for the program's **RunButton_Click** procedure. Figure 4-10 illustrates how the program's window would appear after the program has been run.

```
Select Case expression
    Case expression list
        statement
            .
            .
            .
        statement
    Case expression list
        statement
            .
            .
            .
        statement
    Case Else
        statement
            .
            .
            .
        statement
End Select
```

Where:

expression	is a valid Visual Basic expression.
expression list	is an expression or expressions to match the **Select Case** expression against.
statement	is a valid Visual Basic statement.

Figure 4-9   The Visual Basic Select Case statement.

Listing 4-4-1:

```
DefInt A-Z
```

Listing 4-4-2:

```
Sub RunButton_Click ()

    Number = 3
    Select Case Number
        Case Is < 1
            Print "The number is less than 1"
```

```
        Case 1
            Print "The number is a 1"
        Case 2
            Print "The number is a 2"
        Case 3 To 5
            Print "The number is a 3, 4, or 5"
        Case 7, 10
            Print "The number is a 7 or 10"
        Case 8
            Print "The number is an 8"
        Case 9
            Print "The number is a 9"
        Case Else
            Print "The number is a 6 or greater than 10"
    End Select

End Sub
```

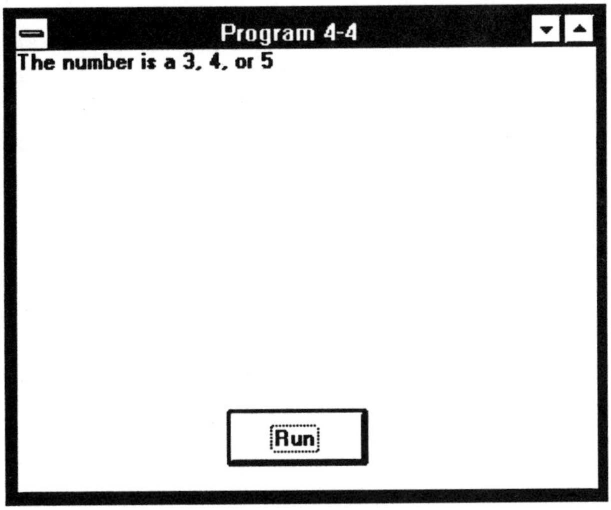

Figure 4-10   A sample Select Case program.

While...Wend Statements

The Visual Basic **While...Wend** statement tells the program to execute a statement or a series of statements continuously until a condition is no longer True. Figure 4-11 defines the syntax for the **While...Wend** statement.

```
While expression
    statement
    .

    .

    .
    statement
Wend
```

Where:

expression   is a logical expression.

statement   is a valid Visual Basic statement.

Figure 4-11 The Visual Basic While...Wend statement.

Program 4-5 demonstrates how a Visual Basic **While...Wend** statement is used in a program that displays every odd number between 100 and 200. Listing 4-5-1 presents the code for the form's declaration section, and Listing 4-5-2 the code for the program's **RunButton_Click** procedure. Figure 4-12 illustrates how the program's window would appear after the program has been run.

Listing 4-5-1:

```
DefInt A-Z
```

Listing 4-5-2:

```
Sub RunButton_Click ()

    Number = 101
    While Number < 201

        Print Number;
        Number = Number + 2
        If Number Mod 10 = 1 Then
            Print
        End If
    Wend
End Sub
```

```
┌────────────────────────────────────────────────┐
│ ▬              Program 4-5              ▼ ▲     │
│ 101  103  105  107  109                          │
│ 111  113  115  117  119                          │
│ 121  123  125  127  129                          │
│ 131  133  135  137  139                          │
│ 141  143  145  147  149                          │
│ 151  153  155  157  159                          │
│ 161  163  165  167  169                          │
│ 171  173  175  177  179                          │
│ 181  183  185  187  189                          │
│ 191  193  195  197  199                          │
│                                                  │
│                                                  │
│                    ┌───────┐                     │
│                    │ Run   │                     │
│                    └───────┘                     │
│                                                  │
└────────────────────────────────────────────────┘
```

Figure 4-12 A sample While...Wend program.

To better understand how a Visual Basic **While...Wend** statement works, let's take a closer look at the **RunButton_Click** procedure.

`Number = 101` assigns the value 101 to the integer variable **Number**.

`While Number < 201` checks the value of **Number**. If **Number** is less than 201, the **While...Wend** loop is executed. If **Number** is greater than or equal to 201, the **While...Wend** loop is ignored.

`Print Number;` displays **Number**'s current value.

`Number = Number + 2` increases the value of **Number** to the next odd value.

```
If Number Mod 10 = 1 Then
    Print
End If
```
moves the cursor to the start of the next line if five values have been displayed.

`Wend` tells Visual Basic to loop back to the **Wend**'s associated **While** statement.

You may be wondering what happens if the **While** condition is initially False. The **While...Wend** loop will never be executed. For example, the following **While...Wend** loop would never be executed:

```
While 0
    I = I + 1
Wend
```

The initial condition is False. Consequently, the statement **I = I + 1** will never be executed.

Do...Loop Statements

In addition to **While...Wend** statements, Visual Basic offers the **Do...Loop** statement to construct even more versatile looping structures. The Visual Basic **Do...Loop** statement comes in four basic forms: the **Do...Loop...While** statement, the **Do...Loop...Until** statement, the **Do...While...Loop** statement, and the **Do...Until...Loop** statement. Let's take a more detailed look at each of these four distinct types of **Do...Loop** statements.

Figure 4-13 illustrates how a **Do...Loop...While** statement is constructed. As this figure illustrates, the **Do...Loop...While** statement performs a conditional check at the end of each loop. As long as the **Do...Loop...While** statement's condition holds True, the loop will be repeated. It is important to note that the statements contained inside of the loop will always be executed

```
Do
    statement
    .
    .
    .
    statement
Loop While expression
```

Where:

statement   is a valid Visual Basic statement.

expression   is a logical expression.

Figure 4-13   The Visual Basic Do...Loop...While statement.

at least once. This is caused by the fact that the loop is executed before the conditional check. Consequently, the check is never made until the loop's statements have been executed for the first time.

Program 4-6 demonstrates how the **Do...Loop...While** statement is used in an actual program. Listing 4-6-1 presents the code for the form's declarations section and Listing 4-6-2 presents the code for the program's **RunButton_Click** procedure. Figure 4-14 shows how the program's window would appear after the program has been run.

Listing 4-6-1:

```
DefInt A-Z
```

Listing 4-6-2:

```
Sub RunButton_Click ()

    Number = 101
    Do
        Print Number;
        Number = Number + 2
        If Number Mod 10 = 1 Then
            Print
        End If
    Loop While Number < 201

End Sub
```

To better understand how the **Do...Loop...While** statement works, let's take a closer look at the program's **RunButton_Click** procedure:

`Number = 101` assigns the value of 101 to the integer variable **Number**.

`Do` causes the loop to be executed.

`Print Number;` displays **Number**'s current value.

`Number = Number + 2` increases the value of **Number** to the next odd value.

```
┌─────────────────────────────────────────────────┐
│ ▬            Program 4-6             ▼ ▲ │
├─────────────────────────────────────────────────┤
│ 101  103  105  107  109                          │
│ 111  113  115  117  119                          │
│ 121  123  125  127  129                          │
│ 131  133  135  137  139                          │
│ 141  143  145  147  149                          │
│ 151  153  155  157  159                          │
│ 161  163  165  167  169                          │
│ 171  173  175  177  179                          │
│ 181  183  185  187  189                          │
│ 191  193  195  197  199                          │
│                                                  │
│                                                  │
│                                                  │
│                  ┌────────┐                      │
│                  │  Run   │                      │
│                  └────────┘                      │
│                                                  │
└─────────────────────────────────────────────────┘
```

Figure 4-14 A sample Do...Loop...While program.

```
If Number Mod 10 = 1 Then
    Print
End If
```
moves cursor to the start of the next line if five values have been displayed.

```
Loop While Number < 201
```
checks to see if the last odd value has been displayed. If the last odd value hasn't been displayed, program execution will loop back to the **Do** keyword.

Figure 4-15 illustrates how a **Do...Loop...Until** statement is constructed. As this figure illustrates, the **Do...Loop...Until** statement performs a conditional check at the end of each loop. As long as the **Do...Loop...Until** statement's condition holds False, the loop will be repeated. As with **Do...Loop...While** statements, **Do...Loop...Until** statements will always execute their associated loop statements at least once.

Program 4-7 demonstrates how a **Do...Loop...Until** statement is used in an actual program. Listing 4-7-1 presents the code for the form's declarations section and Listing 4-7-2 presents the code for the program's **RunButton_Click** procedure. Figure 4-16 illustrates how the program's window would appear after the program has been run.

```
Do
    statement
    .
    .
    .
    statement
Loop Until expression
```

Where:

`statement`	is a valid Visual Basic statement.
`expression`	is a logical expression.

Figure 4-15   The Visual Basic Do...Loop...Until statement.

Listing 4-7-1:

```
DefInt A-Z
```

Listing 4-7-2:

```
Sub RunButton_Click ()

    Number = 101
    Do
        Print Number;
        Number = Number + 2
        If Number Mod 10 = 1 Then
            Print
        End If
    Loop Until Number = 201

End Sub
```

To better understand how the **Do...Loop...Until** statement works, let's take a closer look at the program's **RunButton_Click** procedure:

`Number = 101` assigns the value 101 to the integer variable **Number**.

`Do` causes the loop to be executed.

`Print Number;` displays **Number**'s current value.

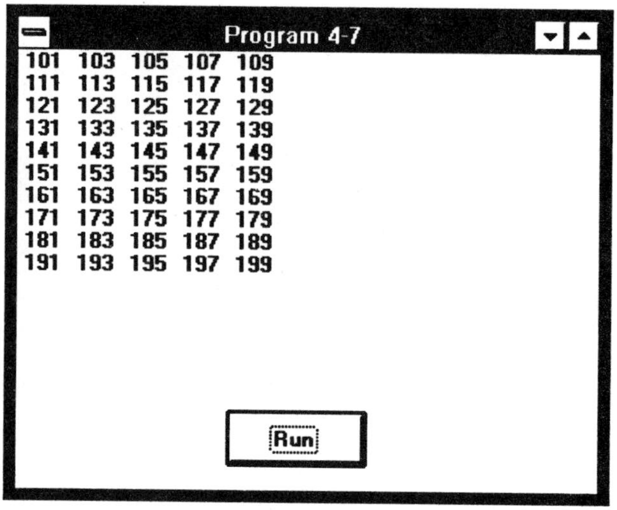

Figure 4-16 A sample Do...Loop...Until program.

`Number = Number + 2` increases the value of **Number** to the next odd value.

```
If Number Mod 10 = 1 Then
    Print
End If
```
moves the cursor to the start of the next line if five values have been displayed.

`Loop Until Number = 201` checks to see if the last odd value has been displayed. If the last odd value hasn't been displayed, program execution will loop back to the **Do** keyword.

Figure 4-17 illustrates how a **Do...While...Loop** statement is constructed. As this figure shows, the **Do...While...Loop** statement performs a conditional check at the start of each loop. As long as the **Do...While...Loop** statement's condition holds True, the loop will be repeated. Because the condition is checked at the start of the loop, it is possible that the loop will never actually be executed. If, for instance, the **Do...While...Loop** statement's condition is initially False, Visual Basic would completely ignore the **Do...While...Loop**.

Program 4-8 demonstrates how the **Do...While...Loop** statement is used in an actual program. Listing 4-8-1 presents the code for the form's declaration section, and Listing 4-8-2

```
Do While expression
    statement
    .
    .
    .
    statement
Loop
```

Where:

expression   is a logical expression.

statement   is a valid Visual Basic statement.

Figure 4-17   The Visual Basic Do...While...Loop statement.

presents the code for the program's **RunButton_Click** procedure. Figure 4-18 illustrates how the program's window would
appear after the program has been run.

Listing 4-8-1:

```
DefInt A-Z
```

Listing 4-8-2:

```
Sub RunButton_Click ()

    Number = 101
    Do While Number < 201
        Print Number;
        Number = Number + 2
        If Number Mod 10 = 1 Then
            Print
        End If
    Loop

End Sub
```

To better understand how the **Do...While...Loop** statement works, let's take a closer look at the program's
RunButton_Click procedure:

Number = 101   assigns the value 101 to the integer variable
Number.

```
┌──────────────────────────────────────────┐
│ ─           Program 4-8              ▼ ▲ │
├──────────────────────────────────────────┤
│ 101 103 105 107 109                       │
│ 111 113 115 117 119                       │
│ 121 123 125 127 129                       │
│ 131 133 135 137 139                       │
│ 141 143 145 147 149                       │
│ 151 153 155 157 159                       │
│ 161 163 165 167 169                       │
│ 171 173 175 177 179                       │
│ 181 183 185 187 189                       │
│ 191 193 195 197 199                       │
│                                           │
│                                           │
│                                           │
│                 ┌───────┐                 │
│                 │  Run  │                 │
│                 └───────┘                 │
│                                           │
└──────────────────────────────────────────┘
```

Figure 4-18 A sample Do...While...Loop statement.

`Do While Number < 201`   checks to see if the last odd value has been displayed. If it has, program execution will continue after the **Loop** keyword.

`Print Number;`   displays **Number**'s current value.

`Number = Number + 2`   increases the value of **Number** to the next odd value.

```
If Number Mod 10 = 1 Then
    Print
End If
```
moves the cursor to the start of the next line if five values have been displayed.

`Loop`   loops execution back to the **Do** keyword.

Figure 4-19 illustrates how a **Do...Until...Loop** statement is constructed. As this figure shows, the **Do...Until...Loop** statement performs a conditional check at the start of each loop. As long as the **Do...Until...Loop** statement's condition holds False, the loop will be repeated. As with **Do...While...Loop** statements, it is possible for **Do...Until...Loop** statements to never be executed.

Program 4-9 demonstrates how the **Do...Until...Loop** statement is used in an actual program. Listing 4-9-1 presents the code for the form's declarations section and Listing 4-9-2

```
Do Until expression
    statement
    .
    .
    .
    statement
Loop
```

Where:

expression   is a logical expression.

statement   is a valid Visual Basic expression.

Figure 4-19 The Visual Basic Do...Until...Loop statement.

presents the code for the program's **RunButton_Click** procedure. Figure 4-20 illustrates how the program's window would appear after the program has been run.

Listing 4-9-1:

```
DefInt A-Z
```

Listing 4-9-2:

```
Sub RunButton_Click ()

    Number = 101
    Do Until Number = 201
        Print Number;
        Number = Number + 2
        If Number Mod 10 = 1 Then
            Print
        End If
    Loop

End Sub
```

To better understand how the **Do...Until...Loop** statement works, let's take a closer look at the program's **RunButton_Click** procedure:

Number = 101 assigns the value 101 to the integer variable **Number.**

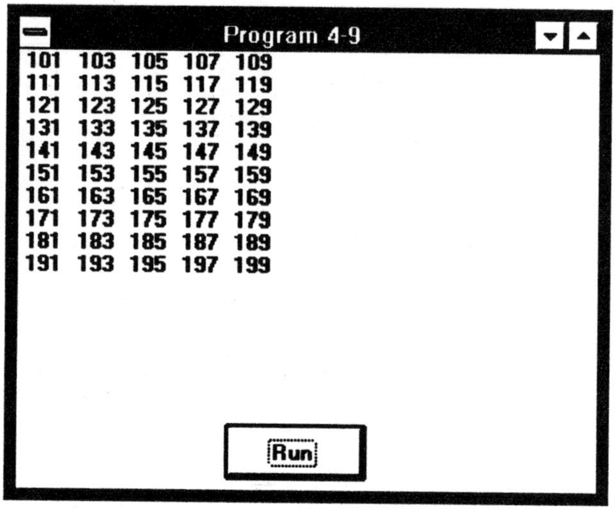

Figure 4-20 A sample Do...Until...Loop program.

`Do Until Number = 201` checks to see if the last odd value has been displayed. If it has, program execution will continue after the **Loop** keyword.

`Print Number;` displays **Number's** current value.

`Number = Number + 2` increases the value of **Number** to the next odd value.

```
If Number Mod 10 = 1 Then
    Print
```
`End If` moves the cursor to the start of the next line if five values have been displayed.

`Loop` loops execution back to the **Do** keyword.

Many times you will want a loop to stop prematurely. Stopping a **Do...Loop** statement prematurely is easily accomplished with an **Exit Do** statement. Essentially, Visual Basic will continue execution after the **Do...Loop** as soon as it encounters an **Exit Do** statement.

Program 4-10 demonstrates how an **Exit Do** statement is used in an actual program. You will note that this program is almost identical to Program 4-9. However, this newer version of the program will terminate the loop after the loop has completed its halfway point. Listing 4-10-1 presents the code

```
┌─────────────────────────────────────────────┐
│ ▬        Program 4-10              ▼  ▲       │
│ 101  103  105  107  109                       │
│ 111  113  115  117  119                       │
│ 121  123  125  127  129                       │
│ 131  133  135  137  139                       │
│ 141  143  145  147  149                       │
│                                               │
│                                               │
│                                               │
│                                               │
│                                               │
│                  ┌────────┐                   │
│                  │ Run    │                   │
│                  └────────┘                   │
└─────────────────────────────────────────────┘
```

Figure 4-21   A sample Exit Do program.

for the form's declarations section and Listing 4-10-2 presents the code for the program's **RunButton_Click** procedure. Figure 4-21 illustrates how the program's window would appear after the program has been run.

Listing 4-10-1:

```
DefInt A-Z
```

Listing 4-10-2:

```
Sub RunButton_Click ()

    Number = 101
    Do Until Number = 201
        Print Number;
        Number = Number + 2
        If Number Mod 10 = 1 Then
            Print
        End If
        If Number = 151 Then Exit Do
    Loop

End Sub
```

To better understand how the **Exit Do** statement works, let's take a closer look at the program's **RunButton_Click** procedure:

`Number = 101`   assigns the value 101 to the integer variable **Number**.

`Do Until Number = 201`   checks to see if the last odd value has been displayed. If it has, program execution will continue after the **Loop** keyword.

`Print Number;`   displays **Number**'s current value.

`Number = Number + 2`   increases the value of **Number** to the next odd value.

```
If Number Mod 10 = 1 Then
    Print
End If
```
`End If`   moves the cursor to the start of the next line if five values have been displayed.

`If Number = 151 Then Exit Do`   exits the loop as soon as the halfway point has been reached.

`Loop`   loops execution back to the **Do** keyword.

For...Next Statements

The Visual Basic **For...Next** statement is used to tell the program to execute one or more statements for a set number of times. Figure 4-22 illustrates how a **For...Next** statement is constructed. As the figure shows, the **For** statement assigns the value of an expression to a variable. After assigning the initial value to the **For** variable, program execution continues by performing an initial check against the **To** expression. If a **Step** wasn't used or a **Step** clause was used and it specified a positive increment, Visual Basic checks to see if the **For** variable is greater than the value of the **To** expression. If it is, Visual Basic will continue execution after the loop's **Next** statement. If the **For** variable is less than or equal to the value of the **To** expression, Visual Basic will execute the loop's statements until its associated **Next** statement is reached. Upon reaching the **Next** statement, Visual Basic will increment the **For** variable by the **Step** amount, check its new value against the **To** expression, and re-execute the loop if the **For** variable is still in range. If a

```
For variable = initial value To ending value [Step
increment/decrement]
    statement
    .
    .
    .
    statement
Next [variable]
```

Where:

`variable`	is a numeric variable. Note that its use after the **Next** keyword is strictly optional. However, specifying the variable after **Next** does provide a certain amount of clarity to the program listing.
`initial value`	is the initial value to be assigned to the variable.
`ending value`	is the final value the value can be equal to and still have Visual Basic execute the loop.
`increment/decrement`	is the value to adjust the variable by after each execution of the loop. If the **Step** clause is omitted, a **Step** value of 1 is assumed.
`statement`	is a valid Visual Basic statement.

Figure 4-22   The Visual Basic For...Next statement.

Step clause was used and it specified a negative value, Visual Basic checks to see if the **For** variable is less than the value of the **To** expression. If it is, Visual Basic will execute the loop's statements until its associated **Next** statement is reached. Upon reaching the **Next** statement, Visual Basic will decrement the **For** variable by the **Step** amount, check its new value against the **To** expression, and re-execute the loop if the **For** variable is still in range.

Program 4-11 demonstrates how a **For...Next** statement is used in an actual program. Because a **Step** clause isn't used in

```
Program 4-11
 1  2  3  4  5  6  7  8  9  10
11 12 13 14 15 16 17 18 19 20
21 22 23 24 25 26 27 28 29 30
31 32 33 34 35 36 37 38 39 40
41 42 43 44 45 46 47 48 49 50
51 52 53 54 55 56 57 58 59 60
61 62 63 64 65 66 67 68 69 70
71 72 73 74 75 76 77 78 79 80
81 82 83 84 85 86 87 88 89 90
91 92 93 94 95 96 97 98 99 100


                    Run
```

Figure 4-23 A sample For...Next program.

the **For...Next** statement, Visual Basic will assume a value of 1 for the **Step** amount. Listing 4-11-1 presents the code for the form's declarations section and Listing 4-11-2 presents the code for the program's **RunButton_Click** procedure. Figure 4-23 illustrates how the program's window would appear after the program has been run.

Listing 4-11-1:

```
DefInt A-Z
```

Listing 4-11-2:

```
Sub RunButton_Click ()

    For I = 1 To 100
        Print I;
        If I Mod 10 = 0 Then
            Print
        End If
    Next

End Sub
```

To better understand how an ascending **For...Next** statement works, let's take a closer look at the program's **RunButton_Click** procedure:

`For I = 1 To 100` assigns the value of **1** to the integer variable **I**. Checks to see if **I** is greater than **100**. If it is, Visual Basic will continue execution after the **Next** statement.

`Print I;` displays **I**'s current value.

```
If I Mod 10 = 0 Then
    Print
End If
```
moves the cursor to the start of the next line if 10 values have been displayed.

`Next` increments **I** by **1** and loops execution back to the **For** statement.

Program 4-12 demonstrates how a **Step** clause is used in a **For...Next** statement. Listing 4-12-1 presents the code for the form's declarations section and Listing 4-12-2 presents the code for the program's **RunButton_Click** procedure. Figure 4-24 illustrates how the program's window would appear after the program has been run.

Listing 4-12-1:

```
DefInt A-Z
```

Listing 4-12-2:

```
Sub RunButton_Click ()

    For I = 1 To 100 Step 2
        Print I;
        If (I + 2) Mod 10 = 1 Then
            Print
        End If
    Next

End Sub
```

To better understand how a **Step** clause is used in a **For...Next** statement, let's take a closer look at the program's **RunButton_Click** procedure:

```
┌──────────────────────────────────────────────────┐
│ ━             Program 4-12             ▼ ▲ │
├──────────────────────────────────────────────────┤
│ 1  3  5  7  9                                      │
│ 11 13 15 17 19                                     │
│ 21 23 25 27 29                                     │
│ 31 33 35 37 39                                     │
│ 41 43 45 47 49                                     │
│ 51 53 55 57 59                                     │
│ 61 63 65 67 69                                     │
│ 71 73 75 77 79                                     │
│ 81 83 85 87 89                                     │
│ 91 93 95 97 99                                     │
│                                                    │
│                                                    │
│                            ┌─────┐                 │
│                            │ Run │                 │
│                            └─────┘                 │
└──────────────────────────────────────────────────┘
```

Figure 4-24 A sample Step clause program.

`For I = 1 To 100 Step 2` assigns the value of **1** to the integer variable **I**. Checks to see if **I** is greater than **100**. If it is, Visual Basic will continue execution after the **Next** statement.

`Print I;` displays **I**'s current value.

```
If (I + 2) Mod 10 = 1 Then
    Print
End If
```
`End If` moves the cursor to the start of the next line if five values have been displayed.

`Next` increments **I** by **2** and loops back to the **For** statement.

Program 4-13 demonstrates how a negative **Step** value is used to create a descending **For...Next** statement. Listing 4-13-1 presents the code for the form's declarations section, and Listing 4-13-2 the code for the program's **RunButton_Click** procedure. Figure 4-25 illustrates how the program's window would appear after the program has been run.

Listing 4-13-1:

```
DefInt A-Z
```

```
┌─────────────────────────────────────────────────┐
│ ▬            Program 4-13              ▼  ▲      │
├─────────────────────────────────────────────────┤
│ 100 99 98 97 96 95 94 93 92 91                  │
│ 90 89 88 87 86 85 84 83 82 81                   │
│ 80 79 78 77 76 75 74 73 72 71                   │
│ 70 69 68 67 66 65 64 63 62 61                   │
│ 60 59 58 57 56 55 54 53 52 51                   │
│ 50 49 48 47 46 45 44 43 42 41                   │
│ 40 39 38 37 36 35 34 33 32 31                   │
│ 30 29 28 27 26 25 24 23 22 21                   │
│ 20 19 18 17 16 15 14 13 12 11                   │
│ 10 9 8 7 6 5 4 3 2 1                            │
│                                                  │
│                                                  │
│                                                  │
│                  ┌─────────┐                     │
│                  │  Run    │                     │
│                  └─────────┘                     │
└─────────────────────────────────────────────────┘
```

Figure 4-25 A sample descending For...Next program.

Listing 4-13-2:

```
Sub RunButton_Click ()

    For I = 100 To 1 Step -1
        Print I;
        If I Mod 10 = 1 Then
            Print
        End If
    Next

End Sub
```

To better understand how a negative **Step** value is used to create a descending **For...Next** statement, let's take a closer look at the program's **RunButton_Click** procedure:

`For I = 100 To 1 Step -1` assigns the value of **100** to the integer variable **I** and checks to see if **I** is less than **1**. If it is, Visual Basic will continue execution after the **Next** statement.

`Print I;` displays **I**'s current value.

`If I Mod 10 = 1 Then`
`    Print`
`End If` moves the cursor to the start of the next line if 10 values have been displayed.

`Next` decrements **I** by **1** and loops execution back to the **For** statement.

Just as **Do...Loop** statements can be prematurely terminated with an **Exit Do** statement, **For...Next** statements can be prematurely terminated with an **Exit For** statement. Similar to the way an **Exit Do** statement works, the **Exit For** statement instructs Visual Basic to break out of the loop as soon as it's encountered.

Program 4-14 demonstrates how an **Exit For** statement is used in an actual program. You will note that this program is almost identical to Program 4-13. However, this newer version of the program will terminate the loop as soon as the **For** variable, **I**, reaches the value of **51**. Listing 4-14-1 presents the code for the form's declarations section and Listing 4-14-2 presents the code for the program's **RunButton_Click** procedure. Figure 4-26 shows how the program's window would appear after the program has been run.

Listing 4-14-1:

```
DefInt A-Z
```

Listing 4-14-2:

```
Sub RunButton_Click ()

    For I = 100 To 1 Step -1
        Print I;
        If I Mod 10 = 1 Then
            Print
        End If
        If I = 51 Then Exit For
    Next

End Sub
```

To better understand how the **Exit For** statement works, let's take a closer look at the program's **RunButton_Click** procedure:

`For I = 100 To 1 Step -1` assigns the value of **100** to the integer variable **I** and checks to see if **I** is less than **1**. If it is, Visual Basic will continue execution after the **Next** statement.

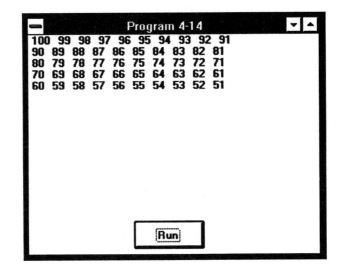

Figure 4-26 A sample Exit For program.

`Print I;`   displays **I**'s current value.

```
If I Mod 10 = 1 Then
    Print
End If
```
`End If`   moves the cursor to the start of the next line if 10 values have been displayed.

`If I = 51 Then Exit For`   terminates the **For...Next** statement if **I** is equal to **51**.

`Next`   decrements **I** by **1** and loops execution back to the **For** statement.

GoTo Statements

Sometimes program execution must branch to a different part of a program without regard for any condition. Visual Basic provides the **GoTo** statement for performing such an unconditional jump. You should be aware, however, that today the use of the **GoTo** statement is considered poor programming practice. Although the **GoTo** statement was necessary for older forms of Basic, the use of the **GoTo** statement is rarely necessary in a Visual Basic program. Perhaps its only acceptable use

```
GoTo line identifier
```

Where:

`line identifier`   is a valid Visual Basic line identifier.

Figure 4-27   The Visual Basic GoTo statement.

today is in implementing critical error handling routines. Always strive to write your programs without using **GoTos**.

Figure 4-27 defines the syntax for the Visual Basic **GoTo** statement. Note that the **GoTo** statement requires a line identifier to direct Visual Basic to where execution is to be branched to.

Program 4-15 demonstrates how a **GoTo** statement is used in an actual program. Listing 4-15 presents the code for the program's **RunButton_Click** procedure. Figure 4-28 illustrates how the program's window would appear after the program has been run.

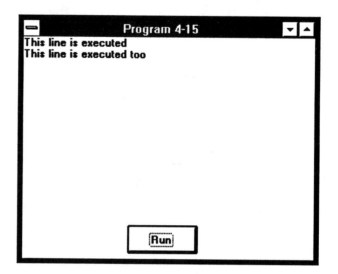

Figure 4-28   A sample GoTo Program.

Listing 4-15:

```
Sub RunButton_Click ()

    Print "This line is executed"
    GoTo Skip
    Print "This line never is!"
Skip:
    Print "This line is executed too"

End Sub
```

Summary

You're now familiar with Visual Basic's program flow structures and know how to use **If...Then, If...Then...Else, Select Case, While...Wend, Do...Loop, For...Next,** and **GoTo** statements in actual programs. Chapter 5 introduces you to subroutines and procedures.

Chapter 5

Subroutines and Procedures

In most programs you write, you will find that certain routines are used repeatedly. Program 5-1, for example, demonstrates how an **If...Then...Else** statement is used over and over to conditionally display messages. Listing 5-1-1 presents the code for the form's declarations section and Listing 5-1-2 presents the code for the program's **RunButton_Click** procedure. Figure 5-1 illustrates how the program's window would appear after the program has been run.

Listing 5-1-1:

```
DefInt A-Z
```

Listing 5-1-2:

```
Sub RunButton_Click ()

    Number = 1
    If Number = 1 Then
        Print "Number is equal to 1"
```

```
    Else
        Print "Number isn't equal to 1"
    End If
    Number = 0
    If Number = 1 Then
        Print "Number is equal to 1"
    Else
        Print "Number isn't equal to 1"
    End If

End Sub
```

The remainder of this chapter shows you how frequently used routines need not be rewritten over and over again by implementing them as either a subroutine or a procedure. Additionally, this chapter also explains function return values, local variables, scope, arguments, and recursion.

Subroutines

A Visual Basic subroutine can eliminate the necessity of repeatedly writing the same section of code over and over again. Figure 5-2 illustrates how a Visual Basic subroutine is constructed. As this figure shows, a subroutine is nothing more

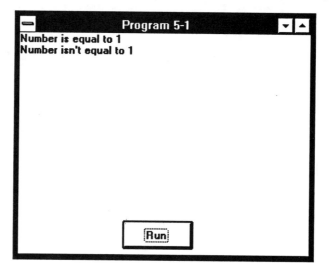

Figure 5-1 A redundant program.

```
line identifier
statement
    .
    .
    .
statement
Return
```

Where:

line identifier   is a valid Visual Basic line identifier.

statement   is a valid Visual Basic statement.

Figure 5-2 A Visual Basic subroutine.

than a line identifier, one or more Visual Basic statements, and a **Return** statement at the end.

To call (branch execution to) the subroutine, Visual Basic provides the **GoSub** statement. Figure 5-3 defines the syntax for the **GoSub** statement. Other than the **GoSub** keyword instead of a **GoTo** keyword, the **GoSub** statement is almost identical to the **GoTo** statement. However, there is one very important difference between the two. The **GoSub** statement not only tells Visual Basic to branch execution to the desired subroutine, it also instructs Visual Basic to return program execution to the point right after the **GoSub** statement as soon as Visual Basic encounters a **Return** statement.

Program 5-2 demonstrates how a subroutine is used in an actual Visual Basic program. Unlike Program 5-1, this newer version uses a subroutine to replace the multiple **If...Then...Else** statements. Listing 5-2-1 presents the code for the form's declarations section, and Listing 5-2-2 the code for the program's **RunButton_Click** procedure. Figure 5-4 illustrates how the program's window would appear after the program has been run.

Listing 5-2-1:

```
DefInt A-Z
```

```
GoSub line identifier
```

Where:

```
line identifier          is a valid Visual Basic line identifier.
```

Figure 5-3 The Visual Basic GoSub statement.

Listing 5-2-2:

```
Sub RunButton_Click ()

    Number = 1
    GoSub Display
    Number = 0
    GoSub Display
    Exit Sub
Display:
    If Number = 1 Then
        Print "Number is equal to 1"
    Else
        Print "Number isn't equal to 1"
    End If
    Return

End Sub
```

Although Program 5-2 is fairly simple, let's take a more detailed look at the program's **RunButton_Click** procedure:

`Number = 1`   assigns the value **1** to the integer variable **Number**.

`GoSub Display`   calls the subroutine **Display**.

`Number = 0`   assigns the value **0** to the integer variable **Number**.

`GoSub Display`   calls the subroutine **Display**.

`Exit Sub`   tells Visual Basic to exit the **Sub** procedure. If this statement was omitted, Visual Basic would continue execution right into the subroutine. If Visual Basic executes the subroutine at this point, it would eventually generate an error because the subroutine wouldn't have been called by a **GoSub** statement.

`Display:`   is the subroutine's identifier.

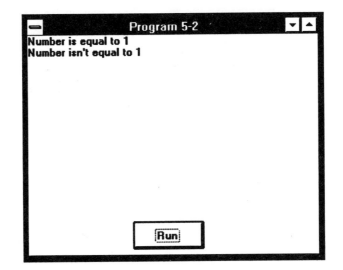

Figure 5-4 A sample subroutine program.

```
If Number = 1 Then
    Print "Number is equal to 1"
Else
    Print "Number isn't equal to 1"
End If
```
`End If`   displays the message **Number is equal to 1** if **Number** is equal to **1**. Otherwise, it displays the message **Number isn't equal to 1**.

`Return`   returns execution to the point right after the calling **GoSub** statement.

Procedures

Although Visual Basic subroutines are preferable to rewriting a lot of redundant code, they are a relic of the past just like **GoTos**. Visual Basic procedures are the way the modern programmer will prefer to go. Not only can a Visual Basic procedure have its own statements, it can have its own variables and in the case of a **Function** procedure they can return a value to the calling part of the program. Essentially, Visual Basic procedures allow the programmer to extend the existing Visual Basic language by defining his own Visual Basic statements and

```
[Static] Sub name[(parameter list)]
statement
   .
   .
   .
[Exit Sub]
   .
   .
   .
statement
End Sub
```

Where:

name	is the **Sub** procedure's name. This name effectively becomes a Visual Basic keyword and can't be used elsewhere in the program.
parameter list	is a list of arguments to be passed to the procedure.
statement	is a valid Visual Basic program statement.

Figure 5-5 A Visual Basic Sub procedure declaration.

functions. Figure 5-5 illustrates the format for defining a **Sub** procedure; Figure 5-6 defines the format for a **Function** procedure.

Figures 5-5 and 5-6 show that Visual Basic **Sub** and **Function** procedures can also have an optional parameter list. A **Sub** or **Function** procedure's parameters are used to pass values to the **Sub** or **Function** procedure. The following are some examples of parameter lists:

```
(Row%, Col%, Message$)
(X As Integer, Y As Integer)
(Name As String * 30)
```

Note in the above examples that the parameters are defined as they would be in a normal variable declaration. Also, note how each variable is separated by a comma.

```
[Static] Function name[(parameter list)][As type]
statement
  .
  .
  .
[Exit Function]
  .
  .
  .
statement
End Function
```

Where:

name	is the **Function** procedure's name. This name effectively becomes a Visual Basic keyword and can't be used elsewhere in the program. Additionally, a **Function** procedure's name follows the same rules as a Visual Basic variable's name. Unless a type declaration character is specified in the name or an **As** clause is used in the statement, Visual Basic will assume the **Function** procedure's type is the same as if it was a variable name and use the current default setting. A data type for a **Function** procedure is necessary to tell Visual Basic the data type of the return value.
parameter list	is a list of arguments to be passed to the procedure.
statement	is a valid Visual Basic program statement.
type	is the data type of the **Function** procedure's return value.

Figure 5-6 The Visual Basic Function procedure.

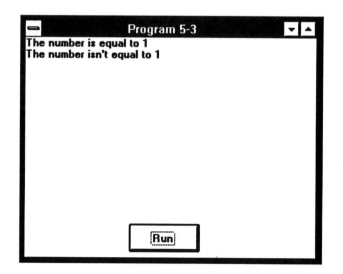

Figure 5-7 A sample Sub procedure program.

Program 5-3 demonstrates how a procedure is used in an actual Visual Basic program. Listing 5-3-1 presents the form's declarations section, Listing 5-3-2 presents the form's **Display** procedure, and Listing 5-3-3 presents the form's **Run-Button_Click** procedure. Figure 5-7 illustrates how the program's window would appear after the program has been run.

While this new version is somewhat similar to the subroutine program presented in Program 5-2, its use of a procedure instead of a subroutine makes it a far superior form of the same program. Although both versions of the same program perform pretty much identical functions, the procedure version is better than the subroutine version because of the way the procedure modularizes the routine. This modularization of the routine has many benefits. It makes the program much easier to read because the routine is distinctly separated from the main part of the Visual Basic program. Moreover, a correctly functioning procedure can save a great deal of time in debugging a program. Once a procedure is developed, it can be used over and over again with little fear that it will somehow not perform its intended function correctly.

Listing 5-3-1:

```
DefInt A-Z
```

Listing 5-3-2:

```
Sub Display (N As Integer)

    If N = 1 Then
        Print "The number is equal to 1"
    Else
        Print "The number isn't equal to 1"
    End If

End Sub
```

Listing 5-3-3:

```
Sub RunButton_Click ()

    Number = 1
    Display Number
    Number = 0
    Display Number

End Sub
```

Although Program 5-3 is a fairly simple example of how a procedure is used with Visual Basic, it demonstrates a number of important points about using a procedure in a program. It's helpful to take a line-by-line look at both the **RunButton_Click** and **Display** procedures:

`Number = 1` assigns the value **1** to the integer variable **Number**.

`Display Number` calls the procedure **Display**. Additionally, the value of the integer variable **Number** is passed as **Display's** one and only argument.

`Number = 0` assigns the value **0** to the integer variable **Number**.

`Display Number` calls the procedure **Display**. Additionally, the value of the integer variable **Number** is passed as **Display's** one and only argument.

`Sub Display (N As Integer)` defines a procedure name **Display** that has one integer parameter identified by **N**.

```
If N = 1 Then
    Print "The number is equal to 1"
Else
    Print "The number isn't equal to 1"
```

`End If` displays the message **The Number is equal to 1** if parameter **N** is equal to **1**. Otherwise, it displays the message **The number isn't equal to 1**.

`End Sub` defines the end of the procedure declaration.

Function Procedure Return Values

Now that you have seen how a simple **Sub** procedure is written, let's take a look at how a simple **Function** procedure is written. As Figure 5-6 illustrated, a data type is specified in the **Function** procedure's header. The data type tells Visual Basic what type of data the **Function** procedure will be returning to the calling program.

Although declaring a **Function** procedure's return type is fairly simple, it is not so obvious how the **Function** procedure's return value is actually returned to the calling program. Fortunately for the Visual Basic programmer, a value is returned by simply assigning the **Function** procedure's return value to the **Function** procedure's name. The **Function** procedure's name acts like a variable with the data type defined as the **Function** procedure's return type. For example, a **Function** procedure named **IntAdd** returns a value of **2** to the calling program as follows:

```
IntAdd = 2
```

This example shows that returning a value to the calling program requires nothing more than a simple assignment statement.

Program 5-4 calls a simple **Function** procedure that multiplies a passed argument by 2 and returns the result. Listing 5-4-1 presents the code for the form's declarations section, Listing 5-4-2 presents the code for the program's **TimesTwo** procedure, and Listing 5-4-3 presents the code for the

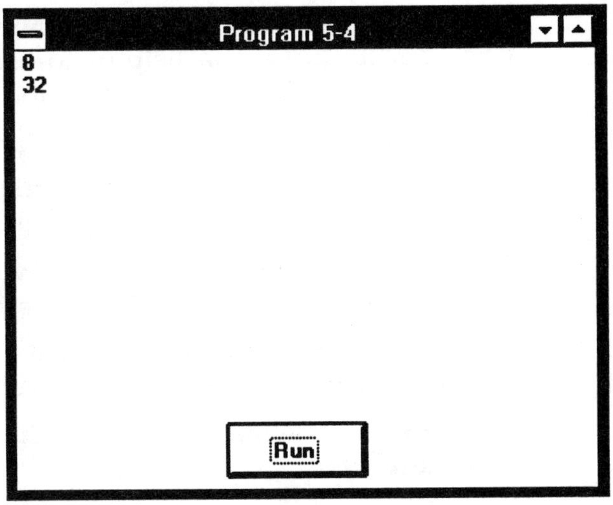

Figure 5-8 A sample Function procedure program.

program's **RunButton_Click** procedure. Figure 5-8 shows how the program's window would appear after the program has been run.

Listing 5-4-1:

```
DefInt A-Z
```

Listing 5-4-2:

```
Function TimesTwo (N As Integer) As Integer

    TimesTwo = N * 2

End Function
```

Listing 5-4-3:

```
Sub RunButton_Click ()

    Print TimesTwo(4)
    Print TimesTwo(16)

End Sub
```

In order to fully understand how the above program performs its task, it is helpful to examine the program's **RunButton_Click** and **TimesTwo** procedures a line at a time:

`Print TimesTwo(4)` displays the result of multiplying **4** by 2.

`Print TimesTwo(16)` displays the result of multiplying **16** by 2.

`Function TimesTwo (N As Integer) As Integer` defines a **Function** procedure named **TimesTwo** that has one integer parameter identified by **N** and returns an integer value.

`TimesTwo = N * 2` multiplies parameter **N** by **2** and assigns it to the **Function** procedure named **TimesTwo**.

`End Function` defines the end of the **TimesTwo Function** procedure.

Local Variables

As stated earlier in this chapter, a Visual Basic **Sub** or **Function** procedure can have its own variables, called local variables. Local variables can be used only inside of the **Sub** or **Function** procedure. The reason for this is scope, a concept that is discussed next. Local variables are declared in a **Sub** or **Function** procedure by either declaring them in a **Dim** statement or by

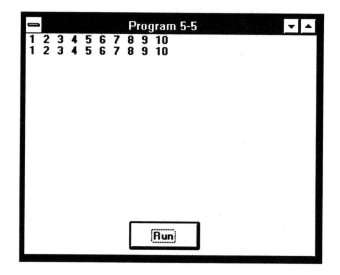

Figure 5-9 A sample local variable program.

simply using the variable in the procedure. Program 5-5 demonstrates how local variables are used in an actual Visual Basic program that uses a local variable **I** to count from 1 to 10 each time the **Sub** procedure **Count** is called. Listing 5-5-1 presents the code for the form's declarations section, Listing 5-5-2 the code for the program's **Count** procedure, and Listing 5-5-3 the code for the program's **RunButton_Click** procedure. Figure 5-9 illustrates how the program's window would appear after the program has been run.

Listing 5-5-1:

```
DefInt A-Z
```

Listing 5-5-2:

```
Sub Count ()

    i = 1
    While i < 11
        Print i;
        i = i + 1
    Wend
    Print

End Sub
```

Listing 5-5-3:

```
Sub RunButton_Click ()

    Count
    Count

End Sub
```

Local variables come in two distinct types: automatic and static. Automatic variables are the default type for Visual Basic local variables. Their chief characteristic is that they do not retain their values between procedure calls. For instance, let's suppose there is a variable **I** in a procedure and at the end of the procedure it had a value of **34**. When the procedure is called again, variable **I** will initially be assigned the value **0**. You should note that Visual Basic (and just about all other forms of

Basic) initially assigns a value of **0** to a numeric variable and a null string (" ") to a string variable.

Unlike an automatic variable, static variables retain their assigned values between procedure calls. If, in our example procedure, the variable **I** had been defined as a static variable, it would still be equal to **34** when the procedure is called again.

Program 5-6 demonstrates how an automatic variable's value isn't retained between procedure calls. This program features a very simple **Sub** procedure called **Count**. Essentially, **Count** displays a local integer variable's value, increments the variable, and returns to the calling program. The program's **RunButton_Click** procedure calls **Count** three times. Each time **Count** is called it will display a value of **0** for the local integer variable. Listing 5-6-1 presents the code for the form's declarations section, Listing 5-6-2 presents the code for the form's **Count** procedure, and Listing 5-6-3 presents the code for the form's **RunButton_Click** procedure. Figure 5-10 illustrates how the program's window would appear after the program has been run.

Listing 5-6-1:

```
DefInt A-Z
```

Listing 5-6-2:

```
Sub Count ()

    Print I
    I = I + 1

End Sub
```

Listing 5-6-3:

```
Sub RunButton_Click ()

    Count
    Count
    Count

End Sub
```

Figure 5-10 An automatic local variable program.

The easiest way to declare a static variable is to use the optional **Static** keyword in the **Sub** or **Function** procedure's definition. If you refer back to Figures 5-5 and 5-6, you will see the necessary syntax for using the **Static** keyword with a **Sub** or **Function** procedure. If the **Sub** or **Function** procedure is defined with the **Static** keyword, Visual Basic assumes that all of the procedure's local variables will be static.

Program 5-7 is a revised version of Program 5-6. Unlike the default automatic variable that was used in Program 5-6's **Count** procedure, this newer version of the **Count** procedure uses the **Static** keyword to make all of its variables static. When this newer version is run, it will display the value **0**, **1**, and **2**. Thus, the revised version does indeed prove that static variables retain their previous values between procedure calls. Listing 5-7-1 presents the code for the form's declarations section, Listing 5-7-2 the code for the program's **Count** procedure, and Listing 5-7-3 the code for the program's **RunButton_Click** procedure. Figure 5-11 illustrates how the program's window would appear after the program has been run.

Listing 5-7-1:

```
DefInt A-Z
```

Listing 5-7-2:

```
Static Sub Count ()

    Print I
    I = I + 1

End Sub
```

Listing 5-7-3:

```
Sub RunButton_Click ()

    Count
    Count
    Count

End Sub
```

Although using the **Static** keyword in a **Sub** or **Function** procedure's definition is the easiest way to make the procedure's variables static, there are times when you may only wish to make certain variables static and others automatic. This can be easily accomplished by omitting the **Static** keyword from the **Sub** or **Function** procedure's definition and

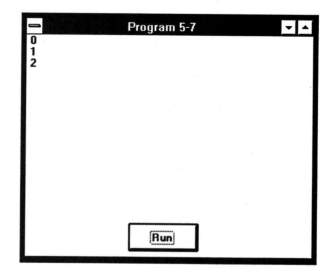

Figure 5-11 A sample static local variable program.

```
Static variable[, variable]...
```

Where:

`variable`	is a valid Visual Basic variable identifier.

Figure 5-12 The Visual Basic Static statement.

using a **Static** statement inside of the procedure. Figure 5-12 defines the syntax for the **Static** statement.

The following are some examples of valid Visual Basic **Static** statements:

```
Static N, J
Static I As Single, S$, First As String * 25
Static A
Static B%, C#, G&, Q
```

Program 5-8 presents a revised version of Programs 5-6 and 5-7. In this latest version, the **Sub** procedure **Count** has an automatic variable, **I**, and a static variable, **J**. You will note that the variable **J** is specifically declared as a static variable in an appropriate **Static** statement. When this program is executed, **J** will retain its value between procedure calls and **I** won't. Listing 5-8-1 presents the code for the form's declarations section, Listing 5-8-2 the code for the program's **Count** procedure, and Listing 5-8-3 the code for the program's **RunButton_Click** procedure. Figure 5-13 illustrates how the program's window would appear after the program has been run.

Listing 5-8-1:

```
DefInt A-Z
```

Listing 5-8-2:

```
Sub Count ()
Static J

    Print I
    I = I + 1
```

```
        Print J
        J = J + 1

End Sub
```

Listing 5-8-3:

```
Sub RunButton_Click ()

        Count
        Count
        Count

End Sub
```

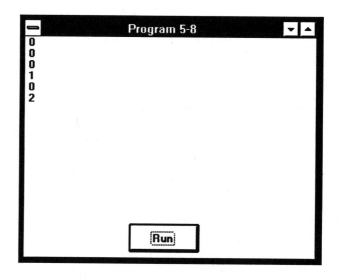

Figure 5-13 A combined automatic and static local variable program.

Scope

The previous section explained that **Sub** and **Function** procedure variables are called local variables because of something called scope. This section examines how a variable's scope affects what parts of a program can access it. If a **Sub** or **Function** procedure variable has a unique identifier, it is called a local variable because only the variable's **Sub** or **Function** procedure can access them. However, a procedure variable that has the same name as either a global, form, or module variable has global scope and is considered to be the same variable. Therefore, both the procedure in question and other procedures can all access the same variable. Program 5-9 illustrates how global scope works in an actual Visual Basic program. This program declares an integer variable **I** in the form's declarations section and is used by the form's **DisplayI** and **RunButton_Click** procedures. Because of Visual Basic's global scoping rules, all instances of **I** are treated as all one variable. Listing 5-9-1 presents the code for the form's declarations section, Listing 5-9-2 the code for the program's **DisplayI** procedure, and Listing 5-9-3 the code for the program's **RunButton_Click** procedure. Figure 5-14 illustrates how the program's window would appear after the program has been run.

Listing 5-9-1:

```
DefInt A-Z

Dim I As Integer
```

Listing 5-9-2:

```
Sub DisplayI ()

    I = 999
    Print I

End Sub
```

Listing 5-9-3:

```
Sub RunButton_Click ()

    I = 32
    DisplayI
    Print I

End Sub
```

Although a programmer can always use unique identifiers to ensure that a procedure's variables are local to the

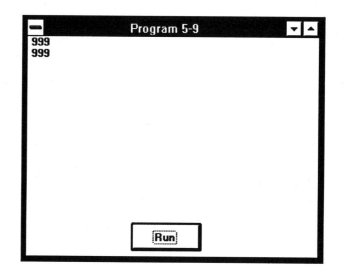

Figure 5-14 A global scope demonstration program.

procedure, variables that are global in other parts of a program can be made local to a procedure by simply declaring them in a **Dim** statement. Program 5-10 presents a revised version of Program 5-9. This newer version of the program makes the integer variable **I** in the form's **DisplayI** procedure local by declaring it in a **Dim** statement. You will note that when this latest version of the program is executed changes to **I** in the **DisplayI** procedure do not affect the global variable **I** in the rest of the program. Thus, this program clearly demonstrates how local variables have no effect on global variables with similar names. Listing 5-10-1 presents the code for the form's declarations section, Listing 5-10-2 the code for the program's **DisplayI** procedure, and Listing 5-10-3 the code for the program's **RunButton_Click** procedure. Figure 5-15 illustrates how the program's window would appear after the program has been run.

Listing 5-10-1:

```
DefInt A-Z

Dim I As Integer
```

Listing 5-10-2:

```
Sub DisplayI ()
Dim I As Integer

     I = 999
     Print I

End Sub
```

Listing 5-10-3:

```
Sub RunButton_Click ()

     I = 32
     DisplayI
     Print I

End Sub
```

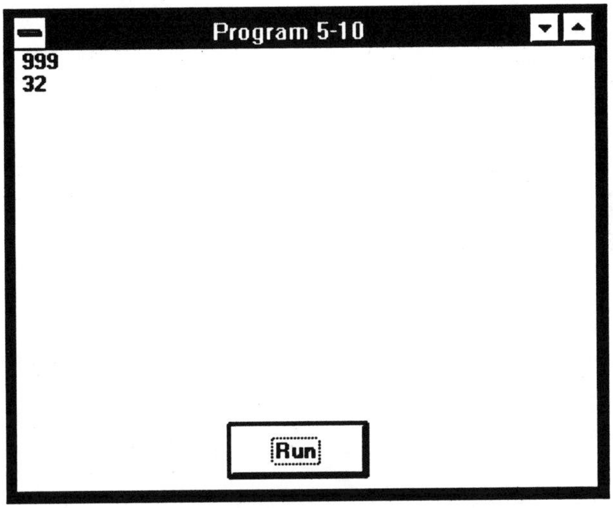

Figure 5-15   A local variable demonstration program.

Arguments

The previous sections have shown that arguments (or parameters) can be passed to either a **Sub** or **Function** procedure. By default, Visual Basic passes arguments by reference. Passing an argument by reference actually passes the argument's memory location to the procedure. With the argument's memory location at its disposal, the **Sub** or **Function** procedure is able to directly access and modify the passed argument. Because a procedure is able to modify a passed argument, the argument's value in the calling program will be changed if any changes take place inside of the procedure. Program 5-11 demonstrates how an argument that is passed by reference is modified by a procedure. Listing 5-11-1 presents the code for the form's declarations section, Listing 5-11-2 the code for the program's **Count** procedure, and Listing 5-11-3 the code for the program's **RunButton_Click** procedure. Figure 5-16 illustrates how the program's window would appear after the program has been run.

Listing 5-11-1:

```
DefInt A-Z
```

Listing 5-11-2:

```
Sub Count (Number As Integer)

    Do
        Print Number
        Number = Number - 1
    Loop Until Number < 0

End Sub
```

Listing 5-11-3:

```
Sub RunButton_Click ()

    N = 10
    Count N
    Print N

End Sub
```

While passing an argument by reference is an acceptable method for many programs, there are times when a variable that has been modified by a procedure can lead to disastrous

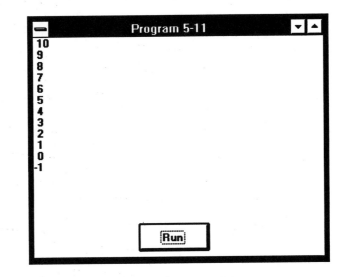

Figure 5-16 A pass-by-reference demonstration program.

consequences in other parts of the program. Accordingly, Visual Basic allows procedure arguments to be passed by value. When an argument is passed by value, only its value is passed to the calling procedure and anything the procedure does to modify the argument will have no effect on the variable in the calling portion of the program. Figure 5-17 defines the syntax for declaring an argument as being passed by value. As this figure illustrates, an argument is passed by value by simply preceding the argument's declaration in the procedure's header with the **ByVal** keyword.

ByVal *name*[**As** *type*]

Where:

name	is a valid Visual Basic variable name.
type	is a Visual Basic data type.

Figure 5-17 Passing an argument by value.

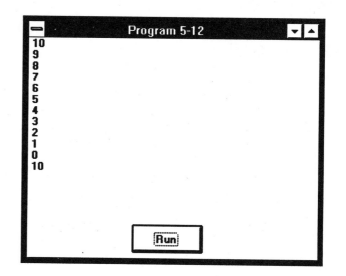

Figure 5-18 A pass-by-value demonstration program.

Program 5-12 is a revised version of Program 5-11. In this newer version, **Count's Number** argument is passed by value instead of by reference. Therefore, the argument isn't changed by **Count**. Listing 5-12-1 presents the code for the form's declarations section, Listing 5-12-2 the code for the program's **Count** procedure, and Listing 5-12-3 the code for the program's **RunButton_Click** procedure. Figure 5-18 illustrates how the program's window would appear after the program has been run.

Listing 5-12-1:

```
DefInt A-Z
```

Listing 5-12-2:

```
Sub Count (ByVal Number As Integer)

    Do
        Print Number
        Number = Number - 1
    Loop Until Number < 0

End Sub
```

Listing 5-12-3:

```
Sub RunButton_Click ()

    N = 10
    Count N
    Print N

End Sub
```

Recursion

Visual Basic **Sub** and **Function** procedures possess **recursion**. Recursion allows a Visual Basic **Sub** or **Function** procedure to call itself repeatedly. Although this may not seem to be an important feature, recursion can greatly simplify writing some of the most important computer programming routines (i.e., quick sort, b-trees, etc.).

Program 5-13 demonstrates how a Visual Basic **Sub** procedure can recursively call itself. Listing 5-13-1 presents the code for the form's declarations section, Listing 5-13-2 the code for the form's **Count** procedure, and Listing 5-13-3 the code for the form's **RunButton_Click** procedure. Figure 5-19 illustrates how the program's window would appear after the program has been run.

Listing 5-13-1:

```
DefInt A-Z
```

Listing 5-13-2:

```
Sub Count (N As Integer)

    Print N
    N = N - 1
    If N > 0 Then
        Count N
    End If

End Sub
```

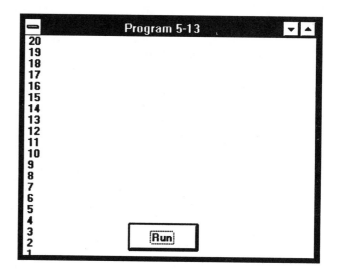

Figure 5-19 A recursion demonstration program.

Listing 5-13-3:

```
Sub RunButton_Click ()

    Count 20

End Sub
```

Although Program 5-13 is quite simple, it's helpful to take a detailed look at how the **Sub** procedure **Count** is used to count backwards from a passed argument.

`Print N`   displays the integer argument **N**'s value.

`N = N - 1`   decrements **N**'s value.

```
If N > 0 Then
    Count N
```
`End If`   checks argument **N**'s value to see if it is still greater than 0. If it is, **Count** calls itself with **N**'s new value for its argument.

This routine could be simplified by a loop; however, there are a number of important computer programming routines that are much easier to write using recursion than using more traditional programming methods. Consequently, it is essential for Visual Basic programmers to understand how recursion works.

Summary

This chapter explained how to use the much out-of-date Basic subroutine to simplify programs that use the same sections of code over and over. Also detailed were Visual Basic's much superior **Sub** and **Function** procedures and how return values, local variables, scope, arguments, and recursion relate to them.

Chapter 6

Arrays

lthough data types differ from each other a great deal, they all share one key characteristic: they can only represent one piece of data at a time. This chapter demonstrates how you can join numerous data items of the same type under one identifier name by declaring the identifier to be an **array**. It discusses both simple and multidimensional arrays and tells you how to pass arrays to procedures and functions.

A Simple Array

Program 6-1 presents a program that demonstrates how a student's grades could be stored in 10 integer variables. After safely tucking away the student's grades in the variables, the program figures the sum of all the grades and uses the result to figure the student's grade average. Listing 6-1-1 presents the code for the form's declarations section and Listing 6-1-2 presents the code for the program's **RunButton_Click** procedure. Figure 6-1 illustrates how the program's window would appear after the program has been run.

Listing 6-1-1:

```
DefInt A-Z
```

Listing 6-1-2:

```
Sub RunButton_Click ()

    G1 = 90
    G2 = 89
    G3 = 100
    G4 = 97
    G5 = 85
    G6 = 99
    G7 = 96
    G8 = 100
    G9 = 94
    G10 = 100
    Total = G1
    Total = Total + G2
    Total = Total + G3
    Total = Total + G4
    Total = Total + G5
    Total = Total + G6
    Total = Total + G7
    Total = Total + G8
    Total = Total + G9
    Total = Total + G10
    Ave = Total \ 10
    Print "The student's grade for the course is:"; Ave

End Sub
```

Although Program 6-1 gets the job done, it is extremely inefficient. Using an array is a far superior method for writing such a program. The first step in using an array is to declare it. Figure 6-2 defines the syntax for declaring a Visual Basic array.

As Figure 6-2 indicates, an array's number of subscripts can be specified in two distinct fashions: specifying the maximum subscript in the array or specifying the range of subscripts in the array. The following are some examples of array declarations that specify the arrays' maximum subscripts:

Dim MonthlyIncome(12)
Dim Days(31)
Dim Students(50)

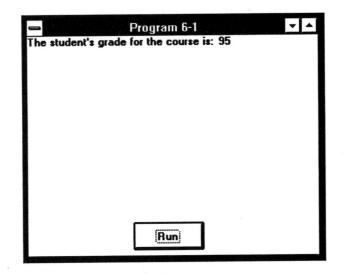

Figure 6-1 A nonarray demonstration program.

The following are some examples of array declarations that specify the subscripts in the arrays with ranges of subscripts:

Dim MonthlyIncome(1 To 12)
Dim Temperatures(-200 To 200)
Dim Students(1 To 50)

`Dim` *identifier*`(`*subscripts*`)`

Where:

identifier	is a valid Visual Basic variable identifier.
subscripts	is either the maximum subscript in the array or a specific range of subscripts for the array.

Figure 6-2 Declaring a Visual Basic array.

If you wanted to declare an array for the grades in Program 6-1, you could use either one of the array declarations below:

Dim Grades(10)
Dim Grades(1 To 10)

While both statements will get the job done, they may not actually perform the same function. The first array declaration specifies the maximum subscript as **10**. This instructs Visual Basic to set aside memory for an array that starts with a default lower limit of either 0 or 1 and ends with a subscript of 10. At the start of the program, Visual Basic always assumes a lower array subscript of 0 for arrays that are declared with their maximum subscript number. By using the **Option Base** statement in a form or module's declarations section before any arrays have been declared, the default lower limit can be changed to 1. Figure 6-3 defines the syntax for the **Option Base** statement.

Although declaring an array by its maximum subscript is the traditional method most older versions of Basic support, declaring an array by a range of subscripts is a superior method. Not only is the ambiguity as to what the array's lower limit might be eliminated by the fact that it is specifically declared, negative subscripts can be used in arrays that have been declared with a range of subscripts.

Figure 6-4 defines the syntax for accessing an array element. The grades for the above example can be accessed as **Grades(1)**, **Grades(2)**, **Grades(3)**, **Grades(4)**, **Grades(5)**, **Grades(6)**, **Grades(7)**, **Grades(8)**, **Grades(9)**, and **Grades(10)**. Furthermore, operations can be performed on these individual array elements just as they would be on individually declared integer variables.

Option Base *lower limit*

Where:

lower limit   is either a 0 or 1.

Figure 6-3 The Visual Basic Option Base statement.

```
identifier(index)
```

Where:

`identifier`	is a previously declared array identifier.
`index`	is a valid element number.

Figure 6-4 Accessing a Visual Basic array element.

Program 6-2 presents a modified version of Program 6-1. This newer version substitutes an integer array for the student's grades. Besides showing how much easier it is to declare an array, Program 6-2 also demonstrates how the student's total grade can be figured much more efficiently with a **For...Next** loop. To accomplish this calculation, the program simply uses the loop counter **I** for the array's index. Thus, each of the array's individual elements are added together to form the total. Listing 6-2-1 presents the code for the form's declarations section and Listing 6-2-2 presents the code for the program's **RunButton_Click** procedure. Figure 6-5 illustrates how the program's window would appear after the program has been run.

Listing 6-2-1:

```
DefInt A-Z

Option Base 1

Dim Grades(10)
```

Listing 6-2-2:

```
Sub RunButton_Click ()

    Grades(1) = 90
    Grades(2) = 89
    Grades(3) = 100
    Grades(4) = 97
    Grades(5) = 85
    Grades(6) = 99
    Grades(7) = 96
```

```
    Grades(8)  =  100
    Grades(9)  =  94
    Grades(10)  =  100
    Total = 0
    For I = 1 To 10
        Total = Total + Grades(I)
    Next
    Ave = Total \ 10
    Print "The student's grade for the course is:"; Ave

End Sub
```

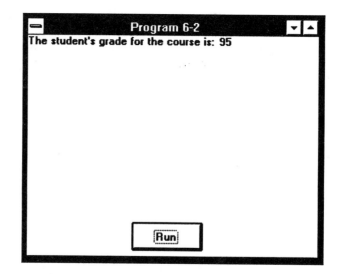

Figure 6-5 An array demonstration program.

Multidimensional Arrays

Although the previous program was useful for demonstrating how arrays are used in Visual Basic, it wasn't all that practical. The program demonstrates how a student's course average could be figured by totaling the student's scores and then figuring the average score. It is very unlikely, however, that a class would ever have just one student. Consequently, a useful program would have to be written in such a way that it could figure the course averages for a number of students. Program 6-3 presents a variation of Program 6-2 that could figure the average score for more than a single student. Listing 6-3-1 presents the code for the form's declarations section, and Listing 6-3-2 the code for the program's **RunButton_Click** procedure. Figure 6-6 illustrates how the program's window would appear after the program has been run.

Listing 6-3-1:

```
DefInt A-Z

Dim Student1(1 To 10), Student2(1 To 10)
```

Listing 6-3-2:

```
Sub RunButton_Click ()

    Student1(1) = 90
    Student1(2) = 89
    Student1(3) = 100
    Student1(4) = 97
    Student1(5) = 85
    Student1(6) = 99
    Student1(7) = 96
    Student1(8) = 100
    Student1(9) = 94
    Student1(10) = 100
    Student2(1) = 85
    Student2(2) = 75
    Student2(3) = 90
    Student2(4) = 88
    Student2(5) = 87
    Student2(6) = 93
    Student2(7) = 95
    Student2(8) = 97
    Student2(9) = 99
    Student2(10) = 100

    Total1 = 0
    Total2 = 0
    For I = 1 To 10
        Total1 = Total1 + Student1(I)
        Total2 = Total2 + Student2(I)
    Next

    Ave1 = Total1 \ 10
    Ave2 = Total2 \ 10
```

```
    Print "Student No. 1's grade for the course is:";
Ave1
    Print "Student No. 2's grade for the course is:";
Ave2

End Sub
```

Program 6-3 declares a separate array for each of the students in the course. Although this program is functionally correct, it is far from being the most efficient Visual Basic program. A more efficient method for representing Program 6-3's student data would be to define it as a multidimensional array. Figure 6-7 defines the syntax for declaring a multidimensional array. Although this figure shows how a two-dimensional array is declared, multidimensional Visual Basic arrays are by no means limited to only two dimensions: three-dimensional arrays are common in a wide variety of programs.

Accessing a multidimensional array element is slightly different from accessing a single-dimensional array element. Figure 6-8 defines the syntax for accessing a multidimensional array element.

Program 6-4 presents a slightly modified version of Program 6-3. This newer version of the program substitutes a multidimensional array for the two individual arrays. Listing

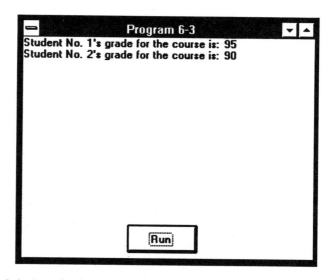

Figure 6-6 A multiple-student demonstration program.

```
Dim identifier(subscripts,subscripts)
```

Where:

`identifier`	is a valid Visual Basic variable identifier.
`subscripts`	is either an array dimension's maximum subscript or a specific range of subscripts for the array dimension.

Figure 6-7 Declaring a multidimensional Visual Basic array.

6-4-1 presents the code for the form's declarations section and Listing 6-4-2 presents the code for the program's **RunButton_Click** procedure. Figure 6-9 illustrates how the program's window would appear after the program has been run.

Listing 6-4-1:

```
DefInt A-Z

Dim Student(1 To 2, 1 To 10)
```

Listing 6-4-2:

```
Sub RunButton_Click ()

    Student(1, 1) = 90
    Student(1, 2) = 89
    Student(1, 3) = 100
    Student(1, 4) = 97
    Student(1, 5) = 85
    Student(1, 6) = 99
    Student(1, 7) = 96
    Student(1, 8) = 100
    Student(1, 9) = 94
    Student(1, 10) = 100
    Student(2, 1) = 85
    Student(2, 2) = 75
    Student(2, 3) = 90
    Student(2, 4) = 88
```

```
Student(2, 5) = 87
Student(2, 6) = 93
Student(2, 7) = 95
Student(2, 8) = 97
Student(2, 9) = 99
Student(2, 10) = 100

Total1 = 0
Total2 = 0
For I = 1 To 10
    Total1 = Total1 + Student(1, I)
    Total2 = Total2 + Student(2, I)
Next

Ave1 = Total1 \ 10
Ave2 = Total2 \ 10
Print "Student No. 1's grade for the course is:";
Ave1
Print "Student No. 2's grade for the course is:";
Ave2

End Sub
```

While Program 6-4 is a step in the right direction, it is wasteful to use four variables to figure the two students' course averages. Program 6-5 demonstrates an even simpler version of the program. It uses a nested (one inside the other) **For...Next** loop to calculate the course averages. Listing 6-5-1 presents the code for the form's declarations section, and Listing 6-5-2 the code for the program's **RunButton_Click** procedure. Figure 6-10 illustrates how the program's window would appear after the program has been run.

---

identifier(*index,index*)

Where:

identifier	is a previously declared array identifier.
index	is a valid element number

Figure 6-8 Accessing a multidimensional Visual Basic array element.

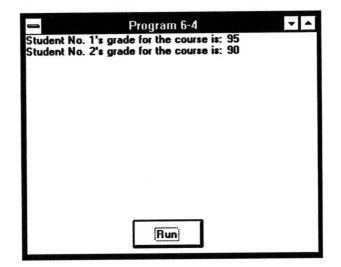

Figure 6-9 A multidimensional array demonstration program.

Listing 6-5-1:

```
DefInt A-Z

Dim Student(1 To 2, 1 To 10)
```

Listing 6-5-2:

```
Sub RunButton_Click ()

    Student(1, 1) = 90
    Student(1, 2) = 89
    Student(1, 3) = 100
    Student(1, 4) = 97
    Student(1, 5) = 85
    Student(1, 6) = 99
    Student(1, 7) = 96
    Student(1, 8) = 100
    Student(1, 9) = 94
    Student(1, 10) = 100
    Student(2, 1) = 85
    Student(2, 2) = 75
    Student(2, 3) = 90
    Student(2, 4) = 88
    Student(2, 5) = 87
    Student(2, 6) = 93
```

```
    Student(2, 7) = 95
    Student(2, 8) = 97
    Student(2, 9) = 99
    Student(2, 10) = 100

For I = 1 To 2
    Total = 0
    For J = 1 To 10
        Total = Total + Student(I, J)
    Next
    Ave = Total \ 10
    Print "Student no."; I; "'s grade for the
course is:", Ave
Next

End Sub
```

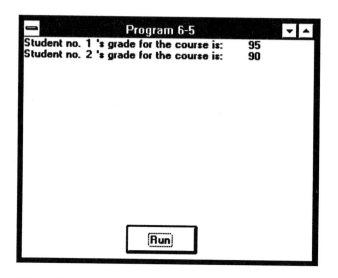

Figure 6-10 An improved multidimensional array program.

Passing Arrays To Sub and Function Procedures

Although passing a regular Visual Basic variable to a **Sub** or **Function** procedure is fairly simple, passing an array to a procedure takes a little more planning. Passing an array as an argument is fairly simple, but how the **Sub** or **Function** procedure actually handles the passed array is a little more complex.

```
identifier([dimensions])
```

Where:

`identifier`	is the name of a previously declared array.
`dimensions`	is the number of dimensions in the array. Note that this is strictly optional and is used to maintain compatibility with other forms of Basic.

Figure 6-11 An array argument.

Figure 6-11 defines the syntax for passing an array as a procedure argument.

Once a **Sub** or **Function** procedure has the array argument at its disposal, it is confronted with a dilemma: what is the size of the array and what are the array's lowest subscript and highest subscript? All of this can be determined quite easily with the Visual Basic **LBound** and **UBound** functions. The **LBound** function returns an array dimension's lowest subscript number. The **UBound** function returns an array dimension's highest subscript number. Figure 6-12 defines the syntax for the **LBound** function and Figure 6-13 defines the syntax for the **UBound** function. As these illustrations show, you must tell these two functions the dimension in question for multidimensional arrays.

```
LBound(array[, dimension])
```

Where:

`array`	is a previously declared array.
`dimension`	is the dimension to return the lowest subscript for.

Figure 6-12 The Visual Basic LBound function.

```
UBound(array[, dimension])
```

Where:

array   is a previously declared array.

dimension   is the dimension to return the
                               highest subscript for.

Figure 6-13 The Visual Basic UBound function.

Program 6-6 demonstrates how an array is passed to a procedure in an actual Visual Basic program. Additionally, Program 6-6 shows how the **LBound** and **UBound** functions are used to manipulate an array in a procedure. Listing 6-6-1 presents the code for the form's declarations section, Listing 6-6-2 the code for the program's **TotalArray** function, and Listing 6-6-3 the code for the program's **RunButton_Click** procedure. Figure 6-14 illustrates how the program's window would appear after the program is run.

Listing 6-6-1:

```
DefInt A-Z

Dim Student(1 To 2, 1 To 10)
```

Listing 6-6-2:

```
Function TotalArray (A(), N) As Integer

    T = 0
    For I = LBound(A, 2) To UBound(A, 2)
        T = T + A(N, I)
    Next
    TotalArray = T

End Function
```

Listing 6-6-3:

```
Sub RunButton_Click ()

    Student(1, 1) = 90
```

```
Student(1, 2) = 89
Student(1, 3) = 100
Student(1, 4) = 97
Student(1, 5) = 85
Student(1, 6) = 99
Student(1, 7) = 96
Student(1, 8) = 100
Student(1, 9) = 94
Student(1, 10) = 100
Student(2, 1) = 85
Student(2, 2) = 75
Student(2, 3) = 90
Student(2, 4) = 88
Student(2, 5) = 87
Student(2, 6) = 93
Student(2, 7) = 95
Student(2, 8) = 97
Student(2, 9) = 99
Student(2, 10) = 100

For I = 1 To 2
    Ave = TotalArray(Student(), I) \ 10
    Print "Student no."; I; "'s grade for the
course is:", Ave
Next

End Sub
```

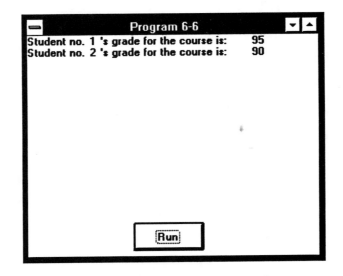

Figure 6-14 Passing an array to a Visual Basic procedure.

Summary

This chapter has shown you how multiple data items of the same type can be grouped together as single-dimensional and multidimensional arrays. Additionally, such topics as passing arrays to **Sub** or **Function** procedures and using the **LBound** and **UBound** functions to manipulate arrays were covered.

Chapter *7*

Records

lthough arrays are an extremely useful programming tool, many programs work with related data of different types. Visual Basic offers a user-defined data type called **records** that allows you to group together data of different types. This chapter introduces you to records and record arrays.

Before we examine the details of Visual Basic records, let's take a look at Program 7-1. This program builds on the programs presented in Chapter 6. Instead of just displaying the course averages, it also displays the students' name. The names and the averages are related data, but they are represented by vastly different data types. Listing 7-1-1 presents the code for the form's declarations section and Listing 7-1-2 presents the code for the program's **RunButton_Click** procedure. Figure 7-1 illustrates how the program's window would appear after the program has been run.

Listing 7-1-1:

```
DefInt A-Z
```

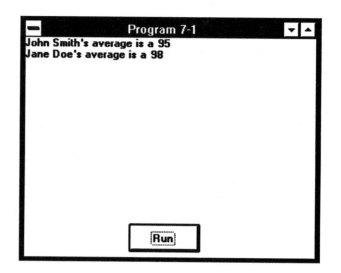

Figure 7-1 A nonrecord demonstration program.

Listing 7-1-2:

```
Sub RunButton_Click ()

    Name1$ = "John Smith"
    Ave1 = 95
    Name2$ = "Jane Doe"
    Ave2 = 98
    Print Name1$; "'s average is a"; Ave1
    Print Name2$; "'s average is a"; Ave2

End Sub
```

Record Basics

The first step in using a record in a Visual Basic program is to define the record's data type in the program's global module. Figure 7-2 defines the syntax for declaring a Visual Basic record type.

As Figure 7-2 illustrates, a Visual Basic record declaration is constructed from one or more field declarations. Figure 7-3 defines the syntax for a field declaration. You should note from Figure 7-3 that arrays can't be used as a field declaration; however, Visual Basic will permit you to use a previously defined record type for a field declaration.

```
Type data type identifier
    field declaration
    .
    .
    .
    field declaration
End Type
```

Where:

data type identifier   is a valid Visual Basic identifier.

field declaration   is a valid field declaration.

Figure 7-2 Declaring a Visual Basic type.

The following examples illustrate valid Visual Basic record declarations:

```
Type MailItem

    Name1 As String * 30
    Name2 As String * 30
    Name3 As String * 30
    State As String * 2
    Zip1 As String * 5
    Zip2 As String * 4

End Type

Type Student

    Name As String * 30
    Ave As Integer

End Type
```

To use a record variable, it must be specifically declared in a **Dim, ReDim, Static,** or **Global** statement. Some examples of record variable declarations are:

```
Dim S1 As Student, S2 As Student
Static M As MailItem
Global A As Student, M As MailItem
```

```
field identifier As data type
```

Where:

```
field identifier
```
is a valid Visual Basic identifier.

```
data type
```
is either **Integer, Long, Single, Double, Currency, String,** or a previously defined record type. Arrays are not allowed as record fields.

Figure 7-3 Declaring a Visual Basic record field.

Figure 7-4 defines how a record variable's field is referenced in an assignment statement or an expression. A desired field is referenced by separating the variable's name and the field's name with a period (.).

Some examples of valid Visual Basic record variable references appear below:

```
Item.Name1 = "John Smith"
Item.Address = "375 Sleepy Lane"
S1.Name = "Jane Doe"
S1.Ave = Total \ 10
```

Program 7-2 demonstrates how Program 7-1 can be rewritten to take advantage of Visual Basic's support for record data types. Even though it is only a simple example of how Visual Basic record types are used in an actual program, it shows how related data can be joined together in a single entry, thereby

```
variable identifier.field identifier
```

Where:

```
variable identifier
```
is the record variable's name.

```
field identifier
```
is the field name.

Figure 7-4 Record variable field references.

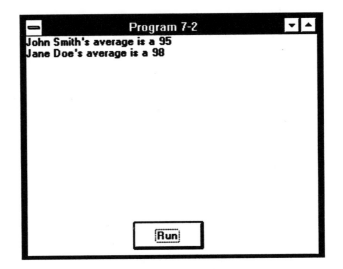

Figure 7-5 A record demonstration program.

eliminating the necessity of using separate variables for each field. Listing 7-2-1 presents the code for the program's global module, Listing 7-2-2 the code for the form's declarations section, and Listing 7-2-3 the code for the program's **Run-Button_Click** procedure. Figure 7-5 illustrates how the program's window would appear after the program has been run.

Listing 7-2-1:

```
DefInt A-Z

Type Student
    SName As String * 30
    Ave As Integer
End Type
```

Listing 7-2-2:

```
DefInt A-Z

Dim S1 As Student, S2 As Student
```

Listing 7-2-3:

```
Sub RunButton_Click ()

    S1.SName = "John Smith"
    S1.Ave = 95
    S2.SName = "Jane Doe"
    S2.Ave = 98
    Print RTrim$(S1.SName); "'s average is a"; S1.Ave
    Print RTrim$(S2.SName); "'s average is a"; S2.Ave

End Sub
```

Record Arrays

Wouldn't it be nice if Visual Basic supported record arrays in a program? Fortunately, Visual Basic fully supports record arrays. Figure 7-6 defines the syntax for declaring a record array in a **Dim** statement. As you can see from this illustration, there is virtually no difference between this type of array declaration and any other array declaration.

Referencing a particular record field while using record arrays in a program is a little different than you might expect. Figure 7-7 defines the syntax for referencing a field in a record array. Note how the array index comes before the period (.) and not after the field name as you might expect.

Program 7-3 is a variation of Program 7-2. It utilizes a record array to store the student data. Listing 7-3-1 presents the code for the program's global module, Listing 7-3-2 the code

---

```
identifier(subscripts[, subscripts]...) As record type
```

Where:

identifier	is a valid Visual Basic identifier.
subscripts	is either the dimension's maximum number of subscripts or a range of subscripts.
record type	is a previously defined record type.

Figure 7-6 Declaring a record array.

```
variable identifier(index[, index]...).field identifier
```

Where:

`variable identifier`   is a valid Visual Basic identifier.

`index`   is the dimension's element number.

`field identifier`   is the field name.

Figure 7-7   Record array field references.

for the form's declarations section, and Listing 7-3-3 the code for the program's **RunButton_Click** procedure. Figure 7-8 illustrates how the program's window would appear after the program has been run.

Listing 7-3-1:

```
DefInt A-Z

Type Student
    SName As String * 30
    Ave As Integer
End Type
```

Listing 7-3-2:

```
DefInt A-Z

Dim S(1 To 2) As Student
```

Listing 7-3-3:

```
Sub RunButton_Click ()

    S(1).SName = "John Smith"
    S(1).Ave = 95
    S(2).SName = "Jane Doe"
    S(2).Ave = 98
    Print RTrim$(S(1).SName); "'s average is a"; S(1).Ave
    Print RTrim$(S(2).SName); "'s average is a"; S(2).Ave

End Sub
```

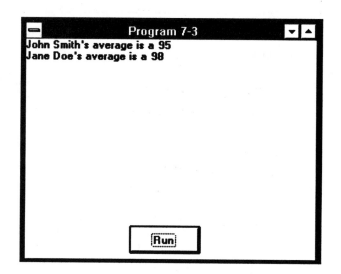

Figure 7-8 A record array demonstration program.

Summary

This chapter has familiarized you with Visual Basic records. You learned how to define a record type, declare a record variable, and reference a record variable's field. The chapter concluded with a discussion of record arrays.

Chapter 8

Forms and Controls

T hroughout this book's previous seven chapters, you have become familiar with Visual Basic's forms and controls. Although you may be aware of what they are at this point, it is necessary to take a more detailed look at these Visual Basic objects in order to exploit their many features to the fullest. Accordingly, this chapter provides a more in-depth look at both forms and controls.

Forms

Essentially, a Visual Basic form is a Windows window. Although a form is an optional part of a Visual Basic program, a formless program probably wouldn't be of much practical use. Because Microsoft chose to implement Visual Basic forms using an object-oriented programming approach, the beginning Visual Basic programmer should look at a Visual Basic form as a super record type. Indeed, all Visual Basic forms have fieldlike data items called properties. Figure 8-1 presents a list of the properties that a Visual Basic form has to offer.

AutoRedraw	FillColor	Height	ScaleHeight
BackColor	FillStyle	hWnd	ScaleLeft
BorderStyle	FontBold	Icon	ScaleMode
Caption	FontItalic	Image	ScaleTop
ControlBox	FontName	Left	ScaleWidth
CurrentX	FontSize	LinkMode	Tag
CurrentY	FontStrikeThru	LinkTopic	Top
DrawMode	FontTransparent	MaxButton	Visible
DrawStyle	FontUnderline	MinButton	Width
DrawWidth	ForeColor	MousePointer	WindowState
Enabled	hDC	Picture	

Figure 8-1 The Visual Basic form properties.

As Figure 8-1 illustrates, the Visual Basic form properties are chiefly used to control a form's appearance at run time. Although these form properties can be initially set at design time with Visual Basic's Properties Bar, many can be initialized or reset at run time. Figure 8-2 defines the syntax for referencing a form property. You should note how similar this is to referencing a record field.

Program 8-1 demonstrates how a form's properties are used in an actual Visual Basic program by doubling the size of a form's font. Listing 8-1 presents the code for the form's **RunButton_Click** procedure. Figure 8-3 shows how the program's window would appear after the program has been run.

Listing 8-1:

```
Sub RunButton_Click ()

    FS = Form1.FontSize
    Print "This is"; FS; "point type."
    Form1.FontSize = FS * 2
    Print "This is"; FontSize; "point type."

End Sub
```

Because a form is an object class, it has a number of special procedures associated with it. These special procedures are

```
[form.]property
```

Where:

form   is the name of the form. If omitted,
                        Visual Basic will assume *form* is the
                        current form.

property   is the name of the property to be
                        referenced.

Figure 8-2 Referencing a form property.

called methods and are called just like any other Visual Basic procedure except you preface them with the form's name and a period (.). Figure 8-4 defines the syntax for calling a method and Figure 8-5 presents a list of the Visual Basic **Form** methods.

Program 8-2 demonstrates how a form's methods are used in an actual Visual Basic program. This program will alternately display and erase text from a form's client area by clicking a command button. Listing 8-2-1 presents the code for the form's declarations section and Listing 8-2-2 presents the code for the form's **RunButton_Click** procedure. Figure 8-6 illustrates how the program's window would appear after the button has been pressed once, and Figure 8-7 how the

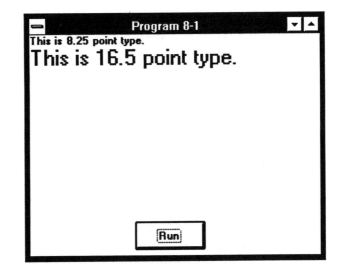

Figure 8-3 A form property demonstration program.

```
[form.]method [arguments]
```

Where:

form	is the name of the form. If omitted, Visual Basic will assume *form* is the current form.
method	is the name of the method to be called.
arguments	are any required or optional arguments that are to be passed to the method.

Figure 8-4 Calling a form's method.

program's window would appear after the button has been pressed a second time.

Listing 8-2-1:

```
DefInt A-Z
```

Listing 8-2-2:

```
Sub RunButton_Click ()
Static Flag

    Flag = Not Flag
    If Flag Then
        For I = 1 To 10
            Form1.Print "*******************************"
        Next
    Else
        Form1.Cls
    End If

End Sub
```

In addition to properties and methods, a Visual Basic **Form** also has events. An event is just like a method except that the event is called by Windows and not by the Visual Basic program. Essentially, Windows calls a form's event procedure whenever it detects an event has occurred and the event in question affects the form. For example, if the user was to click

Circle	Move	PSet	Show
Cls	Point	Refresh	TextHeight
Hide	Print	Scale	TextWidth
Line	PrintForm	SetFocus	

Figure 8-5 The Form methods.

the mouse in the form's client area, Windows would call the form's **Click** event. Figure 8-8 presents a complete list of the **Form** events.

Program 8-3 demonstrates how **Form** events are used in an actual Visual Basic program. This program will clear the program's window whenever the form is double clicked. Listing 8-3-1 presents the code for the form's declarations section, Listing 8-3-2 presents the code for the form's **Form_DblClick** procedure, and Listing 8-3-3 the code for the form's **RunButton_Click** procedure. Figure 8-9 illustrates how the program's window would appear after the button has been pressed; Figure 8-10 shows how the program's window would appear after the button has been pressed a second time.

Listing 8-3-1:

```
DefInt A-Z
```

Listing 8-3-2:

```
Sub Form_DblClick ()

    Cls

End Sub
```

Listing 8-3-3:

```
Sub RunButton_Click ()

    For I = 1 To 10
        Form1.Print "******************************"
    Next

End Sub
```

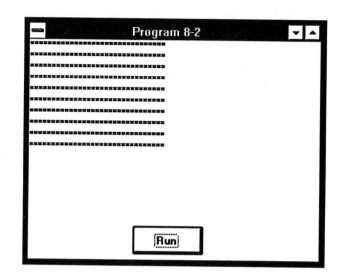

Figure 8-6 A Form method demonstration program (1 of 2).

Because a **Form** is a data object, it can be passed to either a **Sub** or **Function** procedure as an argument just like any other variable. Figure 8-11 defines the syntax for declaring a **Form** argument in a **Sub** or **Function** procedure's header. As this figure illustrates, a **Form** argument is declared just like any

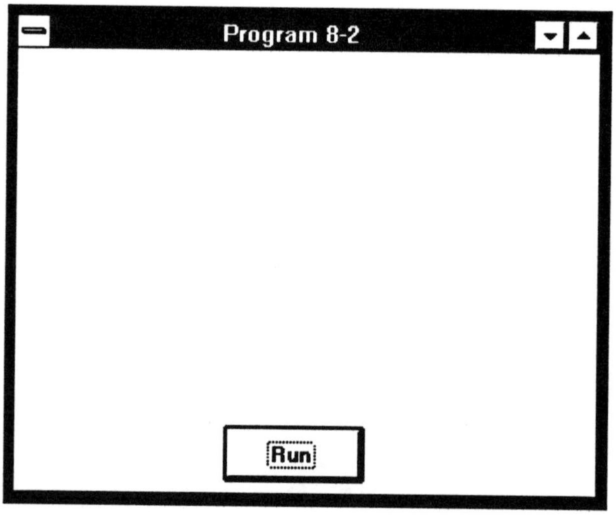

Figure 8-7 A Form method demonstration program (2 of 2).

Click	KeyDown	LinkExecute	MouseMove
DblClick	KeyPress	LinkOpen	MouseUp
DragDrop	KeyUp	Load	Paint
DragOver	LinkClose	LostFocus	Resize
GotFocus	LinkError	MouseDown	Unload

Figure 8-8 The Form events.

other procedure argument except the argument's data type is specified with the **Form** keyword.

Program 8-4 demonstrates how a **Form** can be used as a procedure argument. This program includes a procedure that can double a form's font size. Listing 8-4-1 presents the code for the form's declarations section, Listing 8-4-2 the code for the form's **RunButton_Click** procedure, and Listing 8-4-3 the code for the program's **DoubleSize** procedure. Figure 8-12 illustrates how the program's window would appear after the program has been run.

Listing 8-4-1:

```
DefInt A-Z
```

Listing 8-4-2:

```
Sub RunButton_Click ()

    Print "Font Size ="; FontSize
    DoubleSize Form1
    Print "Font Size ="; FontSize

End Sub
```

Listing 8-4-3:

```
Sub DoubleSize (F As Form)

    F.FontSize = F.FontSize * 2

End Sub
```

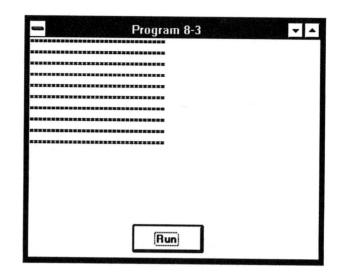

Figure 8-9 A Form event demonstration program (1 of 2).

You should note that even though a **Form** can be used as a procedure argument, it can't be used in any other type of variable declarations. In other words, all **Forms** must be created at design time. Furthermore, you can't assign the value of one **Form** to another. Although, as Program 8-4 demonstrated, you can assign values for a **Form**'s properties and call a **Form**'s methods.

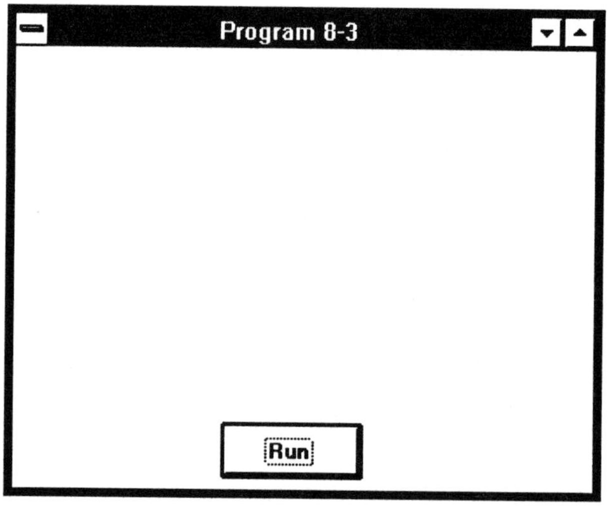

Figure 8-10 A Form event demonstration program (2 of 2)

identifier **As Form**

Where:

identifier   is a valid Visual Basic identifier.

Figure 8-11   Declaring a Form procedure argument.

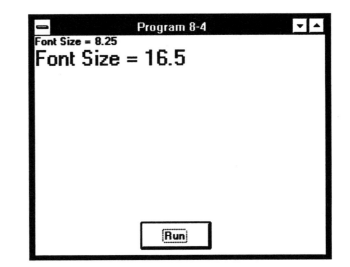

Figure 8-12   A Form procedure argument demonstration program.

Controls

In addition to the **Form** data type, Visual Basic features a **Control** data type. Whereas a Visual Basic **Form** is used to represent a window, a **Control** data type is used to represent one of many different Windows controls. The Windows controls that Visual Basic offers include check boxes, combo boxes, command buttons, directory list boxes, drive list boxes, file list boxes, frames, horizontal scroll bars, labels, list boxes, menus, option buttons, picture boxes, text boxes, timers, and vertical scroll bars.

Because Visual Basic controls are defined by object classes, they have properties just like forms. Like a form's properties, a control's properties are often used to set a control's appear-

```
[control.]property
```

Where:

`control`	is the name of the control. If omitted, Visual Basic will assume *control* is the current control.
`property`	is the name of the property to be referenced.

Figure 8-13 Referencing a control property.

ance at run time. Although control properties can be set at design time with the Visual Basic Properties Bar, many can be initialized and reset at run time. Figure 8-13 defines the syntax for referencing a control property. You should note how similar this is to referencing a record field or a form property.

Program 8-5 demonstrates how a control's properties are used by doubling the size of a control's font. Listing 8-5-1 presents the code for the form's declarations section and Listing 8-5-2 presents the code for the form's **RunButton_Click** procedure. Figure 8-14 illustrates how the program's window would appear before the command button is clicked, and Figure 8-15 how the program's window would appear after the command button is clicked.

Listing 8-5-1:

```
DefInt A-Z
```

Listing 8-5-2:

```
Sub RunButton_Click ()

    RunButton.FontSize = RunButton.FontSize * 2

End Sub
```

Like a form, Visual Basic controls have a number of methods associated with them. Figure 8-16 defines the syntax for calling a method. You will note how calling a control method is virtually identical to calling a form method.

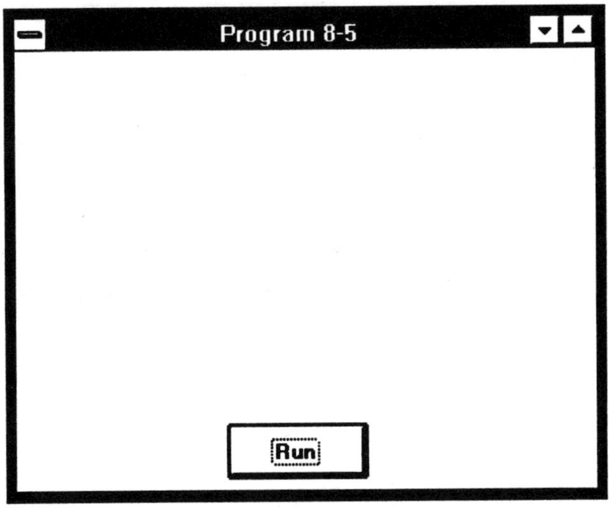

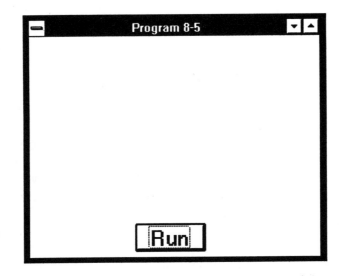

Figure 8-14   A control property demonstration program (1 of 2).

Program 8-6 demonstrates how a control's methods are used in an actual Visual Basic program. This program will move the program's command button to the window's upper left corner when the command button is clicked. Listing 8-6-1 presents the code for the form's declarations section, and Listing 8-6-2 the code for the form's **RunButton_Click** procedure.

Figure 8-15   A control property demonstration program (2 of 2).

```
[control.]method [arguments]
```

Where:

control	is the name of the control If omitted, Visual Basic will assume *control* is the current control.
method	is the name of the method to be called.
arguments	are any required or optional arguments that are passed to the method.

Figure 8-16 Calling a control's method.

Figure 8-17 illustrates how the program's window would appear before the command button is clicked; Figure 8-18 shows how the program's window would appear after the command button is clicked.

Listing 8-6-1:

```
DefInt A-Z
```

Listing 8-6-2:

```
Sub RunButton_Click ()

    RunButton.Move 0, 0

End Sub
```

As you already know from this book's extensive use of the **Click** event, Visual Basic controls have events. As with a form's event, a control's event is called by Windows whenever it detects an event has occurred and the event in question affects the control. For example, if the user clicks a command button with the mouse, Windows will call the control's **Click** event.

Program 8-7 demonstrates how **Control** events are used in an actual Visual Basic program. This program will change a command button's caption to **Click** whenever the button is

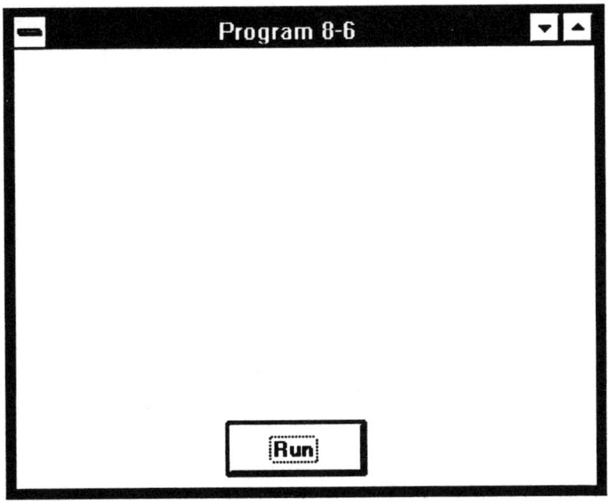

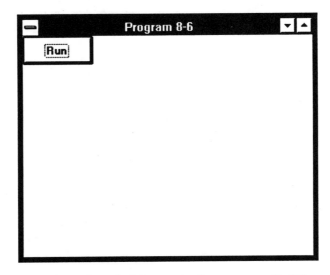

Figure 8-17 A Control method demonstration program (1 of 2).

clicked and change the caption to a key's character whenever a key is pressed. Listing 8-7-1 presents the code for the form's declarations section, Listing 8-7-2 the code for the form's **RunButton_Click** procedure, and Listing 8-7-3 the code for the form's **RunButton_KeyPress** procedure. Figure 8-19 illustrates how the program's window would appear after the

Figure 8-18 A Control method demonstration program (2 of 2).

button has been clicked; Figure 8-20 shows how the program's window would appear after a key has been pressed.

Listing 8-7-1:

```
DefInt A-Z
```

Listing 8-7-2:

```
Sub RunButton_Click ()

    RunButton.Caption = "Click"

End Sub
```

Listing 8-7-3:

```
Sub RunButton_KeyPress (KeyAscii As Integer)

    RunButton.Caption = Chr$(KeyAscii)

End Sub
```

Like a **Form**, a **Control** can be passed to either a **Sub** or **Function** procedure as an argument. Figure 8-21 defines the syntax for declaring a **Control** argument in a **Sub** or **Function** procedure's header. As this figure illustrates, a **Control** argu-

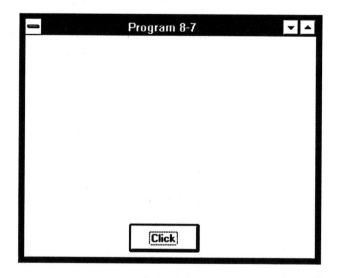

Figure 8-19 A Control event demonstration program (1 of 2).

ment is declared just like any other procedure argument except the argument's data type is specified with the **Control** keyword.

Program 8-8 demonstrates how a **Control** can be used as a procedure argument. This program includes a procedure that can double a control's font size. Listing 8-8-1 presents the code for the form's declarations section, Listing 8-8-2 the code for the form's **RunButton_Click** procedure, and Listing 8-8-3 the code for the **DoubleSize** procedure. Figure 8-22 illustrates how the program's window would appear before the command button is clicked, and Figure 8-23 how the program's window would appear after the command button has been clicked.

Listing 8-8-1:

```
DefInt A-Z
```

Listing 8-8-2:

```
Sub RunButton_Click ()

    DoubleSize RunButton

End Sub
```

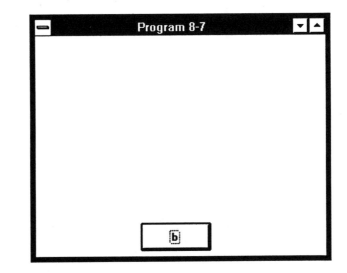

Figure 8-20 A Control event demonstration program (2 of 2).

```
identifier As Control
```

Where:

```
identifier
```
is a valid Visual Basic identifier.

Figure 8-21   Declaring a Control procedure argument.

Listing 8-8-3:

```
Sub DoubleSize (C As Control)

    C.FontSize = C.FontSize * 2

End Sub
```

Many times you might want to write a generic procedure that will work with more than one **Control** type. Visual Basic provides a special **TypeOf...Is** logical expression to determine a control's actual type. Figure 8-24 defines the syntax for using a **TypeOf...Is** expression in an **If...Then...Else** statement.

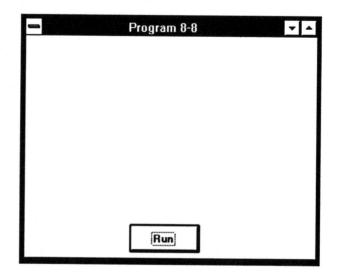

Figure 8-22   A Control procedure argument demonstration program (1 of 2).

Program 8-9 demonstrates how the **TypeOf...Is** expression is used to determine the type of a **Control** argument. Listing 8-9-1 presents the code for the form's declarations section, Listing 8-9-2 the code for the form's **RunButton_Click** procedure, and Listing 8-9-3 the code for the program's **Display** procedure. Figure 8-25 illustrates how the program's window would appear before the command button is clicked, and Figure 8-26 how the program's window would appear after the program's command button is clicked.

Listing 8-9-1:

```
DefInt A-Z
```

Listing 8-9-2:

```
Sub RunButton_Click ()

    Display Text1
    Display Label1

End Sub
```

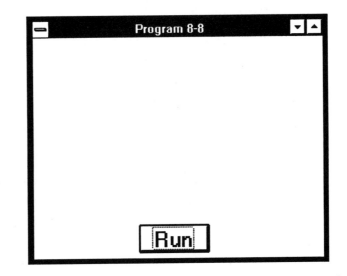

Figure 8-23 A Control procedure argument demonstration program (2 of 2).

```
If TypeOf control Is controltype Then
    statement
    .
    .
    .
    statement
EndIf
```

Where:

control	is a control that is passed as a procedure argument.
controltype	is either **CheckBox, ComboBox, CommandButton, DirListBox, DriveListBox, FileListBox, Frame, HScrollBar, Label, ListBox, Menu, OptionButton, PictureBox, TextBox, Timer,** or **VScrollBar.**
statement	is a valid Visual Basic statement.

Figure 8-24 The Visual Basic TypeOf...Is expression.

Listing 8-9-3:

```
Sub Display (C As Control)

    If TypeOf C Is Label Then
        C.Caption = "Label"
    ElseIf TypeOf C Is TextBox Then
        C.Text = "Text Box"
    End If

End Sub
```

As with **Forms, Controls** can only be used as a procedure argument and not in any other type of variable declarations. Additionally, you can't assign a value of one **Control** to another.

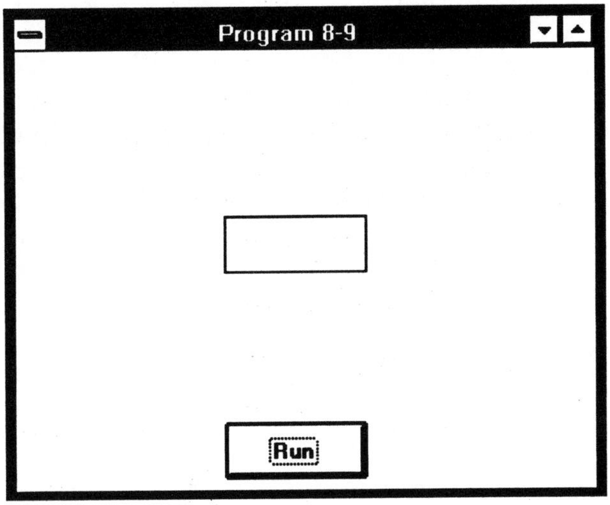

Figure 8-25   A TypeOf...Is demonstration program (1 of 2).

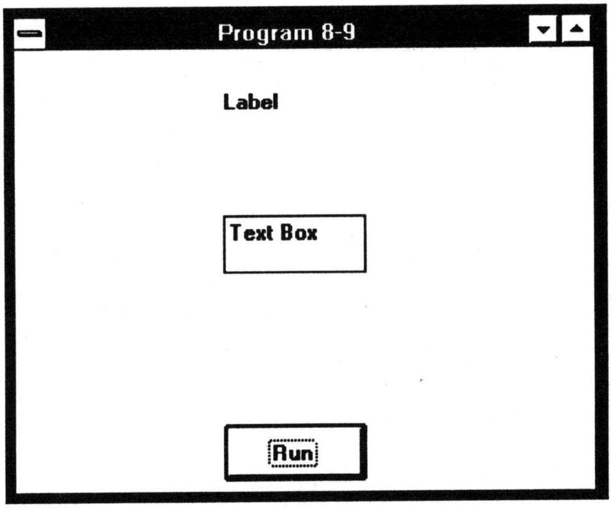

Figure 8-26   A TypeOf...Is demonstration program (2 of 2).

Summary

In this chapter you have learned how Visual Basic uses object classes to represent Windows windows and controls. You also learned how forms and controls have properties, methods, and events. Finally, this chapter detailed how both forms and controls can be passed as procedure arguments.

Chapter 9

Text File Input/Output

The Visual Basic programming language supports two basic types of disk files: text files and binary files. Data that is sent to and retrieved from text files is in the same format (ASCII strings) as data that is sent to the display. Consequently, you would have little trouble reading data in a text file by simply listing it. However, data sent to and retrieved from a binary file uses the same format that Visual Basic uses to store the data in the computer's internal memory. As a result, binary data files are virtually impossible to read.

Text Files

The first step in using a text disk file is to **open** it. Appropriately enough, the Visual Basic statement that opens a file is the **Open** statement. Figure 9-1 defines the syntax for using the **Open** statement to open a disk file. As this figure indicates, a text file can be opened in one of three distinct ways: for output, for input, and for append. When a file is opened for output, it allows you to write data to the file. If there is an existing file

```
Open file [For mode] [Access access] [lock] As
[#]filenumber [Len = reclen]
```

Where:

`file`	is the name of the file to be opened.
`mode`	is the file mode to be used when opening the file. For text files, *mode* is either **Input, Output,** or **Append.**
`access`	is the type of operations that are permitted on the open file if running under a network environment. The Visual Basic *access* types are **Read, Write,** and **Read Write.**
`lock`	is the type of operations that other processes are permitted on the open file under a network environment. The Visual Basic *lock* types are **Shared, Lock Read, Lock Write,** and **Lock Read Write.**
`filenumber`	is the file number to be assigned to this file. While a file is in an open state, it must have a unique file number to perform other actions on the file. Allowable values for the *filenumber* parameter are from 1 to 255.
`reclen`	is the file's buffer size. The default size for a text file is 512. Allowable values for the *reclen* parameter are from 1 to 32,767.

Figure 9-1 The Visual Basic Open statement.

with the same name, the old file's contents will be lost. When an existing file is opened for input, it permits you to read data from the file. Opening a file for append is similar to opening it

```
Print #filenumber, expression[{;|,} expression]...
```

Where:

`filenumber`	is the number of a file that has been previously opened for either output or append.
`expression`	is a valid Visual Basic expression.

Figure 9-2 The Visual Basic Print # statement.

for output, but the **file pointer** (an internal pointer that points to the current location being accessed in a file) is set to the end of the file. Thus, any of the file's existing contents will be preserved and any new data will be written directly after the old data.

Once a file is open, it can be written to and read from by using the Visual Basic **Print #** and **Input #** statements. Figure 9-2 defines the syntax for the **Print #** statement and Figure 9-3 defines the syntax for the **Input #** statement. Note how both of these statements require a file number. Visual Basic uses the specified file number to direct input and output to the correct disk file.

After a data file's input/output operations have been completed, the file must be closed with the Visual Basic **Close** statement. Figure 9-4 defines the syntax for the **Close** statement.

Program 9-1 demonstrates how a Visual Basic text file is accessed in an actual program. When the command button is

```
Input #filenumber,variable[,variable]...
```

Where:

`filenumber`	is the number of a file that has been previously opened for input.
`variable`	is a Visual Basic variable.

Figure 9-3 The Visual Basic Input # statement.

```
Close [[#] filenumber [, [#] filenumber] ...]
```

Where:

filenumber   is the number of a file to be closed.
                              If a file number isn't specified with
                              the **Close** statement, all files will be
                              closed.

Figure 9-4 The Visual Basic Close statement.

clicked, the program starts by opening a text file, writing 10 lines of data to the file, and closing the file. With the data safely stored away on disk, the program continues by reopening the text file, reading and displaying the 10 lines of data, and then reclosing the file. Note the program's use of the Visual Basic **Eof** function. **Eof** returns True if a specified file's file pointer is located at the end of the file's data. Otherwise, the **Eof** function returns False. By using the **Eof** function in a **While...Wend** loop, the program easily reads in all of the file's data. It simply continues to read data until **Eof** returns True. Listing 9-1-1 presents the code for the form's declarations section, and Listing 9-1-2 the code for the program's **RunButton_Click** proce-

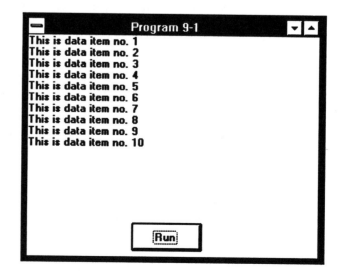

Figure 9-5 A text file demonstration program.

dure. Figure 9-5 illustrates how the program's window would appear after the program has been run.

Listing 9-1-1:

```
DefInt A-Z
```

Listing 9-1-2:

```
Sub RunButton_Click ()

    Open "TEXTDEMO.DAT" For Output As 1
    For I = 1 To 10
        Print #1, "This is data item no."; I
    Next I
    Close 1
    Open "TEXTDEMO.DAT" For Input As 1
    While Not EOF(1)
        Input #1, A$
        Print A$
    Wend
    Close 1

End Sub
```

Summary

In this chapter, you learned how a text file is opened, written to, read from, and closed.

Chapter 10

Binary File Input/Output

T his chapter discusses binary data files—the most efficient way to store numeric data types. In a binary file, data is stored on disk in the same format that it is stored in the computer's memory. Because a data item's binary representation almost always requires less memory than its ASCII counterpart, storing data in a binary file greatly reduces the amount of disk space required to store the data.

Another benefit of storing data in binary files has to do with the fact that Visual Basic is fully aware of the size of a data item. For example, Visual Basic stores integers as two binary bytes. An ASCII string representation of an integer requires from one (as in 0) to six (as in -19999) characters. Consequently, a Visual Basic program can never extract an integer from the middle of a text file. Without first reading all of the preceding data items, the program doesn't know where the data item is located in a text file. The method of reading the preceding data items in order to access data in a text file is call **sequential access**. Because the Visual Basic program knows just how large each data item is in a binary file, it can position the file pointer directly on a desired data item and either read its contents or replace it with a new data item. This method for accessing data is called **random access**. It stands to reason that, in all but the simplest of files, the random access method is usually the preferred method for accessing data.

Binary Files

The easiest way to randomly access disk data with Visual Basic is through the use of binary files. Opening a binary file is almost identical to opening a text file. As with a text file, a binary file is opened with the Visual Basic **Open** statement. Figure 10-1 defines the syntax for opening a binary file with the **Open** statement.

You should note that Visual Basic allows the programmer to perform both input and output on a file that has been opened with the binary format. Data is input from a binary file with the **Get** statement and output to the file with the **Put** statement. Figure 10-2 defines the syntax the **Get** statement uses to read data from a binary file, and Figure 10-3 the syntax the **Put** statement uses to write data to a binary file. As both of these illustrations show, you must specify the file position for the data item to be input or output. The file position is the data item's exact byte position in the file. Byte positions can be calculated with the following formula:

(data item number − 1) * data item size + 1

The data item's size can be determined with the Visual Basic **Len** function. Figure 10-4 defines the syntax for the **Len** function. Essentially, the **Len** function returns the size of a Visual Basic variable.

Program 10-1 demonstrates how a binary file can be used to perform random access. The program starts by creating a binary file of integers and filling the file with dummy integer values. It continues by reopening the file and reading and displaying the dummy values back in reverse order. Obviously, reading a file backward would be impossible to do with a text file. Although this is a rather simple example of randomly accessing a data file, it clearly shows some of the power offered by random access files. Listing 10-1-1 presents the code for the

```
Open file [For mode] [Access access] [lock] As
[#] filenumber [Len = reclen]
```

Where:

file	is the name of the file to be opened.
mode	is the file mode to be used when opening the file. For binary files, *mode* must be **Binary**.
access	is the type of operations that are permitted on the open file if running under a network environment. The Visual Basic *access* types are **Read**, **Write**, and **Read Write**.
lock	is the type of operations that other processes are permitted on the open file under a network environment. The Visual Basic *lock* types are **Shared**, **Lock**, **Read**, **Lock Write**, and **Lock Read Write**.
filenumber	is the file number to be assigned to the file. While a file is in an open state, it must have a unique file number to perform other actions on the file. Allowable values for the *filenumber* parameter are from 1 to 255.
reclen	is the file's buffer size. Visual Basic ignores the **Len** = *reclen* clause for binary files.

Figure 10-1 Opening a binary file.

form's declarations section, and Listing 10-1-2 the code for the program's **RunButton_Click** procedure. Figure 10-5 illustrates how the program's window would appear after the program has been run.

```
Get [#] filenumber, [byteposition], variable
```

Where:

`filenumber`	is the number of a previously opened binary file.
`byteposition`	is the data item's actual byte position in the file. If *byteposition* is omitted, Visual Basic will read the next data item from the file.
`variable`	is the variable to read the data into.

Figure 10-2 The Visual Basic Get statement.

```
Put [#] filenumber, [byteposition], variable
```

Where:

`filenumber`	is the number of a previously opened binary file.
`byteposition`	is the data item's actual byte position in the file. If *byteposition* is omitted, Visual Basic will write the data item at the file's current position.
`variable`	is the variable that holds the data to be written.

Figure 10-3 The Visual Basic Put statement.

```
Len(variable)
```

Where:

`variable`	is the variable whose size is to be returned.

Figure 10-4 The Visual Basic Len statement.

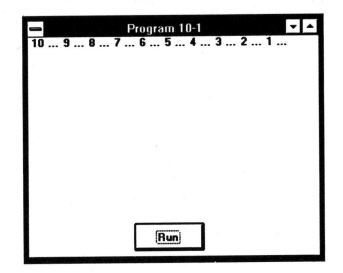

Figure 10-5 A binary file demonstration program.

Listing 10-1-1:

```
DefInt A-Z
```

Listing 10-1-2:

```
Sub RunButton_Click ()

    Open "TEXTDEMO.DAT" For Binary As 1
    For I = 1 To 10
        Put 1, , I
    Next I
    Close 1
    Open "TEXTDEMO.DAT" For Binary As 1
    For I = 10 To 1 Step -1
        Get 1, (I - 1) * Len(I) + 1, Rec
        Print Rec; "...";
    Next I
    Print
    Close 1

End Sub
```

Summary

In this chapter, you learned how random access files can be implemented with Visual Basic's binary file type. The chapter discussed such topics as opening a binary file, reading data from a binary file, and writing data to a binary file. In addition, the chapter explained how a data item's byte position in a binary file can be calculated.

PART II

THE VISUAL BASIC OBJECTS

This section of *The Power of Visual Basic* closely examines the Visual Basic objects: forms and controls. Chapter 11 offers an in-depth look at each of the Visual Basic controls; Chapter 12 presents a complete reference guide for the Visual Basic properties, methods, and events.

The Visual Basic Objects

T his chapter provides the reader with a detailed reference guide to the many Windows controls that are offered with the Visual Basic programming language. Furthermore, this chapter takes a detailed look at the many data objects that Visual Basic predefines. To explain what they are and how they are used in Visual Basic programs, this chapter describes each of the Visual Basic objects as follows:

Illustration:

Presents an example of what the object looks like.

Description:

Describes a object's purpose and how it is used in a Visual Basic program.

Properties:

Offers a complete list of the object's associated properties.

Methods:

Presents a complete list of the object's associated methods.

Events:

Provides a complete list of the object's associated events.

The Check Box Control

Illustration:

The following figure is an example of a Visual Basic form with three check box controls:

```
┌─────────────────────────────────────────────────┐
│ [—]                    Form1                [▼][▲]│
├─────────────────────────────────────────────────┤
│                                                   │
│                   ☒ Check1                         │
│                                                   │
│                                                   │
│                   ☒ Check2                         │
│                                                   │
│                                                   │
│                   ☐ Check3                         │
│                                                   │
│                                                   │
└─────────────────────────────────────────────────┘
```

Description:

The check box control allows the user to select a Yes/No (True/False) option. If a check box control is checked, its **Value** property will be set to True. Otherwise, the check box's **Value** property will be set to False for an unchecked check box. Text can be displayed to the right of a check box control by setting its **Caption** property.

Properties:

BackColor	FontItalic	Index	Top
Caption	FontName	Left	Value
CtlName	FontSize	MousePointer	Visible
DragIcon	FontStrikethru	Parent	Width
DragMode	FontUnderline	TabIndex	
Enabled	ForeColor	TabStop	
FontBold	Height	Tag	

Methods:

Drag	Move	Refresh	SetFocus

Events:

Click	GotFocus	KeyPress	LostFocus
DragOver	KeyDown	KeyUp	

The Clipboard Object

Description:

The clipboard object is used to access the Windows clipboard. It is accessed via the identifier name of **Clipboard** and is used to copy, cut, and paste both text and graphics within a Visual Basic program or between different Windows applications. It is important to note that the Windows clipboard will only remember the last data item copied or cut to it. Once another data item is either copied or cut to the **Clipboard**, its previous contents will be lost.

Methods:

Clear	GetFormat	SetData
GetData	GetText	SetText

The Combo Box Control

Illustration:

The figure below is an example of a Visual Basic form with a combo box control:

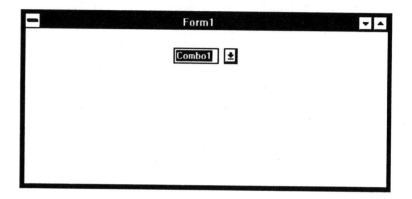

Description:

As its name implies, the combo box control is a combination of two other Windows controls: the text box and the list box. The combo box's **Text** property can be set either by typing the text into the combo box's text box or by pulling down the combo box's list box with the arrow to the right of the text box and clicking the desired list box item.

Properties:

BackColor	FontSize	ListCount	Sorted
CtlName	FontStrikethru	ListIndex	TabIndex
DragIcon	FontUnderline	MousePointer	TabStop
DragMode	ForeColor	Parent	Tag
Enabled	Height	SelLength	Text
FontBold	Index	SelStart	Top
FontItalic	Left	SelText	Visible
FontName	List	Style	Width

Methods:

AddItem	**Move**	**RemoveItem**
Drag	**Refresh**	**SetFocus**

Events:

Change	**DragDrop**	**GotFocus**	**KeyUp**
Click	**DragOver**	**KeyDown**	**LostFocus**
DblClick	**DropDown**	**KeyPress**	

The Command Button Control

Illustration:

The figure that follows is an example of a Visual Basic form with a command button control:

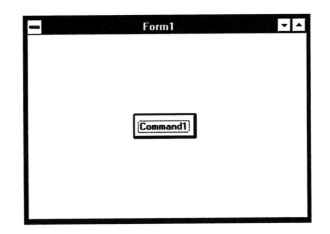

Description:

The command button control is used to allow the user to select an operation when the button is either clicked with the mouse or an appropriate key is pressed. A command button control can be clicked with the ESC key if the control's **Cancel** property is set to True or the command button control can be clicked with the ENTER key if the control's **Default** property is set to True. A command button control's text is set with the **Caption** property.

Properties:

BackColor	Enabled	Height	Tag
Cancel	FontBold	Index	Top
Caption	FontItalic	Left	Value
CtlName	FontName	MousePointer	Visible
Default	FontSize	Parent	Width
DragIcon	FontStrikethru	TabIndex	
DragMode	FontUnderline	TabStop	

Methods:

Drag	Move	Refresh	SetFocus

Events:

Click	DragOver	KeyDown	KeyUp
DragDrop	GotFocus	KeyPress	LostFocus

The Debug Object

Description:

To facilitate debugging a program, Visual Basic defines an object with an identifier of **Debug**. The **Debug** object is used to display values in the Visual Basic Immediate window.

Method:

Print

The Directory List Box Control

Illustration:

An example of a Visual Basic form with a directory list box control follows:

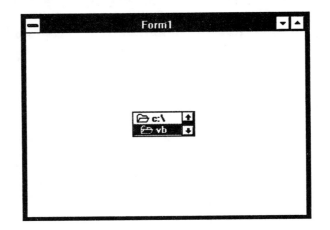

Description:

The directory list box control is used to display and select from a hierarchical list of directories. The current directory is set to the directory list box's currently selected directory. The directory list box's **Path** property can be used to set the current directory at run time. Additionally, the list of directories is accessed with the **List, ListCount,** and **ListIndex** properties.

Properties:

BackColor	FontName	Left	TabIndex
CtlName	FontSize	List	TabStop
DragIcon	FontStrikethru	ListCount	Tag
DragMode	FontUnderline	ListIndex	Top
Enabled	ForeColor	MousePointer	Visible
FontBold	Height	Parent	Width
FontItalic	Index	Path	

Methods:

Drag	**Move**	**Refresh**	**SetFocus**

Events:

Change	**DragOver**	**KeyPress**	**MouseDown**
Click	**GotFocus**	**KeyUp**	**MouseMove**
DragDrop	**KeyDown**	**LostFocus**	**MouseUp**

The Drive List Box

Illustration:

An example of a Visual Basic form with a drive list box control appears below:

Description:

The drive list box control is used to display and select from a list of valid drives. Normally, the drive list box control only displays the current drive; however, by clicking the arrow to the right of the drive list box control, Windows will display a list of all valid drives. The current drive is set to the drive list box's currently selected drive. The drive list box's **Drive** property can be used to set the current drive at run time. In addition, the list of drives can be accessed with the **List, ListCount,** and **ListIndex** properties.

Properties:

BackColor	FontItalic	Index	TabIndex
CtlName	FontName	Left	TabStop
DragIcon	FontSize	List	Tag
DragMode	FontStrikethru	ListCount	Top
Drive	FontUnderline	ListIndex	Visible
Enabled	ForeColor	MousePointer	Width
FontBold	Height	Parent	

Methods:

Drag	Move	Refresh	SetFocus

Events:

Change	DragOver	KeyDown	KeyUp
DragDrop	GotFocus	KeyPress	LostFocus

The File List Box Control

Illustration:

The following figure is an example of a Visual Basic form with a file list box control:

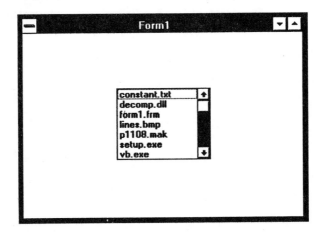

Description:

The file list box control is used to display and select from a list of the current directory's files. The list of files is accessed with the **List, ListCount,** and **ListIndex** properties.

Properties:

Archive	FontName	List	System
BackColor	FontSize	ListCount	TabIndex
CtlName	FontStrikethru	ListIndex	TabStop
DragIcon	FontUnderline	MousePointer	Tag
DragMode	ForeColor	Normal	Top
Enabled	Height	Parent	Visible
FileName	Hidden	Path	Width
FontBold	Index	Pattern	
FontItalic	Left	ReadOnly	

Methods:

Drag	Move	Refresh	SetFocus

Events:

Click	GotFocus	LostFocus	PathChange
DblClick	KeyDown	MouseDown	PatternChange
DragDrop	KeyPress	MouseMove	
DragOver	KeyUp	MouseUp	

The Frame Control

Illustration:

The figure that follows is an example of a Visual Basic form with a frame control:

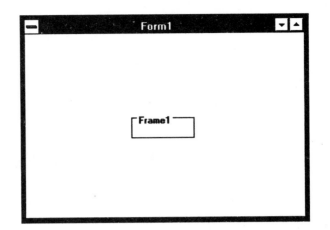

Description:

The frame control is used to group together one or more controls. Controls are grouped together by first drawing the frame control on the form and then drawing the controls inside of the frame control. The most common use for a frame control is to group together option buttons.

Properties:

BackColor	FontBold	ForeColor	TabIndex
Caption	FontItalic	Height	Tag
CtlName	FontName	Index	Top
DragIcon	FontSize	Left	Visible
DragMode	FontStrikethru	MousePointer	Width
Enabled	FontUnderline	Parent	

Methods:

Drag	Move	Refresh

Events:

DragDrop	DragOver

The Label Control

Illustration:

The figure below is an example of a Visual Basic form with a label control:

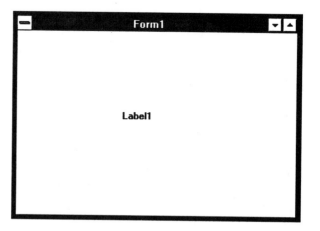

Description:

The label control is used to display text somewhere in a Window. Unlike a text box control, the label control's text cannot be changed directly by the user. It can be changed at run time by changing the label control's **Caption** property.

Properties:

Alignment	Enabled	Height	Parent
AutoSize	FontBold	Index	TabIndex
BackColor	FontItalic	Left	Tag
BorderStyle	FontName	LinkItem	Top
Caption	FontSize	LinkMode	Visible
CtlName	FontStrikethru	LinkTimeout	Width
DragIcon	FontUnderline	LinkTopic	
DragMode	ForeColor	MousePointer	

Methods:

Drag	**LinkPoke**	**Move**
LinkExecute	**LinkRequest**	**Refresh**

Events:

Change	**DragDrop**	**LinkError**	**MouseMove**
Click	**DragOver**	**LinkOpen**	**MouseUp**
DblClick	**LinkClose**	**MouseDown**	

The List Box Control

Illustration:

An example of a Visual Basic form with a list box control follows:

Description:

The list box control allows the user to make a selection from a list of items. Items can be added to the list with the AddItem method and removed from the list with the **RemoveItem** method. Additionally, the list of items can be accessed with the **List**, **ListCount**, and **ListIndex** properties.

Properties:

BackColor	FontName	Left	TabIndex
CtlName	FontSize	List	TabStop
DragIcon	FontStrikethru	ListCount	Tag
DragMode	FontUnderline	ListIndex	Text
Enabled	ForeColor	MousePointer	Top
FontBold	Height	Parent	Visible
FontItalic	Index	Sorted	Width

Methods:

AddItem	Move	RemoveItem
Drag	Refresh	SetFocus

Events:

Click	DragOver	KeyPress	MouseDown
DblClick	GotFocus	KeyUp	MouseMove
DragDrop	KeyDown	LostFocus	MouseUp

The Menu Control

Illustration:

The figure that appears below is an example of a Visual Basic form with a menu control:

Description:

The menu control is used to add a menu system to a Visual Basic form. To create a menu control, you must use Visual Basic's Menu Design Window. The following figure illustrates how the Menu Design Window appeared as the menu for the above example illustration was created:

```
┌─────────────────────────────────────────────┐
│ ▬            Menu Design Window              │
├─────────────────────────────────────────────┤
│  Caption: [&File          ]        ┌─────┐  │
│                                    │ Done │  │
│  CtlName: [FileMenu        ]       └─────┘  │
│                                    ┌──────┐ │
│                                    │Cancel│ │
│   Index: [    ]   Accelerator: [(none)  ▼]  │
│                                             │
│  ☐ Checked    ☒ Enabled      ☒ Visible      │
│  ┌──┬──┬──┬──┐ ┌──────┐ ┌──────┐ ┌──────┐  │
│  │← │→ │↑ │↓ │ │ Next │ │Insert│ │Delete│  │
│  └──┴──┴──┴──┘ └──────┘ └──────┘ └──────┘  │
│  &File                                      │
│  ····&Open                                  │
│  ····&Close                                 │
│  ····E&xit                                  │
│  &Edit                                      │
│  ····&Copy                                  │
│  ····Cu&t                                   │
│                                             │
└─────────────────────────────────────────────┘
```

When using Visual Basic's Menu Design window to create a menu, you should keep the following rules in mind:

1. Unindented menu items appear on the menu bar.

2. Menu items that are indented once will appear in the last menu bar item's menu.

3. Menu items that are indented more than once will appear in a submenu off of the last menu item.

4. A separator bar is created by setting a menu item's **Caption** property to a hyphen (-).

All menu items respond to a **Click** event. If a menu item has a menu below it, Windows will drop the menu down. Otherwise, Windows will call the menu item's **Click** event procedure.

Properties:

Caption	CtlName	Index	Tag
Checked	Enabled	Parent	Visible

Events:

Click

The Option Button Control

Illustration:

An example of a Visual Basic form with a group of option button controls follows:

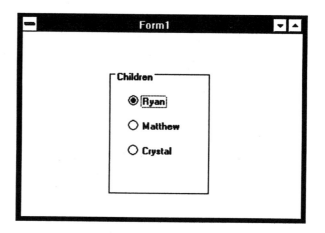

Description:

The option button control allows the user to turn an option on or off. Option button controls can be grouped together by first drawing either a frame control or a picture box control and then drawing the option button controls inside of the previously created control. When option button controls are grouped together, only one will be "on" at a time. All other option button controls in the group will be "off."

Properties:

BackColor	FontItalic	Index	Top
Caption	FontName	Left	Value
CtlName	FontSize	MousePointer	Visible
DragIcon	FontStrikethru	Parent	Width
DragMode	FontUnderline	TabIndex	
Enabled	ForeColor	TabStop	
FontBold	Height	Tag	

Methods:

Drag	Move	Refresh	SetFocus

Events:

Click	DragOver	KeyPress
DblClick	GotFocus	KeyUp
DragDrop	KeyDown	LostFocus

The Picture Box Control

Illustration:

The figure below is an example of a Visual Basic form with a picture box control:

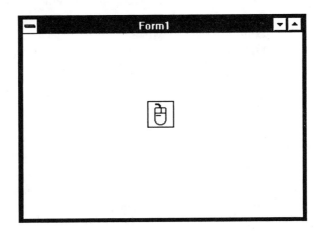

Description:

As its name implies, the picture box control is used to display a picture in a window. A picture box control can display a bitmap, an icon, or a metafile. It can also be used with graphics statements and **Print** statements. In addition, a picture box control can be used to group together option button controls.

Properties:

AutoRedraw	Enabled	Height	ScaleLeft
AutoSize	FillColor	Image	ScaleMode
BackColor	FillStyle	Index	ScaleTop
BorderStyle	FontBold	Left	ScaleWidth
CtlName	FontItalic	LinkItem	TabIndex
CurrentX	FontName	LinkMode	TabStop
CurrentY	FontSize	LinkTimeout	Tag
DragIcon	FontStrikethru	LinkTopic	Top
DragMode	FontTransparent	MousePointer	Visible
DrawMode	FontUnderline	Parent	Width
DrawStyle	ForeColor	Picture	
DrawWidth	hDC	ScaleHeight	

Methods:

Circle	LinkPoke	Print	TextHeight
Cls	LinkRequest	PSet	TextWidth
Drag	LinkSend	Refresh	
Line	Move	Scale	
LinkExecute	Point	SetFocus	

Events:

Change	GotFocus	LinkError	MouseUp
Click	KeyDown	LinkOpen	Paint
DblClick	KeyPress	LostFocus	
DragDrop	KeyUp	MouseDown	
DragOver	LinkClose	MouseMove	

The Printer Object

Description:

The printer object is used to send output to the default system printer. Visual Basic assigns an identifier of **Printer** for the printer object.

Properties:

CurrentX	FontBold	FontTransparent	ScaleLeft
CurrentY	FontCount	FontUnderline	ScaleMode
DrawMode	FontItalic	ForeColor	ScaleTop
DrawStyle	FontName	hDC	ScaleWidth
DrawWidth	Fonts	Height	Width
FillColor	FontSize	Page	
FillStyle	FontStrikethru	ScaleHeight	

Methods:

Circle	NewPage	Scale
EndDoc	Print	TextHeight
Line	PSet	TextWidth

The Screen Object

Description:

The screen object is used to activate a specific form or control at run time. Visual Basic assigns an identifier of **Screen** to the screen object.

Properties:

ActiveControl	FontCount	Height	Width
ActiveForm	Fonts	MousePointer	

The Scroll Bar Controls

Illustration:

The following figure is an example of a Visual Basic form with scroll bar controls:

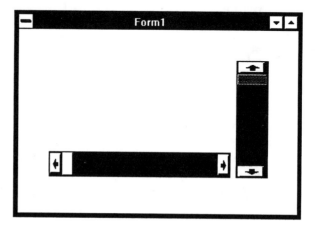

Description:

The Visual Basic scroll bar controls are used either as an input device or as a quantity indicator. Scroll bar controls can be either horizontal or vertical and the range of values they represent can vary depending upon their **Max** and **Min** properties. A scroll bar's **Value** property holds the current position of the scroll box. The scroll bar's **SmallChange** property holds the amount the **Value** property is adjusted by if the user clicks the scroll bar's arrows; the scroll bar's **LargeChange** property holds the amount the **Value** property is adjusted by if the user clicks the scroll bar itself.

Properties:

CtlName	**Index**	**MousePointer**	**Tag**
DragIcon	**LargeChange**	**Parent**	**Top**
DragMode	**Left**	**SmallChange**	**Value**
Enabled	**Max**	**TabIndex**	**Visible**
Height	**Min**	**TabStop**	**Width**

Methods:

Drag	**Move**	**Refresh**	**SetFocus**

Events:

Change	**DragOver**	**KeyDown**	**KeyUp**
DragDrop	**GotFocus**	**KeyPress**	**LostFocus**

The Text Box Control

Illustration:

The figure below is an example of a Visual Basic form with a text box control:

Description:

The text box control is used either to display information or allow the user to enter information. A multiline text box control is created by setting the control's **MultiLine** property to True.

Properties:

BackColor	**FontSize**	**LinkTimeout**	**TabIndex**
BorderStyle	**FontStrikethru**	**LinkTopic**	**TabStop**

CtlName	FontUnderline	MousePointer	Tag
DragIcon	ForeColor	MultiLine	Text
DragMode	Height	Parent	Top
Enabled	Index	ScrollBars	Visible
FontBold	Left	SelLength	Width
FontItalic	LinkItem	SelStart	
FontName	LinkMode	SelText	

Methods:

Drag	LinkPoke	Move	SetFocus
LinkExecute	LinkRequest	Refresh	

Events:

Change	GotFocus	KeyUp	LinkOpen
DragDrop	KeyDown	LinkClose	LostFocus
DragOver	KeyPress	LinkError	

The Timer Control

Illustration:

An example of a Visual Basic form with a timer control follows:

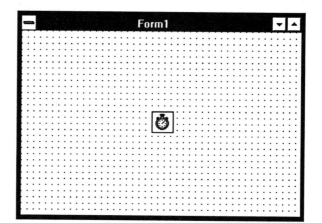

You should note that the above illustration shows the timer control at design time and not at run time, the reason being that the timer control is invisible at run time.

Description:

The timer control runs a procedure at a specified time interval. The procedure Windows calls is the timer control's **Timer** event procedure and the time interval is specified by the timer control's **Interval** property.

Properties:

CtlName	Index	Parent
Enabled	Interval	Tag

Events:

Timer

Chapter 12

The Visual Basic Properties, Methods, and Events

T his chapter provides the reader with a detailed reference guide to the many properties, methods, and events that the Visual Basic programming language offers for manipulating forms and controls. To show how they are used in Visual Basic programs, this section describes each of the Visual Basic properties, methods, and events as follows:

Summary:

Presents an exact syntactic model for each of the Visual Basic properties, methods, and events.

Description:

Describes a property, a method, or an event's purpose and how it is used in an application program.

See Also:

Lists any similar or related Visual Basic properties, methods, or events.

Example:

Illustrates how a Visual Basic property, method, or event could actually be used in an application program.

ActiveControl Property

Summary:

Screen.ActiveControl

Description:

The **ActiveControl** property returns the control that has the focus. You should note that the **ActiveControl** property is always used with the **Screen** object.

See Also:

ActiveForm

Example:

The following program demonstrates how the **ActiveControl** property is used by clearing the text in the currently active text box control whenever the form is clicked. Listing 12-1 presents the code for the form's **Form_Click** event. Figure 12-1 illustrates how the program's window would appear after the program has been run.

Listing 12-1:

```
Sub Form_Click ()
    If TypeOf Screen.ActiveControl Is TextBox Then
        Screen.ActiveControl.Text = ""
    End If
End Sub
```

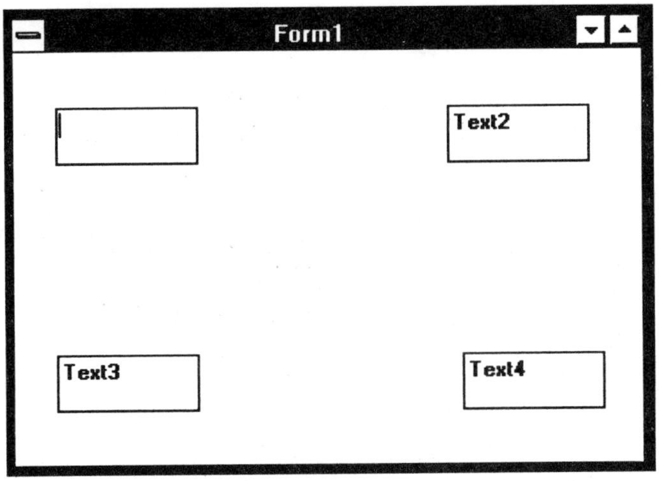

*Figure 12-1 An **ActiveControl** demonstration program.*

ActiveForm Property

Summary:

Screen.ActiveForm

Description:

The **ActiveForm** property returns the form that has the focus. You should note that the **ActiveForm** property is always used with the **Screen** object.

See Also:

ActiveControl

Example:

The program that follows demonstrates how the **ActiveForm** control property is used in an actual program by doubling the font size for the currently active form whenever the form is clicked. Listing 12-2-1 presents the code for the **Double-FontSize** procedure and Listing 12-2-2 presents the code for the form's **Form_Click** event. Figure 12-2 shows how the

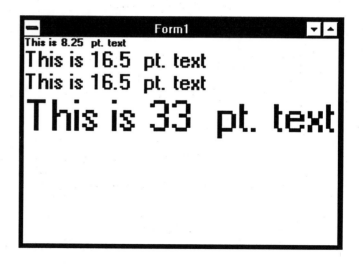

*Figure 12-2 An **ActiveForm** demonstration program.*

program's window would appear after the program has been run.

Listing 12-2-1:

```
Sub DoubleFontSize ()

    Screen.ActiveForm.FontSize =
    Screen.ActiveForm.FontSize * 2

End Sub
```

Listing 12-2-2:

```
Sub Form_Click ()

    Print "This is"; FontSize; " pt. text"
    DoubleFontSize
    Print "This is"; FontSize; " pt. text"

End Sub
```

AddItem Method

Summary:

control.**AddItem** *item*[*,index*]

`control`	is either a combo box or list box control.
`item`	is the string expression to be added to the list.
`index`	is the item's position in the list.

Description:

The **AddItem** method adds a string expression to either a combo box or a list box's item list. The string expression is specified by *item* and the combo box or list box control is specified by *control*. An optional *index* parameter can be specified and tells Visual Basic the item's position in the list. You should note that the first item in a list is always 0. If the optional *index* parameter is omitted from the statement, Visual Basic will add the item in its proper sorted order if the control's **Sorted** property is set to True or at the end of the list if the control's **Sorted** property is set to False.

See Also:

RemoveItem, Sorted

Example:

The following program demonstrates how the **AddItem** method is used by creating a three-item list box control. Listing 12-3 presents the code for the form's **Form_Load** event. Figure 12-3 illustrates how the program's window would appear after the program has been run.

Listing 12-3:

```
Sub Form_Load ()

    List1.AddItem "Ryan"
    List1.AddItem "Matthew"
    List1.AddItem "Crystal"

End Sub
```

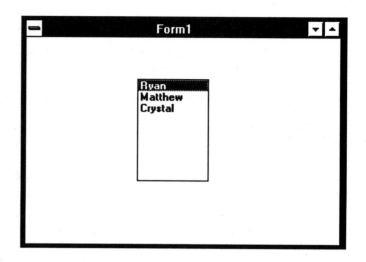

*Figure 12-3 An **AddItem** demonstration program.*

Alignment Property

Summary:

```
[form.] [label.]Alignment [ = setting]
```

form	is the label's form.
label	is the appropriate label.
setting	is the new alignment setting.

Description:

The **Alignment** property is used to either set or return a label's text alignment. Visual Basic supports three **Alignment** values:

Value	Description
0	Left justify
1	Right justify
2	Center

You should note that Visual Basic left-justifies label text by default.

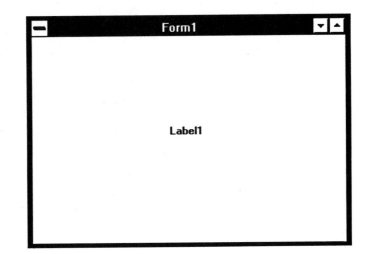

Figure 12-4 An **Alignment** *demonstration program.*

Example:

The program that follows demonstrates how the **Alignment** property is used by centering a label's text. Listing 12-4 presents the code for the form's **Form_Click** event. Figure 12-4 illustrates how the program's window would appear after the program has been run.

Listing 12-4:

```
Sub Form_Load ()

    Label1.Alignment = 2

End Sub
```

Archive Property

Summary:

```
[form.] filelistbox.Archive [ = flag]
```

form	is the file list box's form.
filelistbox	is the appropriate file list box.
flag	is the new archive attribute setting.

Description:

The **Archive** property is used to either set or return a file list box's archive attribute setting. If the **Archive** property is set to True (the default), Visual Basic will display files with their archive attributes set in the file list box. If the **Archive** property is set to False, Visual Basic will not display files with their archive attributes set in the file list box.

See Also:

Hidden, Normal, ReadOnly, and **System**

Example:

The following program demonstrates how the **Archive** property is used by toggling a file list box's **Archive** property on and off whenever the form is clicked. Listing 12-5 presents the code for the form's **Form_Click** event. Figure 12-5 illustrates how the program's window would appear after the program has been run.

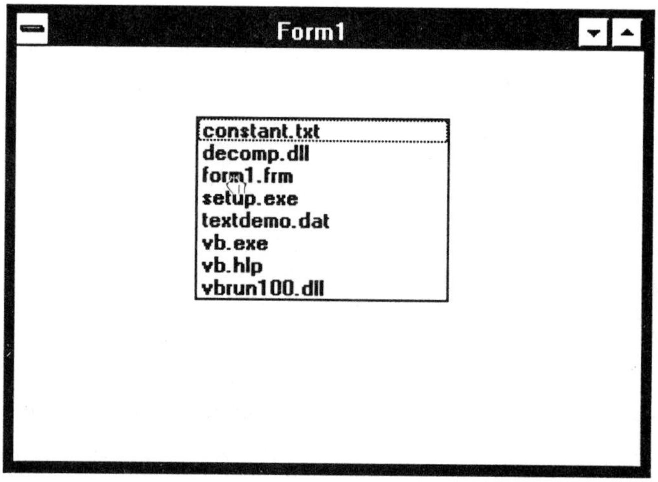

Figure 12-5 An **Archive** *demonstration program.*

Listing 12-5:

```
Sub Form_Click ()

    File1.Archive = Not File1.Archive

End Sub
```

AutoRedraw Property

Summary:

[*form.*] [*picturebox.*]**AutoRedraw**[= *flag*]

form	is the appropriate form.
picturebox	is the appropriate picture box.
flag	is the new setting for the **AutoRedraw** property.

Description:

The **AutoRedraw** property is used to either set or return a form or a picture box's automatic repainting setting. If the **AutoRedraw** property is set to True, Visual Basic will constantly maintain a form or a picture box's image as a bitmap. Whenever the form or picture box needs to be repainted, Visual Basic can restore the image completely from the saved bitmap. If the **AutoRedraw** property is set to False, Visual Basic will not maintain a copy of the form or picture box's image in memory. Therefore, Visual Basic will call the form or picture box's **Paint** event whenever the image must be redrawn.

Example:

The program that follows demonstrates how the **AutoRedraw** property is used to maintain a portion of a form's image. Listing 12-6 presents the code for the form's **Form_Click** event. Figure 12-6 illustrates how the program's window would appear after the program has been run.

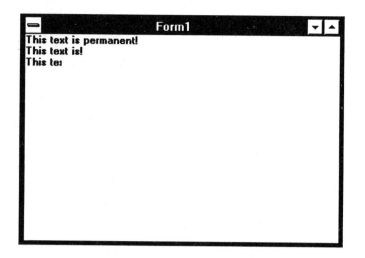

*Figure 12-6 An **AutoRedraw** demonstration program.*

Listing 12-6:

```
Sub Form_Click ()

    AutoRedraw = -1
    Print "This text is permanent!"
    Print "This text is!"
    AutoRedraw = 0
    Print "This text isn't!"

End Sub
```

AutoSize Property

Summary:

[*form.*]{*label.*|*picturebox.*}**AutoSize**[= *flag*]

form   is the label or picture box's form.

label   is the appropriate label.

picturebox   is the appropriate picture box.

flag   is the new setting for the **AutoSize** property.

Description:

The **AutoSize** property is used to either set or return a label or a picture box's automatic resize setting. If the **AutoSize** property is set to True, Visual Basic will automatically resize the label or picture box to fit its contents. If the **AutoSize** property is set to False, Visual Basic will maintain the size of a control. If the control's contents exceed its size, the control's contents are clipped to fit into the area.

Example:

The following program demonstrates how the **AutoSize** property is used by setting a label's **AutoSize** property to True when the form is clicked. Listing 12-7 presents the code for the form's **Form_Click** event. Figure 12-7 illustrates how the program's window would appear after the program has been run.

Listing 12-7:

```
Sub Form_Click ()

    Label1.AutoSize = -1

End Sub
```

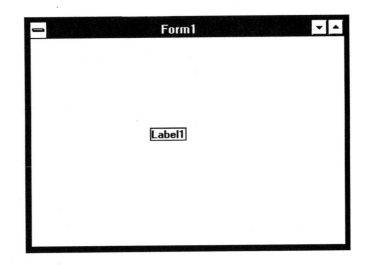

*Figure 12-7 An **AutoSize** demonstration program.*

BackColor Property

Summary:

[*form.*] [*control.*]**BackColor** [= *color*]

form	is the appropriate form.
control	is the appropriate control.
color	is the new background color.

Description:

The **BackColor** property sets and returns the background color for either a form, a check box, a combo box, a command button, a directory list box, a drive list box, a file list box, a frame, a label, a list box, an option button, a picture box, or a text box.

See Also:

ForeColor, QBColor, and **RGB**

Example:

The program below demonstrates how the **BackColor** property is used by setting a form's background color to yellow. Listing 12-8 presents the code for the form's **Form_Click** event. Figure 12-8 illustrates how the program's window would appear after the program has been run.

Listing 12-8:

```
Sub Form_Click ()

    BackColor = RGB(255, 255, 0)
    Print "I now have a yellow background"

End Sub
```

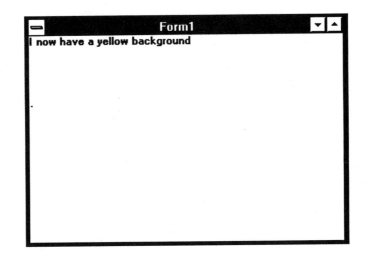

*Figure 12-8 A **BackColor** demonstration program.*

BorderStyle Property

Summary:

[*form.*] [*control.*]**BorderStyle**[= *style*]

form	is the appropriate form.
control	is the appropriate control.
style	is the new border style.

Description:

The **BorderStyle** sets and returns the border style for either a form, a label, a picture box, or a text box. You should note that a form or a picture box border style can only be set at design time. Visual Basic supports these form border styles:

Style	Description
0	No border.
1	Fixed single. (Cannot be resized.)
2	Sizable border. (Default.)
3	Fixed double. (Cannot be resized.)

Visual Basic supports these label, text box, and picture box styles:

Style	Description
0	None. (Label default.)
1	Fixed single. (Picture box and text box default.)

Example:

The following program demonstrates how the **BorderStyle** property is used by alternately changing a label's border style from none to fixed single and vice versa. Listing 12-9 presents the code for the form's **Form_Click** event. Figure 12-9 illustrates how the program's window would appear after the program has been run.

Listing 12-9:

```
Sub Form_Click ()

    If Label1.BorderStyle = 1 Then
        Label1.BorderStyle = 0
    Else
        Label1.BorderStyle = 1
    End If

End Sub
```

Cancel Property

Summary:

```
[form.] commandbutton.Cancel [ = flag]
```

flag   is the new cancel setting.

Description:

The **Cancel** property determines whether or not a command button responds to the ESC key. If a command button's **Cancel**

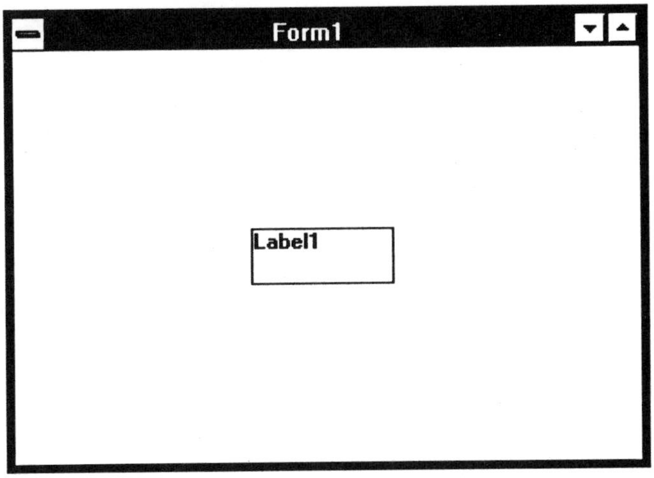

*Figure 12-9 A **BorderStyle** demonstration program.*

property is set to True, Visual Basic will call its **Click** event whenever the ESC key is pressed. If a command button's **Cancel** property is set to False, the command button will ignore all ESC key presses. You should note that only one command button per form can have its **Cancel** button set to True. Visual Basic will automatically set any other of the form's command buttons' **Cancel** properties to False when another command button's **Cancel** property is set to True. The default setting for all command buttons is to have their **Cancel** property set to False.

Example:

The program that appears below demonstrates how the **Cancel** property is used in an actual program by having a "Cancel" command button display a message each time the ESC key is pressed. Listing 12-10-1 presents the code for the form's **Form_Load** event, Listing 12-10-2 the code for the form's **Command1_Click** event, and Listing 12-10-3 the code for the form's **Command2_Click** event. Figure 12-10 shows how the program's window would appear after the program has been run.

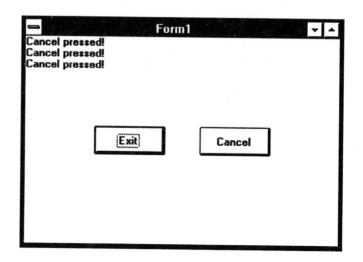

*Figure 12-10 A **Cancel** demonstration program.*

Listing 12-10-1:

```
Sub Form_Load ()

    Command2.Cancel = -1

End Sub
```

Listing 12-10-2:

```
Sub Command1_Click ()

    End

End Sub
```

Listing 12-10-3:

```
Sub Command2_Click ()

    Print "Cancel pressed!"

End Sub
```

Caption Property

Summary:

```
[form.][control.]Caption[ = string]
```

form   is the appropriate form.

control   is the appropriate control.

string   is the form or control's new caption.

Description:

The **Caption** property sets or returns the text associated with either a form or a control. In the case of a form, the text is the form's title bar. In the case of a control, it is either the text that appears beside the control or in the control. When setting the **Caption** property, the new text is specified by *string*.

Example:

The program that follows demonstrates how the **Caption** property is used in an actual property to change a form's title bar. Each time the form is clicked, the title bar will be appropriately changed. Listing 12-11-1 presents the code for the form's declarations section, and Listing 12-11-2 the code for the form's **Form_Click** event. Figure 12-11 illustrates how the program's window would appear after the program has been run.

Listing 12-11:

```
DefInt A-Z

Dim N As Integer
```

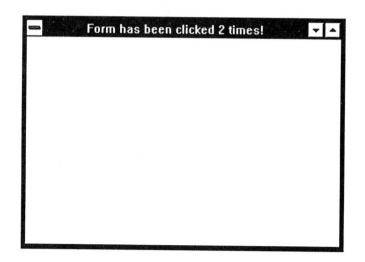

Figure 12-11 A **Caption** *demonstration program.*

Listing 12-11-2:

```
Sub Form_Click ()

    N = N + 1
    Caption = "Form has been clicked" + Str$(N) +
    " times!"

End Sub
```

Change Event

Summary:

Sub *control_***Change(**[*Index* **As Integer**]**)**

control   is the desired control.

index   is the control's index in an array of controls.

Description:

The **Change** event is called by Visual Basic to signal to the program that a control has changed. The table that follows explains the type of controls that feature a **Change** event and why Visual Basic calls the event:

Control	Reason For Event
Combo Box[1]	Called when the user enters data or the control's **Text** property has been changed.
Directory List Box	Called when the user selects a new directory or the control's **Path** property has been changed.
Drive List Box	Called when the user selects a new drive or the control's **Drive** property has been changed.
Label	Called when a DDE link updates the control or the control's **Caption** property has been changed.
Picture Box	Called when a DDE link updates the control or the control's **Picture** property has been changed.
Scroll Bars	Called when the user moves the scroll box or the control's **Value** property has been changed.
Text Box	Called when the user enters data or the control's **Text** property has been changed.

[1]Will only be called if the combo box's **Style** property is set for either 0 (Dropdown Combo) or 1 (Simple Combo).

Example:

The following program shows how the **Change** event is used to reset a form's background color according the position of a horizontal scroll bar. Listing 12-12-1 presents code the form's **Form_Load** event and Listing 12-12-2 presents the code for the form's **HScroll1_Change** event. Figure 12-12 illustrates how the program's window would appear after the program has been run.

Listing 12-12-1:

```
Sub Form_Load ()

    HScroll1.Min = 0
    HScroll1.Max = 255
```

```
        HScroll1.Value = 0
        HScroll1.SmallChange = 1
        HScroll1.LargeChange = 25

End Sub
```

Listing 12-12-2:

```
Sub HScroll1_Change ()

        BackColor = RGB(HScroll1.Value, 0, 0)

End Sub
```

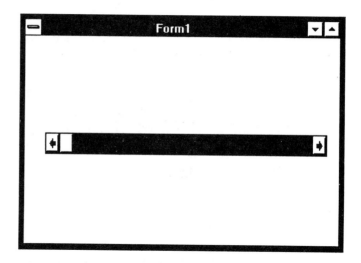

Figure 12-12 A **Change** *demonstration program.*

Checked Property

Summary:

menuitem.**Checked**[= *flag*]

menuitem	is the desired menu item.
flag	is the **Checked** property's new setting.

Description:

The **Checked** property determines whether or not a check mark is displayed next to a menu item. If the menu item's **Checked** property is set to True, a check mark will be displayed next to the menu item. If the menu item's **Checked** property is set to False (the default), a check mark will not be displayed next to the menu item. When setting the **Checked** property, its new value is passed in the *flag* parameter.

Example:

The program below demonstrates how the **Checked** property is used to turn on a check mark beside a menu item. Listing 12-13 presents the code for the form's **FileSave_Click** event. Figure 12-13 shows the Menu Design Window that is used to build the demonstration program.

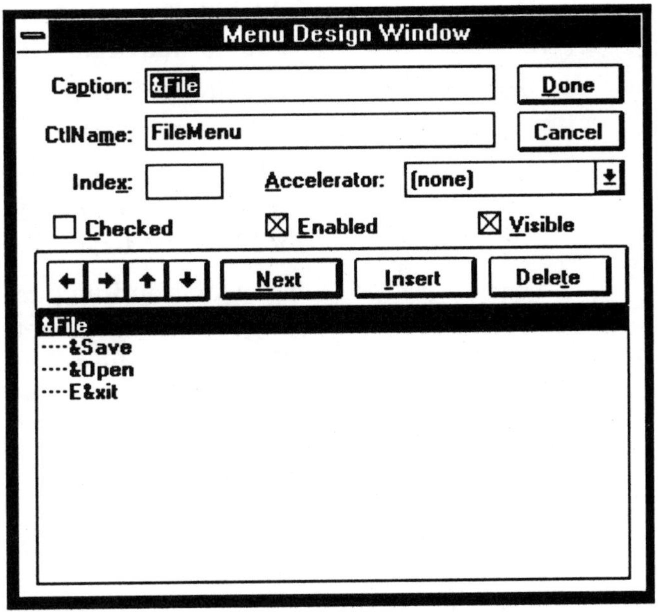

Figure 12-13 A sample Menu Design Window.

Listing 12-13:

```
Sub FileSave_Click ()

    FileSave.Checked = -1

End Sub
```

Circle Method

Summary:

[object.] **Circle** *[**Step**] (x,y), radius[, [color] [, [start] [, [end] [, aspect]]]]*

object	is either a form, a picture box, or the **Printer** object.
x, y	is the center of the circle's starting coordinate. If the **Step** keyword is used in the statement, the *x,y* coordinates are considered relative to **CurrentX** and **Current Y**.
radius	is the radius of the circle.
color	is the RGB color value to be used when drawing the circle.
start	is the arc's starting position. The valid range for this parameter is -2Pi radians to 2Pi radians. The default starting position is 0.
end	is the arc's ending position. The valid range for this parameter is -2Pi radians to 2Pi radians. The default ending position is 2Pi radians.
aspect	is the circle's aspect ratio. The default aspect ratio is 1.0.

Description:

The **Circle** method draws a circle, an ellipse, or an arc on either a form, a picture box, or the **Printer** object.

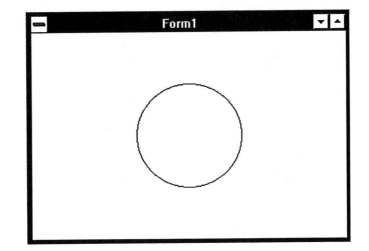

*Figure 12-14 A **Circle** demonstration program.*

See Also:

CurrentX, CurrentY, DrawMode, DrawWidth, FillColor, FillStyle, ForeColor, QBColor, and **RGB**

Example:

The program that follows demonstrates how the **Circle** method is used to draw a circle on a form. Listing 12-14 presents the code for the form's **Form_Click** event. Figure 12-14 illustrates how the program's window would appear after the program has been run.

Listing 12-14:

```
Sub Form_Click ()

    Circle (ScaleWidth / 2, ScaleHeight / 2),
    ScaleHeight / 4

End Sub
```

Clear Method

Summary:

```
Clipboard.Clear
```

Description:

The **Clear** method is used to clear the **Clipboard** object's current contents.

Example:

The following program demonstrates how the **Clear** method is used in an actual program by clearing the **Clipboard**'s contents when the form is clicked. Listing 12-15-1 presents the code for the form's **Form_Load** event, and Listing 12-15-2 the code for the form's **Form_Click** event. Figure 12-15 shows how the program's window would appear after the program has been run.

Listing 12-15-1:

```
Sub Form_Load ()

    Clipboard.SetText "Click the form to clear the
    Clipboard"
    Text1.Text = Clipboard.GetText()

End Sub
```

Listing 12-15-2:

```
Sub Form_Click ()

    Clipboard.Clear
    Clipboard.SetText ""
    Text1.Text = Clipboard.GetText()

End Sub
```

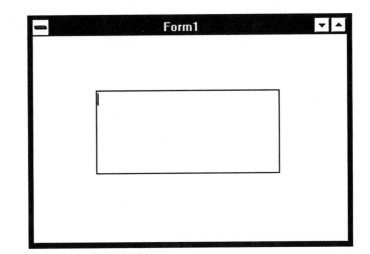

*Figure 12-15 A **Clear** demonstration program.*

Click Event

Summary:

```
Sub Form_Click( )
```

or

```
Sub control_Click([Index As Integer])
```

control   is the desired control.

index   is the control's index in an array of controls.

Description:

The **Click** event is called by Visual Basic to signal the program that a form, a check box, a combo box, a command button, a directory list box, a file list box, a label, a list box, a menu, an option button, or a picture box has been clicked.

Example:

The program below shows how the **Click** event is used by displaying a message whenever a command button is clicked. Listing 12-16 presents the code for the **Command1_Click**

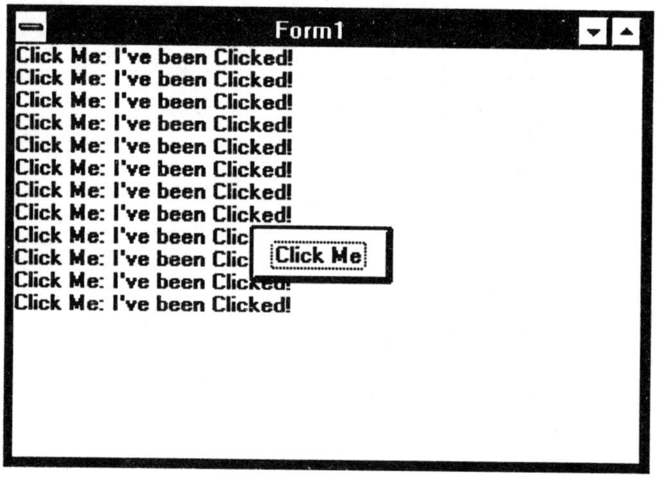

Figure 12-16 A **Click** *demonstration program.*

event. Figure 12-16 illustrates how the program would appear after the program has been run.

Listing 12-16:

```
Sub Command1_Click ()

    Print "Click Me: I've been Clicked!"

End Sub
```

Cls Method

Summary:

[{form.|picturebox.}]**Cls**

form   is the desired form.

picturebox   is the desired picture box.

Description:

The **Cls** method erases any text or graphics from a form or a picture box control. After clearing the form or picture box,

Visual Basic sets both **CurrentX** and **CurrentY** to 0. You should note that any text or graphics displayed while the **AutoRedraw** property is equal to True will be preserved if the **Cls** method is called while **AutoRedraw** is equal to False.

See Also:

AutoRedraw, CurrentX, and **CurrentY**

Example:

The program that appears below demonstrates how the **Cls** method is used to erase 10 lines of text from a form. Listing 12-17-1 presents code for the form's **Form_Click** event and Listing 12-17-2 the code for the form's **Form_Paint** event. Figure 12-17 illustrates how the form appears before the **Click** event is executed; Figure 12-18 shows how the form appears after the **Click** event is executed.

Listing 12-17-1:

```
Sub Form_Click ()

    Cls

End Sub
```

Listing 12-17-2:

```
Sub Form_Paint ()
Dim I As Integer

    For I = 1 To 10
        Print "10 lines of junk"
    Next I

End Sub
```

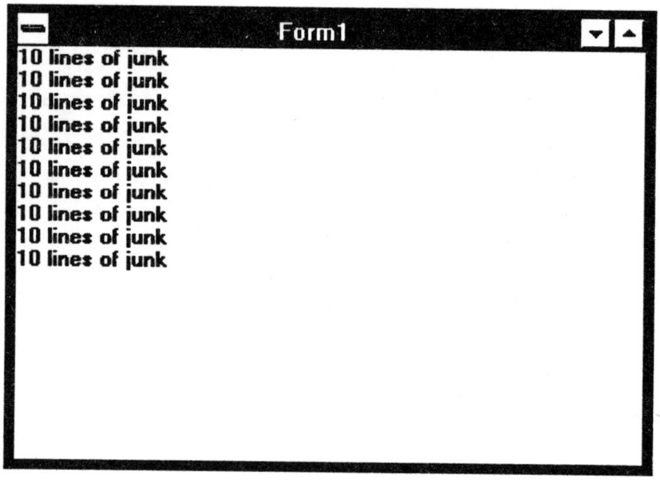

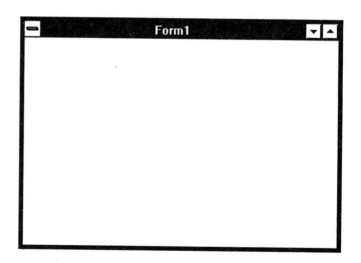

*Figure 12-17 A **Cls** demonstration program (1 of 2).*

*Figure 12-18 A **Cls** demonstration program (2 of 2).*

ControlBox Property

Summary:

[*form*.] **ControlBox**

form   is the desired form.

Description:

The **ControlBox** property determines if a form has a Control-menu box. If **ControlBox** is set to True, the form will have a Control-menu box. If **ControlBox** is set to False, the form will not have a Control-menu box. You should note that the **ControlBox** property is read-only at run time.

Example:

The following program demonstrates how the **ControlBox** property is used to create a form without a Control-menu box. Listing 12-18 presents the code for the form's **Command1_Click** event. Figure 12-19 illustrates how the program's window would appear after the program has been run.

Listing 12-18:

```
Sub Command1_Click ()

     End

End Sub
```

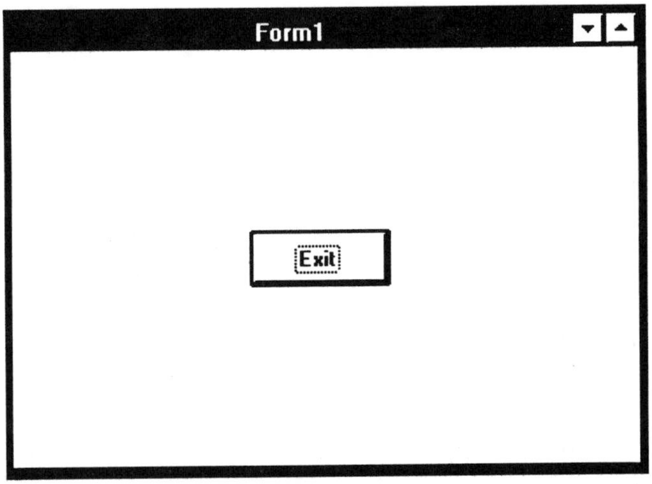

*Figure 12-19 A **ControlBox** demonstration program.*

CtlName Property

Description:

The **CtlName** property is used to assign a name to a check box, a combo box, a command button, a directory list box, a drive list box, a file list box, a frame, a horizontal scroll bar, a label, a list box, a menu, an option button, a picture box, a text box, a timer, or a vertical scroll bar. The **CtlName** property is only available at design time.

CurrentX Property

Summary:

{ [*form.*] [*picturebox.*] **Printer.** } **CurrentX** [= *x*]

form   is the desired form.

picturebox   is the desired picture box.

x   is the new horizontal position.

Description:

The **CurrentX** property sets or returns the current horizontal position when displaying or printing text and graphics to either a form, a picture box, or the **Printer** object.

Example:

The program that follows demonstrates the **CurrentX** property by displaying a message to the right of a form's center. Listing 12-19 presents the form's **Form_Click** event. Figure 12-20 shows how the program's window would appear after the program has been run.

Listing 12-19:

```
Sub Form_Click ()

    CurrentX = ScaleWidth / 2
    Print "I'm to the right of center"

End Sub
```

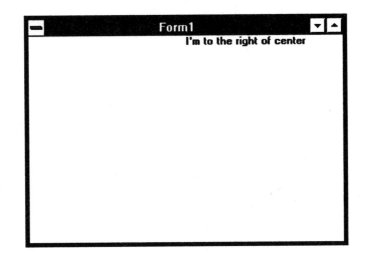

*Figure 12-20 A **CurrentX** demonstration program.*

CurrentY Property

Summary:

`{[form.] [picturebox.] Printer.}CurrentY[ = y]`

form	is the desired form.
picturebox	is the desired picture box.
y	is the new vertical position.

Description:

The **CurrentY** property sets or returns the current vertical position when displaying or printing text and graphics to either a form, a picture box, or the **Printer** object.

Example:

The following program demonstrates the **CurrentY** property by displaying a message just below the form's center. Listing 12-20 presents the code for the form's **Form_Click** event. Figure 12-21 illustrates how the program's window would appear after the program has been run.

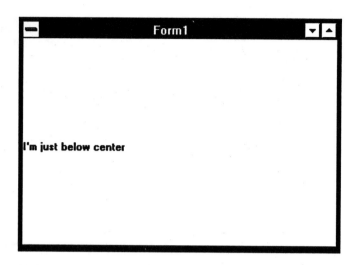

Figure 12-21 A **CurrentY** *demonstration program.*

Listing 12-20:

```
Sub Form_Click ()

    CurrentY = ScaleHeight / 2
    Print "I'm just below center"

End Sub
```

DblClick Event

Summary:

Sub Form_DblClick( )

or

Sub *control*_**DblClick(**[*Index* **As Integer**]**)**

control   is the desired control.

index   is the control's index in an array of controls.

Description:

The **DblClick** event is called by Visual Basic to signal the program that a form, a combo box, a directory list box, a file

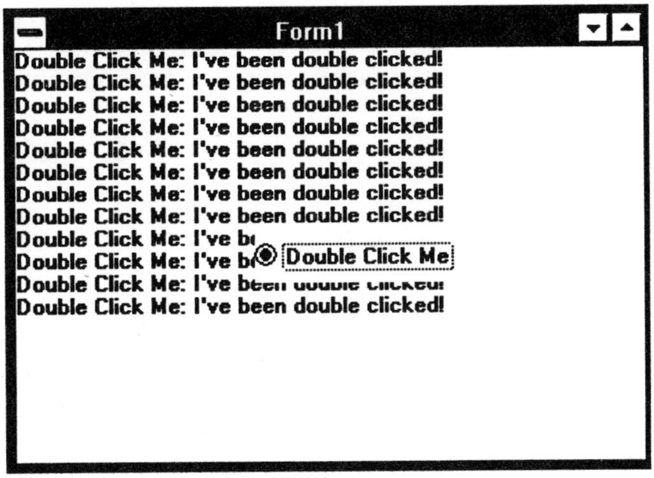

*Figure 12-22 A **DblClick** demonstration program.*

list box, a label, a list box, an option button, or a picture box has been double clicked.

Example:

The program below demonstrates how the **DblClick** event is used in an actual program by displaying a message whenever an option button is double clicked. Listing 12-21 presents the code for the **Option1_DblClick** event. Figure 12-22 illustrates how the program would appear after the program has been run.

Listing 12-21:

```
Sub Option1_DblClick ()

    Print "Double Click Me: I've been double clicked!"

End Sub
```

Default Property

Summary:

[form.] commandbutton.**Default**[= *flag*]

form	is the command button's form.
commandbutton	is the desired command button.
flag	is the new default flag.

Description:

The **Default** property determines whether or not a command button responds to the ENTER key. If a command button's **Default** property is set to True, Visual Basic will call its **Click** event whenever the ENTER key is pressed. If a command button's **Default** property is set to False, the command button will ignore all ENTER key presses. You should note that only one command button per form can have its **Default** button set to True. Visual Basic will automatically set any other of the form's command buttons' **Default** property to False when a command button's **Default** property is set to True. The default setting is for all command buttons is to have their **Default** property set to False.

Example:

The program that appears below shows how the **Cancel** property is used in an actual program by having a "Default" command button display a message each time the ENTER key is pressed. Listing 12-22-1 presents the code for the form's **Form_Load** event, Listing 12-22-2 the code for the form's **Command1_Click** event, and Listing 12-22-3 the code for the form's **Command2_Click** event. Figure 12-23 illustrates how the program's window would appear after the program has been run.

Listing 12-22-1:

```
Sub Form_Load ()

    Command2.Default = -1

End Sub
```

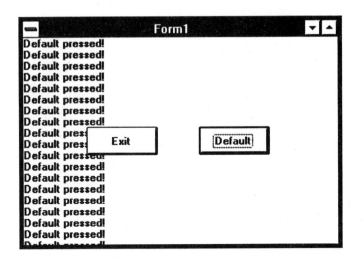

*Figure 12-23 A **Default** demonstration program.*

Listing 12-22-2:

```
Sub Command1_Click ()

    End

End Sub
```

Listing 12-22-3:

```
Sub Command2_Click ()

    Print "Default pressed!"

End Sub
```

Drag Method

Summary:

`[control.]`**Drag** `[action]`

`control`   is the control to be dragged.

`action`   is the drag action Visual Basic is to perform.

Description:

The **Drag** method begins, ends, or cancels a dragging action on a Visual Basic control. The type of action to be performed is specified by *action* and can be one of the following values:

Action	Description
0	Cancel the drag operation.
1	Begin the drag operation.
2	Drop the dragged control.

See Also:

DragDrop,   DragIcon,   DragMode,   DragOver, and **MousePointer**

Example:

The following program demonstrates how the **Drag** method is used by starting a dragging operation when the mouse button is pressed on a label control and dropping the control when the

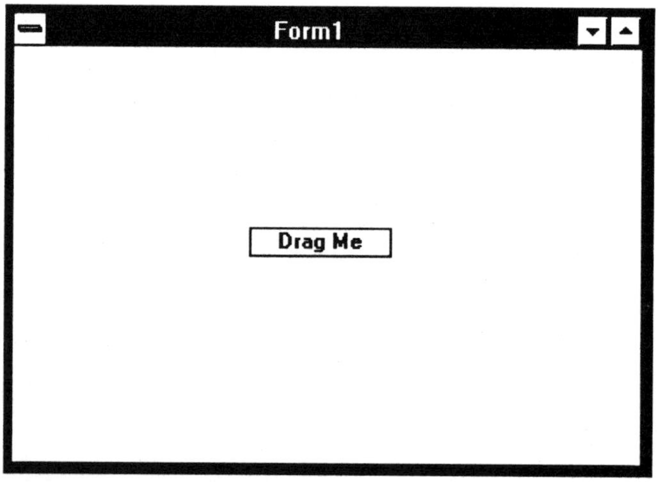

*Figure 12-24 A **Drag** demonstration program (1 of 2).*

mouse button is released. Listing 12-23-1 presents the code for the form's **Form_DragDrop** event, Listing 12-23-2 the code for the form's **Label1_MouseDown** event, and Listing 12-23-3 the code for the form's **Label1_MouseUp** event. Figure 12-24 shows how the program's window appears before the control is dragged, and Figure 12-25 how it appears after the control is dropped.

Listing 12-23-1:

```
Sub Form_DragDrop (Source As Control, X As Single, Y
As Single)

    Source.Left = X
    Source.Top = Y

End Sub
```

Listing 12-23-2:

```
Sub Label1_MouseDown (Button As Integer, Shift As
Integer, X As Single, Y As Single)

    Label1.Drag 1

End Sub
```

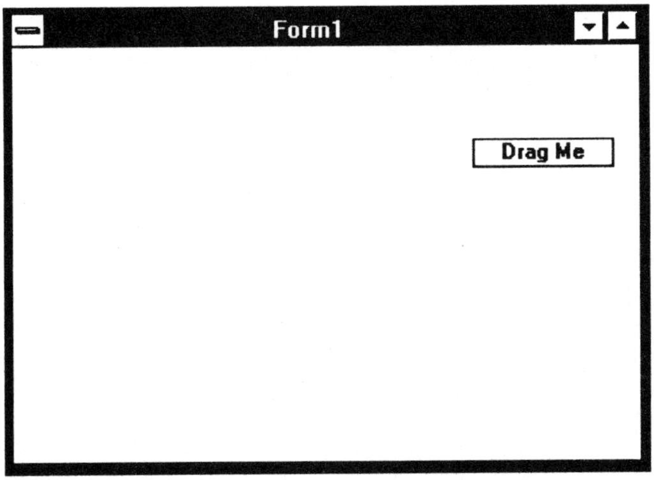

*Figure 12-25 A **Drag** demonstration program (2 of 2).*

Listing 12-23-3:

```
Sub Label1_MouseUp (Button As Integer, Shift As
Integer, X As Single, Y As Single)

    Label1.Drag 2

End Sub
```

DragDrop Event

Summary:

```
Sub Form_DragDrop(source As Control, x As Control, y
As Single)
```

or

```
Sub control_DragDrop([index As Integer,] source As
Control, x As Single, y As Single)
```

source	is the control that was dropped.
x	is the mouse pointer's *x*-coordinate when the control was dropped.
y	is the mouse pointer's *y*-coordinate when the control was dropped.
control	is the desired control.
index	is the control's index in an array of control's.

Description:

The **DragDrop** event is used by Visual Basic to tell the program when a control has been dropped on a form, a check box, a combo box, a command button, a directory list box, a drive list box, a file list box, a frame, a horizontal scroll bar, a list box, an option button, a picture box, a text box, or a vertical scroll bar.

See Also:

Drag, DragIcon, DragMode, DragOver, and **MousePointer**

Example:

The program that follows demonstrates how the **DragDrop** method is used by moving a dragged control to its new position and displaying a message about what just occurred. Listing 12-24-1 presents the code for the form's **Form_Load** and Listing 12-24-2 the code for the form's **Form_DragDrop** event. Figure 12-26 illustrates how the program's window would appear after the program has been run.

Listing 12-24-1:

```
Sub Form_Load ()

    Label1.DragMode = 1

End Sub
```

Listing 12-24-2:

```
Sub Form_DragDrop (Source As Control, X As Single, Y
As Single)

    Print "Something was dropped at"; X; ","; Y
    Source.Left = X
    Source.Top = Y

End Sub
```

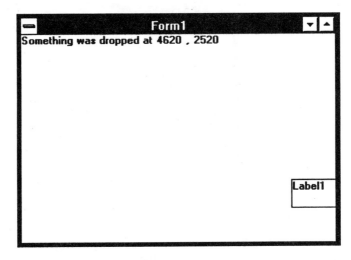

*Figure 12-26 A **DragDrop** demonstration program.*

DragIcon Property

Summary:

[*form.*] *control*.**DragIcon**[= *icon*]

form	is the control's form.
control	is the desired control.
icon	is the new icon.

Description:

The **DragIcon** property is used to set or return the mouse pointer that Visual Basic will use when dragging operations are being performed on a check box, a combo box, a command button, a directory list box, a drive list box, a file list box, a frame, a horizontal scroll bar, a label, a list box, an option button, a picture box, a text box, or a vertical scroll bar.

See Also:

Drag, DragDrop, DragMode, DragOver, LoadPicture, and **MousePointer**

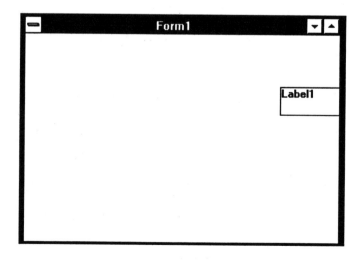

Figure 12-27 A **DragIcon** *demonstration program.*

Example:

The program that appears below demonstrates how the **DragIcon** property is used by setting a label control's drag icon to a new pointer. Listing 12-25-1 presents the code for the form's **Form_Load** event, and Listing 12-25-2 the code for the form's **Form_DragDrop** event. Figure 12-27 shows how the program's window would appear after the program has been run.

Listing 12-25-1:

```
Sub Form_Load ()

    Label1.DragIcon =
    LoadPicture("c:\vb\icons\arrows\point01.ico")
    Label1.DragMode = 1

End Sub
```

Listing 12-25-2:

```
Sub Form_DragDrop (Source As Control, X As Single, Y
As Single)

    Source.Left = X
    Source.Top = Y

End Sub
```

DragMode Property

Summary:

[*form.*] *control.***DragMode** [= *mode*]

form   is the control's form.

control   is the desired control.

mode   is the new mode.

Description:

The **DragMode** property is used to set or return a control's drag mode. If the **DragMode** property is set to 0 (the default), the control must be dragged manually with the **Drag** method. If the **DragMode** property is set to 1, the control will be dragged automatically and Visual Basic will handle the details of the drag operation.

See Also:

Drag, DragDrop, DragIcon, DragMode, DragOver, and **MousePointer**

Example:

The below program shows how the **DragMode** property is used by setting a label control for automatic dragging. Listing 12-26-1 presents the code for the form's **Form_Load** event; Listing 12-26-2 presents the code for the form's **Form_DragDrop** event. Figure 12-28 illustrates how the program's window would appear after the program has been run.

Listing 12-26-1:

```
Sub Form_Load ()

    Label1.DragMode = 1

End Sub
```

Listing 12-26-2:

```
Sub Form_DragDrop (Source As Control, X As Single, Y As Single)

    Source.Left = X
    Source.Top = Y

End Sub
```

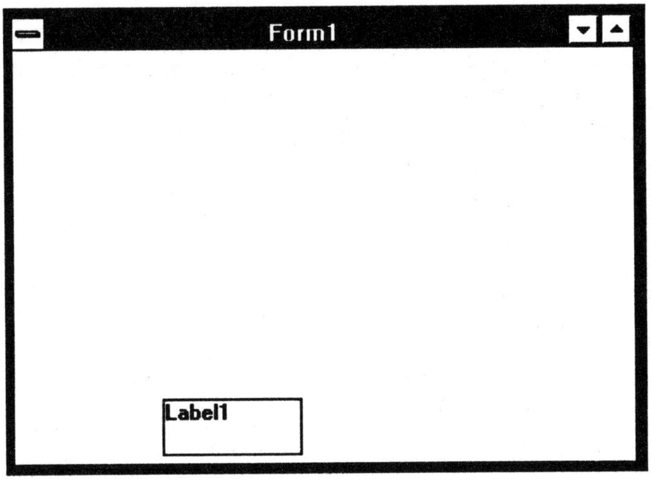

*Figure 12-28 A **DragMode** demonstration program.*

DragOver Event

Summary:

```
Sub Form_DragOver(source As Control, x As Single, y
As Single, state As Integer)
```

or

```
Sub control_DragOver([index As Integer,] source As
Control, x As Single, y As Single, state  As Integer)
```

source	is the control being dragged.
x	is the mouse pointer's current *x*-coordinate.
y	is the mouse pointer's current *y*-coordinate.
state	is the state of the control.
control	is the desired control.
index	is the control's index in an array of controls.

Description:

The **DragOver** event is called by Visual Basic to tell the program when a control is being dragged over a form, a check box, a combo, box, a command button, a directory list box, a drive list box, a file list box, a frame, a horizontal scroll bar, a label, a list box, an option button, a picture box, a text box, or a vertical scroll bar. The **DragOver** event passes the dragged control's current state in the *state* parameter as follows:

State	Description
0	The dragged control has just entered the form or control.
1	The dragged control has just left the form or control.
2	The dragged control is over the form or control.

See Also:

Drag, DragDrop, DragIcon, DragMode, and **MousePointer**

Example:

The following program demonstrates how the **DragOver** event is used by displaying appropriate messages when a dragged control is entering and leaving another control. Listing 12-27-1 presents the code for the form's **Form_Load** event, Listing 12-27-2 presents the code for the form's **Form_DragDrop** event, and Listing 12-27-3 the code for the form's **Label2_DragOver** event. Figure 12-29 shows how the program's window would appear after the program has been run.

Listing 12-27-1:

```
Sub Form_Load ()

    Label1.DragMode = 1

End Sub
```

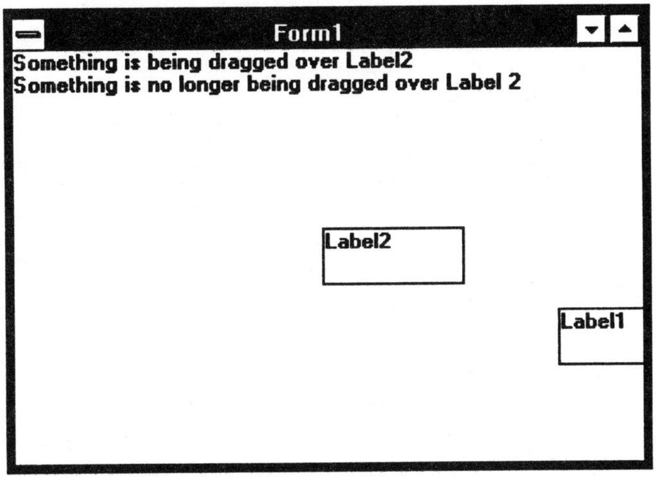

Figure 12-29 A **DragOver** *demonstration program.*

Listing 12-27-2:

```
Sub Form_DragDrop (Source As Control, X As Single, Y
As Single)

    Source.Left = X
    Source.Top = Y

End Sub
```

Listing 12-27-3:

```
Sub Label2_DragOver (Source As Control, X As Single,
Y As Single, State As Integer)

    If State = 0 Then
        Print "Something is being dragged over Label2"
    End If
    If State = 1 Then
        Print "Something is no longer being dragged
        over Label 2"
    End If

End Sub
```

DrawMode Property

Summary:

{[*form*.] [*picturebox*.] **Printer**.}**DrawMode**[= *mode*]

form	is the desired form.
picturebox	is the desired picture box.
mode	is the new drawing mode.

Description:

The **DrawMode** property sets or returns the drawing mode for a form, a picture box, or the **Printer** object. The new drawing mode is set with the *mode* parameter and can be any one of the following values:

Mode	Description
1	Blackness—All graphics output will be in black.
2	Not Merge Pen—All graphics output will be in the inverse of Merge Pen (Mode 15).
3	Mask Not Pen—All graphics output will be in the combination of the colors common to the display color and the inverse of the pen color.
4	Not Copy Pen—All graphics output will be in the inverse of the pen color.
5	Mask Pen Not—All graphics output will be in the combination of the colors common to the pen color and the inverse of the display color.
6	Invert—All graphics output will be in the inverse of the display color.
7	Xor Pen—All graphics output will be in the combination of colors in the pen color and the display color, but not in both.
8	Not Mask Pen—All graphics output will be in the inverse of the Mask Pen color.

(continued)

Mode	Description
9	Mask Pen—All graphics output will be in the combination of the colors common to the pen color and the display color.
10	Not Xor Pen—All graphics output will be in the inverse of the Xor Pen color.
11	Nop—Nothing will be drawn in this mode.
12	Merge Not Pen—All graphics output is a combination of the display color and the inverse of the pen color.
13	Copy Pen—All graphics output is in the **ForeColor** property's color. (This is Visual Basic's default setting.)
14	Merge Pen Not—All graphics output is in the combination of the pen color and the inverse of the display color.
15	Merge Pen—All graphics output is in the combination of the pen color and the display color.
16	Whiteness—All graphics output is in white.

Example:

The program that follows demonstrates how the **DrawMode** property is used by alternately setting a form's drawing mode from Blackness to Whiteness whenever the left mouse button is pressed. Listing 12-28-1 presents the code for the form's **Form_Load** event, Listing 12-28-2 the code for the form's **Form_MouseDown** event, and Listing 12-28-3 the code for the form's **Form_MouseMove** event. Figure 12-30 illustrates how the program's window would appear after the program has been run.

Listing 12-28-1:

```
Sub Form_Load ()

    DrawMode = 1

End Sub
```

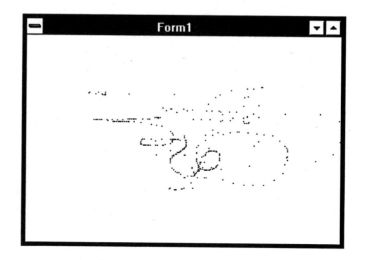

*Figure 12-30 A **DrawMode** demonstration program.*

Listing 12-28-2:

```
Sub Form_MouseDown (Button As Integer, Shift As
Integer, X As Single, Y As Single)

    If Button = 1 Then
        If DrawMode = 1 Then
            DrawMode = 16
        Else
            DrawMode = 1
        End If
    End If

End Sub
```

Listing 12-28-3:

```
Sub Form_MouseMove (Button As Integer, Shift As
Integer, X As Single, Y As Single)

    PSet (X, Y)

End Sub
```

DrawStyle Property

Summary:

`{[form.] [picturebox.] |Printer.}DrawStyle[ = style]`

form	is the desired form.
picturebox	is the desired picture box.
style	is the new style.

Description:

The **DrawStyle** property sets or returns the line style for a form, a picture box, or the **Printer** object. The new drawing style is set with the *style* parameter and can be any one of the below values:

Style	*Description*
0	Solid (This is Visual Basic's default setting.)
1	Dash
2	Dot
3	Dash–dot
4	Dash–dot–dot
5	Invisible
6	Inside solid

Example:

The program that follows demonstrates how the **DrawStyle** property is used by drawing a line with each of the Visual Basic drawing styles. Listing 12-29 presents the code for the form's **Form_Click** event. Figure 12-31 shows how the program's window would appear after the program has been run.

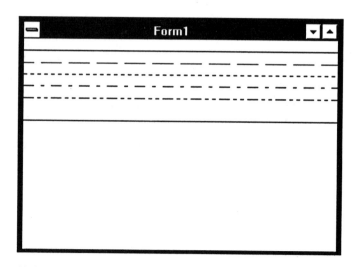

Figure 12-31 A **DrawStyle** *demonstration program.*

Listing 12-29:

```
Sub Form_Click ()
Dim I As Integer

    For I = 0 To 6
        DrawStyle = I
        Line (0, (I + 1) * 200)-(ScaleWidth, (I + 1) * 200)
    Next I

End Sub
```

DrawWidth Property

Summary:

{[*form*.] [*picturebox*.] | **Printer**.}**DrawWidth**[= *width*]

form   is the desired form.

picturebox   is the desired picture box.

width   is the new drawing width.

Description:

The **DrawWidth** property sets and returns the drawing width for a form, a picture box, or the **Printer** object.

Example:

The following program demonstrates how the **DrawWidth** property is used by drawing a series of 10 lines with each a little thicker than the last. Listing 12-30 presents the code for the form's **DrawWidth** property. Figure 12-32 illustrates how the program's window would appear after the program has been run.

Listing 12-30:

```
Sub Form_Click ()
Dim I As Integer

    For I = 1 To 10
        DrawWidth = I
        Line (0, (I + 1) * 200)-(ScaleWidth, (I + 1) * 200)
    Next I

End Sub
```

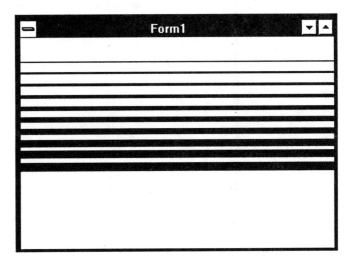

*Figure 12-32 A **DrawWidth** demonstration program.*

Drive Property

Summary:

drivelistbox.**Drive** [= *drive*]

drivelistbox   is the desired drive list box.

drive   is a string expression that specifies the new drive.

Description:

The **Drive** property sets and returns the selected drive for a drive list box.

Example:

The program that follows shows how the **Drive** property is used to set the selected drive to drive C: by clicking a command button. Listing 12-31 presents the code for the form's **Command1_Click** event. Figure 12-33 shows how the program's window would appear after the program has been run.

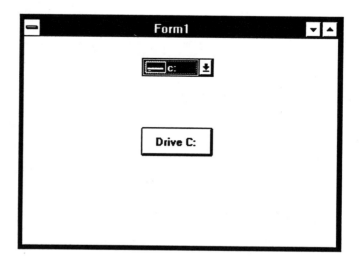

Figure 12-33 A **Drive** *demonstration program.*

Listing 12-31:

```
Sub Command1_Click ()

    Drive1.Drive = "C:"

End Sub
```

DropDown Event

Summary:

Sub *control*_**DropDown**([*Index* **As Integer**])

control is the desired control.

index is the control's index in an array of controls.

Description:

The **DropDown** event is called by Visual Basic to tell the program that a combo box's list box is about to drop down.

Example:

The program below demonstrates how the **DropDown** event is used by displaying an appropriate message when a combo box drops down. Listing 12-32-1 presents the code for the form's **Form_Load** event, and Listing 12-32-2 the code for the form's **Combo1_DropDown** event. Figure 12-34 illustrates how the program's window would appear after the program has been run.

Listing 12-32-1:

```
Sub Form_Load ()

    Combo1.AddItem "Ryan"
    Combo1.AddItem "Matthew"
    Combo1.AddItem "Crystal"

End Sub
```

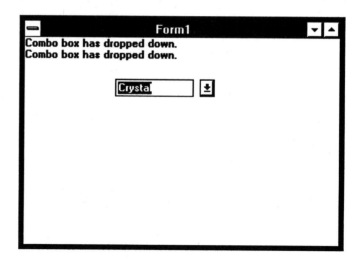

*Figure 12-34 A **DropDown** demonstration program.*

Listing 12-32-2:

```
Sub Combo1_DropDown ()

    Print "Combo box has dropped down."

End Sub
```

Enabled Property

Summary:

[*form.*] [*control.*]**Enabled**[= *flag*]

form   is the desired form.

control   is the desired control.

flag   is the new enabled/disabled setting.

Description:

The **Enabled** property determines whether or not a form, a check box, a combo box, a command button, a directory list box, a drive list box, a file list box, a frame, a horizontal scroll bar, a label, a list box, a menu, an option button, a picture box,

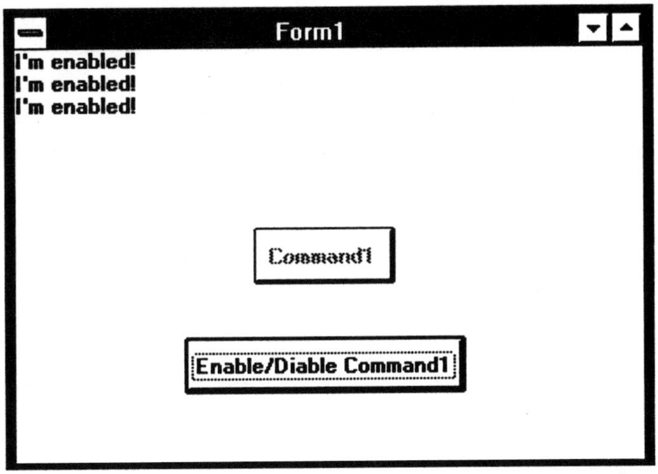

Figure 12-35 An **Enabled** *demonstration program.*

a text box, a timer, or a vertical scroll bar responds to events. If the **Enabled** property is set to True, the form or control will respond to events. If the **Enabled** property is set to False, the form or control will not respond to events.

Example:

The program that appears below shows how the **Enabled** property is used by alternately enabling and disabling a command button when another command button is clicked. Listing 12-33-1 presents the code for the form's **Command1_Click** event, and Listing 12-33-2 the code for the form's **Command2_Click** event. Figure 12-35 illustrates how the program's window would appear after the program has been run.

Listing 12-33-1:

```
Sub Command1_Click ()

    Print "I'm enabled!"

End Sub
```

Listing 12-33-2:

```
Sub Command2_Click ()

    Command1.Enabled = Not Command1.Enabled

End Sub
```

EndDoc Method

Summary:

```
Printer.EndDoc
```

Description:

The **EndDoc** method ends a document sent to the printer. You should note that the **EndDoc** method can only be used with the **Printer** object. Normally, the **EndDoc** method will generate a form feed; however, a form feed will not be generated if **EndDoc** is called immediately after **NewPage**.

See Also:

NewPage

Example:

The following program demonstrates how the **EndDoc** method is used by ending a short print job. Listing 12-34 presents the code for the form's **Command1_Click** event. Figure 12-36 illustrates how the program's window would appear after the program has been run.

Listing 12-34:

```
Sub Command1_Click ()

    Printer.Print "This is an EndDoc demo"
    Printer.EndDoc

End Sub
```

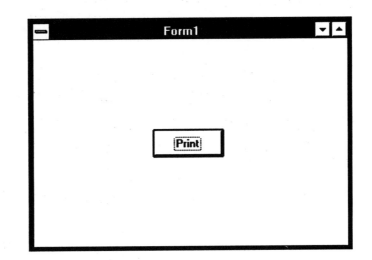

Figure 12-36 An **EndDoc** *demonstration program.*

FileName Property

Summary:

[*form.*] [*filelistbox.*] **FileName** [= *filename*]

form	is the desired form.
filelistbox	is the desired file list box.
filename	is a string expression that specifies the new file name.

Description:

The **FileName** property sets or returns the currently selected file name for a file list box.

Example:

The following program demonstrates how the **FileName** property is used by displaying a file list box's currently selected file as a label control's caption. Listing 12-35 presents the code for the form's **File1_Click** event. Figure 12-37 shows how the program's window would appear after the program has been run.

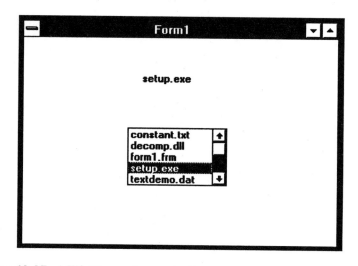

Figure 12-37 A **FileName** *demonstration program.*

Listing 12-35:

```
Sub File1_Click ()

    Label1.Caption = File1.FileName

End Sub
```

FillColor Property

Summary:

{[*form.*] [*picturebox.*] |**Printer.**}**FillColor**[= *color*]

form   is the desired form.

picturebox   is the desired picture box.

color   is the new fill color.

Description:

The **FillColor** property sets and returns the current fill color for a form, a picture box, or the **Printer** object. The **FillColor** property's value is used to fill in figures drawn with the **Circle** and **Line** methods. You should note that for the **FillColor**

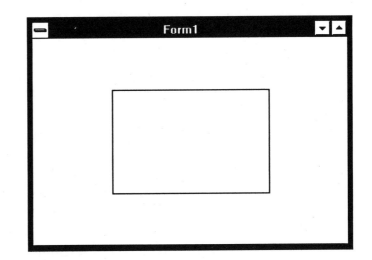

Figure 12-38 A **FillColor** *demonstration program.*

property to take effect the object's **FillStyle** property must be changed from its **Transparent** setting.

See Also:

FillStyle

Example:

The program that follows shows how the **FillColor** property is used to fill in a box with yellow. Listing 12-36 presents the code for the form's **Form_Click** event. Figure 12-38 illustrates how the program's window would appear after the program has been run.

Listing 12-36:

```
Sub Form_Click ()

    FillStyle = 0
    FillColor = QBColor(14)
    Line (ScaleWidth / 4, ScaleHeight /
    4)-(ScaleWidth - ScaleWidth / 4, ScaleHeight -
    ScaleHeight / 4), , B

End Sub
```

FillStyle Property

Summary:

```
{[form.][picturebox.]|Printer.}FillStyle[ = style]
```

form   is the desired form.

picturebox   is the desired picture box.

style   is the object's new fill style.

Description:

The **FillStyle** property sets and returns the current fill style for a form, a picture box, or the **Printer** object. The **FillStyle** property's new value is set with the *style* parameter and can be any one of the following values:

Style	Description
0	Solid
1	Transparent (This is the Visual Basic default.)
2	Horizontal line
3	Vertical line
4	Upward diagonal
5	Downward diagonal
6	Cross
7	Diagonal cross

See Also:

FillColor

Description:

The program that appears below demonstrates how the **FillStyle** property is used to fill in a box with series of different fill styles. Listing 12-37 presents the code for the form's

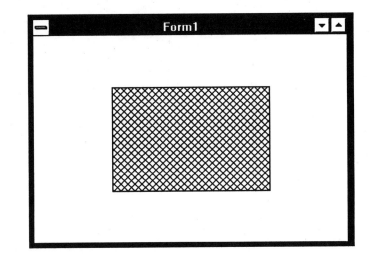

Figure 12-39 A **FillStyle** *demonstration program.*

Form_Click event. Figure 12-39 shows how the program's window would appear after the program has been run.

Listing 12-37:

```
Sub Form_Click ()
Static S As Integer

    FillStyle = S
    S = (S + 1) Mod 8
    Cls
    Line (ScaleWidth / 4, ScaleHeight /
    4)-(ScaleWidth - ScaleWidth / 4, ScaleHeight -
    ScaleHeight / 4), , B

End Sub
```

FontBold Property

Summary:

{[*form.*] [*control.*]|**Printer.**}**FontBold**[= *flag*]

form   is the desired form.

control   is the desired control.

flag   is the new font bold setting.

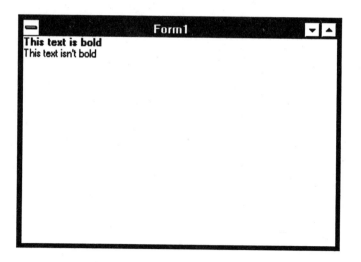

*Figure 12-40 A **FontBold** demonstration program.*

Description:

The **FontBold** property sets or returns the font bold setting for a form, a check box, a combo box, a command button, a directory list box, a drive list box, a file list box, a frame, a label, a list box, an option button, a picture box, a text box, or the **Printer** object. If **FontBold** is set to True (the default), text will be displayed or printed in bold. If **FontBold** is set to False, text will not be displayed or printed in bold.

Example:

The following program shows how the **FontBold** property is used by displaying both bold and nonbold text. Listing 12-38 presents the code for the form's **Form_Click** event. Figure 12-40 illustrates how the program's window would appear after the program has been run.

Listing 12-38:

```
Sub Form_Click ()

    Print "This text is bold"
```

```
FontBold = 0
Print "This text isn't bold"
```

End Sub

FontCount Property

Summary:

`{Printer|Screen}.FontCount`

Description:

The **FontCount** property returns the number of fonts that are available for either the **Screen** or **Printer** objects.

Example:

The program below demonstrates how the **FontCount** property is used by displaying the number of screen fonts and the number of printer fonts. Listing 12-39 presents the code for the form's **Form_Click** event. Figure 12-41 shows how the program's window will appear after the program has been run.

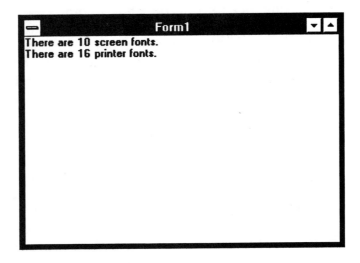

Figure 12-41 A **FontCount** *demonstration program.*

Listing 12-39:

```
Sub Form_Click ()

    Print "There are"; Screen.FontCount; "screen
    fonts."
    Print "There are"; Printer.FontCount; "printer
    fonts."

End Sub
```

FontItalic Property

Summary:

{*form.*] [*control.*] | **Printer.**} *FontBold*[= *flag*]

form   the desired form.

control   the desired control.

flag   is the new font italicized setting.

Description:

The **FontItalic** property sets or returns the font italicized setting for a form, a check box, a combo box, a command button, a directory list box, a drive list box, a file list box, a frame, a label, a list box, an option button, a picture box, a text box, or the **Printer** object. If **FontItalic** is set to True, text will be displayed or printed in italics. If **FontItalic** is set to False (the default), text will not be displayed or printed in italics.

Example:

The program that follows demonstrates how the **FontItalic** property is used by displaying both italicized and non-italicized text. Listing 12-40 presents the code for the form's **Form_Click** event. Figure 12-42 illustrates how the program's window would appear after the program has been run.

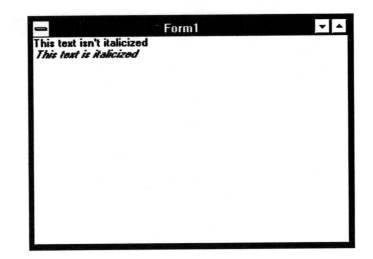

Figure 12-42 A **FontItalic** *demonstration program.*

Listing 12-40:

```
Sub Form_Click ()

    Print "This text isn't italicized"
    FontItalic = -1
    Print "This text is italicized"

End Sub
```

FontName Property

Summary:

`{[[form.] [control.]|Printer.}FontName[ = font]`

form	is the desired form.
control	is the desired control.
font	is a string expression that specifies the new font name.

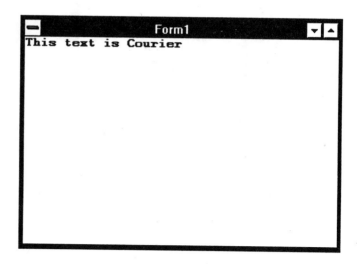

Figure 12-43 A **FontName** *demonstration program.*

Description:

The **FontName** property sets and returns the font name for a form, a check box, a combo box, a command button, a directory list box, a drive list box, a file list box, a frame, a label, a list box, an option button, a picture box, a text box, or the **Printer** object.

Example:

The below program demonstrates how the **FontName** parameter is used by displaying a message in Courier. Listing 12-41 presents the code for the form's **Form_Click** event. Figure 12-43 shows how the program's window would appear after the program has been run.

Listing 12-41:

```
Sub Form_Click ()

    FontName = "Courier"
    Print "This text is Courier"

End Sub
```

Fonts Property

Summary:

`{Printer|Screen}.Fonts(`*index*`)`

index   is the array index.

Description:

The **Fonts** property returns the string representation of a font name for either the **Printer** object or the **Screen** object. The font is specified by *index* and is any value from 0 to **FontCount** - 1. The **Fonts** property is only available at run time and is read-only.

See Also:

FontCount and **FontName**

Example:

The program that appears below shows how the **Fonts** property is used by displaying all of the **Screen** object's font names in their respective fonts. Listing 12-42 presents the code for the form's **Form_Click** event. Figure 12-44 illustrates how the program's window would appear after the program has been run.

Listing 12-42:

```
Sub Form_Click ()
Dim I As Integer, F As String

    For I = 0 To Screen.FontCount - 1
        FontName = Screen.Fonts(I)
        Print "This is "; FontName
    Next I

End Sub
```

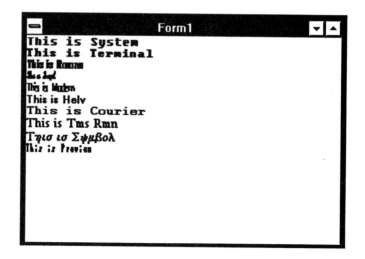

*Figure 12-44 A **Fonts** demonstration program.*

FontSize Property

Summary:

`{[form.][control.]|Printer.}FontSize[ = size]`

form   is the desired form.

control   is the desired control.

size   is the font's new point size.

Description:

The **FontSize** property sets or returns the current font size for a form, a check box, a command button, a combo box, a directory list box, a drive list box, a file list box, a frame, a label, a list box, an option button, a picture box, a text box, or the **Printer** object.

Example:

The following program demonstrates how the **FontSize** property is used by doubling a font's size. Listing 12-43 presents the code for the form's **Form_Click** event. Figure 12-45 shows how

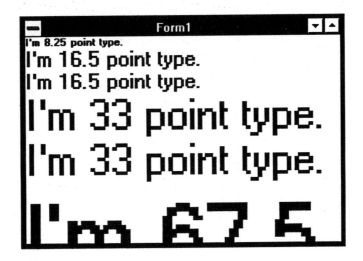

*Figure 12-45 A **FontSize** demonstration program.*

the program's window would appear after the program has been run.

Listing 12-43:

```
Sub Form_Click ()

    Print "I'm"; FontSize; "point type."
    FontSize = FontSize * 2
    Print "I'm"; FontSize; "point type."

End Sub
```

FontStrikethru Property

Summary:

{[*form*.] [*control*.]|**Printer**.}**FontStrikethru**[= *flag*]

form   is the desired form.

control   is the desired control.

flag   is the new font strikethru setting.

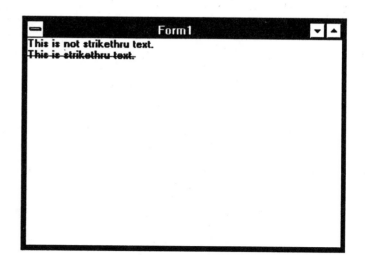

Figure 12-46 A **FontStrikethru** *demonstration program.*

Description:

The **FontStrikethru** property sets or returns the font strikethru setting for a form, a check box, a combo box, a command button, a directory list box, a drive list box, a file list box, a frame, a label, a list box, an option button, a picture box, a text box, or the **Printer** object. If **FontStrikethru** is set to True, text will be displayed with a line through it. If **FontStrikethru** is set to False (the default), text will not be displayed with a line through it.

Example:

The program below shows how the **FontStrikethru** property is used by displaying text that has strikethru. Listing 12-44 presents the code for the form's **Form_Click** event. Figure 12-46 illustrates how the program's window would appear after the program has been run.

Listing 12-44:

```
Sub Form_Click ()

    Print "This is not strikethru text."
```

```
FontStrikethru = -1
Print "This is strikethru text."

End Sub
```

FontTransparent Property

Summary:

`{[form.][picturebox.]|Printer.}FontTransparent[ = flag]`

form	is the desired form.
picturebox	is the desired picture box.
flag	is the new font transparency setting.

Description:

The **FontTransparent** property sets or returns the font transparency setting for a form, a picture box, or the **Printer** object. If **FontTransparent** is set to True (the default), only the face of text characters will be displayed. If **FontTransparent** is set to False, both the background and the face of text characters will be displayed.

Example:

The following program demonstrates how the **FontTransparent** property is used by displaying both transparent and non-transparent text. Listing 12-45 presents the code for the form's **Form_Click** event. Figure 12-47 shows how the program's window would appear after the program has been run.

Listing 12-45:

```
Sub Form_Click ()
Dim I As Integer

    Line (ScaleWidth / 4, ScaleHeight /
    4)-(ScaleWidth - ScaleWidth / 4, ScaleHeight -
    ScaleHeight / 4), , BF
    CurrentX = 0
```

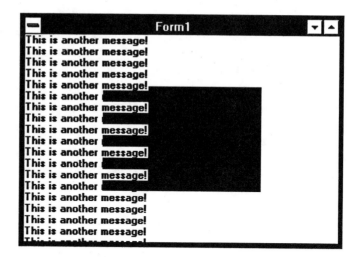

Figure 12-47 A **FontTransparent** *demonstration program.*

```
    CurrentY = 0
    For I = 1 To 30
        If I Mod 2 = 0 Then
            FontTransparent = -1
        Else
            FontTransparent = 0
        End If
        Print "This is another message!"
    Next I

End Sub
```

FontUnderline Property

Summary:

`{[form.][control.]|`**Printer.**`}`**FontUnderline**

form	is the desired form.
control	is the desired control.
flag	is the new font underline setting.

Description:

The **FontUnderline** property sets or returns the font underline setting for a form, a check box, a combo box, a command button, a directory list box, a drive list box, a file list box, a frame, a label, a list box, an option button, a picture box, a text box, or the **Printer** object. If **FontUnderline** is set to True, text will be displayed or printed with an underline. If **FontUnderline** is set to False (the default), text will not be displayed or printed with an underline.

Example:

The program that follows demonstrates how the **FontUnderline** property is used by displaying both underlined and non-underlined text. Listing 12-46 presents the code for the form's **Form_Click** event. Figure 12-48 illustrates how the program's window would appear after the program has been run.

Listing 12-46:

```
Sub Form_Click ()

    Print "This text isn't underlined!"
    FontUnderline = -1
    Print "This text is underlined!"

End Sub
```

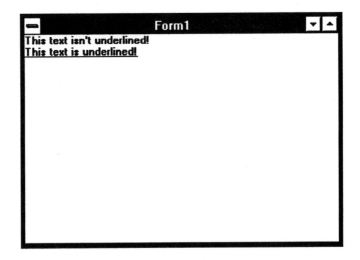

Figure 12-48 A **FontUnderline** *demonstration program.*

ForeColor Property

Summary:

[*form.*] [*control.*] **ForeColor** [= *color*]

form   is the desired form.

control   is the desired control.

color   is the new foreground color.

Description:

The **ForeColor** property sets or returns the foreground color for a form, a check box, a combo box, a command button, a directory list box, a drive list box, a file list box, a frame, a label, a list box, an option button, a picture box, or a text box.

See Also:

BackColor, QBColor, and **RGB**

Example:

The program that appears below shows how the **ForeColor** property is used by setting the foreground color for a series of messages to 16 distinct colors. Listing 12-47 presents the code for the form's **Form_Click** event. Figure 12-49 illustrates how the program's window would appear after the program has been run.

Listing 12-47:

```
Sub Form_Click ()
Dim I As Integer

    For I = 0 To 15
        ForeColor = QBColor(I)
        Print "This message is printed in color #"; I
    Next I

End Sub
```

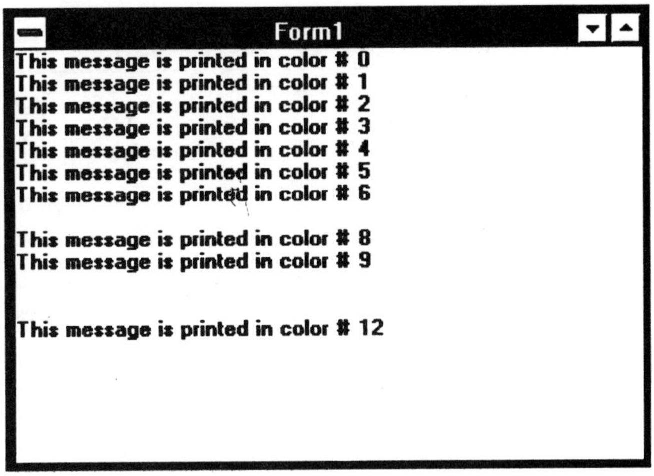

Figure 12-49 A **ForeColor** *demonstration program.*

FormName Property

Description:

The **FormName** property is used to assign a name to a form. The **FormName** property is only available at design time.

GetData Method

Summary:

```
Clipboard.GetData([format])
```

format	is the picture format to retrieve from the clipboard.

Description:

The **GetData** method returns a picture from the clipboard. The type of picture to retrieve is specified with the *format* parameter and can be one of these values:

Format	Description
2	Bitmap (The default.)
3	Metafile
8	Device-independent bitmap

You should note that if the clipboard doesn't hold a picture with the specified format no picture will be returned.

Example:

The below program demonstrates the **GetData** method by retrieving a bitmap from the clipboard. Listing 12-48 presents the code for the form's **Form_Click** event. Figure 12-50 illustrates how the program's window would appear after the program has been run.

Listing 12-48:

```
Sub Form_Click ()

    Picture = Clipboard.GetData ()

End Sub
```

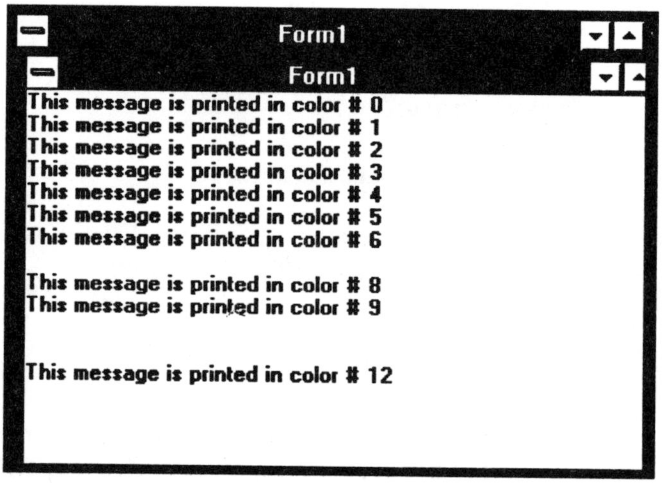

*Figure 12-50 A **GetData** demonstration program.*

GetFormat Method

Summary:

```
Clipboard.GetFormat(format)
```

format   is the clipboard format to check for.

Description:

The **GetFormat** method checks the clipboard to see if a data item of a specified format is present. The format to check for is specified by *format* and can be any one of these values:

Format	Description
&HBF00	Dynamic data exchange link
1	Text
2	Bitmap
3	Metafile
8	Device-independent bitmap

If an item of the specified format is present in the clipboard, Visual Basic will return True. Otherwise, Visual Basic will return False to indicate the clipboard's contents are of a different format or the clipboard is empty.

Example:

The program that follows demonstrates the **GetFormat** method by checking to see if the clipboard contains text. Listing 12-49 presents the code for the form's **Form_Click** event. Figure 12-51 illustrates how the program's window would appear after the program has been run.

Listing 12-49:

```
Sub Form_Click ()

    If Clipboard.GetFormat(1) Then
```

```
                    Print "There is text in the clipboard"
              Else
                    Print "There is no text in the clipboard"
              End If

       End Sub
```

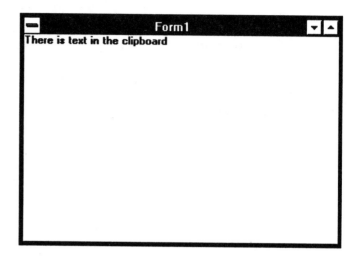

*Figure 12-51 A **GetFormat** demonstration program.*

GetText Method

Summary:

Clipboard.GetText([*format*])

format   is the data format to be retrieved.

Description:

The **GetText** method retrieves a text string from the clipboard.
The data format of the text string to be retrieved is specified by
format and can be one of these values:

Format	Description
&HBF00	Dynamic data exchange link.
1	Text (The default.)

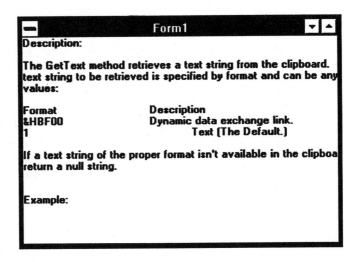

*Figure 12-52 A **GetText** demonstration program.*

If a text string of the proper format isn't available in the clipboard, Visual Basic will return a null string.

Example:

The program below shows how the **GetText** method is used by retrieving and displaying a text string from the clipboard. Listing 12-50 presents the code for the form's **Form_Click** event. Figure 12-52 illustrates how the program's window would appear after the program has been run.

Listing 12-50:

```
Sub Form_Click ()

    Clip$ = Clipboard.GetText(1)
    Print Clip$

End Sub
```

GotFocus Event

Summary:

```
Sub Form_GotFocus() Sub control_Gotfocus([index As
Integer])
```

`control`	is the desired control.
`index`	is the control's index in an array of controls.

Description:

The **GotFocus** event is called by Visual Basic to tell the program that a form, a check box, a combo box, a command button, a directory list box, a drive list box, a file list box, a horizontal scroll bar, a list box, an option button, a picture box, a text box, or a vertical scroll bar has received the focus.

Example:

The following program demonstrates how the **GotFocus** event is used by displaying an appropriate message whenever a command button receives the focus. Listing 12-51 presents the code for the form's **Command2_GotFocus** event. Figure 12-53 shows how the program's window would appear after the program has been run.

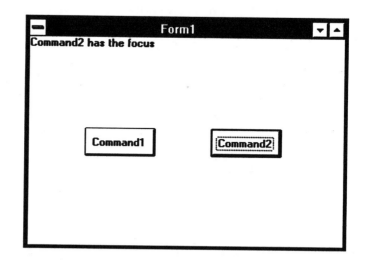

*Figure 12-53 A **GotFocus** demonstration program.*

Listing 12-51:

```
Sub Command2_GotFocus ()

    Print "Command2 has the focus"

End Sub
```

hDC Property

Summary:

{[*form*.] [*picturebox*.] | **Printer.**}**hDC**

form   is the desired form.

picturebox   is the desired picture box.

Description:

The **hDC** property returns the current device context handle for a form, a picture box, or the **Printer** object. You should note that the **hDC** property is transient in nature and its current value should be retrieved before using it in the program.

Example:

The program that follows shows how the **hDC** property is used by displaying a form's current device context. Listing 12-52 presents the code for the form's **Form_Click** event. Figure 12-54 illustrates how the program's window would appear after the program has been run.

Listing 12-52:

```
Sub Form_Click ()

    Print "The form's hDC is"; hDC

End Sub
```

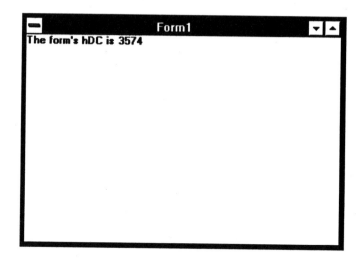

Figure 12-54 An **hDC** *demonstration program.*

Height Property

Summary:

{[*form.*][*control.*]|**Printer.**|**Screen.**}**Height**[= *height*]

form   is the desired form.

control   is the desired control.

height   is the form or control's new height.

Description:

The **Height** property sets and returns the height for a form, a check box, a combo box, a command button, a directory list box, a drive list box, a file list box, a frame, a horizontal scroll bar, a label, a list box, an option button, a picture box, a text box, or a vertical scroll bar. Additionally, the **Height** property returns the height of the **Screen** object and the **Printer** object.

See Also:

Width

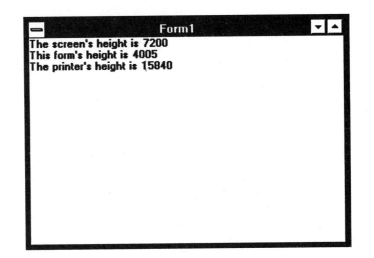

Figure 12-55 A **Height** *demonstration program.*

Example:

The program that appears below demonstrates how the **Height** property is used by displaying the height of the **Screen** object, the form, and the **Printer** object. Listing 12-53 presents the code for the form's **Form_Click** event. Figure 12-55 shows how the program's window would appear after the program has been run.

Listing 12-53:

```
Sub Form_Click ()

    Print "The screen's height is"; Screen.Height
    Print "This form's height is"; Height
    Print "The printer's height is"; Printer.Height

End Sub
```

Hidden Property

Summary:

*[form.]filelistbox.***Hidden**[= *flag*]

form	is the file list box's form.
filelistbox	is the desired file list box.
flag	is the new hidden attribute setting.

Description:

The **Hidden** property is used to either set or return a file list box's hidden attribute setting. If the **Hidden** property is set to True, Visual Basic will display files with their hidden attributes set in the file list box. If the **Hidden** property is set to False (the default), Visual Basic will not display files with their hidden attributes set in the file list box.

See Also:

Archive, Normal, ReadOnly, and **System**

Example:

The below program shows how the **Hidden** property is used by setting a file list box's hidden attribute to True. Listing 12-54

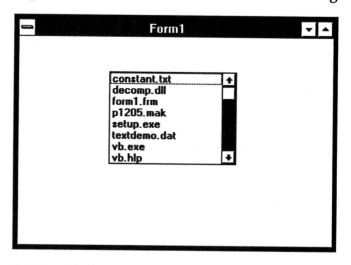

*Figure 12-56 A **Hidden** demonstration program.*

presents the code for the form's **Form_Click** event. Figure 12-56 illustrates how the program's window would appear after the program has been run.

Listing 12-54:

```
Sub Form_Click ()

    File1.Hidden = -1

End Sub
```

Hide Method

Summary:

```
[form.]Hide
```

`form`   is the desired form.

Description:

The **Hide** method hides a form from the screen by erasing it from the screen and setting its **Visible** property to False. If the specified form hasn't been loaded, Visual Basic will load the form but not display it.

See Also:

Show and **Visible**

Example:

The following program demonstrates how the **Hide** method is used by hiding a form. Listing 12-55 presents the code for the form's **Form_Click** event. Figure 12-57 illustrates how the program's window would appear after the program has been run.

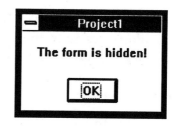

*Figure 12-57 A **Hide** demonstration program.*

Listing 12-55:

```
Sub Form_Click ()

    Hide
    Msg$ = "The form is hidden!"
    MsgBox Msg$
    Show

End Sub
```

hWnd Property

Summary:

*[form.]***hWnd**

form   is the desired form.

Description:

The **hWnd** property returns a program's Windows handle. You should note that the **hWnd** property is only available at run time.

Example:

The program that follows demonstrates how the **hWnd** property is used by displaying a program's Windows handle. Listing 12-56 presents the code for the form's **Form_Click** event. Figure 12-58 shows how the program's window would appear after the program has been run.

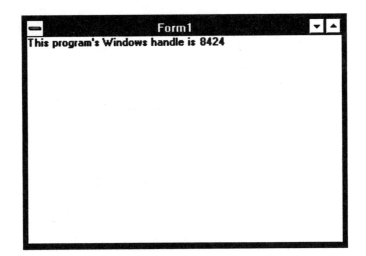

*Figure 12-58 A **hWnd** demonstration program.*

Listing 12-56:

```
Sub Form_Click ()

    Print "This program's Windows handle is"; hWnd

End Sub
```

Icon Property

Summary:

`[`*form.*`]`**Icon**

form   is the desired form.

Description:

The **Icon** property returns a form's icon. A form's icon is set at design time, but the **Icon** property is available for reading at run time.

Example:

The program that follows shows how the **Icon** property is used by displaying a form's icon in a picture box. Listing 12-57

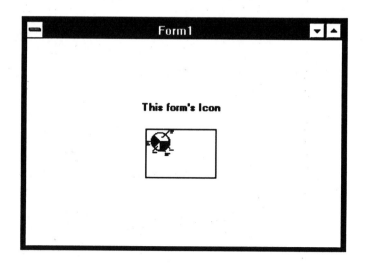

Figure 12-59   An **Icon** *demonstration program.*

presents the code for the form's **Form_Click** event. Figure 12-59 illustrates how the program's window would appear after the program has been run.

Listing 12-57:

```
Sub Form_Click ()

    Picture1.Picture = Icon

End Sub
```

Image Property

Summary:

[*form.*] [*picturebox.*]**Image**

form　　　　　is the desired form.

picturebox　　is the desired picture box.

Description:

The **Image** property returns a persistent bitmap handle for a form or a picture box.

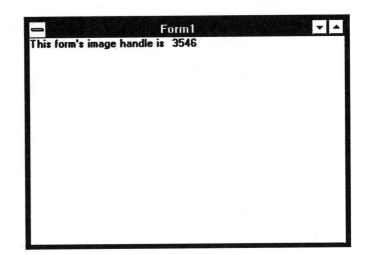

Figure 12-60 An **Image** *demonstration program.*

Example:

The program that follows demonstrates how the **Image** property is used by displaying a form's persistent bitmap handle. Listing 12-58 presents the code for the form's **Form_Click** event. Figure 12-60 illustrates how the program's window would appear after the program has been run.

Listing 12-58:

```
Sub Form_Click ()

    Print "This form's image handle is "; Image

End Sub
```

Index Property

Summary:

[form.]control[(index)].**Index**

form	is the control's form.
control	is the desired control.
index	is the control's index.

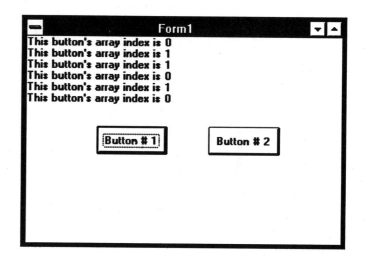

*Figure 12-61 An **Index** demonstration program.*

Description:

The **Index** property returns a control's array index. As you might suspect, the control must be part of an array of controls (a collection of controls with the same **CtlName**). Although the **Index** property can be set at design time, it is read only at run time.

Example:

The following program shows how the **Index** property is used to display a control's array index whenever the control is clicked. Listing 12-59 presents the code for the form's **Command1._Click** event. Figure 12-61 illustrates how the program's window would appear after the program has been run.

Listing 12-59:

```
Sub Command1_Click (Index As Integer)

    Print "This button's array index is";
    Command1(Index).Index

End Sub
```

Interval Property

Summary:

```
[form.] timer.Interval [ = interval]
```

form   is the timer's form.

timer   is the desired timer.

interval   is the timer's new interval in milliseconds.

Description:

The **Interval** property sets and returns the time interval Visual Basic is to use between calls to a timer control's **Timer** event. The interval is specified by *interval* and can be any value from 0 to 65,535 milliseconds. Setting the **Interval** property to 0 effectively disables the timer control.

Example:

The program below demonstrates how the **Interval** property is used to display a message every 10 seconds. Listing 12-60-1 presents the code for the form's **Form_Load** event, and Listing 12-60-2 the code for the form's **Timer1_Timer** event. Figure 12-62 shows how the program's window would appear after the program has been run.

Listing 12-60-1:

```
Sub Form_Load ()

    Timer1.Interval = 10000

End Sub
```

Listing 12-60-2:

```
Sub Timer1_Timer ()

    Print "10 seconds have elapsed!"

End Sub
```

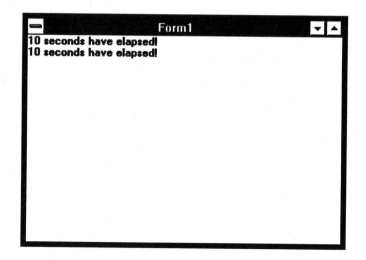

*Figure 12-62 An **Interval** demonstration program.*

KeyDown Event

Summary:

Sub Form_KeyDown(*keycode* **As Integer,** *shift* **As Integer**)

or

Sub *control_***KeyDown**([*index* **As Integer,**] *keycode* **As Integer,** *shift* **As Integer**)

keycode	is the pressed key's key code.
shift	is the state of the SHIFT, CTRL, and ALT keys.
control	is the desired control.
index	is the control's index in an array of controls.

Description:

The **KeyDown** event is called by Visual Basic to tell the program when a key has been pressed in a form, a check box, a combo box, a command button, a directory list box, a drive list box, a file list box, a horizontal scroll bar, a list box, an option button, a picture box, a text box, or a vertical scroll bar. You should note that the key code returned by the **KeyDown** event isn't the same as the key's ASCII code. The key codes Visual Basic returns can be found in the CONSTANT.TXT file. Visual Basic returns the value of the shift keys in the *shift* argument as follows:

Shift	*Description*
SHIFT	1
CTRL	2
ALT	4

See Also:

KeyPress and **KeyUp**

Example:

The program that appears below shows how the **KeyDown** event is used by displaying the key code and shift state for a form's key presses. Listing 12-61 presents the code for the form's **Form_KeyDown** control. Figure 12-63 illustrates how

```
Form1

A key has been pressed!
Key Code: 17
Shift Flags: 2
A key has been pressed!
Key Code: 66
Shift Flags: 2
A key has been pressed!
Key Code: 16
Shift Flags: 1
A key has been pressed!
Key Code: 68
Shift Flags: 1
A key has been pressed!
Key Code: 13
Shift Flags: 0
```

*Figure 12-63 A **KeyDown** demonstration program.*

the program's window would appear after the program has been run.

Listing 12-61:

```
Sub Form_KeyDown (KeyCode As Integer, Shift As Integer)

    Print "A key has been pressed!"
    Print "Key Code:"; KeyCode
    Print "Shift Flags:"; Shift

End Sub
```

KeyPress Event

Summary:

Sub Form_KeyPress(*asciicode* **As Integer**)

or

Sub *control*_**KeyPress**([*index* **As Integer**,] *asciicode* **As Integer**)

asciicode	is the key's ASCII code.
control	is the desired control.
index	is the control's index in an array of controls.

Description:

The **KeyPress** event is called by Visual Basic to tell the program when a key has been pressed and released in a form, a check box, a combo box, a command button, a directory list box, a drive list box, a file list box, a horizontal scroll bar, a list box, an option button, a picture box, a text box, or a vertical scroll bar.

See Also:

KeyDown and **KeyUp**

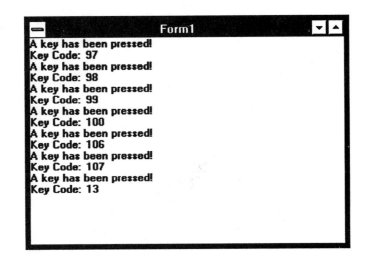

Figure 12-64 A **KeyPress** *demonstration program.*

Example:

The following program shows how the **KeyPress** event is used by displaying the ASCII code for a variety of key presses. Listing 12-62 presents the code for the form's **KeyPress** event. Figure 12-64 illustrates how the program's window would appear after the program has been run.

Listing 12-62:

```
Sub Form_KeyPress (KeyAscii As Integer)

    Print "A key has been pressed!"
    Print "Key Code:"; KeyAscii

End Sub
```

KeyUp Event

Summary:

Sub Form_KeyUp(*keycode* **As Integer,** *shift* **As Integer)**

or

Sub *control_***KeyUp**([*index* **As Integer,**] *keycode* **As Integer,** *shift* **As Integer)**

`keycode`	is the released key's key code.
`shift`	is the state of the SHIFT, CTRL, and ALT keys.
`control`	is the desired control.
`index`	is the control's index in an array of controls.

Description:

The **KeyUp** event is called by Visual Basic to tell the program when a key has been released in a form, a check box, a combo box, a command button, a directory list box, a drive list box, a file list box, a horizontal scroll bar, a list box, an option button, a picture box, a text box, or a vertical scroll bar. You should note that the key code returned by the **KeyUp** event isn't the same as the key's ASCII code. The key codes Visual Basic returns can be found in the CONSTANT.TXT file. Visual Basic returns the value of the shift keys in the *shift* argument as follows:

Shift	*Description*
SHIFT	1
CTRL	2
ALT	4

See Also:

KeyDown and **KeyPress**

Example:

The program that follows demonstrates how the **KeyUp** event is used by displaying the key code and shift state for a form's key releases. Listing 12-63 presents the code for the form's **Form_KeyUp** control. Figure 12-65 shows how the program's window would appear after the program has been run.

Listing 12-63:

```
Sub Form_KeyUp (KeyCode As Integer, Shift As Integer)

    Print "A key has been released!"
    Print "Key Code:"; KeyCode
    Print "Shift Flags:"; Shift

End Sub
```

LargeChange Property

Summary:

[*form.*]{*hscrollbar*|*vscrollbar*}.**LargeChange**[= *change*]

form	is the scroll bar's form.
hscrollbar	is the desired horizontal scroll bar.
vscrollbar	is the desired vertical scroll bar.
change	is the new amount of change.

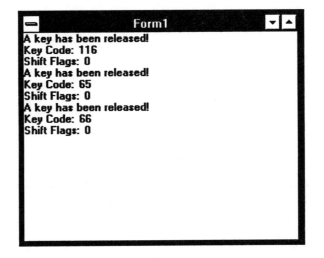

Figure 12-65 A **KeyUp** *demonstration program.*

Description:

The **LargeChange** property sets and returns the amount of change that occurs to a scroll bar's **Value** property when the scroll bar is clicked between the scroll box and a scroll arrow.

See Also:

SmallChange

Example:

The program that appears below shows how the **LargeChange** property is used to regulate the amount of scrolling that occurs when a user clicks the scroll bar between the scroll bar's box and a scroll arrow. Listing 12-64-1 presents the code for the form's **Form_Load** event, and Listing 12-64-2 the code for the form's **HScroll1_Change** event. Figure 12-66 illustrates how the program's window would appear after the program has been run.

Listing 12-64-1:

```
Sub Form_Load ()

    Label1.Caption = Str$(HScroll1.Value)
    HScroll1.Max = 200
    HScroll1.LargeChange = 10

End Sub
```

Listing 12-64-2:

```
Sub HScroll1_Change ()

    Label1.Caption = Str$(HScroll1.Value)

End Sub
```

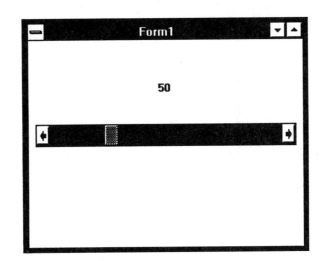

*Figure 12-66 A **LargeChange** demonstration program.*

Left Property

Summary:

```
[form.] [control.]Left[ = x]
```

form	is the desired form.
control	is the desired control.
x	is the new *x*-coordinate.

Description:

The **Left** property sets or returns the *x*-coordinate for a form, a check box, a combo box, a command button, a directory list box, a drive list box, a file list box, a frame, a horizontal scroll bar, a label, a list box, an option button, a picture box, a text box, or a vertical scroll bar. A form's **Left** property is always in twips. A control's **Left** property is expressed using its container's coordinate system.

See Also:

Top

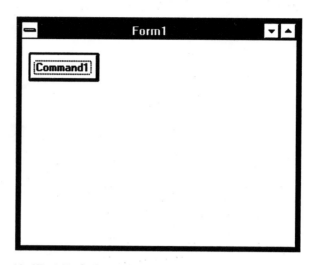

*Figure 12-67 A **Left** demonstration program (1 of 2).*

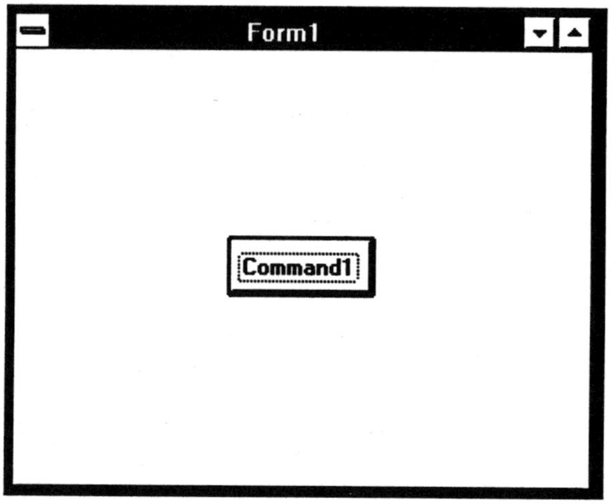

*Figure 12-68 A **Left** demonstration program (2 of 2).*

Example:

The program that follows demonstrates how the **Left** property is used by centering a command button in a form. Listing 12-65 presents the code for the form's **Command1_Click** event. Figure 12-67 shows how the program's window would appear before the command button is clicked, and Figure 12-68 how the program's window would appear after the command button is clicked.

Listing 12-65:

```
Sub Command1_Click ()

    Command1.Left = Form1.ScaleWidth / 2 -
    Command1.Width / 2
    Command1.Top = Form1.ScaleHeight / 2 -
    Command1.Height / 2

End Sub
```

Line Method

Summary:

```
[object.]Line [[Step](x1, y1)] - [Step](x2,
y2)[,[color],B[F]]]
```

`object`	is the desired form, picture box, or **Printer** object.
Step	tells Visual Basic that *x1, y1* are relative to the current graphics position.
`x1, y1`	is the line's starting coordinates.
Step	tells Visual Basic that *x2, y2* are relative to the line's starting coordinates.
`x2, y2`	is the line's ending coordinates.
`color`	is the color Visual Basic is to use when drawing the line. If omitted, Visual Basic will use the **ForeColor** property.
B	tells Visual Basic to draw a box using *x1, y1* and *x2, y2* as opposite corners of the box.
F	tells Visual Basic to fill in the box with the color specified by *color*.

Description:

The **Line** method is used to draw a line or a box on a form, a picture box, or the **Printer** object.

See Also:

CurrentX, CurrentY, DrawMode, DrawWidth, FillColor, FillStyle, ForeColor, QBColor, and **RGB**

Example:

The following program demonstrates how the **Line** method is used by drawing a filled-in box on a form. Listing 12-66 presents the code for the form's **Form_Click** event. Figure 12-69 illustrates how the program window would appear after the program has been run.

Listing 12-66:

```
Sub Form_Click ()

    Line (ScaleWidth / 4, ScaleHeight / 4)-(ScaleWidth -
    ScaleWidth / 4, ScaleHeight - ScaleHeight / 4), , B

End Sub
```

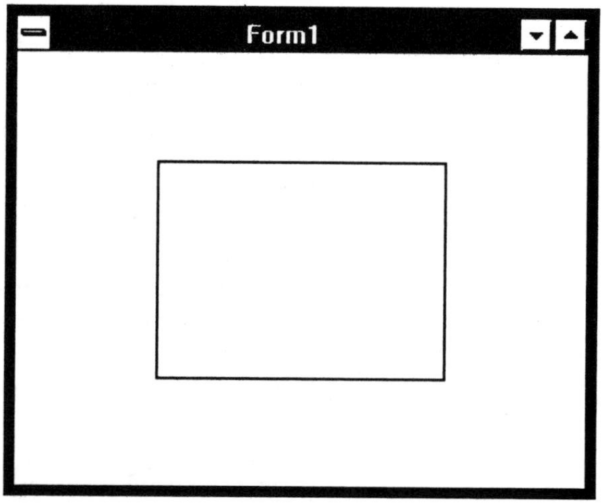

Figure 12-69 A **Line** *demonstration program.*

LinkClose Event

Summary:

Sub Form_LinkClose( )

or

Sub *control***_LinkClose(**[*index* **As Integer**]**)**

control   is the desired control.

index   is the control's index in an array of controls.

Description:

The **LinkClose** event is called by Visual Basic to tell the program that a DDE (dynamic data exchange) conversation for a form, a label, a picture box, or a text box has terminated.

Example:

The programs that follow show how the **LinkClose** event is used by displaying an appropriate message when a DDE conversation has terminated. Listing 12-67-1 presents the code for the server program's **Form_Load** event, Listing 12-67-2 the code for the server program's **Command1_Click** event, Listing 12-68-1 the code for the client program's **Form_Load** event, and Listing 12-68-2 the code for the client program's **Text1_LinkClose** event. Figure 12-70 illustrates how the desktop would appear after the DDE conversation has been terminated by the user pressing the server program's command button.

Listing 12-67-1:

```
Sub Form_Load ()

    LinkTopic = "Demo"
    LinkMode = 1

End Sub
```

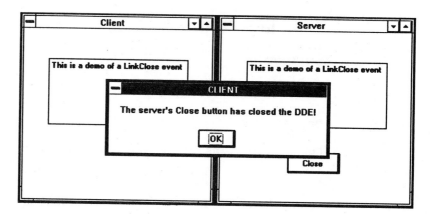

Figure 12-70 A **LinkClose** *demonstration program.*

Listing 12-67-2:

```
Sub Command1_Click ()

    LinkMode = 0

End Sub
```

Listing 12-68-1:

```
Sub Form_Load ()

    Text1.LinkTopic = "Server|Demo"
    Text1.LinkItem = "Text1"
    Text1.LinkMode = 1

End Sub
```

Listing 12-68-2:

```
Sub Text1_LinkClose ()

    MsgBox "The server's Close button has closed the
    DDE!"
    Text1.LinkMode = 0

End Sub
```

LinkError Event

Summary:

```
Sub Form_LinkError(error As Integer)
```

or

```
Sub control_LinkError([index As Integer,] error As
Integer)
```

error	is the DDE error code.
control	is the desired control.
index	is the control's index in an array of controls.

Description:

The **LinkError** event is called by Visual Basic whenever an error occurs in a DDE conversation. The error code is passed as the *error* argument and can be any one of the following:

Error	*Description*
1	Data was requested in the wrong format.
2	Data was requested before a DDE conversation had started.
3	An attempt to perform a DDE without first starting the DDE conversation.
4	An attempt to change an item without a DDE conversation.
5	An attempt to poke data without first starting the DDE conversation.
6	The client attempted to continue with the DDE conversation after the server's **LinkMode** was set to 0.
7	Too many DDE conversations.

(continued)

Error	Description
8	A string was too long to send and was truncated accordingly.
9	An invalid control array element was specified in a DDE conversation.
10	An unexpected DDE message was received.
11	Not enough memory for a DDE conversation.
12	A server attempted to perform client operations.

LinkExecute Event

Summary:

```
Sub Form_LinkExecute(command As String, cancel As
Integer)
```

command   is the command string passed from the
                client.

cancel   is used to indicate if a command was
                accepted or not.

Description:

The **LinkExecute** event is used by Visual Basic to tell a form that a command string has been passed to it from a client. Before exiting from the **LinkExecute** event, the event's code should set the *cancel* argument to indicate whether or not the operation was successful. If the operation was successful, the *cancel* argument should be set to 0. Otherwise, the *cancel* argument should be set to a nonzero value to indicate an unsuccessful operation.

Example:

The programs that follow demonstrate how the **LinkExecute** event is used by alternately appending periods and asterisks to a text box's contents through a **LinkExecute** command. Listing 12-69-1 presents the code for the server program's **Form_Load** event, and Listing 12-69-2 the code for the server program's **Form_LinkExecute** event; Listing 12-70-1 presents the code for the client program's **Form_Load** event, and Listing 12-70-2 the code for the client program's **Command1_Click** event. Figure 12-71 shows how the desktop would appear after the **LinkExecute** event has occurred several times.

Listing 12-69-1:

```
Sub Form_Load ()

    LinkTopic = "Demo"
    LinkMode = 1

End Sub
```

Listing 12-69-2:

```
Sub Form_LinkExecute (CmdStr As String, Cancel As
Integer)

    If CmdStr = "Periods" Then
        Text1.Text = Text1.Text + "..."
    End If
    If CmdStr = "Asterisks" Then
        Text1.Text = Text1.Text + "***"
    End If
    Cancel = 0

End Sub
```

Listing 12-70-1:

```
Sub Form_Load ()

    Text1.LinkTopic = "Server|Demo"
    Text1.LinkItem = "Text1"
    Text1.LinkMode = 1

End Sub
```

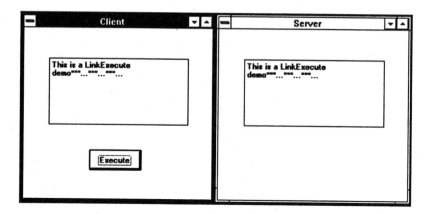

*Figure 12-71 A **LinkExecute** demonstration program.*

Listing 12-70-2:

```
Sub Command1_Click ()

Static Flag As Integer

    If Flag Then
        Text1.LinkExecute "Periods"
    Else
        Text1.LinkExecute "Asterisks"
    End If
    Flag = Not Flag

End Sub
```

LinkExecute Method

Summary:

control.**LinkExecute** *command*

control   is a control that's part of a DDE
               conversation.

command   is a string expression to be sent to the DDE
               server.

Description:

The **LinkExecute** method is used to send a command string from a DDE client control to a DDE server form. Upon receipt of the **LinkExecute** command string, the server's **LinkExecute** event will be called.

Example:

The following programs demonstrate how the **LinkExecute** method is used by alternately instructing the server to display periods and asterisks in the server's text box control. Listing 12-71-1 presents the code for the server program's **Form_Load** event, and Listing 12-71-2 the code for the server program's **Form_LinkExecute** event; Listing 12-72-1 presents the code for the client program's **Form_Load** event, and Listing 12-72-2 the code for the client program's **Command1_Click** event. Figure 12-72 illustrates how the desktop would appear after the **LinkExecute** event has occurred several times.

Listing 12-71-1:

```
Sub Form_Load ()

    LinkTopic = "Demo"
    LinkMode = 1

End Sub
```

Listing 12-71-2:

```
Sub Form_LinkExecute (CmdStr As String, Cancel As
Integer)

    If CmdStr = "Periods" Then
        Text1.Text = Text1.Text + "..."
    End If
    If CmdStr = "Asterisks" Then
        Text1.Text = Text1.Text + "***"
    End If
    Cancel = 0

End Sub
```

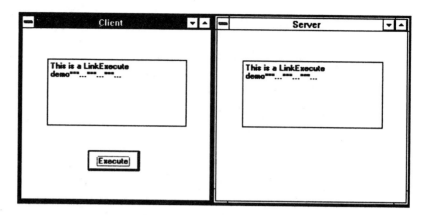

Figure 12-72 A **LinkExecute** *demonstration program.*

Listing 12-72-1:

```
Sub Form_Load ()

    Text1.LinkTopic = "Server|Demo"
    Text1.LinkItem = "Text1"
    Text1.LinkMode = 1

End Sub
```

Listing 12-72-2:

```
Sub Command1_Click ()
Static Flag As Integer

    If Flag Then
        Text1.LinkExecute "Periods"
    Else
        Text1.LinkExecute "Asterisks"
    End If
    Flag = Not Flag

End Sub
```

LinkItem Property

Summary:

[*form*.]{*label*|*picturebox*|*textbox*}**LinkItem**[= *item*]

form   is the client control's form.

`label`	is the desired label.
`picturebox`	is the desired picture box.
`textbox`	is the desired text box.
`item`	is a string expression that specifies the server's data item.

Description:

The **LinkItem** property sets or returns the data item that is linked to the control on the server's side of a DDE conversation. You should note that the server's data item must possess a data type that is compatible with the client control.

Example:

The programs that follow show how the **LinkItem** property is used to specify a server's data item during a DDE conversation. Listing 12-73 presents the code for the server program's **Form_Load** event, and Listing 12-74 the code for the client program's **Form_Load** event. Figure 12-73 illustrates how the desktop would appear after the DDE conversation has started.

Listing 12-73:

```
Sub Form_Load ()

    LinkTopic = "Demo"
    LinkMode = 1

End Sub
```

Listing 12-74:

```
Sub Form_Load ()

    Text1.LinkTopic = "Server|Demo"
    Text1.LinkItem = "Text1"
    Text1.LinkMode = 1

End Sub
```

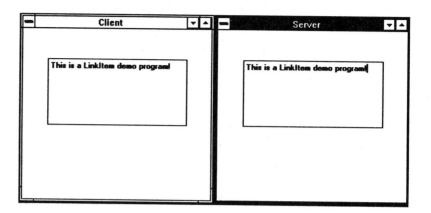

Figure 12-73 A **LinkItem** *demonstration program.*

LinkMode Property

Summary:

[*form.*] [*control.*]**LinkMode** [= *mode*]

form	is the desired form.
control	is the desired label, picture box, or text box control.
mode	is the desired link mode.

Description:

The **LinkMode** property sets and returns the type of link for a DDE conversation. The type of link is specified by *mode* and can be one of the following values for a Visual Basic form:

Mode	Description
0	No DDE can take place.
1	The form can act as a DDE server and any label, picture box, or text box control can act as a data item during a DDE conversation. (Default)

For a control, *mode* can be any one of the following values:

Mode	Description
0	No DDE link in progress. (Default)
1	This is a hot link and the control will be updated whenever the server's data item is changed.
2	This is a cold link and the control will only be updated when the **LinkRequest** method is called.

Example:

The programs below demonstrate how the **LinkMode** property is used to establish a hot DDE link. Listing 12-75 presents the code for the server program's **Form_Load** event, and Listing 12-76 the code for the client program's **Form_Load** event. Figure 12-74 shows how the desktop would appear after the DDE conversation has started.

Listing 12-75:

```
Sub Form_Load ()

    LinkTopic = "Demo"
    LinkMode = 1

End Sub
```

Listing 12-76:

```
Sub Form_Load ()

    Text1.LinkTopic = "Server|Demo"
    Text1.LinkItem = "Text1"
    Text1.LinkMode = 1

End Sub
```

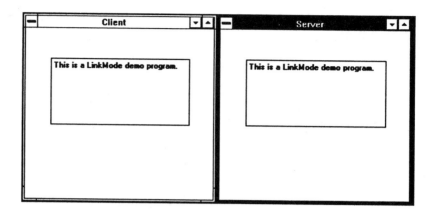

*Figure 12-74 A **LinkMode** demonstration program.*

LinkOpen Event

Summary:

Sub Form_LinkOpen(*cancel* **As Integer**)

or

Sub *control*_**LinkOpen**([*index* **As Integer**,] *cancel* **As Integer**)

cancel	specifies whether or not the DDE conversation is to take place.
control	is the desired label, picture box, or text box control.
index	is the control's index in an array of controls.

Description:

The **LinkOpen** event is called by Visual Basic to tell the program when a DDE conversation is about to be established. The conversation can be aborted by setting the *cancel* argument to a nonzero value. Otherwise, the *cancel* argument should remain set to its default 0 value to establish the DDE conversation.

See Also:

LinkClose

Example:

The programs that appear below show how the **LinkOpen** event is used by displaying a message box when a DDE conversation is about to be established. Listing 12-77 gives the code for the server program's **Form_Load** event, Listing 12-78-1 the code for the client program's **Form_Load** event, and Listing 12-78-2 the code for the client program's **Text_LinkOpen** event. Figure 12-75 illustrates how the desktop would appear as the DDE conversation is about to be established.

Listing 12-77:

```
Sub Form_Load ()

    LinkTopic = "Demo"
    LinkMode = 1

End Sub
```

Listing 12-78-1:

```
Sub Form_Load ()

    Text1.LinkTopic = "Server|Demo"
    Text1.LinkItem = "Text1"
    Text1.LinkMode = 1

End Sub
```

Listing 12-78-2:

```
Sub Text1_LinkOpen (Cancel As Integer)

    MsgBox "A DDE conversation has started!"

End Sub
```

*Figure 12-75 A **LinkOpen** demonstration program.*

LinkPoke Method

Summary:

`control.LinkPoke`

`control`   is the desired label, picture box, or text box
                 control.

Description:

The **LinkPoke** method sends the current contents of a client
control to the server application. The following table details
which property is sent for the three types of Visual Basic client
controls:

Control	Property
Label	**Caption**
Picture Box	**Picture**
Text Box	**Text**

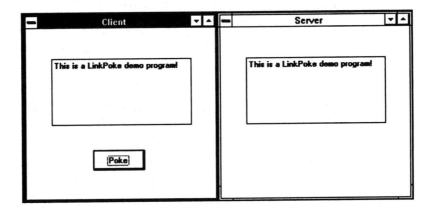

*Figure 12-76 A **LinkPoke** demonstration program.*

Example:

The programs below demonstrate how the **LinkPoke** method is used by sending a client control's current contents to the server whenever a command button is pressed. Listing 12-79 presents the code for the server program's **Form_Load** event, Listing 12-80-1 the code for the client program's **Form_Load** event, and Listing 12-80-2 the code for the client program's **Command1_Click** event. Figure 12-76 shows how the desktop would appear after the client control's contents have been poked to the server application.

Listing 12-79:

```
Sub Form_Load ()

    LinkTopic = "Demo"
    LinkMode = 1

End Sub
```

Listing 12-80-1:

```
Sub Form_Load ()

    Text1.LinkTopic = "Server|Demo"
    Text1.LinkItem = "Text1"
    Text1.LinkMode = 1

End Sub
```

Listing 12-80-2:

```
Sub Command1_Click ()

    Text1.LinkPoke

End Sub
```

LinkRequest Method

Summary:

`control.LinkRequest`

`control`   is the desired label, picture box, or text box
control.

Description:

The **LinkRequest** method is used by the client application to
request data for one of its client controls from the server
application. This method is particularly useful if the client
control and the server only have a cold link established. If the
DDE conversation is taking place via a cold link, no data will
be transferred to the client control until it is specifically re-
quested with the **LinkRequest** method.

Example:

The programs that follow demonstrate how the **LinkRequest**
method is used by transferring data from the server to the client
control whenever a command button is pressed. Listing 12-81
presents the code for the server program's **Form_Load** event,
Listing 12-82-1 the code for the client program's **Form_Load**
event, and Listing 12-82-2 the code for the client program's
Command1_Click event. Figure 12-77 illustrates how the
desktop would appear after data has been transferred via the
LinkRequest method.

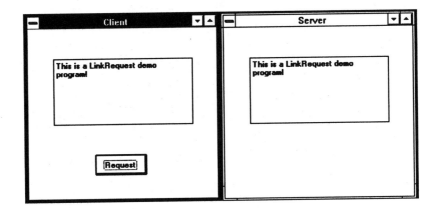

Figure 12-77 **A LinkRequest** *demonstration program.*

Listing 12-81:

```
Sub Form_Load ()

    LinkTopic = "Demo"
    LinkMode = 1

End Sub
```

Listing 12-82-1:

```
Sub Form_Load ()

    Text1.LinkTopic = "Server|Demo"
    Text1.LinkItem = "Text1"
    Text1.LinkMode = 2

End Sub
```

Listing 12-82-2:

```
Sub Command1_Click ()

    Text1.LinkRequest

End Sub
```

LinkSend Method

Summary:

picturebox.**LinkSend**

picturebox　　　is the desired picture box control.

Description:

The **LinkSend** method is used to send the contents of a picture box control to a client control in a DDE conversation. Even with a hot link, Visual Basic doesn't automatically update the client control when changes have been made to the server's picture box control. Thus, the picture box's contents must be periodically transferred to the client application via the **LinkSend** method.

Example:

The following program demonstrates how the **LinkSend** method is used to send the contents of a picture box control to the client application whenever a command button is pressed. Listing 12-83-1 presents the code for the server program's **Form_Load** event, Listing 12-83-2 the code for the server program's **Command1_Click** event, and Listing 12-84 the code for the client program's **Form_Load** event. Figure 12-78 shows

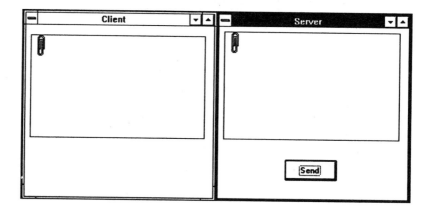

*Figure 12-78 A **LinkSend** demonstration program.*

how the desktop would appear after the picture box control's contents have been transferred with the **LinkSend** method.

Listing 12-83-1:

```
Sub Form_Load ()

    LinkTopic = "Demo"
    LinkMode = 1
    Picture1.Picture =
    LoadPicture("c:\vb\icons\office\clip01.ico")

End Sub
```

Listing 12-83-2:

```
Sub Command1_Click ()

    Picture1.LinkSend

End Sub
```

Listing 12-84:

```
Sub Form_Load ()

    Picture1.LinkTopic = "Server|Demo"
    Picture1.LinkItem = "Picture1"
    Picture1.LinkMode = 1

End Sub
```

LinkTimeout Property

Summary:

[*form.*] {*label* | *picturebox* | *textbox*} **.LinkTimeout** [= *tenths*]

form	is the desired form.
label	is the desired label.
picturebox	is the desired picture box.
textbox	is the desired text box.
tenths	is the new time out delay in tenths of a second.

Description:

The **LinkTimeout** property sets and returns the amount of time Visual Basic will wait for a DDE transfer to take place before issuing an error message. Visual Basic uses a default value of 5 seconds for all DDE transfers. If the **LinkTimeout** property is set to -1, Visual Basic will wait indefinitely for the DDE transfer to take place.

Example:

The programs that appear below show how the **LinkTimeout** property is used by setting a client control for an indefinite time-out delay. Listing 12-85 presents the code for the server program's **Form_Load** event; Listing 12-86 presents the code for the client program's **Form_Load** event. Figure 12-79 illustrates how the desktop would appear after the programs have been run.

Listing 12-85:

```
Sub Form_Load ()

    LinkTopic = "Demo"
    LinkMode = 1

End Sub
```

Listing 12-86:

```
Sub Form_Load ()

    Text1.LinkTopic = "Server|Demo"
    Text1.LinkItem = "Text1"
    Text1.LinkMode = 1
    Text1.LinkTimeout = -1

End Sub
```

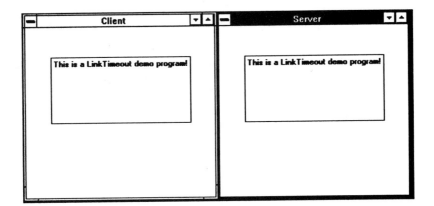

Figure 12-79 A **LinkTimeout** *demonstration program.*

LinkTopic Property

Summary:

`[form.] [control.]`**LinkTopic**`[ = topic]`

`form`   is the desired server form.

`control`   is the desired client control.

`topic`   is the DDE conversation's new link topic.

Description:

The **LinkTopic** property sets and returns a DDE conversation's link topic. The topic is specified by the string argument *topic*. For a server form, the *topic* argument specifies just the topic. For a client control, the *topic* argument specifies the server application's name and the topic separated by the pipe character (|).

Example:

The programs below demonstrate how the **LinkTopic** property is used to initiate a DDE conversation properly. Listing 12-87 specifies the server program's **Form_Load** event, and

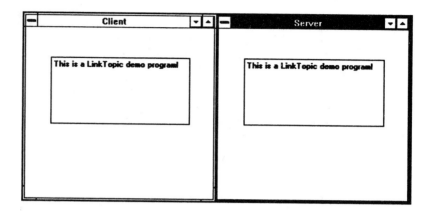

*Figure 12-80 A **LinkTopic** demonstration program.*

Listing 12-88 the client program's **Form_Load** event. Figure 12-80 shows how the desktop would appear after these two programs have been run.

Listing 12-87:

```
Sub Form_Load ()

    LinkTopic = "Demo"
    LinkMode = 1

End Sub
```

Listing 12-88:

```
Sub Form_Load ()

    Text1.LinkTopic = "Server|Demo"
    Text1.LinkItem = "Text1"
    Text1.LinkMode = 1

End Sub
```

List Property

Summary:

*[form.]control.***List***(index)* [= *item*]

form	is the control's form.
control	is the desired control.
index	is the list item's index in an array of list items.
item	is a string expression.

Description:

The **List** property is an array of strings that are used to hold the contents of a combo box, a list box, a directory list box, a drive list box, or a file list box. Except for a directory list box, the valid range of *index* values extend from 0 to **ListCount** - 1. The valid range of *index* values for a directory list box are from -*n* to **ListCount** - 1. Where -1 is the current directory, -2 is the current directory's parent directory, and so on.

See Also:

ListCount

Example:

The following program shows how the **List** property is used by displaying a list box's complete item list. Listing 12-89-1 presents the code for the program's **Form_Load** event, and Listing 12-89-2 the code for the program's **Form_Click** event. Figure 12-81 illustrates how the program's window would appear after the program has been run.

Listing 12-89-1:

```
Sub Form_Load ()

    List1.AddItem ("Ryan")
    List1.AddItem ("Matthew")
    List1.AddItem ("Chrissy")

End Sub
```

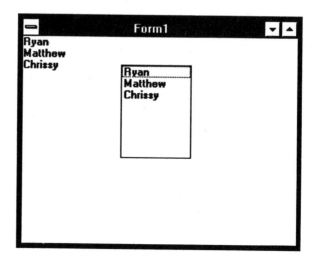

*Figure 12-81 A **List** demonstration program.*

Listing 12-89-2:

```
Sub Form_Click ()
    Dim I As Integer

    For I = 0 To 2
        Print List1.List(I)
    Next I

End Sub
```

ListCount Property

Summary:

[*form.*]*control*.**ListCount**

form   is the control's form.

control   is the desired control.

Description:

The **ListCount** property returns the number of items in a combo box, a directory list box, a drive list box, a file list box, or a list box.

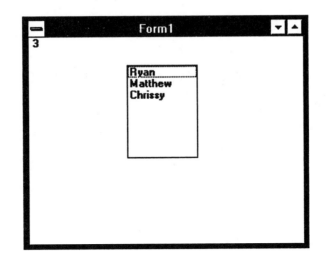

*Figure 12-82 A **ListCount** demonstration program.*

See Also:

List

Example:

The program that follows demonstrates how the **ListCount** property is used by displaying the number of items in a list box's list. Listing 12-90-1 presents the code for the form's **Form_Load** event, and Listing 12-90-2 the code for the form's **Form_Click** event. Figure 12-82 shows how the program's window would appear after the program has been run.

Listing 12-90-1:

```
Sub Form_Load ()

    List1.AddItem ("Ryan")
    List1.AddItem ("Matthew")
    List1.AddItem ("Chrissy")

End Sub
```

Listing 12-90-2:

```
Sub Form_Click ()

    Print List1.ListCount

End Sub
```

ListIndex Property

Summary:

[*form.*] *control*.**ListIndex**[= *index*]

form	is the control's form.
control	is the desired control.
index	is the index of the new currently selected item.

Description:

The **ListIndex** property sets and returns the index of the currently selected item for a combo box, a directory list box, a drive list box, a file list box, or a list box. Visual Basic sets the

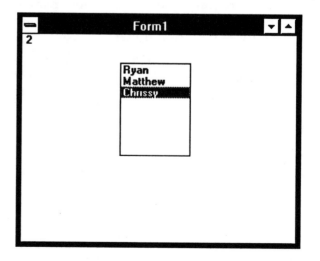

Figure 12-83 A **ListIndex** *demonstration program.*

ListIndex property to -1 to indicate either an empty list or a list without a selected item.

Example:

The program below demonstrates how the **ListIndex** property is used by displaying the index of the currently selected item. Listing 12-91-1 presents the code for the program's **Form_Load** event, and Listing 12-91-2 the code for the program's **Form-_Click** event. Figure 12-83 illustrates how the program's window would appear after the program has been run.

Listing 12-91-1:

```
Sub Form_Load ()

    List1.AddItem ("Ryan")
    List1.AddItem ("Matthew")
    List1.AddItem ("Chrissy")

End Sub
```

Listing 12-91-2:

```
Sub Form_Click ()

    Print List1.ListIndex

End Sub
```

Load Event

Summary:

```
Sub Form_Load( )
```

Description:

The **Load** event is called by Visual Basic to tell the program when a form is being loaded. Consequently, the **Load** event is commonly used to perform any initialization the form may need.

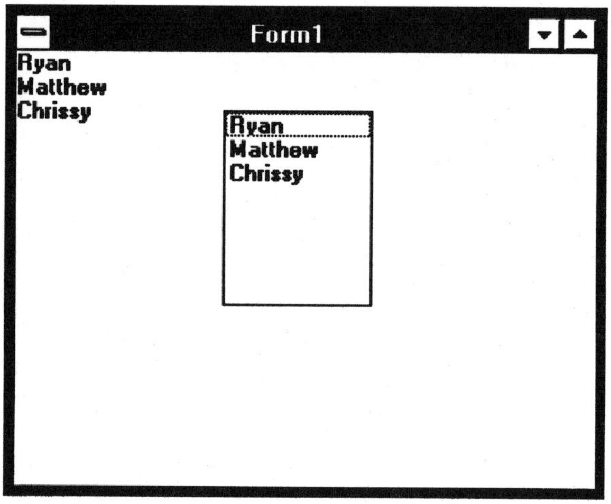

*Figure 12-84 A **Load** demonstration program.*

Example:

The program that appears below demonstrates how the **Load** event is used by displaying a message box when a form is being loaded. Listing 12-92 gives the code for the program's **Form_Load** event. Figure 12-84 illustrates how the program's window would appear after the program has been run.

Listing 12-92:

```
Sub Form_Load ()

    MsgBox "The form has been loaded"

End Sub
```

LostFocus Event

Summary:

Sub Form_LostFocus( )

or

Sub *control*_**LostFocus**([*index* **As Integer**])

`control`	is the desired control.
`index`	is the control's index in an array of controls.

Description:

The **LostFocus** event is called by Visual Basic to tell the program that a form, a check box, a combo box, a command button, a directory list box, a drive list box, a file list box, a horizontal scroll bar, a list box, an option button, a picture box, a text box, or a vertical scroll bar has lost the focus.

See Also:

GotFocus and **SetFocus**

Example:

The following program shows how the **LostFocus** event is used by displaying a message whenever a command button loses the focus. Listing 12-93 presents the code for the program's **Command1_LostFocus** event. Figure 12-85 illustrates how the program's window would appear after the program has been run.

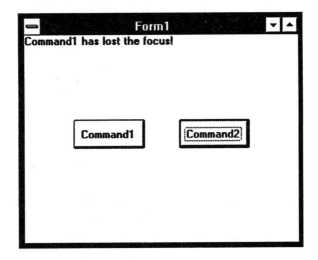

*Figure 12-85 A **LostFocus** demonstration program.*

Listing 12-93:

```
Sub Command1_LostFocus ()

    Print "Command1 has lost the focus!"

End Sub
```

Max Property

Summary:

`[form.]{horizontalscrollbar|verticalscrollbar}.Max[ = limit]`

form	is the scroll bar's form.
horizontalscrollbar	is the desired horizontal scroll bar.
verticalscrollbar	is the desired vertical scroll bar.
limit	is the scroll bar's new maximum value.

Description:

The **Max** property is used to set or return a scroll bar's upper limit. The new upper limit is specified by the *limit* parameter and must be in the range of -32,768 to 32,767. Visual Basic assigns a default value of 32,767 to all scroll bars.

See Also:

Min

Example:

The program that follows demonstrates how the **Max** value is used by displaying a message when a scroll bar's upper limit has been reached. Listing 12-94-1 presents the code for the program's **Form_Load** event; Listing 12-94-2 specifies the code for the program's **HScroll1_Change** event. Figure 12-86 shows how the program's window would appear after the program has been run.

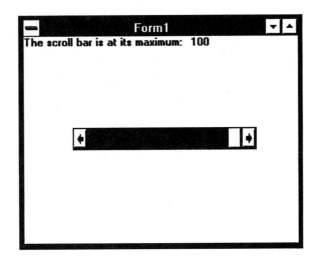

*Figure 12-86 A **Max** demonstration program.*

Listing 12-94-1:

```
Sub Form_Load ()

    HScroll1.Max = 100

End Sub
```

Listing 12-94-2:

```
Sub HScroll1_Change ()

    If HScroll1.Value = HScroll1.Max Then
        Print "The scroll bar is at its maximum: ";
        HScroll1.Max
    End If

End Sub
```

MaxButton Property

Summary:

[*form.*]**MaxButton**

form   is the desired form.

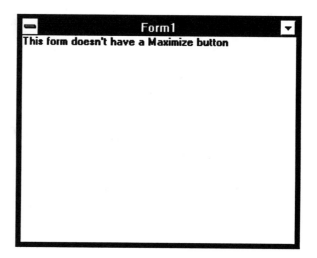

Figure 12-87 A **MaxButton** *demonstration program.*

Description:

The **MaxButton** property is used to specify whether or not a form has a Maximize button. If the **MaxButton** property is set to True (the default), the form will have a Maximize button. If the **MaxButton** property is set to False, the form will not have a Maximize button. You should note that the **MaxButton** property is read-only at run time.

See Also:

MinButton

Example:

The program that follows demonstrates how the **MaxButton** property is used by displaying an appropriate message as to whether or not the form has a Maximize button. Listing 12-95 presents the code for the program's **Form_Paint** event. Figure 12-87 illustrates how the program's window would appear after the program has been run.

Listing 12-95:

```
Sub Form_Paint ()

    If MaxButton Then
        Print "This form has a Maximize button"
    Else
        Print "This form doesn't have a Maximize
        button"
    End If

End Sub
```

Min Property

Summary:

[form.]{horizontalscrollbar|verticalscrollbar}.**Min**[= *limit*]

form	is the scroll bar's form.
horizontalscrollbar	is the desired horizontal scroll bar.
verticalscrollbar	is the desired vertical scroll bar.
limit	is the scroll bar's new minimum value.

Description:

The **Min** property is used to set or return a scroll bar's lower limit. The new lower limit is specified by the *limit* parameter and must be in the range of -32,768 to 32,767. Visual Basic assigns a default value of 32,767 to all scroll bars.

See Also:

Max

Example:

The program that appears below demonstrates how the **Min** value is used by displaying a message when a scroll bar's lower

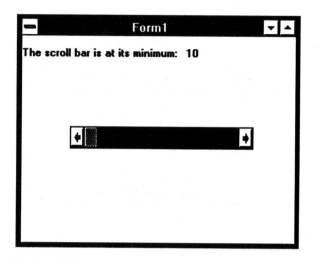

*Figure 12-88 A **Min** demonstration program.*

limit has been reached. Listing 12-96-1 presents the code for the program's **Form_Load** event, and Listing 12-96-2 the code for the program's **HScroll1_Change** event. Figure 12-88 shows how the program's window would appear after the program has been run.

Listing 12-96-1:

```
Sub Form_Load ()

    HScroll1.Min = 10

End Sub
```

Listing 12-96-2:

```
Sub HScroll1_Change ()

    If HScroll1.Value = HScroll1.Min Then
        Print "The scroll bar is at its minimum: ";
        HScroll1.Min
    End If

End Sub
```

MinButton Property

Summary:

[*form.*]**MinButton**

form   is the desired form.

Description:

The **MinButton** property is used to specify whether or not a form has a Minimize button. If the **MinButton** property is set to True (the default), the form will have a Minimize button. If the **MinButton** property is set to False, the form will not have a Minimize button. You should note that the **MinButton** property is read-only at run time.

See Also:

MaxButton

Example:

The following program demonstrates how the **MinButton** property is used by displaying an appropriate message as to whether or not the form has a Minimize button. Listing 12-97 gives the program's **Form_Paint** event. Figure 12-89 illustrates how the program's window would appear after the program has been run.

Listing 12-97:

```
Sub Form_Paint ()

    If MinButton Then
        Print "This form has a Minimize button"
    Else
        Print "This form doesn't have a Minimize
        button"
    End If

End Sub
```

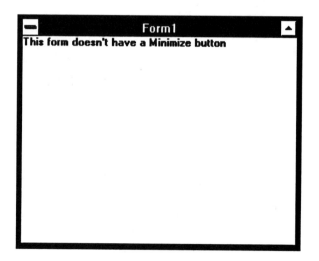

*Figure 12-89 A **MinButton** demonstration program.*

MouseDown Event

Summary:

```
Sub Form_MouseDown(button As Integer, shift As
Integer, x As Single, y As Single)
```

or

```
Sub control_MouseDown([index As Integer,] button As
Integer, shift As Integer, x As Single, y As Single)
```

button	specifies which mouse button is down.
shift	specifies which, if any, keyboard shift keys are down.
x,y	is the mouse pointer's current coordinates.
control	is the desired control.
index	is the control's index in an array of controls.

Description:

The **MouseDown** event is called by Visual Basic to tell the program when a mouse button has been pressed in a form, a file list box, a label, a list box, or a picture box. The mouse button that has been pressed is specified in the *button* parameter as follows:

Button	Description
1	Left button
2	Right button
4	Center button

You should note that only one button will be reported at a time. If more than one mouse button has been pressed, Visual Basic will call the **MouseDown** event multiple times.

The **MouseDown** event also reports if any of the shift keys are being pressed. The state of the shift keys is reported in the *shift* parameter as follows:

Shift	Description
1	SHIFT
2	CTRL
4	ALT

You should note that Visual Basic will report multiple shift key presses in the *shift* parameter.

See Also:

MouseMove and **MouseUp**

Example:

The program that follows shows how the **MouseDown** event is used by displaying which mouse button was pressed, the state of the shift keys, and the mouse pointer's location whenever the mouse button is pressed in a form. Listing 12-98 presents the code for the program's **Form_MouseDown** event. Figure 12-90 illustrates how the program's window would appear after the program has been run.

Listing 12-98:

```
Sub Form_MouseDown (Button As Integer, Shift As
Integer, X As Single, Y As Single)

    Print "Button: ";
    Select Case Button
        Case 1
            Print "Left"
        Case 2
            Print "Right"
        Case 4
            Print "Center"
    End Select
    Print "Shift Keys: ";
    If Shift And 1 Then
        Print "SHIFT ";
    End If
    If Shift And 2 Then
        Print "CTRL ";
    End If
    If Shift And 4 Then
        Print "ALT ";
    End If
    Print
    Print "X,Y:"; X; ","; Y

End Sub
```

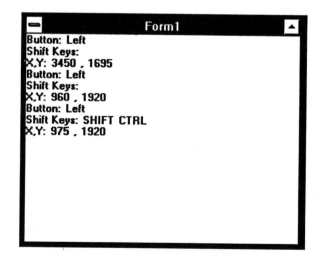

*Figure 12-90 A **MouseDown** demonstration program.*

MouseMove Event

Summary:

```
Sub Form_MouseMove(button As Integer, shift As
Integer, x As Single, y As Single)
```

or

```
Sub control_MouseMove([index As Integer,] button As
Integer, shift As Integer,  x As Single, y As Single)
```

button	specifies which, if any, mouse buttons are down.
shift	specifies which, if any, keyboard shift keys are down.
x,y	is the mouse pointer's current coordinates.
control	is the desired control.
index	is the control's index in an array of controls.

Description:

The **MouseMove** event is called by Visual Basic to tell the program when the mouse pointer has moved in a form, a file list box, a label, a list box, or a picture box. The **MouseMove** event reports if any mouse buttons are being pressed. The state of the mouse buttons is specified in the *button* parameter as follows:

Shift	*Description*
1	Left
2	Right
4	Center

You should note that Visual Basic will report multiple mouse button presses in the *button* parameter.

The **MouseMove** event also reports if any shift keys are being pressed. The state of the shift keys is reported in the *shift* parameter as follows:

Shift	Description
1	SHIFT
2	CTRL
4	ALT

You should note that Visual Basic will report multiple shift key presses in the *shift* parameter.

See Also:

MouseDown and **MouseUp**

Example:

The program that appears below demonstrates how the **MouseMove** event is used by displaying the state of the mouse buttons, the state of the shift keys, and the mouse pointer's location whenever the mouse is moved in a form. Listing 12-99 presents the code for the program's **Form_MouseMove** event. Figure 12-91 shows how the program's window would appear after the program has been run.

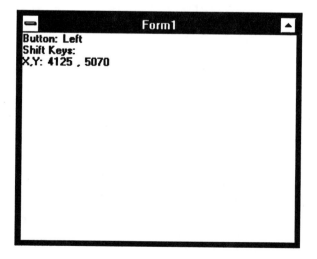

*Figure 12-91 A **MouseMove** demonstration program.*

Listing 12-99:

```
Sub Form_MouseMove (Button As Integer, Shift As
Integer, X As Single, Y As Single)

    CurrentX = 0
    CurrentY = 0
    FontTransparent = 0
    Print "Button: ";
    Select Case Button
        Case 1
            Print "Left      "
        Case 2
            Print "Right     "
        Case 4
            Print "Center    "
        Case Else
            Print "          "
    End Select
    Print "Shift Keys: ";
    If Shift And 1 Then
        Print "SHIFT ";
    End If
    If Shift And 2 Then
        Print "CTRL ";
    End If
    If Shift And 4 Then
        Print "ALT ";
    End If
    Print "                      "
    Print "X,Y:"; X; ","; Y; "                "

End Sub
```

MousePointer Property

Summary:

{[*form*.][*control*.]|**Screen.**}**MousePointer**[= *pointer*]

form   is the desired form.

control   is the desired control.

pointer   is the new mouse pointer.

Description:

The **MousePointer** property is used to set or return the type of mouse pointer for a form, a check box, a combo box, a command button, a directory list box, a drive list box, a file list box, a frame, a horizontal scroll bar, a label, a list box, an option button, a picture box, the **Screen** object, a text box, or a vertical scroll bar. A new mouse pointer is set with the *pointer* parameter and can be any one of the following values:

Pointer	Description
0	Shape determined by the control. (The default.)
1	Arrow.
2	Cross-hair.
3	I-beam.
4	Icon.
5	Arrow pointing north
6	Arrow pointing northeast and southwest.
7	Arrow pointing north and south.
8	Arrow pointing northwest and southeast.
9	Arrow pointing west and east.
10	Up arrow.
11	Hourglass.
12	No drop.

Example:

The program that follows shows how the **MousePointer** is used by changing a form's mouse pointer to a hourglass. Listing 12-100 presents the code for the program's **Form_Load** event. Figure 12-92 illustrates how the program's window would appear after the program has been run.

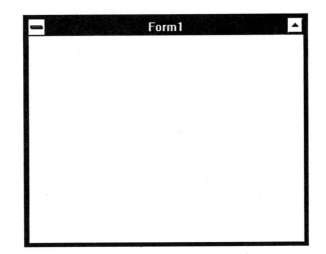

Figure 12-92 A **MousePointer** *demonstration program.*

Listing 12-100:

```
Sub Form_Load ()

    MousePointer = 11

End Sub
```

MouseUp Event

Summary:

Sub Form_MouseUp(*button* **As Integer,** *shift* **As Integer,** *x* **As Single,** *y* **As Single)**

or

Sub *control*_**MouseUp**([*index* **As Integer,**] *button* **As Integer,** *shift* **As Integer,** *x* **As Single,** *y* **As Single)**

button	specifies which mouse button has been released.
shift	specifies which, if any, keyboard shift keys are down.

`x,y`	is the mouse pointer's current coordinates.
`control`	is the desired control.
`index`	is the control's index in an array of controls.

Description:

The **MouseUp** event is called by Visual Basic to tell the program when a mouse button has been released in a form, a file list box, a label, a list box, or a picture box. The mouse button that has been released is specified in the *button* parameter as follows:

Button	Description
1	Left button
2	Right button
4	Center button

You should note that only one button will be reported at a time. If more than one mouse button has been released, Visual Basic will call the **MouseUp** event multiple times.

The **MouseUp** event also reports if any of the shift keys are being pressed. The state of the shift keys is reported in the *shift* parameter as follows:

Shift	Description
1	SHIFT
2	CTRL
4	ALT

You should note that Visual Basic will report multiple shift key presses in the *shift* parameter.

See Also:

MouseDown and **MouseMove**

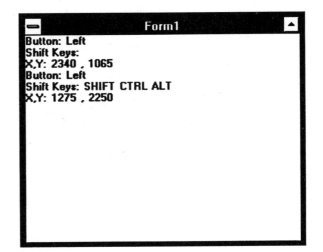

*Figure 12-93   A **MouseUp** demonstration program.*

Example:

The following program demonstrates how the **MouseUp** event is used by displaying which mouse button was released, the state of the shift keys, and the mouse pointer's location whenever the mouse button is released in a form. Listing 12-101 presents the code for the program's **Form_MouseUp** event. Figure 12-93 illustrates how the program's window would appear after the program has been run.

Listing 12-101:

```
Sub Form_MouseUp (Button As Integer, Shift As
Integer, X As Single, Y As Single)

    Print "Button: ";
    Select Case Button
        Case 1
            Print "Left"
        Case 2
            Print "Right"
        Case 4
            Print "Center"
    End Select
    Print "Shift Keys: ";
    If Shift And 1 Then
```

```
        Print "SHIFT ";
    End If
    If Shift And 2 Then
        Print "CTRL ";
    End If
    If Shift And 4 Then
        Print "ALT ";
    End If
    Print
    Print "X,Y:"; X; ","; Y

End Sub
```

Move Method

Summary:

[*form.*] [*control.*]**Move** *left*[, *top*[, *width*[, *height*]]]

form	is the desired form.
control	is the desired control.
left	is the form or control's new *x*-coordinate.
top	is the form or control's new *y*-coordinate.
width	is the form or control's new width.
height	is the form or control's new height.

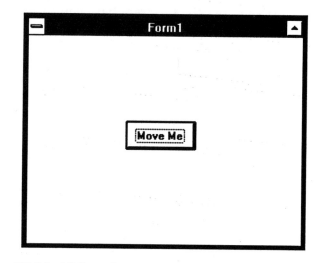

Figure 12-94 A **Move** *demonstration program (1 of 2).*

Description:

The **Move** method is used to move and/or resize a form, a check box, a combo box, a command button, a directory list box, a drive list box, a file list box, a frame, a horizontal scroll bar, a label, a list box, an option button, a picture box, a text box, or a vertical scroll bar. When moving a form or a control in a frame, the *left* and *top* parameters are expressed in twips. When moving a control on a form or picture box control, the *left* and *top* parameters are expressed in the form or picture box's coordinate system.

Example:

The program that follows demonstrates how the **Move** method is used by moving a command button to the upper left corner of a form. Listing 12-102 gives the code for the program's **Command1_Click** event. Figure 12-94 shows how the program's window would appear before the command button is clicked, and Figure 12-95 how the program's window would appear after the command button is clicked.

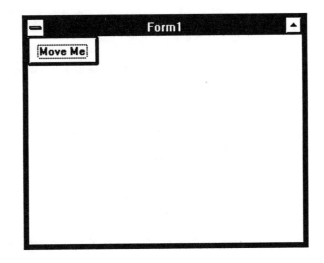

Figure 12-95 A **Move** *demonstration program (2 of 2).*

Listing 12-102:

```
Sub Command1_Click ()

    Command1.Move 0, 0

End Sub
```

MultiLine Property

Summary:

*[form.] textbox.***MultiLine**

form   is the text box control's form.

textbox   is the desired text box.

Description:

The **MultiLine** property determines whether or not a text box supports multiple lines of text. The **MultiLine** property is read-only at run time and returns True if the text box is a multiline text box. Otherwise, the **MultiLine** property returns False to indicate a single-line text box. By default, all text boxes are single-line.

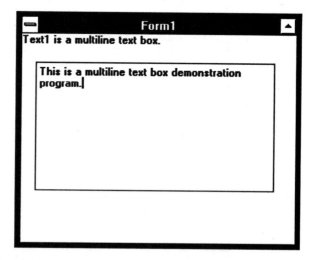

*Figure 12-96 A **MultiLine** demonstration program.*

Example:

The program below shows how the **MultiLine** property is used to create a multiline text box. Listing 12-103 presents the code for the program's **Form_Click** event. Figure 12-96 illustrates how the program's window would appear after the program has been run.

Listing 12-103:

```
Sub Form_Click ()

    If Text1.MultiLine Then
        Print "Text1 is a multiline text box."
    Else
        Print "Text1 isn't a multiline text box."
    End If

End Sub
```

NewPage Method

Summary:

`Printer.NewPage`

Description:

The **NewPage** method is used to send a form feed to the printer. Additionally, the **NewPage** property increments the **Printer** object's **Page** property.

See Also:

EndDoc and **Page**

Example:

The program that follows demonstrates how the **NewPage** method is used by sending a form feed to the printer whenever a command button is pressed. Listing 12-104 presents the code for the program's **Command1_Click** event. Figure 12-97

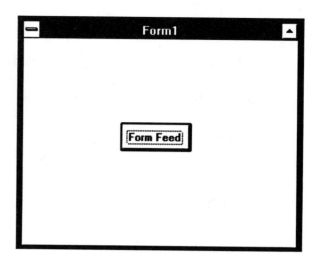

*Figure 12-97 A **NewPage** demonstration program.*

shows how the program's window would appear after the program has been run.

Listing 12-104:

```
Sub Command1_Click ()

    Printer.NewPage
    Printer.EndDoc

End Sub
```

Normal Property

Summary:

[*form.*] *filelistbox*.**Normal**[= *flag*]

form　　　　　　is the file list box's form.

filelistbox　　is the desired file list box.

flag　　　　　　is the new normal attribute setting.

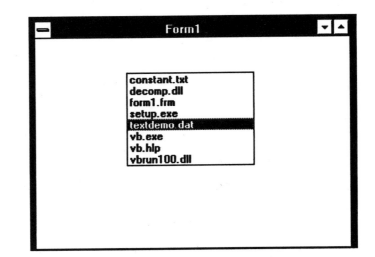

Figure 12-98 A **Normal** *demonstration program.*

Description:

The **Normal** property is used to either set or return a file list box's normal attribute setting. If the **Normal** property is set to True (the default), Visual Basic will display files with their normal attributes set in the file list box. If the **Normal** property is set to False, Visual Basic will not display files with their hidden attributes set in the file list box.

See Also:

Archive, Hidden, ReadOnly, and **System**

Example:

The following program demonstrates how the **Normal** property is used by setting a file list box's normal attribute to True. Listing 12-105 presents the code for the form's **Form_Click** event. Figure 12-98 illustrates how the program's window would appear after the program has been run.

Listing 12-105:

```
Sub Form_Click ()

    File1.Normal = -1

End Sub
```

Page Property

Summary:

`Printer.Page`

Description:

The **Page** property is used to determine which page the **Printer** object is printing to. Visual Basic starts counting pages either from the start of the program or since the last call to **EndDoc**. The **Page** property is incremented each time the **NewPage** method is called or a **Print** statement causes the text to be printed on the next page.

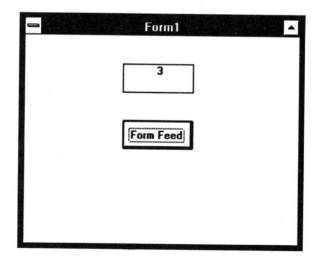

Figure 12-99 A **Page** *demonstration program.*

See Also:

EndDoc and **NewPage**

Example:

The program that follows demonstrates how the **Page** property is used by displaying the current page in a label control after a form feed is sent to the **Printer** object. Listing 12-106 presents the code for the program's **Command1_Click** event. Figure 12-99 shows how the program's window would appear after the program has been run.

Listing 12-106:

```
Sub Command1_Click ()

    Printer.NewPage
    Label1.Caption = Str$(Printer.Page)

End Sub
```

Paint Event

Summary:

Sub Form_Paint( )

or

Sub *picturebox***_Paint(**[*index* **As Integer**]**)**

picturebox	is the desired picture box control.
index	is the picture box control's index in an array of controls.

Description:

The **Paint** event is called by Visual Basic when all or part of a form or picture box control must be redrawn. Typically, a form or picture box must be redrawn whenever it has moved, been resized, or because another window that covered the form or picture box has been moved. A **Paint** event can be invoked by

*Figure 12-100 A **Paint** demonstration program.*

using the **Refresh** method. You should note that Visual Basic will automatically redraw the form or picture box if the **AutoRedraw** property has been set to True.

See Also:

AutoRedraw and **Refresh**

Example:

The program that appears below shows how the **Paint** event is used by redrawing a box on a form whenever the form's **Paint** event is called. Listing 12-107 gives the code for the program's **Form_Paint** event. Figure 12-100 illustrates how the program's window would appear after the program has been run.

Listing 12-107:

```
Sub Form_Paint ()

    Line (ScaleWidth / 4, ScaleHeight / 4)-(ScaleWidth -
    ScaleWidth / 4, ScaleHeight - ScaleHeight / 4), , BF

End Sub
```

Parent Property

Summary:

```
control.Parent
```

`control`   is the desired control.

Description:

The **Parent** property returns the parent form for a check box, a combo box, a command button, a directory list box, a drive list box, a file list box, a frame, a horizontal scroll bar, a label, a list box, a menu, an option button, a picture box, a text box, a timer, or a vertical scroll bar.

Example:

The program below demonstrates how the **Parent** property is used by clearing a form's client area whenever a command button is pressed. Listing 12-108-1 presents the code for the program's **Form_Paint** event, and Listing 12-108-2 the code for the program's **Command1_Click** event. Figure 12-101 illustrates how the program's window appears before the command button is pressed; Figure 12-102 shows how the program's window appears after the command button is pressed.

Listing 12-108-1:

```
Sub Form_Paint ()
    Dim I As Integer

    For I = 1 To 10
        Print "I'm a nothing line"
    Next I

End Sub
```

Listing 12-108-2:

```
Sub Command1_Click ()

    Command1.Parent.Cls

End Sub
```

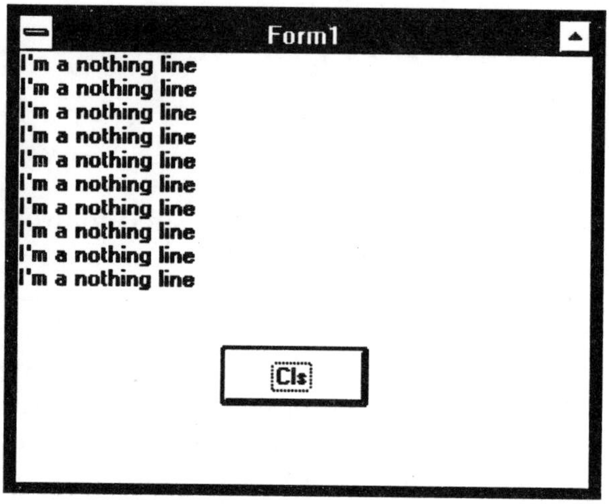

*Figure 12-101 A **Parent** demonstration program (1 of 2).*

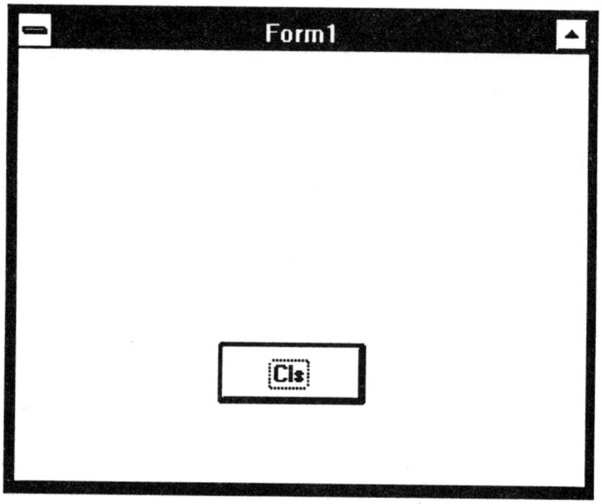

*Figure 12-102 A **Parent** demonstration program (2 of 2).*

Path Property

Summary:

```
[form.]{directorylistbox|filelistbox}.Path[ = path]
```

form   is the control's form.

`directorylistbox`	is the desired directory list box.
`filelistbox`	is the desired file list box.
`path`	is a string that specifies the new path.

Description:

The **Path** property sets or returns the current path for either a directory list box or a file list box. You should note that if *path* contains only a drive spec, Visual Basic will set the directory to the specified drive's current directory.

Example:

The following program shows how the **Path** property is used by setting a directory list box's path to the root directory of drive C:. Listing 12-109 presents the code for the form's **Command1_Click** event. Figure 12-103 illustrates how the program's window would appear after the program has been run.

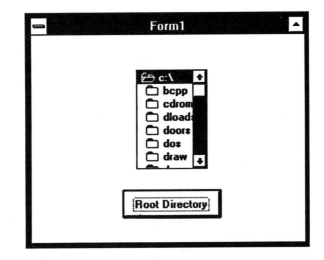

*Figure 12-103 A **Path** demonstration program.*

Listing 12-109:

```
Sub Command1_Click ()

    Dir1.Path = "C:\"

End Sub
```

PathChange Event

Summary:

Sub *filelistbox*_**PathChange**([*index* **As Integer**])

filelistbox   is the desired file list box.

index   is the file list box's index in an array of controls.

Description:

The **PathChange** event is called by Visual Basic to tell the program when a file list box's **Path** property has been changed.

See Also:

Path

Example:

The program that follows demonstrates how the **PathChange** event is used by displaying the current directory in a label control. Listing 12-110-1 presents the code for the program's **File1_PathChange** event, and Listing 12-110-2 the code for the program's **Command1_Click** event. Figure 12-104 illustrates how the program's window would appear after the program has been run.

Listing 12-110-1:

```
Sub File1_PathChange ()

    Label1.Caption = "Path: " + File1.Path

End Sub
```

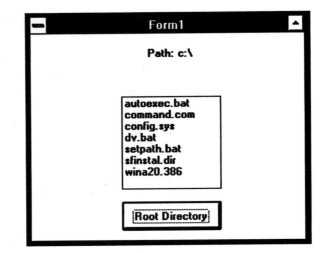

*Figure 12-104 A **PathChange** demonstration program.*

Listing 12-110-2:

```
Sub Command1_Click ()

    File1.Path = "C:\"

End Sub
```

Pattern Property

Summary:

[*form.*] *filelistbox*.**Pattern**[= *files*]

form	is the file list box control's form.
filelistbox	is the desired file list box.
files	is the new directory search string.

Description:

The **Pattern** property sets and returns the directory search string Visual Basic uses when displaying files in a file list box. The directory search string is specified by *files* and the default search string is ***.***.

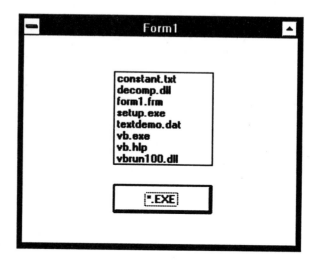

Figure 12-105 A **Pattern** *demonstration program (1 of 2).*

See Also:

PatternChange

Example:

The program that appears below demonstrates how the **Pattern** property is used by displaying only the EXE files in a directory after a command button has been pressed. Listing 12-111 presents the code for the program's **Command1_Click** event. Figure 12-105 shows how the program's window appears before the command button is pressed, and Figure 12-106 how it appears after the command button is pressed.

Listing 12-111:

```
Sub Command1_Click ()

    File1.Pattern = "*.exe"

End Sub
```

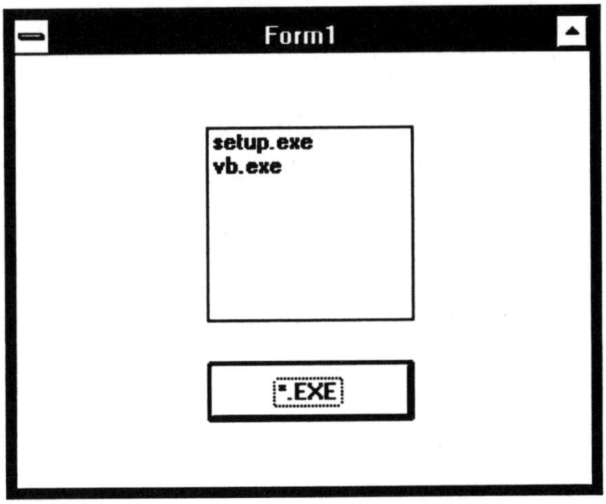

Figure 12-106 A **Pattern** *demonstration program (2 of 2).*

PatternChange Event

Summary:

```
Sub filelistbox_PatternChange([index As Integer])
```

filelistbox is the desired file list box.

index is the file list box's index in an array of controls.

Description:

The **PatternChange** event is called by Visual Basic to tell the program when a file list box's **Pattern** property has been changed.

See Also:

Pattern

Example:

The program below shows how the **PatternChange** event is used by displaying the current directory search string in a label control. Listing 12-112-1 gives the code for the program's **File1_PatternChange** event, and Listing 12-112-2 the code for the program's **Command1_Click** event. Figure 12-107 illustrates how the program's window would appear after the program has been run.

Listing 12-112-1:

```
Sub File1_PatternChange ()

    Label1.Caption = File1.Pattern

End Sub
```

Listing 12-112-2:

```
Sub Command1_Click ()

    File1.Pattern = "*.exe"

End Sub
```

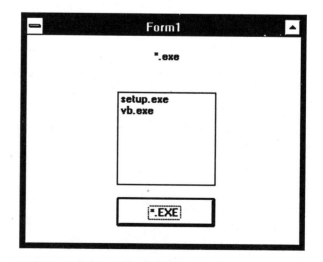

*Figure 12-107 A **PatternChange** demonstration program.*

Picture Property

Summary:

[*form.*] [*picturebox.*]**Picture**[= *picture*]

form   is the desired form.

picturebox   is the desired picture box.

picture   is the new picture.

Description:

The **Picture** property specifies a picture to be displayed in either a form or a picture box. The picture can be specified either at design time with the Properties Bar or at run time with the **LoadPicture** function.

See Also:

LoadPicture

Example:

The following program demonstrates the **Picture** property by displaying an icon in a form. Listing 12-113 presents the code for the program's **Form_Click** event. Figure 12-108 shows how the program's window would appear after the program has been run.

Listing 12-113:

```
Sub Form_Click ()

    Picture =
    LoadPicture("c:\vb\icons\arrows\arw09dn.ico")

End Sub
```

Figure 12-108 A **Picture** *demonstration program.*

Point Method

Summary:

[*form.*] [*picturebox.*] **Point**(*x*, *y*)

form	is the desired form.
picturebox	is the desired picture box.
x,y	is the graphics coordinate.

Description:

The **Point** method returns the RGB color of a graphics point on a form or a picture box control.

Example:

The program that follows demonstrates how the **Point** method is used by displaying the color of a form's upper-left corner and its center. Listing 12-114 presents the code for the program's **Form_Click** event. Figure 12-109 illustrates how the program's window would appear after the program has been run.

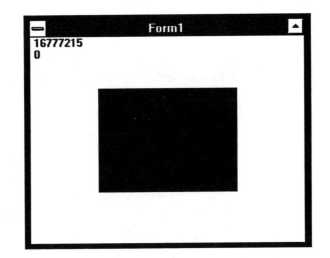

Figure 12-109 A **Point** *demonstration program.*

Listing 12-114:

```
Sub Form_Click ()

    Line (ScaleWidth / 4, ScaleHeight /
    4)-(ScaleWidth - ScaleWidth / 4, ScaleHeight -
    ScaleHeight / 4), , BF
    CurrentX = 0
    CurrentY = 0
    Print Point(0, 0)
    Print Point(ScaleWidth / 2, ScaleHeight / 2)

End Sub
```

Print Method

Summary:

```
{[form.]picturebox.|Printer.}Print
[expressionlist][{;|,}]
```

form	is the desired form.
picturebox	is the desired picture box.
expressionlist	is one or more expressions separated by either a semicolon or a comma.

Description:

The **Print** method is used to print text on a form, a picture box, or the **Printer** object. If the **Print** statement has more than one expression, the expressions must be separated by either a semicolon or a comma. Expressions separated by a semicolon will be printed one after the other. If multiple expressions are separated by a comma, the current print location will be tabbed over to the next print zone before the second expression is printed. If neither a semicolon or a comma is specified at the end of a **Print** statement, Visual Basic will move the cursor to the start of the next line.

Example:

The program that appears below shows how the **Print** method is used by displaying a variety of strings on a form. Listing 12-115 presents the code for the program's **Form_Click** event. Figure 12-110 illustrates how the program's window would appear after the program has been run.

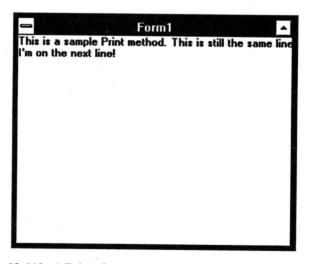

*Figure 12-110 A **Print** demonstration program.*

Listing 12-115:

```
Sub Form_Click ()

    Print "This is a sample Print method.";
    Print " This is still the same line."
    Print "I'm on the next line!"

End Sub
```

PrintForm Method

Summary:

[*form.*] **PrintForm**

form   is the desired form.

Description:

The **PrintForm** method is used to print a form's image on the **Printer** object.

Example:

The below program demonstrates how the **PrintForm** method is used to print a form's image when a command button is pressed. Listing 12-116 presents the code for the program's **Command1_Click** event. Figure 12-111 shows how the program's window would appear after the program has been run.

Listing 12-116:

```
Sub Command1_Click ()

    PrintForm

End Sub
```

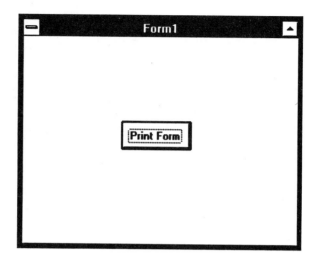

Figure 12-111 A **PrintForm** *demonstration program.*

PSet Method

Summary:

`{[[form.]picturebox.|Printer.}PSet [Step](x, y)[, color]`

form	is the desired form.
picturebox	is the desired picture box.
Step	specifies that the coordinates are relative to the current graphics position.
x, y	is the graphic point's coordinates.
color	is the color to set the point to. If *color* is omitted, Visual Basic will use the current foreground color.

Description:

The **PSet** method sets a graphics point on a form, a picture box, or the **Printer** object to a specified color.

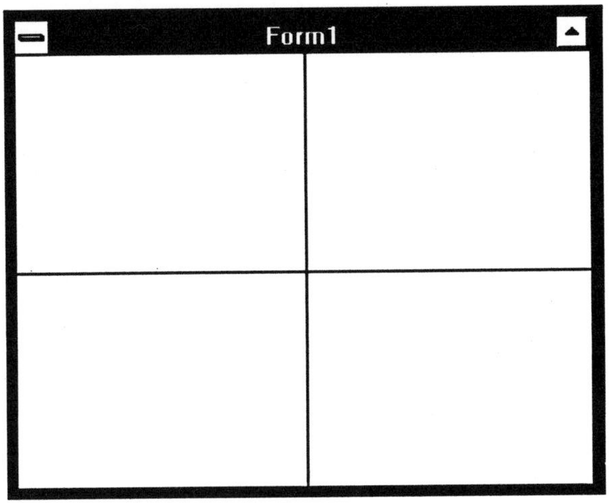

*Figure 12-112 A **PSet** demonstration program.*

Example:

The following program shows how the **PSet** method is used by drawing a vertical line and a horizontal line through the center of a form. Listing 12-117 gives the code for the program's **Form_Click** event. Figure 12-112 illustrates how the program's window would appear after the program has been run.

Listing 12-117:

```
Sub Form_Click ()
    Dim I As Integer, SW As Integer, SH As Integer

    SW = ScaleWidth
    SH = ScaleHeight
    For I = 0 To SW
        PSet (I, SH / 2)
    Next I
    For I = 0 To SH
        PSet (SW / 2, I)
    Next I

End Sub
```

ReadOnly Property

Summary:

[*form.*] *filelistbox*.**ReadOnly**[= *flag*]

form   is the file list box's form.

filelistbox   is the desired file list box.

flag   is the new read-only attribute setting.

Description:

The **ReadOnly** property is used to either set or return a file list box's read-only attribute setting. If the **ReadOnly** property is set to True (the default), Visual Basic will display files with their read-only attributes set in the file list box. If the **ReadOnly** property is set to False, Visual Basic will not display files with their read-only attributes set in the file list box.

See Also:

Archive, Hidden, Normal, and **System**

Example:

The program that follows demonstrates how the **ReadOnly** property is used by setting a file list box's read-only attribute to True. Listing 12-118 presents the code for the program's **Form_Click** event. Figure 12-113 illustrates how the program's window would appear after the program has been run.

Listing 12-118:

```
Sub Form_Click ()

    File1.ReadOnly = -1

End Sub
```

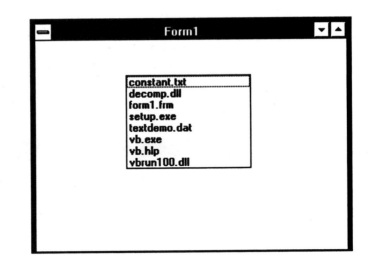

Figure 12-113 A **ReadOnly** *demonstration program.*

Refresh Method

Summary:

`[form.] [control.]`**Refresh**

`form`   is the desired form.

`control`   is the desired control.

Description:

The **Refresh** method forces Visual Basic to refresh a form or a control. This method can be useful to force a repainting of a form or a picture box control. Additionally, **Refresh** is useful for updating file list boxes, directory list boxes, and drive list boxes if you know the file system has changed.

Example:

The program that appears below shows how the **Refresh** method is used by updating a directory list box after a new directory has been created. Listing 12-119 presents the code for the program's **Command1_Click** event. Figure 12-114 illustrates how the program's window appears before the command button is pressed, and Figure 12-115 how it appears after the command button is pressed.

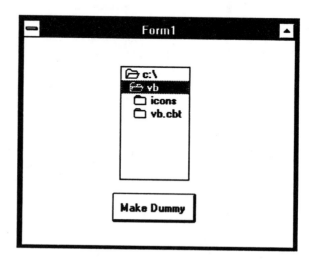

*Figure 12-114 A **Refresh** demonstration program (1 of 2).*

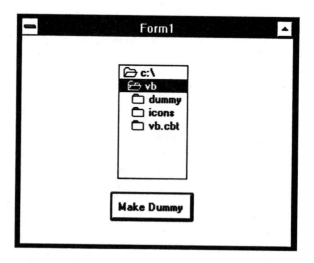

*Figure 12-115 A **Refresh** demonstration program (2 of 2).*

Listing 12-119:

```
Sub Command1_Click ()
    Static Flag As Integer

    If Flag Then
        Exit Sub
    End If
    MkDir "c:\vb\dummy"
    Dir1.Refresh
    Flag = -1

End Sub
```

RemoveItem Method

Summary:

`{listbox|combobox}.RemoveItem index`

listbox	is the desired list box.
combobox	is the desired combo box.
index	is the item's index in the list.

Description:

The **RemoveItem** method removes an item from a list in a list box or a combo box. The item to be removed is specified by *index* and can be any number from 0 to **ListCount** - 1.

See Also:

AddItem

Example:

The program that follows demonstrates how the **RemoveItem** method is used by removing the last item from a list box every time a command button is pressed. Listing 12-120-1 presents the code for the program's **Form_Load** event, and Listing

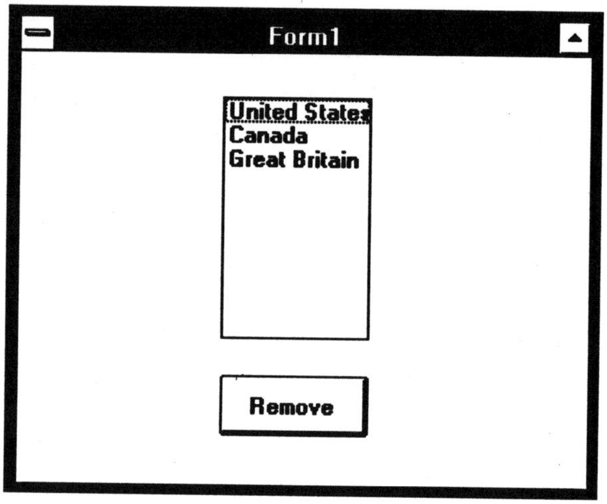

*Figure 12-116 A **RemoveItem** demonstration program (1 of 2).*

12-120-2 the code for the program's **Command1_Click** event. Figure 12-116 shows how the program's window appears before the command button is pressed; Figure 12-117 shows how the program's window appears after the command button is pressed.

Listing 12-120-1:

```
Sub Form_Load ()

    List1.AddItem "United States"
    List1.AddItem "Canada"
    List1.AddItem "Great Britain"

End Sub
```

Listing 12-120-2:

```
Sub Command1_Click ()

    If List1.ListCount <> 0 Then
        List1.RemoveItem List1.ListCount - 1
    End If

End Sub
```

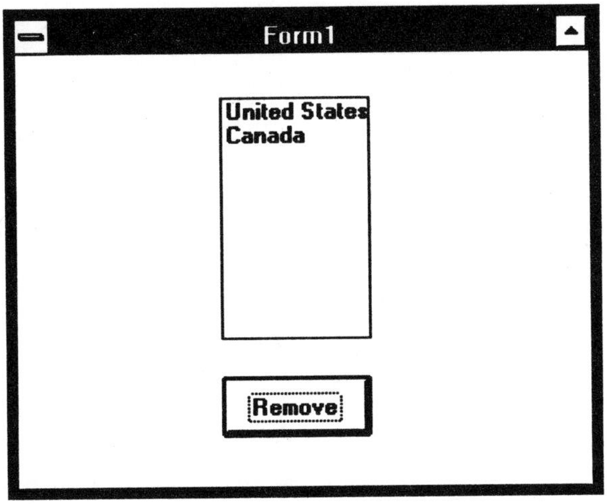

*Figure 12-117 A **RemoveItem** demonstration program (2 of 2).*

Resize Event

Summary:

```
Sub Form_Resize( )
```

Description:

The **Resize** event is called by Visual Basic to tell the program that the form's size has changed.

Example:

The following program demonstrates how the **Resize** event is used by displaying a jumbo-sized command button that fills a form's entire client area. Listing 12-121 presents the code for the program's **Form_Resize** event. Figure 12-118 illustrates how the program's window would appear after the program has been run.

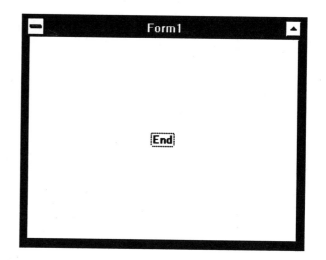

*Figure 12-118 A **Resize** demonstration program.*

Listing 12-121:

```
Sub Form_Resize ()

    Command1.Move 0, 0, ScaleWidth, ScaleHeight

End Sub
```

Scale Method

Summary:

{{[*form.*]*picturebox.*|**Printer.**}**Scale** [(*x1, y1*)-(*x2, y2*)

form	is the desired form.
picturebox	is the desired picture box.
x1, y1	is the object's new upper left coordinates.
x2, y2	is the object's new lower right coordinates.

Description:

The **Scale** method specifies the coordinate system for a form, a picture box, or the **Printer** object. Calling **Scale** without coordinates sets the coordinate system to twips.

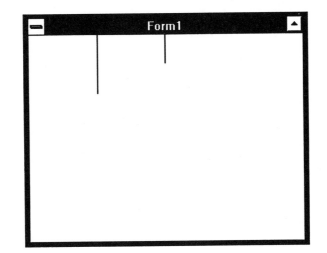

*Figure 12-119 A **Scale** demonstration program.*

Example:

The program that follows demonstrates how the **Scale** method is used by doubling the number of vertical points in a form. Listing 12-122 gives the code for the program's **Form_Click** event. Figure 12-119 shows how the program's window would appear after the program has been run.

Listing 12-122:

```
Sub Form_Click ()

    Line (ScaleWidth / 4, 0)-(ScaleWidth / 4, 1000)
    Scale (0, 0)-(ScaleWidth - 1, ScaleHeight * 2 - 1)
    Line (ScaleWidth / 2, 0)-(ScaleWidth / 2, 1000)

End Sub
```

ScaleHeight Property

Summary:

{[*form.*] [*picturebox.*] | **Printer.**}**ScaleHeight**[= *height*]

form   is the desired form.

`picturebox`   is the desired picture box.

`height`   is the scale's new height.

Description:

The **ScaleHeight** property sets or returns the scale height for a form, a picture box, or the **Printer** object. Positive scale heights run from top to bottom. Negative scale heights run from bottom to top. The scale's height can be set with *height*. You should note that by manually setting a scale's height the **ScaleMode** will be set to 0.

See Also:

ScaleMode and **ScaleWidth**

Example:

The program that appears below shows how the **ScaleHeight** property is used by drawing a line from a form's upper left corner to its lower right corner. Listing 12-123 presents the program's **Form_Click** event. Figure 12-120 illustrates how the

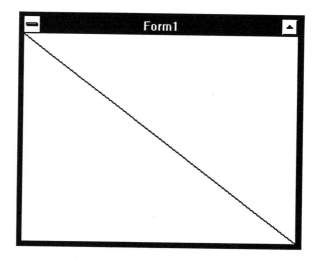

*Figure 12-120 A **ScaleHeight** demonstration program.*

program's window would appear after the program has been run.

Listing 12-123:

```
Sub Form_Click ()

    Line (0, 0)-(ScaleWidth, ScaleHeight)

End Sub
```

ScaleLeft Property

Summary:

{[*form.*] [*picturebox.*]|**Printer.**}**ScaleLeft**[= *x*]

form   is the desired form.

picturebox   is the desired picture box.

x   is the new *x*-coordinate.

Description:

The **ScaleLeft** property sets or returns the leftmost *x*-coordinate for a form, a picture box, or the **Printer** object. A new coordinate can be set with the *x* parameter. By default, **ScaleLeft** is equal to 0.

See Also:

ScaleMode and **ScaleTop**

Example:

The following program demonstrates how the **ScaleLeft** property is used by drawing a line from a form's upper left corner to its lower right corner. Listing 12-124 presents the code for the program's **Form_Click** event. Figure 12-121 illustrates how the program's window would appear after the program has been run.

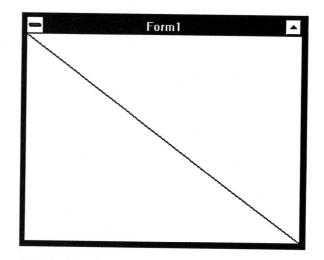

Figure 12-121 A **ScaleLeft** *demonstration program.*

Listing 12-124:

```
Sub Form_Click ()

    Line (ScaleLeft, ScaleTop)-(ScaleWidth,
    ScaleHeight)

End Sub
```

ScaleMode Property

Summary:

{[*form.*] [*picturebox.*]|**Printer.**}**ScaleMode**[= *mode*]

form	is the desired form.
picturebox	is the desired picture box.
mode	is the new coordinate system.

Description:

The **ScaleMode** property sets or returns the coordinate system that is in use by a form, a picture box, or the **Printer** object. The new coordinate system is specified by the *mode* parameter and can be any one of the following values:

Mode	Description
0	User-defined.
1	Twips (1440 twips per logical inch). (Default.)
2	Points (72 points per logical inch).
3	Pixels (1 dot on the monitor).
4	Characters (120 twips per each horizontal unit and 240 twips per each vertical unit.)
5	Inches.
6	Millimeters.
7	Centimeters.

Example:

The following program demonstrates the **ScaleMode** property by changing a form's coordinate system to points. Listing 12-125 presents the code for the program's **Form_Click** event. Figure 12-122 shows how the program's window would appear after the program has been run.

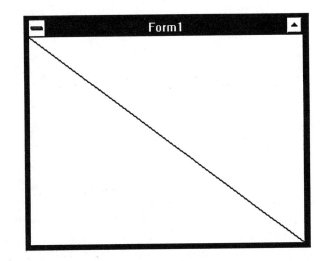

Figure 12-122 A **ScaleMode** *demonstration program.*

Listing 12-125:

```
Sub Form_Click ()

    ScaleMode = 2
    Line (ScaleLeft, ScaleTop)-(ScaleWidth,
    ScaleHeight)

End Sub
```

ScaleTop Property

Summary:

{[*form*.] [*picturebox*.] |**Printer**.}**ScaleTop**[= *y*]

form   is the desired form.

picturebox   is the desired picture box.

y   is the new *y*-coordinate.

Description:

The **ScaleTop** property sets or returns the leftmost *y*-coordinate for a form, a picture box, or the **Printer** object. A new coordinate can be set with the *y* parameter. By default, **ScaleTop** is equal to 0.

See Also:

ScaleLeft and **ScaleMode**

Example:

The program that follows shows how the **ScaleTop** property is used by drawing a line from a form's upper-left corner to its lower-right corner. Listing 12-126 presents the code for the program's **Form_Click** event. Figure 12-123 illustrates how the program's window would appear after the program has been run.

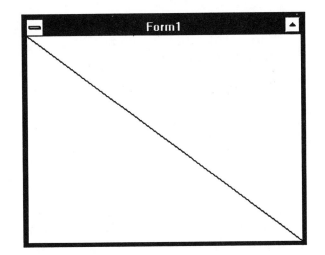

*Figure 12-123 A **ScaleTop** demonstration program.*

Listing 12-126:

```
Sub Form_Click ()

    Line (ScaleLeft, ScaleTop)-(ScaleWidth,
    ScaleHeight)

End Sub
```

ScaleWidth Property

Summary:

{[*form*.] [*picturebox*.]|**Printer**.}**ScaleWidth**[= *width*]

form   is the desired form.

picturebox   is the desired picture box.

width   is the scale's new width.

Description:

The **ScaleWidth** property sets or returns the scale width for a form, a picture box, or the **Printer** object. Positive scale widths run from the left to the right. Negative scale widths run from the right to the left. The scale's width can be set with *width*. You should note that by manually setting a scale's height the **ScaleMode** will be set to 0.

See Also:

ScaleHeight and **ScaleMode**

Example:

The program that appears below demonstrates how the **ScaleWidth** property is used by drawing a line from a form's upper-left corner to its lower-right corner. Listing 12-127 gives the code for the program's **Form_Click** event. Figure 12-124 shows how the program's window would appear after the program has been run.

Listing 12-127:

```
Sub Form_Click ()

    Line (ScaleLeft, ScaleTop)-(ScaleWidth,
    ScaleHeight)

End Sub
```

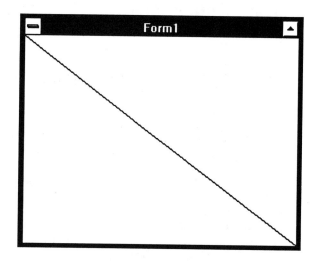

*Figure 12-124 A **ScaleWidth** demonstration program.*

ScrollBars Property

Summary:

`[form.] textbox.`**`ScrollBars`**

form	is the text box control's form.
textbox	is the desired text box.

Description:

The **ScrollBars** property determines what type, if any, scroll bars a text box control has. You should note that the **ScrollBars** property is read-only at run time and only multiline text box controls can have scroll bars. The values returned by the **ScrollBars** property can be any one of these:

Value	Description
0	No scroll bars (Default)
1	Horizontal
2	Vertical
3	Both

Example:

The program below shows how the **ScrollBars** property is used to add both vertical and horizontal scroll bars to a multiline text box control. Listing 12-128 presents the code for the program's **Form_Click** event. Figure 12-125 illustrates how the program's window would appear after the program has been run.

Listing 12-128:

```
Sub Form_Click ()

    Select Case Text1.ScrollBars
        Case 0:
            Text1.Text = "Text1 doesn't have any
            scroll bars!"
```

```
        Case 1:
            Text1.Text = "Text1 has a horizontal
            scroll bar!"
        Case 2:
            Text1.Text = "Text1 has a vertical scroll
            bar!"
        Case 3:
            Text1.Text = "Text1 has a horizontal and a
            vertical scroll bar!"
    End Select

End Sub
```

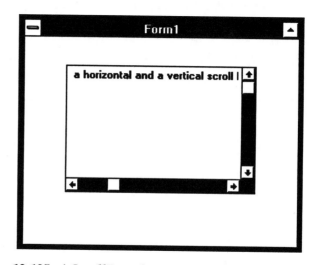

Figure 12-125 A **ScrollBars** *demonstration program.*

SelLength Property

Summary:

[*form.*]{*combobox.*|*textbox.*}**SelLength**[= *length*]

form   is the control's form.

combobox   is the desired combo box.

textbox   is the desired text box.

length   is the selected text's new length.

Description:

The **SelLength** property sets or returns the length of a selected string for a combo box or a text box. The valid range for the **SelLength** property can extend from 0 to the number of characters in the control.

See Also:

SelStart and **SelText**

Example:

The following program demonstrates how the **SelLength** property is used to display the length of a selected string when a form is clicked. Listing 12-129 presents the code for the program's **Form_Click** event. Figure 12-126 shows how the program's window would appear after the program has been run.

Listing 12-129:

```
Sub Form_Click ()

    Print "Selected text length: "; Text1.SelLength

End Sub
```

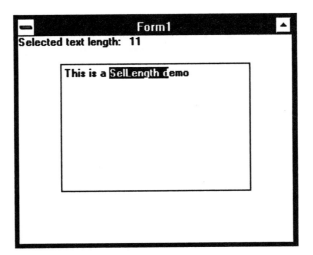

*Figure 12-126 The **SelLength** demonstration program.*

SelStart Property

Summary:

[*form.*] {*combobox.* | *textbox.*}**SelStart**[= *position*]

form	is the control's form.
combobox	is the desired combo box.
textbox	is the desired text box.
position	is the new insertion point.

Description:

The **SelStart** property returns the starting position of a selected string for a combo box or a text box. If there isn't any text selected in the control, the **SelStart** property returns the position of the insertion point in the text string. Whenever a *position* is assigned to the **SelStart** property, Visual Basic will use the *position* value for the new insertion point and set the control's **SelLength** to 0.

See Also:

SelLength and **SelText**

Example:

The program that follows shows how the **SelStart** property is used to display the starting position of a selected string when a form is clicked. Listing 12-130 presents the code for the program's **Form_Click** event. Figure 12-127 illustrates how the program's window would appear after the program has been run.

Listing 12-130:

```
Sub Form_Click ()

    Print "Selected text start: "; Text1.SelStart

End Sub
```

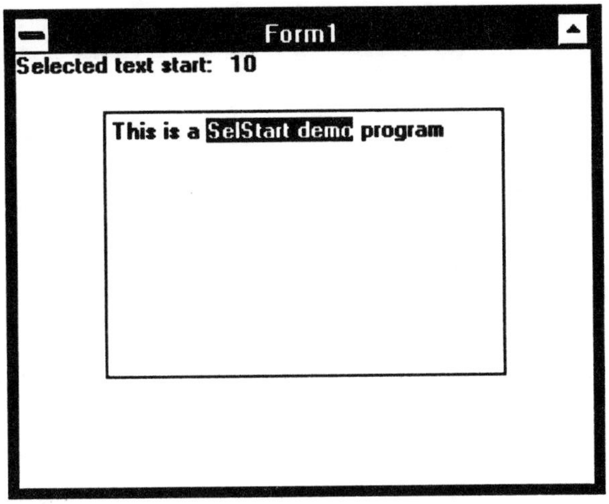

Figure 12-127 A **SelStart** *demonstration program.*

SelText Property

Summary:

[form.] {*combobox.* | *textbox.*} **SelText** [= *string*]

form	is the control's form.
combobox	is desired combo box.
textbox	is the desired text box.
string	is the replacement string.

Description:

The **SelText** property sets or returns the selected string for a combo box or a text box. If there isn't a selected string, the **SelText** property returns a null string (""). If a *string* is assigned to the **SelText** property, the currently selected string will be replaced with the specified string.

See Also:

SelLength and **SelStart**

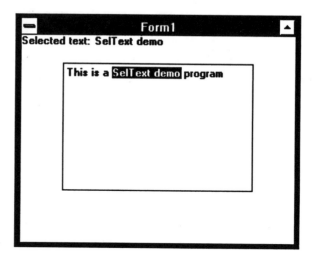

*Figure 12-128 A **SelText** demonstration program.*

Example:

The program that appears below demonstrates how the **SelText** property is used to display a selected string when a form is clicked. Listing 12-131 presents the code for the program's **Form_Click** event. Figure 12-128 shows how the program's window would appear after the program has been run.

Listing 12-131:

```
Sub Form_Click ()

    Print "Selected text: "; Text1.SelText

End Sub
```

SetData Method

Summary:

Clipboard.SetData *picture[, format]*

picture	is the picture to place on the clipboard.
format	is the picture's format.

Description:

The **SetData** method places a picture on the clipboard. The type of picture to save is specified with the *format* parameter and can be one of these values:

Format	Description
2	Bitmap (Default)
3	Metafile
8	Device-independent bitmap

Example:

The below program demonstrates how the **SetData** method is used by saving a form's image on the clipboard. Listing 12-132-1 presents the code for the program's **Form_Load** event, and Listing 12-132-2 the code for the program's **Form_Click** event. Figure 12-129 illustrates how the program's window would appear after the program has been run.

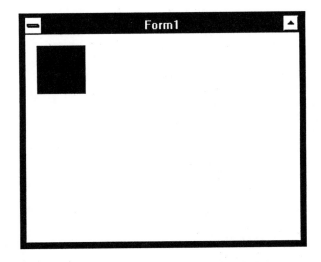

*Figure 12-129 A **SetData** demonstration program.*

Listing 12-132-1:

```
Sub Form_Load ()

    AutoRedraw = -1

End Sub
```

Listing 12-132-2:

```
Sub Form_Click ()
    Static Cnt As Integer

    Select Case Cnt
        Case 0
            Line (200, 200)-(1000, 1000), , BF
        Case 1
            ClipBoard.SetData (Image)
            Cls
        Case 2
            Picture = ClipBoard.GetData()
        Case Else
    End Select
    Cnt = Cnt + 1

End Sub
```

SetFocus Method

Summary:

[*form.*] [*control.*]**SetFocus**

form   is the desired form.

control   is the desired control.

Description:

The **SetFocus** method sets the focus to either a form or a control.

See Also:

GetFocus

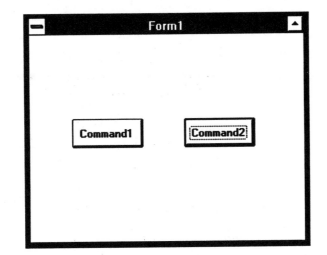

Figure 12-130 A **SetFocus** *demonstration program.*

Example:

The following program shows how the **SetFocus** method is used by setting the focus to the second of two command buttons when a form is clicked. Listing 12-133 gives the code for the program's **Form_Click** event. Figure 12-130 illustrates how the program's window would appear after the program has been run.

Listing 12-133:

```
Sub Form_Click ()

    Command2.SetFocus

End Sub
```

SetText Method

Summary:

Clipboard.SetText *string*[*,format*]

string	is the string to be saved on the clipboard.
format	is the data format.

Description:

The **SetText** method places a string on the clipboard. The string's data format can optionally be specified by *format* and can be one of these values:

Format	Description
&HBF00	Dynamic data exchange link
1	Text (Default)

See Also:

GetText

Example:

The program that follows demonstrates how the **SetText** method is used by saving a text box control's selected text on the clipboard and then displaying it on the same form. Listing 12-134 presents the code for the program's **Form_Click** event. Figure 12-131 illustrates how the program's window would appear after the program has been run.

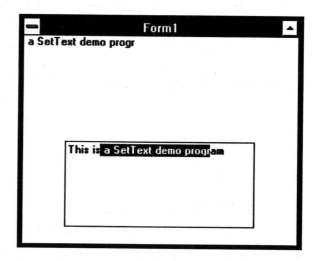

*Figure 12-131 A **SetText** demonstration program.*

Listing 12-134:

```
Sub Form_Click ()

    Clipboard.SetText Text1.SelText
    Print Clipboard.GetText()

End Sub
```

Show Method

Summary:

[*form.*]**Show** [*style*]

form	is the desired form.
style	is the form's style.

Description:

The **Show** method displays a specified form. If the form isn't already loaded into memory, Visual Basic will first load the form and then display it. An optional style can be specified for the form with the *style* parameter and can be one of the following values:

Style	Description
0	Modeless. (Default.)
1	Modal. When a modal form is displayed, no other form in the application can accept input. The modal form must either be hidden or unloaded for other forms to accept input.

See Also:

Hide, Load, and **Unload**

Example:

The program that follows demonstrates how the **Show** method is used to display a form. Listing 12-135 presents the code for **Form1's Form_Click** event. Figure 12-132 shows how the desktop would appear after the program has been run.

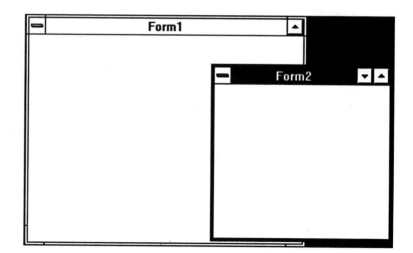

*Figure 12-132 A **Show** demonstration program.*

Listing 12-135:

```
Sub Form_Click ()
    Form2.Show

End Sub
```

SmallChange Property

Summary:

[*form*.] [*hscrollbar*|*vscrollbar*}.**SmallChange**[= *change*]

form	is the scroll bar's form.
hscrollbar	is the desired horizontal scroll bar.
vscrollbar	is the desired vertical scroll bar.
change	is the new amount of change.

Description:

The **SmallChange** property sets and returns the amount of change that occurs to a scroll bar's **Value** property when the scroll bar's arrows are clicked.

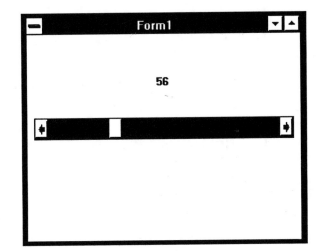

*Figure 12-133 A **SmallChange** demonstration program.*

See Also:

LargeChange

Example:

The below program demonstrates how the **SmallChange** property is used to regulate the amount of scrolling that occurs when a user clicks the scroll bar arrows. Listing 12-136-1 presents the code for the program's **Form_Load** event, and Listing 12-136-2 the code for the program's **HScroll1_Change** event. Figure 12-133 illustrates how the program's window would appear after the program has been run.

Listing 12-136-1:

```
Sub Form_Load ()

    Label1.Caption = Str$(HScroll1.Value)
    HScroll1.Max = 200
    HScroll1.SmallChange = 2

End Sub
```

Listing 12-136-2:

```
Sub HScroll1_Change ()

    Label1.Caption = Str$(HScroll1.Value)

End Sub
```

Sorted Property

Summary:

[*form.*] {*combobox*|*listbox*}.**Sorted**

form	is the control's form.
combobox	is the desired combo box.
listbox	is the desired list box.

Description:

The **Sorted** property determines whether or not the items in a combo box or a list box are sorted alphabetically. If the **Sorted** property is set to True, Visual Basic will maintain a sorted list for the control. If the **Sorted** property is set to False (the

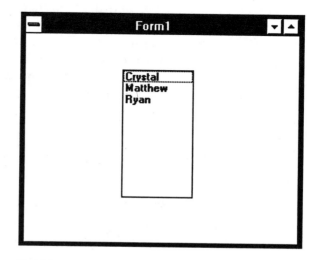

*Figure 12-134 A **Sorted** demonstration program.*

default), Visual Basic will not sort the list for the control. You should note that the **Sorted** property is read-only at run time.

Example:

The following program demonstrates how the **Sorted** property is used to maintain a sorted list box control. Listing 12-137 presents the code for the program's **Form_Load** event. Figure 12-134 shows how the program's window would appear after the program has been run.

Listing 12-137:

```
Sub Form_Load ()

    List1.AddItem "Ryan"
    List1.AddItem "Matthew"
    List1.AddItem "Crystal"

End Sub
```

Style Property

Summary:

`[form.] combobox.Style`

form	is the combo box's form.
combobox	is the desired combo box.

Description:

The **Style** property determines the style of a combo box control. You should note that the **Style** property is read-only at run time and will return one of the following values:

Style	*Description*
0	Dropdown combo box. This type of combo box features an edit area and a list area. The list area can be viewed by clicking the scroll arrow to the right of the edit area. (Default.)

(continued)

Style	Description
1	Simple combo box. This type of combo box features an edit area and a list area. Unlike the dropdown combo box's list area, the simple combo box's list area is displayed at all times.
2	Dropdown list box. This type of combo box features a list area only. The list area can be viewed by clicking the scroll arrow.

Example:

The program that follows shows how the **Style** property is used to create a simple combo box control. Listing 12-138 gives the code for the program's **Form_Load** event. Figure 12-135 illustrates how the program's window would appear after the program has been run.

Listing 12-138:

```
Sub Form_Load ()

    Combo1.AddItem "Ryan"
    Combo1.AddItem "Matthew"
    Combo1.AddItem "Crystal"

End Sub
```

System Property

Summary:

*[form.]filelistbox.***System***[= flag]*

form	is the file list box's form.
filelistbox	is the desired file list box.
flag	is the new system attribute setting.

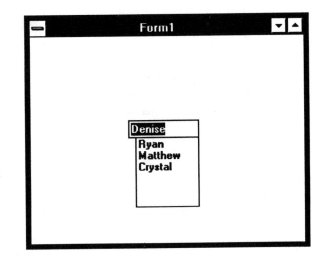

*Figure 12-135 A **Style** demonstration program.*

Description:

The **System** property is used to either set or return a file list box's system attribute setting. If the **System** property is set to True, Visual Basic will display files with their system attributes set in the file list box. If the **System** property is set to False (the default), Visual Basic will not display files with their system attributes set in the file list box.

See Also:

Archive, Hidden, Normal, and **ReadOnly**

Example:

The program that follows demonstrates how the **System** property is used by setting a file list box's system attribute to True. Listing 12-139 presents the code for the program's **Form_Click** event. Figure 12-136 illustrates how the program's window would appear after the program has been run.

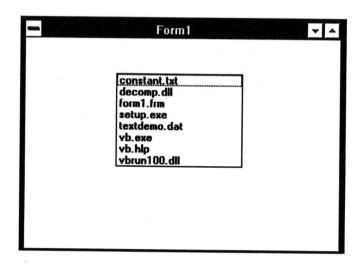

*Figure 12-136 A **System** demonstration program.*

Listing 12-139:

```
Sub Form_Click ()

    File1.System = -1

End Sub
```

TabIndex Property

Summary:

[*form.*] *control*.**TabIndex**[= *index*]

form   is the control's form.

control   is the desired control.

index   is the control's new tab index setting.

Description:

The **TabIndex** property sets or returns the tab stop for a check box, a combo box, a command button, a directory list box, a drive list box, a file list box, a frame, a horizontal scroll bar, a label, a list box, an option button, a picture box, a text box, or a vertical scroll bar. Essentially, a form's tab stops control the order in which Visual Basic moves the focus from control to control as the user presses the TAB key. At design time, Visual Basic assigns the tab stop order as the same order in which you place controls on the form. The tab stops are numbered from 0 to n - 1, where n is the number of controls on the form. A control's position in a sequence of tab stops can be changed with the *index* parameter. After assigning a new tab stop to a control, Visual Basic will automatically renumber the remaining controls to reflect the change.

See Also:

TabStop

Example:

The below program demonstrates how the **TabIndex** property is used to assign the first tab stop to the third command button in a series of five command buttons. Listing 12-140 presents the code for the program's **Form_Load** event. Figure 12-137 shows how the program's window would appear after the program has been run.

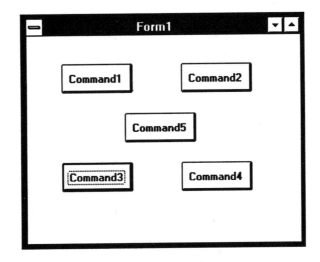

Figure 12-137 A **TabIndex** *demonstration program.*

Listing 12-140:

```
Sub Form_Load ()

    Command3.TabIndex = 0

End Sub
```

TabStop Property

Summary:

[*form.*] *control*.**TabStop**[= *flag*]

form   is the control's form.

control   is the desired control.

flag   is the control's new tab stop setting.

Description:

The **TabStop** property sets or returns whether or not a check box, a combo box, a command button, a directory list box, a drive list box, a file list box, a horizontal scroll bar, a list box, an option button, a picture box, a text box, or a vertical scroll bar can receive the focus due to the user TABing to the control. If the **TabStop** property is set to True (the default), the control can receive the focus through the TAB key. If the **TabStop** property is set to False, the control can't receive the focus through the TAB key.

See Also:

TabIndex

Example:

The following program shows how the **TabStop** property is used to prevent the third command button in a series of five command buttons from receiving the focus. Listing 12-141

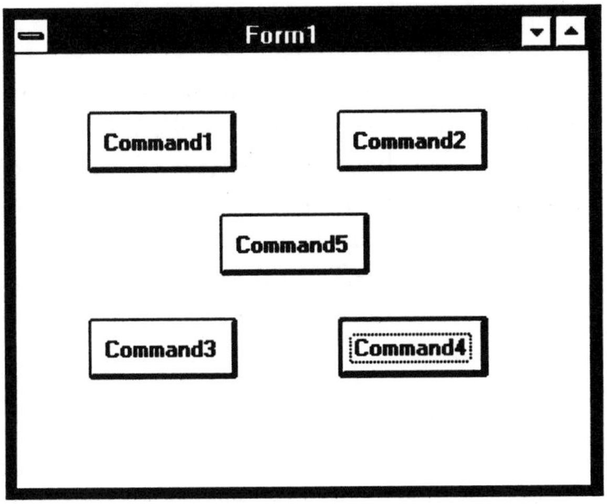

Figure 12-138 A **TabStop** *demonstration program.*

presents the code for the program's **Form_Load** event. Figure 12-138 illustrates how the program's window would appear after the program has been run.

Listing 12-141:

```
Sub Form_Load ()

    Command3.TabStop = 0

End Sub
```

Tag Property

Summary:

[*form.*] [*control.*] **Tag** [= *string*]

form   is the desired form.

control   is the desired control.

string   is the new tag.

Description:

The **Tag** property is used to set and return a temporary string value for a form, a check box, a combo box, a command button, a directory list box, a drive list box, a file list box, a frame, a horizontal scroll bar, a label, a list box, a menu, an option button, a picture box, a text box, a timer, or a vertical scroll bar. By default, the **Tag** property is set to a null string ("").

Example:

The program that follows demonstrates how the **Tag** property is used by setting and displaying a temporary tag value. Listing 12-142-1 presents the code for the program's **Form_Load** event, and Listing 12-142-2 the code for the program's **Form_Click** event. Figure 12-139 illustrates how the program's window would appear after the program has been run.

Listing 12-142-1:

```
Sub Form_Load ()

    Tag = "Form1 Tag"

End Sub
```

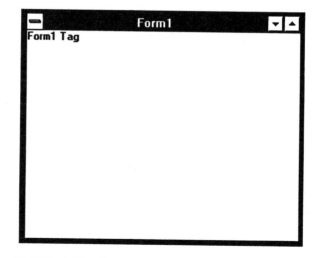

*Figure 12-139 A **Tag** demonstration program.*

Listing 12-142-2:

```
Sub Form_Click ()

    Print Tag

End Sub
```

Text Property

Summary:

*[form.] [combobox.|listbox.|textbox.}***Text**[= *string*]

form	is the control's form.
combobox	is the desired combo box.
listbox	is the desired list box.
textbox	is the desired text box.
string	is the control's new text.

Description:

The **Text** property sets or returns the contents of a combo box, a list box, or a text box. If the control is a combo box, the **Text** property sets or returns the text in the edit area for a dropdown combo or a simple combo or returns the selected item for a dropdown list. If the control is a list box, the **Text** property returns the selected item.

Example:

The program that follows demonstrates how the **Text** property is used by displaying a text box control's text whenever the control's form is clicked. Listing 12-143 gives the code for the program's **Form_Click** event. Figure 12-140 shows how the program's window would appear after the program has been run.

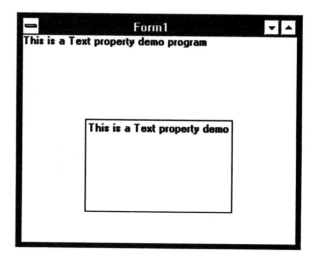

*Figure 12-140 A **Text** demonstration program.*

Listing 12-143:

```
Sub Form_Click ()

    Print Text1.Text

End Sub
```

TextHeight Method

Summary:

`{form.|picturebox.|`**Printer.**`}`**TextHeight**`(string)`

form   is the desired form.

picturebox   is the desired picture box.

string   is the string to return the height of.

Description:

The **TextHeight** method returns the height of a specified *string* as it would be displayed in the current font for a form, a picture box, or the **Printer** object.

See Also:

TextWidth

Example:

The program below shows how the **TextHeight** method is used to center a string in a form's client area. Listing 12-144 presents the code for the program's **Form_Click** event. Figure 12-141 illustrates how the program's window would appear after the program has been run.

Listing 12-144:

```
Sub Form_Click ()
    Dim TH As Integer, TW As Integer, Message As
    String

    Message = "A Centered String!"
    TH = TextHeight(Message)
    TW = TextWidth(Message)
    CurrentY = ScaleHeight / 2 - TH / 2
    CurrentX = ScaleWidth / 2 - TW / 2
    Print Message

End Sub
```

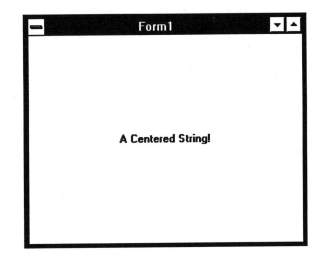

Figure 12-141 A **TextHeight** *demonstration program.*

TextWidth Method

Summary:

{*form.*|*picturebox.*|**Printer.**}**TextWidth**(*string*)

form	is the desired form.
picturebox	is the desired picture box.
string	is the string to return the width of.

Description:

The **TextWidth** method returns the width of a specified *string* as it would be displayed in the current font for a form, a picture box, or the **Printer** object.

See Also:

TextHeight

Example:

The following program demonstrates how the **TextWidth** method is used to center a string in a form's client area. Listing 12-145 presents the code for the program's **Form_Click** event. Figure 12-142 shows how the program's window would appear after the program has been run.

Listing 12-145:

```
Sub Form_Click ()
    Dim TH As Integer, TW As Integer, Message As String

    Message = "A Centered String!"
    TH = TextHeight(Message)
    TW = TextWidth(Message)
    CurrentY = ScaleHeight / 2 - TH / 2
    CurrentX = ScaleWidth / 2 - TW / 2
    Print Message

End Sub
```

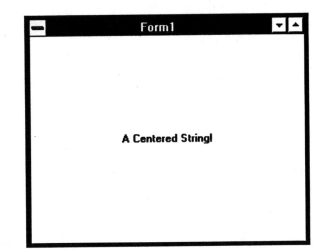

Figure 12-142 A **TextWidth** *demonstration program.*

Timer Event

Summary:

```
Sub timer_Timer([index As Integer])
```

timer   is the desired timer.

index   is the control's index in an array of controls.

Description:

The **Timer** event is called by Visual Basic when a timer control's interval has elapsed. In order for this event to be called, the timer control's **Interval** property must be set to an appropriate value and its **Enabled** property must be set to True.

See Also:

Enabled and **Interval**

Description:

The program that follows shows how the **Timer** event is used to display a message on the form every 10 seconds. Listing

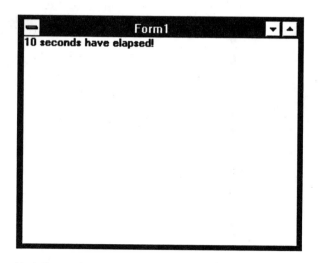

*Figure 12-143 A **Timer** demonstration program.*

12-146-1 presents the code for the program's **Form_Load** event, and Listing 12-146-2 the code for the program's **Timer1_Timer** event. Figure 12-143 illustrates how the program's window would appear after the program has been run.

Listing 12-146-1:

```
Sub Form_Load ()

    Timer1.Interval = 10000

End Sub
```

Listing 12-146-2:

```
Sub Timer1_Timer ()

    Print "10 seconds have elapsed!"

End Sub
```

Top Property

Summary:

[*form.*][*control.*]**Left**[= *y*]

form	is the desired form.
control	is the desired control.
y	is the new *y*-coordinate.

Description:

The **Top** property sets or returns the *y*-coordinate for a form, a check box, a combo box, a command button, a directory list box, a drive list box, a file list box, a frame, a horizontal scroll bar, a label, a list box, an option button, a picture box, a text box, or a vertical scroll bar. A form's **Top** property is always in twips. A control's **Top** property is expressed using its container's coordinate system.

See Also:

Left

Example:

The program that appears below demonstrates how the **Top** property is used by centering a command button in a form. Listing 12-147 presents the code for the program's **Command1_Click** event. Figure 12-144 illustrates how the program's window appears before the command button is clicked; Figure 12-145 shows how it appears after the command button is clicked.

Listing 12-147:

```
Sub Command1_Click ()

    Command1.Left = Form1.ScaleWidth / 2 -
    Command1.Width / 2
    Command1.Top = Form1.ScaleHeight / 2 -
    Command1.Height / 2

End Sub
```

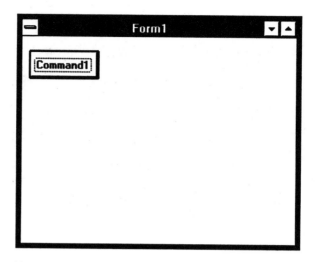

Figure 12-144 A **Top** *demonstration program (1 of 2).*

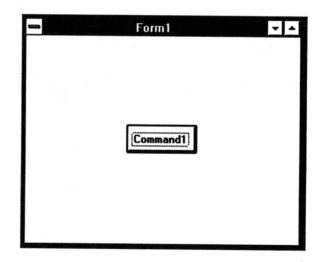

Figure 12-145 A **Top** *demonstration program (2 of 2).*

Unload Event

Summary:

Sub Form_Unload(*cancel* **As Integer**)

cancel　　　　is the event return value.

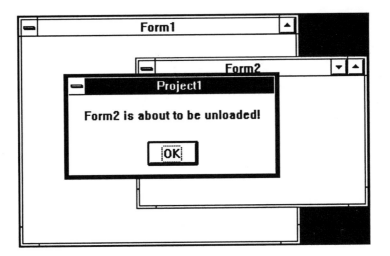

Figure 12-146 An **Unload** *demonstration program.*

Description:

The **Unload** event is called by Visual Basic to tell the program when a form is about to be unloaded. The unloading of the form can be aborted by changing the event's *cancel* parameter to a nonzero value.

Example:

The below program demonstrates how the **Unload** event is used by displaying a message box when a form is about to be unloaded. Listing 12-148-1 gives the code for the first form's **Form_Click** event, and Listing 12-148-2 the code for the second form's **Form_Unload** event. Figure 12-146 illustrates how the desktop appears after the program has been run.

Listing 12-148-1:

```
Sub Form_Click ()

    Form2.Show

End Sub
```

Listing 12-148-2:

```
Sub Form_Unload (Cancel As Integer)

    MsgBox "Form2 is about to be unloaded!"

End Sub
```

Value Property

Summary:

[*form.*] [*control.*]**Value**[= *value*]

form	is the control's form.
control	is the desired control.
value	is the control's new value setting.

Description:

The **Value** property is used to set or return the current state of a check box, an option box, a command button, a horizontal scroll bar, or a vertical scroll bar. For a check box control, the **Value** property can be set to 0 for Off (the default), 1 for On, and 2 for Grayed. For an option button or a command button, the **Value** property is either True or False. For scroll bars, the

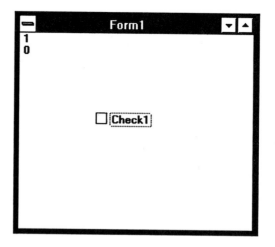

*Figure 12-147 A **Value** demonstration program.*

Value property represents the position of the scroll box and can be any value between -32,768 and 32,767.

Example:

The following program demonstrates how the **Value** property is used by displaying the current state of check button. Listing 12-149 presents the code for the program's **Check1_Click** event. Figure 12-147 shows how the program's window would appear after the program has been run.

Listing 12-149:

```
Sub Check1_Click ()

    Print Check1.Value

End Sub
```

Visible Property

Summary:

[*form.*] [*control.*]**Visible**[= *flag*]

form   is the desired form.

control   is the desired control.

flag   is the form or control's new setting.

Description:

The **Visible** property sets or returns the visual state of a form, a check box, a combo box, a command button, a directory list box, a drive list box, a file list box, a frame, a horizontal scroll bar, a label, a list box, a menu, an option button, a picture box, a text box, or a vertical scroll bar. If the **Visible** property is set to True (the default), the form or control will be displayed. If the **Visible** property is set to False, the form or control will not be displayed.

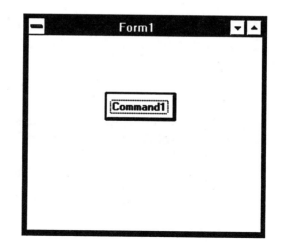

*Figure 12-148 A **Visible** demonstration program.*

Example:

The program that follows shows how the **Visible** property is used to hide and redisplay a command button whenever another command button is pressed. Listing 12-150 presents the code for the program's **Command1_Click** event. Figure 12-148 illustrates how the program's window would appear after the program has been run.

Listing 12-150:

```
Sub Command1_Click ()

    Command2.Visible = Not Command2.Visible

End Sub
```

Width Property

Summary:

{[*form.*] [*control.*] |**Printer.**|**Screen.**}**Width**[= *width*] form   is the desired form.

control   is the desired control.

width   is the form or control's new width.

Description:

The **Width** property sets or returns the width of a form, a check box, a combo box, a command button, a directory list box, a drive list box, a file list box, a frame, a horizontal scroll bar, a label, a list box, an option button, a picture box, a text box, or a vertical scroll bar. Additionally, the **Width** property returns the width of the **Screen** object and the **Printer** object.

See Also:

Height

Example:

The program that appears below demonstrates how the **Width** property is used by displaying the width of the **Screen** object, the form, and the **Printer** object. Listing 12-151 presents the code for the program's **Form_Click** event. Figure 12-149 shows how the program's window would appear after the program has been run.

Listing 12-151:

```
Sub Form_Click ()

    Print "The screen's width is"; Screen.Width
    Print "The form's width is"; Width
    Print "The printer's width is"; Printer.Width

End Sub
```

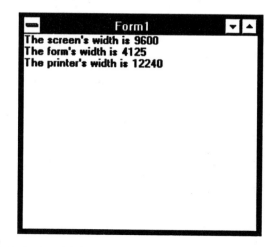

Figure 12-149 A **Width** *demonstration program.*

WindowState Property

Summary:

[*form.*]**WindowState**[= *state*]

form   is the desired form.

state   is the form's new display state.

Description:

The **WindowState** property sets or returns the display state for a form. A new state can be set with the *state* parameter and can be one of these values:

State	Description
0	Normal (Default)
1	Minimized
2	Maximized

*Figure 12-150 A **WindowState** demonstration program.*

Example:

The below program shows how the **WindowState** property is used by minimizing a form when it is clicked. Listing 12-152 gives the code for the program's **Form_Click** event. Figure 12-150 illustrates how the desktop would appear after the form has been clicked.

Listing 12-152:

```
Sub Form_Click ()

    WindowState = 1

End Sub
```

PART III

THE VISUAL BASIC STATEMENTS AND FUNCTIONS

T his section of *The Power of Visual Basic* provides a complete reference guide to Visual Basic's many statements and functions.

Chapter 13

The Visual Basic Statements and Functions

T his chapter provides the reader with a detailed reference guide to the many statements and functions that are built into the Visual Basic programming language. To show how they are used in Visual Basic programs, this section describes each of the Visual Basic statements and functions as follows:

Summary:

Presents an exact syntactic model for each of the Visual Basic statements and functions.

Description:

Describes a statement's or function's purpose and how it is used in an application program.

See Also:

Lists any similar or related Visual Basic statements or functions.

Example:

Illustrates how a Visual Basic statement or function could actually be used in an application program.

Abs Function

Summary:

Abs(*expression*)

expression   is a numeric expression.

Description:

The **Abs** function returns the unsigned value of the specified numeric *expression*.

Example:

The following program demonstrates how the **Abs** function is used on a variety of numeric expressions. Listing 13-1 presents the code for the program's **Form_Click** event. Figure 13-1 illustrates how the program's window would appear after the program has been run.

Listing 13-1:

```
Sub Form_Click ()
    Dim N As Integer

    N = -3
    Print Abs(N)
    Print Abs(-32.333)
    Print Abs(32.3333)

End Sub
```

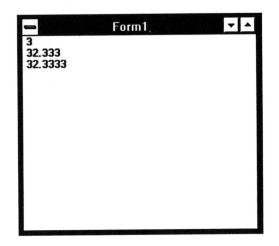

Figure 13-1 An **Abs** *demonstration program.*

AppActivate Statement

Summary:

AppActivate *application*

application   is a string expression.

Description:

The **AppActivate** changes the focus from the current application program to the program whose title is specified by *application*.

Example:

The program that follows demonstrates how the **AppActivate** statement is used to change the focus from one program to another. Listing 13-2 presents the code for the program's **Form_Click** event. Figure 13-2 shows how the desktop would appear after the program has been run.

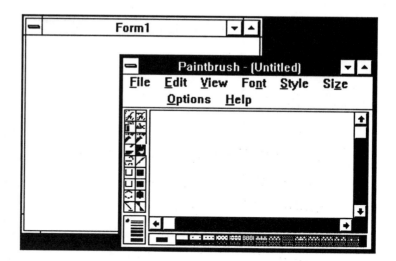

*Figure 13-2 An **AppActivate** demonstration program.*

Listing 13-2:

```
Sub Form_Click ()

    AppActivate "Paintbrush - (Untitled)"

End Sub
```

Asc Function

Summary:

Asc(*expression*)

expression   is a string expression.

Description:

The **Asc** function returns the ASCII code of the first character of the specified string *expression*. You should note that the string must be at least one character long or an error will result.

See Also:

Chr$

*Figure 13-3 An **Asc** demonstration program.*

Example:

The program that appears below shows how the **Asc** function is used on a variety of string expressions. Listing 13-3 presents the code for the program's **Form_Click** event. Figure 13-3 illustrates how the program's window would appear after the program has been run.

Listing 13-3:

```
Sub Form_Click ()

    A$ = "Visual Basic is pretty neat"
    Print Asc(" ")
    Print Asc(A$)

End Sub
```

Atn Function

Summary:

Atn(*expression*)

expression   is a numeric expression.

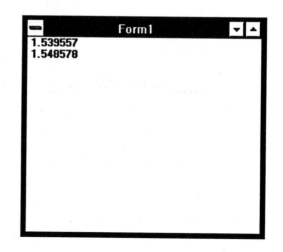

*Figure 13-4 An **Atn** demonstration program.*

Description:

The **Atn** function returns the arctangent of a numeric *expression*. The return value will be in radians. If the numeric *expression* was an **Integer** or a **Single**, a single-precision result will be returned. Otherwise, Visual Basic will return a double-precision result.

See Also:

Tan

Example:

The following program demonstrates how the **Atn** function is used on a variety of numeric expressions. Listing 13-4 presents the code for the program's **Form_Click** event. Figure 13-4 shows how the program's window would appear after the program has been run.

Listing 13-4:

```
Sub Form_Click ()

    Print Atn(32)
    Print Atn(45)

End Sub
```

Beep Statement

Summary:

Beep

Description:

The **Beep** statements generates a beep on the computer's speaker.

Example:

The following program shows how the **Beep** statement is used by beeping whenever the form is clicked. Listing 13-5-1 gives the code for the program's **Form_Paint** event, and Listing 13-5-2 presents the code for the program's **Form_Click** event. Figure 13-5 illustrates how the program's window would appear after the program has been run.

Listing 13-5-1:

```
Sub Form_Paint ()

    Print "Click me and I'll beep!"

End Sub
```

*Figure 13-5 A **Beep** demonstration program.*

Listing 13-5-2:

```
Sub Form_Click ()

    Beep

End Sub
```

Call Statement

Summary:

Call *name*[(*argument*[, *argument*]...)]

name	is the name of the procedure.
argument	is one of more arguments to be passed to the procedure.

Description:

The **Call** statement calls a **Sub** procedure or a dynamic-link library procedure specified by *name* and passes one or more *argument*s to the procedure. You should note that using the **Call** statement isn't strictly required and is provided by Visual Basic to maintain compatibility with older forms of Basic.

*Figure 13-6 A **Call** demonstration program.*

See Also:

Declare

Example:

The program that follows shows how the **Call** statement is used by calling a **Sub** procedure. Listing 13-6-1 presents the code for the program's **Form_Click** event; Listing 13-6-2 gives the code for the program's **DisplayTimesTwo** procedure. Figure 13-6 illustrates how the program's window would appear after the program has been run.

Listing 13-6-1:

```
Sub Form_Click ()

    N = 2
    Call DisplayTimesTwo(N)
    Call DisplayTimesTwo(4)
    Call DisplayTimesTwo(N * 4)

End Sub
```

Listing 13-6-2:

```
Sub DisplayTimesTwo (N)

    Print N * 2

End Sub
```

CCur Function

Summary:

CCur (*expression*)

expression   is a numeric expression.

Description:

The **CCur** function converts the result of a numeric *expression* to a currency result.

Example:

The program that appears below demonstrates the **CCur** function by converting the results of a variety of expressions to currency values. Listing 13-7 presents the code for the program's **Form_Click** event. Figure 13-7 shows how the program's window would appear after the program has been run.

Listing 13-7:

```
Sub Form_Click ()

    N@ = CCur(22 / 7)
    Print N@
    Print 22 / 7
    Print CCur(22 / 7)
    Print 22@ / 7@

End Sub
```

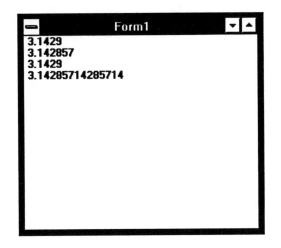

Figure 13-7 A **CCur** *demonstration program.*

CDbl Function

Summary:

`CDbl(expression)`

`expression`   is a numeric expression.

Description:

The **CDbl** function converts the result of a numeric *expression* to a double-precision result.

Example:

The following program demonstrates the **CDbl** function by converting the results of a variety of expressions to double precision. Listing 13-8 presents the code for the program's **Form_Click** event. Figure 13-8 illustrates how the program's window would appear after the program has been run.

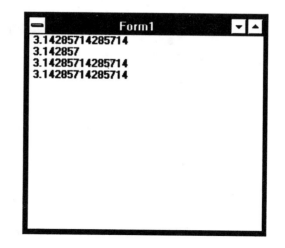

*Figure 13-8 A **CDbl** demonstration program.*

Listing 13-8:

```
Sub Form_Click ()

    N# = CDbl(22 / 7)
    Print N#
    Print 22 / 7
    Print CDbl(22 / 7)
    Print 22# / 7#

End Sub
```

ChDir Statement

Summary:

ChDir *path*

path   is the path for the new default directory.

Description:

The **ChDir** statement changes the current default directory to the one specified by the string expression *path*.

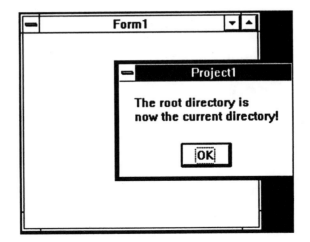

Figure 13-9 A **ChDir** *demonstration program.*

See Also:

ChDrive, CurDir$, Dir$, MkDir, and **RmDir**

Example:

The following program demonstrates the **ChDir** statement by changing the default directory for the C: drive. Listing 13-9 presents the code for the program's **Form_Click** event. Figure 13-9 shows how the program's window would appear after the program has been run.

Listing 13-9:

```
Sub Form_Click ()

    ChDir "C:\"
    MsgBox "The root directory is " + Chr$(13) +
    Chr$(10) + "now the current directory!"

End Sub
```

ChDrive Statement

Summary:

ChDrive *drive*

drive   is the new current drive.

Description:

The **ChDrive** statement changes the current drive to the one specified by the string expression *drive*.

See Also:

ChDir, CurDir, Dir$, MkDir, and **RmDir**

Example:

The program that follows demonstrates how the **ChDrive** statement is used by changing the current drive to the A: drive. Listing 13-10 presents the code for the program's **Form_Click** event. Figure 13-10 illustrates how the program's window would appear after the program has been run.

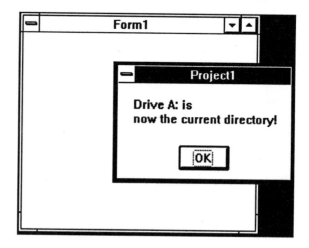

*Figure 13-10 A **ChDrive** demonstration program.*

Listing 13-10:

```
Sub Form_Click ()

    ChDrive "A:"
    MsgBox "Drive A: is " + Chr$(13) + Chr$(10) +
    "now the current directory!"

End Sub
```

Chr$ Function

Summary:

Chr$(*asciicode*)

asciicode   is a number from 0 to 255.

Description:

The **Chr$** function returns a single-character string result. The character's ASCII code is specified by *asciicode*.

See Also:

Asc

Example:

The program that appears below demonstrates the **Chr$** function by displaying 1000 random characters. Listing 13-11 gives the code for the program's **Form_Click** statement. Figure 13-11 shows how the program's window would appear after the program has been run.

Listing 13-11:

```
Sub Form_Click ()
    Dim I As Integer

    For I = 1 To 1000
        Print Chr$(Int(Rnd * 224) + 32);
        If I Mod 50 = 0 Then
```

```
        Print
    End If
Next I

End Sub
```

*Figure 13-11 A **Chr$** demonstration program.*

CInt Function

Summary:

CInt(*expression*)

expression   is a numeric expression.

Description:

The **CInt** function converts the result of a numeric *expression* to an integer result. You should note that *expression*'s fractional part is rounded before it is converted.

See Also:

Fix and **Int**

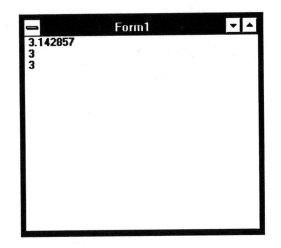

Figure 13-12 A **CInt** *demonstration program.*

Example:

The below program demonstrates the **CInt** function by converting the results of a variety of expressions to integers. Listing 13-12 presents the code for the program's **Form_Click** event. Figure 13-12 illustrates how the program's window would appear after the program has been run.

Listing 13-12:

```
Sub Form_Click ()

    N% = 22 / 7
    Print 22 / 7
    Print CInt(22 / 7)
    Print N%

End Sub
```

CLng Function

Summary:

CLng(*expression*)

expression   is a numeric expression.

Description:

The **CLng** function converts the result of a numeric *expression* to a long-integer result. You should note that *expression*'s fractional part is rounded before it is converted.

Example:

The following program demonstrates the **CLng** function by converting the results of a variety of expressions to long integers. Listing 13-13 presents the code for the program's **Form_Click** event. Figure 13-13 shows how the program's window would appear after the program has been run.

Listing 13-13:

```
Sub Form_Click ()

    N& = 22 / 7
    Print 22 / 7
    Print CLng(22 / 7)
    Print N&

End Sub
```

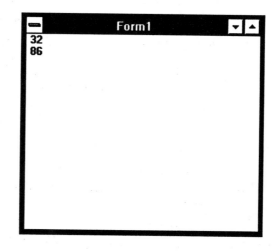

Figure 13-13 A **CLng** *demonstration program.*

Close Statement

Summary:

Close [[#] *number* [, [#] *number*] ...]

number   is the number of an open file.

Description:

The **Close** statement closes one or more open files as specified by their appropriate *number*(s). If the **Close** statement is used without any arguments, all open files will be closed.

See Also:

Open

Example:

The program that follows demonstrates the **Close** statement by opening and closing a text file for both input and output. Listing 13-14 presents the code for the program's **Form_Click** event. Figure 13-14 illustrates how the program's window would appear after the program has been run.

Listing 13-14:

```
Sub Form_Click ()
    Dim I As Integer

    Open "TEXTDEMO.DAT" For Output As 1
    For I = 1 To 10
        Print #1, "This is data item no."; I
    Next I
    Close 1
    Open "TEXTDEMO.DAT" For Input As 1
    While Not EOF(1)
        Input #1, A$
        Print A$
    Wend
    Close 1

End Sub
```

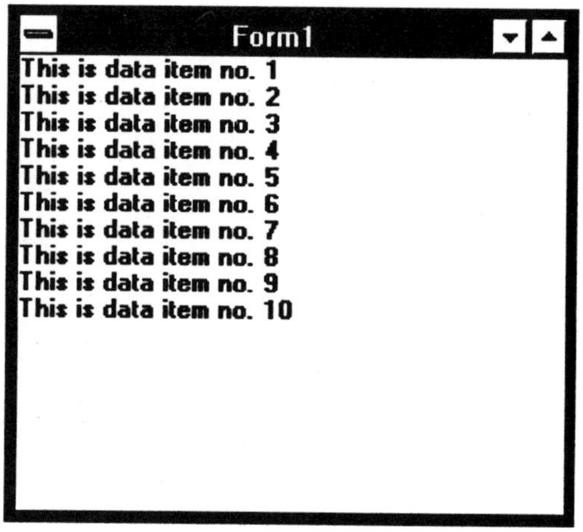

*Figure 13-14 A **Close** demonstration program.*

Command$ Function

Summary:

`Command$`

Description:

The **Command$** function returns the command line that is passed to the program when it is executed. A command line can be passed to the Visual Basic environment with Visual Basic's **/CMD** switch.

Example:

The program that follows demonstrates the **Command$** function by displaying the command line that was passed to the program. Listing 13-15 presents the code for the program's **Form_Click** event. Figure 13-15 shows how the program's window would appear after the program has been run.

*Figure 13-15 A **Command$** demonstration program.*

Listing 13-15:

```
Sub Form_Click ()

    Print Command$

End Sub
```

Const Statement

Summary:

[**Global**] **Const** *identifier* = *expression*[, *identifier* = *expression*] . . .

Global   is used to declare a constant in the global module that may be used by all of the program's modules.

identifier   is a Visual Basic identifier.

expression   is a constant expression.

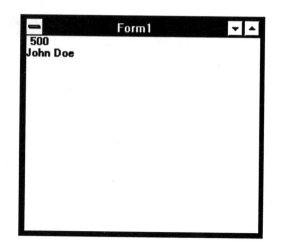

*Figure 13-16 A **Const** demonstration program.*

Description:

The **Const** statement is used to assign the value of a constant *expression* to an *identifier*. Once the constant *expression* has been assigned to the *identifier*, Visual Basic will replace all instances of the *identifier* with the constant *expression*'s value. You should note that the constart's *identifier* must follow the naming rules that apply to a Visual Basic variable.

Example:

The below program demonstrates the **Const** statement by defining a few constants and displaying their values. Listing 13-16-1 presents the form's declarations section, and Listing 13-16-2 the code for the program's **Form_Click** event. Figure 13-16 illustrates how the program's window would appear after the program has been run.

Listing 13-16-1:

```
Const Number% = 500, UName$ = "John Doe"
```

Listing 13-16-2:

```
Sub Form_Click ()

    Print Number%
    Print UName$

End Sub
```

Cos Function

Summary:

Cos(*expression*)

expression   is a numeric expression.

Description:

The **Cos** function returns the cosine for the angle specified (in radians) by *expression*.

See Also:

Atn, Sin, and **Tan**

Example:

The following program shows how the **Cos** function is used by calculating the cosine for a few angles. Listing 13-17 presents the code for the program's **Form_Click** event. Figure 13-17 illustrates how the program's window would appear after the program has been run.

Listing 13-17:

```
Sub Form_Click ()

    Print Cos(2.5)
    Print Cos(.25)

End Sub
```

*Figure 13-17 A **Cos** demonstration program.*

CSng Function

Summary:

CSng (*expression*)

expression   is a numeric expression.

Description:

The **CSng** function converts the result of a numeric *expression* to a single-precision result. If necessary, **CSng** will round the value before the conversion.

See Also:

CCur, CDbl, CInt, and **CLng**

Example:

The program that follows demonstrates the **CSng** function by converting the results of a variety of expressions to single precision. Listing 13-18 gives the code for the program's

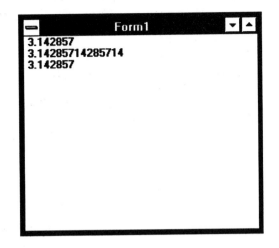

*Figure 13-18 A **CSng** demonstration program.*

Form_Click event. Figure 13-18 illustrates how the program's window would appear after the program has been run.

Listing 13-18:

```
Sub Form_Click ()

    N = CSng(22# / 7#)
    Print N
    Print 22# / 7#
    Print 22 / 7

End Sub
```

CurDir$ Function

Summary:

CurDir$ [(*drive*)]

drive   is a string expression.

Description:

The **CurDir$** function returns the current path for a drive. A drive can be optionally specified with the *drive* parameter. If the *drive* parameter is omitted, Visual Basic will return the path for the current drive.

See Also:

ChDir, ChDrive, MkDir, and **RmDir**

Example:

The program that appears below demonstrates the **CurDir$** function by displaying the path for the currently selected drive. Listing 13-19 presents the code for the program's **Form_Click** event. Figure 13-19 shows how the program's window would appear after the program has been run.

Listing 13-19:

```
Sub Form_Click ()

    Print CurDir$

End Sub
```

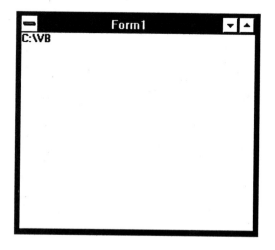

Figure 13-19 A **CurDir$** *demonstration program.*

Date$ Function

Summary:

`Date$`

Description:

The **Date$** function returns the current date as a 10-character string (*mm-dd-yyyy*).

See Also:

Date$ Statement

Example:

The following program demonstrates the **Date$** function by displaying the current system date. Listing 13-20 presents the code for the program's **Form_Click** event. Figure 13-20 illustrates how the program's window would appear after the program has been run.

*Figure 13-20 A **Date$** function demonstration program.*

Listing 13-20:

```
Sub Form_Click ()

    Print Date$

End Sub
```

Date$ Statement

Summary:

Date$ = *expression*

expression   is a string expression.

Description:

The **Date$** statement sets the date for the system clock. The new date is specified by *expression* and is a string with one of these formats:

mm-dd-yy
mm-dd-yyyy
mm/dd/yy
mm/dd/yyyy

See Also:

Date$ Function

Example:

The following program shows how the **Date$** statement is used by setting the system clock twice. Listing 13-21 presents the code for the program's **Form_Click** event. Figure 13-21 illustrates how the program's window would appear after the program has been run.

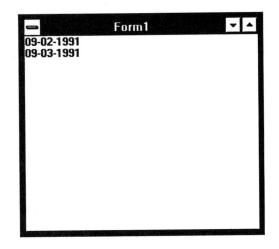

*Figure 13-21 A **Date$** statement demonstration program.*

Listing 13-21:

```
Sub Form_Click ()

    Date$ = "09/02/1991"
    Print Date$
    Date$ = "09/03/1991"
    Print Date$

End Sub
```

DateSerial Function

Summary:

DateSerial(*year, month, day*)

year   is a numeric expression.

month   is a numeric expression.

day   is a numeric expression.

Description:

The **DateSerial** function returns a double-precision serial number based on a specific date. The date is specified by the function's three parameters: *year*, *month*, and *day*. The valid range of dates the **DateSerial** function can handle extends from January 1, 1753 to December 31, 2078.

See Also:

DateValue, Day, Month, Now, Weekday, and **Year**

Example:

The program that follows demonstrates the **DateSerial** function by displaying a date's serial number. Listing 13-22 presents the code for the program's **Form_Click** event. Figure 13-22 illustrates how the program's window would appear after the program has been run.

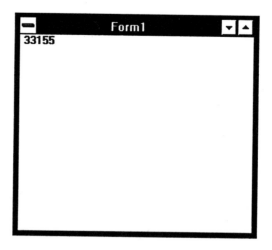

Figure 13-22 A **DateSerial** *demonstration program.*

Listing 13-22:

```
Sub Form_Click ()

    Print DateSerial(1990, 10, 9)

End Sub
```

DateValue Function

Summary:

DateValue(*date*)

date   is a string expression.

Description:

The **DateValue** function returns a serial number for a specific *date*. The string argument *date* can be any of six different formats. The following are examples of how the date 10/09/90 could be specified:

```
10/09/1990
10/09/90
October 9, 1990
Oct 9, 1990
9-Oct-1990
9 October 90
```

See Also:

DateSerial, Day, Month, Now, WeekDay, and **Year**

Example:

The program that follows demonstrates the **DateValue** function by displaying a date's serial number. Listing 13-23 gives the code for the program's **Form_Click** event. Figure 13-23 shows how the program's window would appear after the program has been run.

Figure 13-23 A **DateValue** *demonstration program.*

Listing 13-23:

```
Sub Form_Click ()

    Print DateValue("10/09/90")

End Sub
```

Day Function

Summary:

Day(*serialnumber*)

serialnumber   is a numeric expression.

Description:

The **Day** function returns the day of the month that is represented by a serial number. The serial number is specified by
serialnumber.

See Also:

Hour, Minute, Month, Now, Second, Weekday, and **Year**

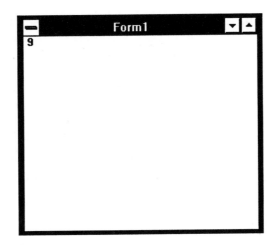

Figure 13-24 A **Day** *demonstration program.*

Example:

The following program demonstrates the **Day** function by displaying a serial number's day of the month. Listing 13-24 presents the code for the program's **Form_Click** event. Figure 13-24 illustrates how the program's window would appear after the program has been run.

Listing 13-24:

```
Sub Form_Click ()

    Print Day(33155)

End Sub
```

Declare Statement

Summary:

Declare Sub *name* **Lib** *libname* [**Alias** *aliasname*] [([*argumentlist*])]

or

```
Declare Function name [Lib libname] [Alias
aliasname]][([argumentlist])] [As type]
```

name	is the procedure's name.
libname	is the name of the procedure's dynamic-link library.
aliasname	is the procedure's name in the dynamic-link library.
argumentlist	is a list of the procedure's arguments.

Description:

The **Declare** statement is used to declare a prototype for a dynamic-link library procedure. The procedure's name is specified by *name* and must follow the Visual Basic naming rules. Should the procedure's name in the dynamic-link library be the same as a Visual Basic reserved word, a procedure, or a global variable or constant, or have an invalid character, the procedure's name in the dynamic-link library can be specified with *aliasname* and a more acceptable name can be specified with *name*.

The procedure's arguments are specified by *argumentlist* and must have the following syntax:

```
[ByVal] variablename[( )] [ As type] [, [ByVal]
variablename[( )] [ As type]]...
```

You should note how the **ByVal** keyword can be used to specify an argument that is passed by value instead of by reference.

Example:

The program that follows shows how the **Declare** statement is used by declaring a prototype for a dynamic-link library procedure. Listing 13-25-1 presents the code for the form's declarations section; Listing 13-25-2 gives the code for the program's **Form_Click** event. Figure 13-25 illustrates how the program's window would appear after the program has been run.

Figure 13-25 A **Declare** *demonstration program.*

Listing 13-25-1:

```
Declare Function IsZoomed Lib "User" (ByVal hWnd%) As
Integer
```

Listing 13-25-2:

```
Sub Form_Click ()

    If IsZoomed(hWnd) Then
        Print "The form is maximized"
    Else
        Print "The form isn't maximized"
    End If

End Sub
```

DefCur Statement

Summary:

DefCur *range*[*, range*]

range   is either a single letter or a range of letters
                     (*letter-letter*).

Description:

The **DefCur** statement sets the Visual Basic variable identifier defaults for either a single letter or a range of letters to **Currency**. Once a variable identifier default has been set with the **DefCur** statement, any variable names that begin with the default character will be considered a **Currency** variable. The exceptions to this naming convention are variable identifiers that use type declaration characters and ones that have been specifically declared in a statement such as a **Dim** statement. You should note that the **DefCur** statement only affects the variables in the statement's form or module.

See Also:

DefDbl, DefInt, DefLng, DefSng, and **DefStr**

Example:

The program below demonstrates how the **DefCur** statement is used to set the Visual Basic variable identifier defaults to **Currency**. Listing 13-26-1 presents the code for the form's declarations section and Listing 13-26-2 the code for the program's **Form_Click** event. Figure 13-26 illustrates how the

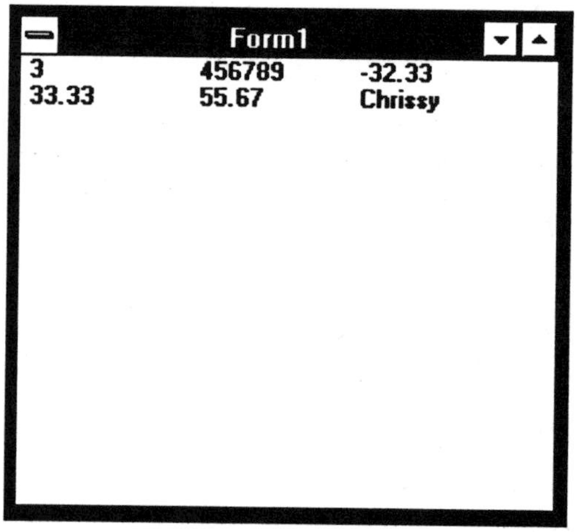

Figure 13-26 A **DefCur** *demonstration program.*

program's window would appear after the program has been run.

Listing 13-26-1:

```
DefCur A-Z
```

Listing 13-26-2:

```
Sub Form_Click ()

    I% = 3
    L& = 456789
    S! = -32.33
    D# = 33.33
    C = 55.67
    N$ = "Chrissy"
    Print I%, L&, S!
    Print D#, C, N$

End Sub
```

DefDbl Statement

Summary:

DefDbl *range*[, *range*]

range   is either a single letter or a range of letters (*letter-letter*).

Description:

The **DefDbl** statement sets the Visual Basic variable identifier defaults for either a single letter or a range of letters to **Double**. Once a variable identifier default has been set with the **DefDbl** statement, any variable names that begin with the default character will be considered a **Double** variable. The exceptions to this naming convention are variable identifiers that use type declaration characters and ones that have been specifically declared in a statement such as a **Dim** statement. You should note that the **DefDbl** statement only affects the variables in the statement's form or module.

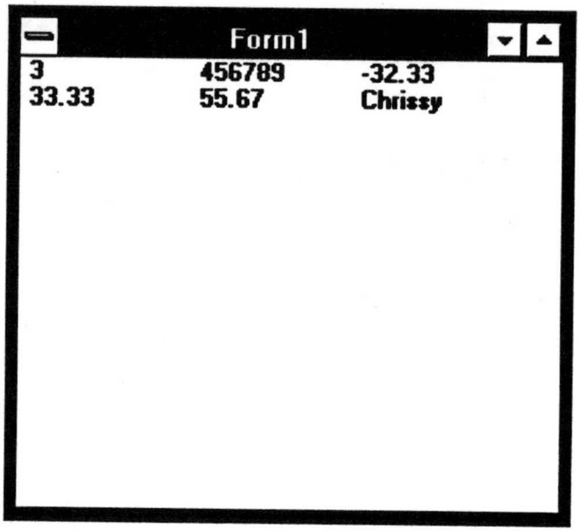

Figure 13-27 A **DefDbl** *demonstration program.*

See Also:

DefCur, DefInt, DefLng, DefSng, and **DefStr**

Example:

The following program demonstrates how the **DefDbl** statement is used to set the Visual Basic variable identifier defaults to **Double**. Listing 13-27-1 presents the form's declarations section, and Listing 13-27-2 the program's **Form_Click** event. Figure 13-27 shows how the program's window would appear after the program has been run.

Listing 13-27-1:

```
DefDbl A-Z
```

Listing 13-27-2:

```
Sub Form_Click ()

    I% = 3
    L& = 456789
    S! = -32.33
    D = 33.33
```

```
C@ = 55.67
N$ = "Chrissy"
Print I%, L&, S!
Print D, C@, N$
```

End Sub

DefInt Statement

Summary:

DefInt *range*[, *range*]

range   is either a single letter or a range of letters (*letter-letter*).

Description:

The **DefInt** statement sets the Visual Basic variable identifier defaults for either a single letter or a range of letters to **Integer**. Once a variable identifier default has been set with the **DefInt** statement, any variable names that begin with the default character will be considered an **Integer** variable. The exceptions to this naming convention are variable identifiers that use type declaration characters and ones that have been specifically declared in a statement such as a **Dim** statement. You should note that the **DefInt** statement only affects the variables in the statement's form or module.

See Also:

DefCur, DefDbl, DefLng, DefSng, and **DefStr**

Example:

The program that follows shows how the **DefInt** statement is used to set the Visual Basic variable identifier defaults to **Integer**. Listing 13-28-1 presents the code for the form's declarations section, and Listing 13-28-2 the code for the form's **Form_Click** event. Figure 13-28 illustrates how the program's window would appear after the program has been run.

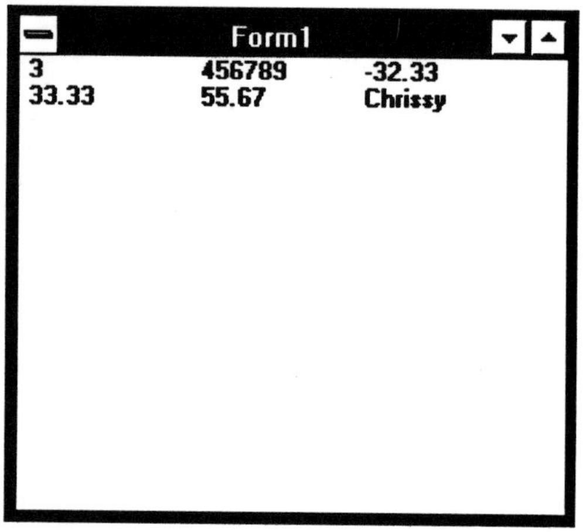

Figure 13-28 A **DefInt** *demonstration program.*

Listing 13-28-1:

```
DefInt A-Z
```

Listing 13-28-2:

```
Sub Form_Click ()

    I = 3
    L& = 456789
    S! = -32.33
    D# = 33.33
    C@ = 55.67
    N$ = "Chrissy"
    Print I, L&, S!
    Print D#, C@, N$

End Sub
```

DefLng Statement

Summary:

DefLng *range[, range]*

range　　　　　　is either a single letter or a range of letters
　　　　　　　　　(*letter-letter*).

Description:

The **DefLng** statement sets the Visual Basic variable identifier defaults for either a single letter or a range of letters to **Long**. Once a variable identifier default has been set with the **DefLng** statement, any variable names that begin with the default character will be considered a **Long** variable. The exceptions to this naming convention are variable identifiers that use type declaration characters and ones that have been specifically declared in a statement such as a **Dim** statement. You should note that the **DefLng** statement only affects the variables in the statement's form or module.

See Also:

DefCur, DefDbl, DefInt, DefSng, and **DefStr**

Example:

The program that appears below demonstrates how the **DefLng** statement is used to set the Visual Basic variable identifier defaults to **Long**. Listing 13-29-1 presents the code for the form's declarations section; Listing 13-29-2 gives the code for the program's **Form_Click** event. Figure 13-29 shows

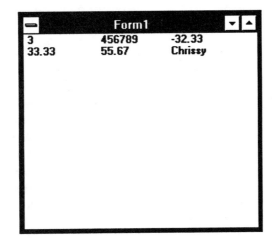

Figure 13-29 A **DefLng** *demonstration program.*

how the program's window would appear after the program has been run.

Listing 13-29-1:

```
DefLng A-Z
```

Listing 13-29-2:

```
Sub Form_Click ()

    I% = 3
    L = 456789
    S! = -32.33
    D# = 33.33
    C@ = 55.67
    N$ = "Chrissy"
    Print I%, L, S!
    Print D#, C@, N$

End Sub
```

DefSng Statement

Summary:

DefSng *range*[, *range*]

range   is either a single letter or a range of letters (*letter-letter*).

Description:

The **DefSng** statement sets the Visual Basic variable identifier defaults for either a single letter or a range of letters to **Single**. Once a variable identifier default has been set with the **DefSng** statement, any variable names that begin with the default character will be considered a **Single** variable. The exceptions to this naming convention are variable identifiers that use type declaration characters and ones that have been specifically declared in a statement such as a **Dim** statement. You should note that the **DefSng** statement only affects the variables in the

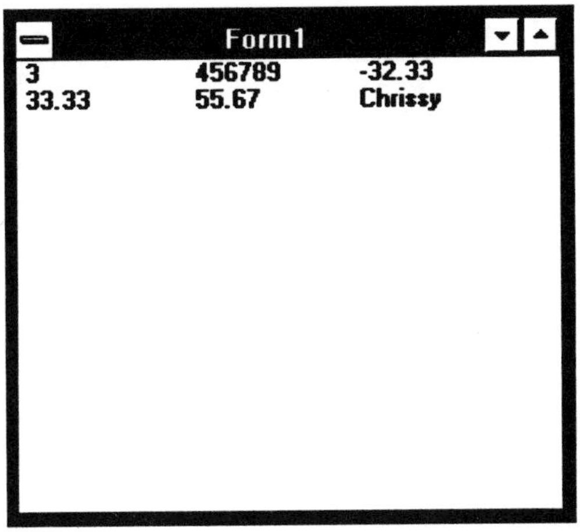

*Figure 13-30 A **DefSng** demonstration program.*

statement's form or module. Additionally, Visual Basic initially sets all variable identifier defaults to **Single**. Consequently, the **DefSng** statement is only necessary to reset a default that has been previously overridden.

See Also:

DefCur, DefDbl, DefInt, DefLng, and **DefStr**

Example:

The below program shows how the **DefSng** statement is used to set the Visual Basic defaults to **Single**. Listing 13-30-1 presents the code for the program's declarations section, and Listing 13-30-2 the code for the program's **Form_Click** event. Figure 13-30 illustrates how the program's window would appear after the program has been run.

Listing 13-30-1:

```
DefSng A-Z
```

Listing 13-30-2:

```
Sub Form_Click ()

    I% = 3
    L& = 456789
    S = -32.33
    D# = 33.33
    C@ = 55.67
    N$ = "Chrissy"
    Print I%, L&, S
    Print D#, C@, N$

End Sub
```

DefStr Statement

Summary:

DefStr *range[, range]* . . .

range   is either a single letter or a range of letters (*letter-letter*).

Description:

The **DefStr** statement sets the Visual Basic variable identifier defaults for either a single letter or a range of letters to **String**. Once a variable identifier default has been set with the **DefStr** statement, any variable names that begin with the default character will be considered a **String** variable. The exceptions to this naming convention are variable identifiers that use type declaration characters and ones that have been specifically declared in a statement such as a **Dim** statement.

See Also:

DefCur, DefDbl, DefInt, DefLng, and **DefSng**

Example:

The following program demonstrates how the **DefStr** statement is used to set the Visual Basic variable identifier defaults

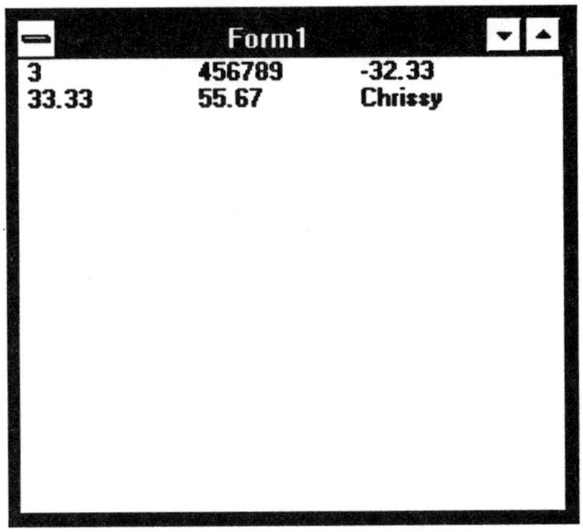

*Figure 13-31   A **DefStr** demonstration program.*

to **String**. Listing 13-31-1 gives the code for the form's declarations section, and Listing 13-31-2 the code for the program's **Form_Click** event. Figure 13-31 illustrates how the program's window would appear after the program has been run.

Listing 13-31-1:

```
DefStr A-Z
```

Listing 13-31-2:

```
Sub Form_Click ()

    I% = 3
    L& = 456789
    S! = -32.33
    D# = 33.33
    C@ = 55.67
    N = "Chrissy"
    Print I%, L&, S!
    Print D#, C@, N

End Sub
```

Dim Statement

Summary:

```
Dim [Shared] identifier[(subscripts)] [As
type] [,identifier[(subscripts)] [As type]]...
```

Shared	is used to maintain compatibility with older forms of Basic. It is ignored by Visual Basic.
identifier	is a variable identifier.
subscripts	is either the maximum subscript or a range of subscripts for each dimension in an array.
type	is either an elementary data type (**Integer, Long, Single, Double, Currency,** or **String**) or a previously defined record type.

Description:

The **Dim** statement specifically declares variables in a Visual Basic program. Each variable in a **Dim** statement can either be an elementary data type or a previously defined record type. Furthermore, a variable can be declared as an array.

See Also:

Global, Option Base, ReDim, and **Static**

Example:

The program that follows demonstrates the **Dim** statement by declaring an integer array variable, an integer variable, and a fixed-length string variable. Listing 13-32-1 presents the code for the form's declarations section, and Listing 13-32-2 the code for the program's **Form_Click** event. Figure 13-32 shows how

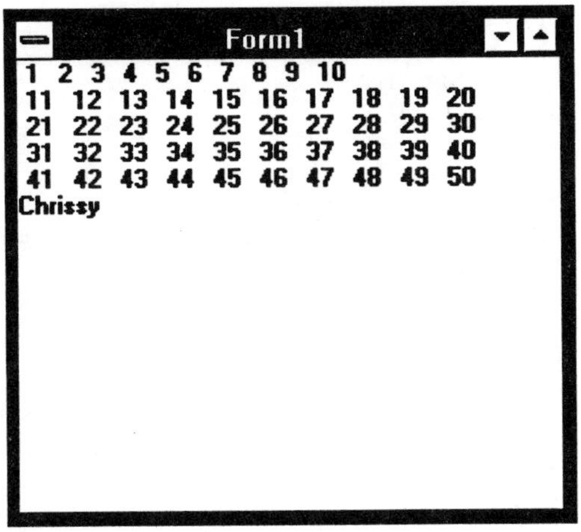

*Figure 13-32 A **Dim** demonstration program.*

the program's window would appear after the program has been run.

Listing 13-32-1:

```
Dim A(1 To 50) As Integer, I As Integer, FirstName As
String * 10
```

Listing 13-32-2:

```
Sub Form_Click ()

    For I = 1 To 50
        A(I) = I
    Next
    For I = 1 To 50
        Print A(I);
        If A(I) Mod 10 = 0 Then
            Print
        End If
    Next
    FirstName = "Chrissy"
    Print FirstName

End Sub
```

Dir$ Function

Summary:

`Dir$[(filespec)]`

`filespec`   is a string expression.

Description:

The **Dir$** function returns the next file name that matches a specified file specification. The file specification is passed as *filespec* and is only used for the **Dir$** function's first call. Subsequent calls to the **Dir$** function will continue to look for file names that match the previously passed file specification. The file specification string can contain the DOS wildcard characters (***** and **?**). When no more filenames match the file specification, Visual Basic will return a null string.

See Also:

ChDir and **CurDir$**

Example:

The program that appears below demonstrates the **Dir$** function by displaying the current directory's files a file at a time as the form is clicked. Listing 13-33 presents the code for the program's **Form_Click** event. Figure 13-33 illustrates how the program's window would appear after the program has been run.

Listing 13-33:

```
Sub Form_Click ()
    Static I As Integer

    If I Then
        Print Dir$
    Else
        Print Dir$("*.*")
        I = -1
    End If

End Sub
```

*Figure 13-33 A **Dir$** demonstration program.*

Do...Loop Statement

Summary:

```
Do
    statement
    .
    .
    [Exit Do]
    .
    .
    statement
Loop [{While|Until} expression]
```

or

```
Do [{While|Until} expression]
    statement
    .
    .
    [Exit Do]
    .
    .
    statement
Loop
```

statement	is a Visual Basic program statement.
expression	is a logical expression.

```
┌─────────────────────────────────────────────┐
│ ═      Form1                          ▼  ▲  │
│ 1  2  3  4  5  6  7  8  9  10                │
│ 11 12 13 14 15 16 17 18 19 20               │
│ 21 22 23 24 25 26 27 28 29 30               │
│ 31 32 33 34 35 36 37 38 39 40               │
│ 41 42 43 44 45 46 47 48 49 50               │
│ 51 52 53 54 55 56 57 58 59 60               │
│ 61 62 63 64 65 66 67 68 69 70               │
│ 71 72 73 74 75 76 77 78 79 80               │
│ 81 82 83 84 85 86 87 88 89 90               │
│ 91 92 93 94 95 96 97 98 99 100              │
│                                             │
│                                             │
│                                             │
│                                             │
└─────────────────────────────────────────────┘
```

*Figure 13-34 A **Do...Loop** demonstration program.*

Description:

The **Do...Loop** statement is an iteration structure used to implement loops in a Visual Basic program. An optional test for a logical expression can be performed either at the beginning or at the end of the loop. Moreover, the loop will be re-executed if the expression is True and the **While** keyword is used or if the expression is False and the **Until** keyword is used. If the optional test is omitted from the **Do...Loop** structure, the loop will repeat indefinitely. A **Do...Loop** can be prematurely exited with an **Exit Do** statement.

Example:

The below program shows how the **Do...Loop** statement is used by counting from 1 to 100. Listing 13-34 presents the code for the program's **Form_Click** event. Figure 13-34 illustrates how the program's window would appear after the program has been run.

Listing 13-34:

```
Sub Form_Click ()
    Dim I As Integer

    I = 0
    Do
        I = I + 1
        Print I;
        If I Mod 10 = 0 Then
            Print
        End If
    Loop Until I = 100

End Sub
```

DoEvents Function

Summary:

```
DoEvents( )
```

Description:

The **DoEvents** function returns the number of Visual Basic forms that are loaded. However, the **DoEvents** function serves an even more important task by yielding program execution to the Windows environment so other applications can process events. Accordingly, the **DoEvents** function should be used in Visual Basic program loops to keep other applications running.

Example:

The following program demonstrates how the **DoEvents** function is used in an indefinite idle loop to keep Windows functioning properly. Listing 13-35-1 is the program's **Main** procedure, Listing 13-35-2 is the program's **Form_Paint** event, and Listing 13-35-3 is the program's **Form_Click** event. Figure 13-35 shows how the program's window would appear after the program has been run.

*Figure 13-35 A **DoEvents** demonstration program.*

Listing 13-35-1:

```
Sub Main ()

    Form1.Show
    While DoEvents()
    Wend

End Sub
```

Listing 13-35-2:

```
Sub Form_Paint ()

    Print "Click me to end the program!"

End Sub
```

Listing 13-35-3:

```
Sub Form_Click ()

    End

End Sub
```

End Statement

Summary:

End

Description:

The **End** statement ends program execution. In addition, the **End** statement closes all files and destroys the program's forms and variables.

Example:

The program that follows demonstrates the **End** statement by ending program execution when a form is clicked. Listing 13-36-1 presents the code for the program's **Form_Paint** event, and Listing 13-36-2 the code for the program's **Form_Click** event. Figure 13-36 illustrates how the program's window would appear after the program has been run.

*Figure 13-36 An **End** demonstration program.*

Listing 13-36-1:

```
Sub Form_Paint ()

    Print "Click me to end the program!"

End Sub
```

Listing 13-36-2:

```
Sub Form_Click ()

    End

End Sub
```

Environ$ Function

Summary:

Environ$ *(expression)*

expression   is an expression.

Description:

The **Environ$** function returns an environment string from the DOS environment-string table. If *expression* is a string, Visual Basic will search for a matching environment-string name. If a match is found, Visual Basic will return the corresponding environment string. Otherwise, Visual Basic will return the environment-string name followed by an equal sign (=). If *expression* is numeric, Visual Basic searches for the environment string whose position in the environment-string table is determined by *expression*. If an environment string is found in the specified position, its value will be returned. Otherwise, Visual Basic will return a null string ("").

Example:

The program that follows demonstrates the **Environ$** function by displaying the current environment-string table. Listing 13-37 presents the code for the program's **Form_Click** event.

*Figure 13-37 An **Environ$** demonstration program.*

Figure 13-37 shows how the program's window would appear after the program has been run.

Listing 13-37:

```
Sub Form_Click ()
    Dim I As Integer

    I = 1
    While Environ$(I) <> ""
        Print Environ$(I)
        I = I + 1
    Wend

End Sub
```

Eof Function

Summary:

Eof(*filenumber*)

filenumber   is the number of a previously opened file.

Description:

The **Eof** function is used to determine if a file's file pointer has reached the end of the file. The file must have been previously opened and is specified by *filenumber*. If the end of the file has been reached, the **Eof** function returns True. Otherwise, the **Eof** function returns False.

See Also:

Open

Example:

The below program shows how the **Eof** function is used by reading in a text file until the end of the file has been reached. Listing 13-38 presents the code for the program's **Form_Click** event. Figure 13-38 illustrates how the program's window would appear after the program has been run.

Listing 13-38:

```
Sub Form_Click ()
    Dim I As Integer

    Open "TEXTDEMO.DAT" For Output As 1
    For I = 1 To 10
        Print #1, "This is data item no."; I
    Next I
    Close 1
    Open "TEXTDEMO.DAT" For Input As 1
    While Not EOF(1)
        Input #1, A$
        Print A$
    Wend
    Close 1

End Sub
```

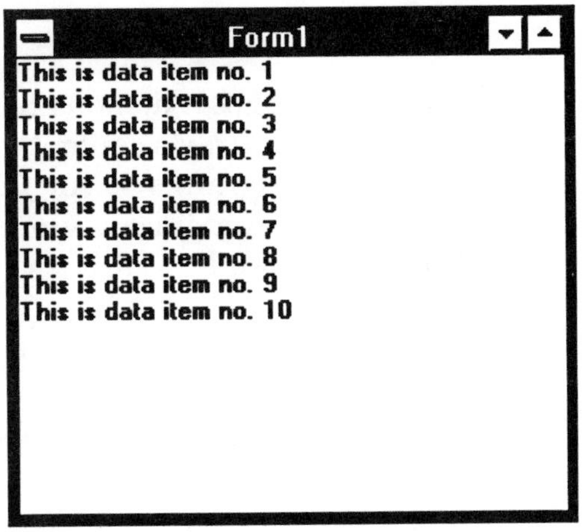

*Figure 13-38 A **Eof** demonstration program.*

Erase Statement

Summary:

Erase *array*[*,array*]...

array	is the name of a previously dimensioned array.

Description:

The **Erase** statement effectively erases a previously dimensioned array. If an array is a static array, all of its elements will be set to zero for a numeric array or to null strings for a string array. If an array is a dynamic array, it will be completely erased from memory. Once an array has been erased, it can be redimensioned with the **Dim** statement.

See Also:

Dim, **ReDim**, and **Static**

Example:

The following program demonstrates the **Erase** statement by erasing a numeric array's contents. Listing 13-39 presents the code for the program's **Form_Click** event. Figure 13-39 illustrates how the program's window would appear after the program has been run.

Listing 13-39:

```
Sub Form_Click ()
    Static A(1 To 10) As Integer
    Dim I As Integer

    For I = 1 To 10
        A(I) = I
    Next I
    For I = 1 To 10
        Print A(I);
    Next I
    Print
    Erase A
    For I = 1 To 10
        Print A(I);
    Next I
    Print

End Sub
```

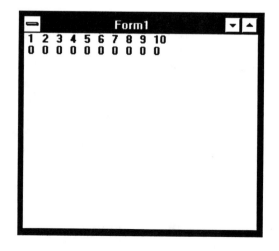

*Figure 13-39 An **Erase** demonstration program.*

Error$ Statement

Summary:

Error$[(*errorcode*)]

errorcode   is a numeric expression.

Description:

The **Error$** function returns an error message for a specified error code. The error code is specified by *errorcode*. If the *errorcode* parameter is omitted, the **Error$** function will return the error message for the last run-time error.

See Also:

Err Function, **Err** Statement, **Erl**, and **Error**

Example:

The program that follows demonstrates how the **Error$** function is used by displaying the error messages for error codes 1 through 10. Listing 13-40 presents the code for the program's **Form_Click** event. Figure 13-40 shows how the program window would appear after the program has been run.

Listing 13-40:

```
Sub Form_Click ()
    Dim I As Integer

    For I = 1 To 10
        Print Error$(I)
    Next I

End Sub
```

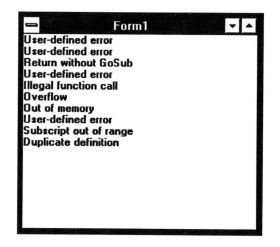

*Figure 13-40 An **Error$** demonstration program.*

Error Statement

Summary:

Error *errorcode*

errorcode   is a numeric expression.

Description:

The **Error** statement simulates a Visual Basic error. The error to be simulated is specified by *errorcode* and can be any value between 1 and 32,767.

See Also:

Err Function, **Err** Statement, **Erl**, and **Error$**

Example:

The program that follows shows how the **Error** statement can be used to generate an error message. Listing 13-41 gives the code for the program's **Form_Click** event. Figure 13-41 illustrates how the program's window would appear after the program has been run.

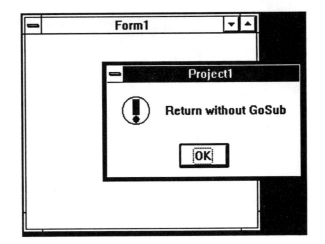

*Figure 13-41 An **Error** demonstration program.*

Listing 13-41:

```
Sub Form_Click ()

    Error 3

End Sub
```

Erl Function

Summary:

```
Erl
```

Description:

The **Erl** function returns the line number for where the last error occurred. Because line numbers are not required with Visual Basic, a value of 0 will be returned if the program line does not have a line number.

See Also:

Err Function, **Err** Statement, **Error$**, and **Error**

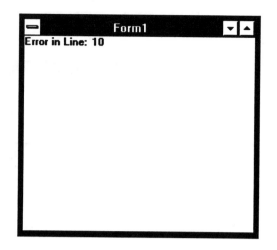

*Figure 13-42 An **Erl** demonstration program.*

Example:

The below program demonstrates the **Erl** function by displaying the line number for the program line that causes an error. Listing 13-42 presents the code for the program's **Form_Click** event. Figure 13-42 illustrates how the program's window would appear after the program has been run.

Listing 13-42:

```
Sub Form_Click ()

    On Error GoTo Handler

10  N = 100 / 0

    Exit Sub

Handler:
    Print "Error in Line:"; Erl
    Resume Next

End Sub
```

Err Function

Summary:

```
Err
```

Description:

The **Err** function returns the error code for the last error that occurred.

See Also:

Erl, **Err** Statement, **Error$**, and **Error**

Example:

The following program demonstrates the **Err** function by displaying the error code for the last error that occurred. Listing 13-43 presents the code for the program's **Form_Click** event. Figure 13-43 shows how the program's window would appear after the program has been run.

Listing 13-43:

```
Sub Form_Click ()

    On Error GoTo Handler

10  N = 100 / 0

    Exit Sub

Handler:
    Print "Error:"; Err
    Resume Next

End Sub
```

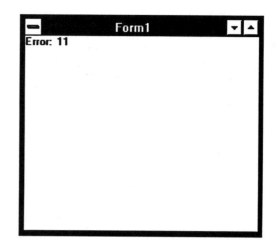

*Figure 13-43 An **Err** function demonstration program.*

Err Statement

Summary:

```
Err = errorcode
```

errorcode   is a numeric expression.

Description:

The **Err** statement forces Visual Basic's last error code to a specified value. The new error code is specified by *errorcode*. You should note that unlike Visual Basic's **Error** statement, the **Err** statement doesn't actually generate the specified error.

See Also:

Erl, **Err** Function, **Error$**, and **Error**

Description:

The program that follows shows how the **Err** statement is used to set a new error code. Listing 13-44 gives the code for the program's **Form_Click** event. Figure 13-44 illustrates how the

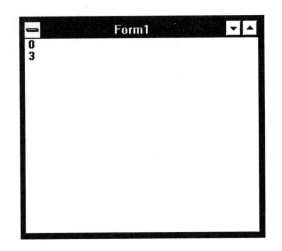

*Figure 13-44 An **Err** statement demonstration program.*

program's window would appear after the program has been run.

Listing 13-44:

```
Sub Form_Click ()

    Print Err
    Err = 3
    Print Err

End Sub
```

Exp Function

Summary:

Exp(*power*)

power   is a numeric expression.

Description:

The **Exp** function returns the value of *e* (the base of natural logarithms) raised to a specified *power*.

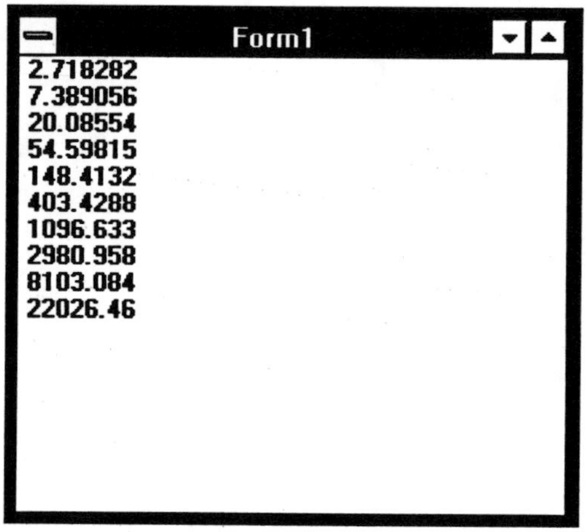

*Figure 13-45 An **Exp** demonstration program.*

See Also:

Log

Example:

The program that appears below demonstrates the **Exp** function by displaying the exponent for a number of values. Listing 13-45 presents the code for the program's **Form_Click** event. Figure 13-45 illustrates how the program's window would appear after the program has been run.

Listing 13-45:

```
Sub Form_Click ()
    Dim I As Integer

    For I = 1 To 10
        Print Exp(I)
    Next I

End Sub
```

FileAttr Function

Summary:

FileAttr(*filenumber, attribute*)

filenumber	is the number of a previously opened file.
attribute	tells Visual Basic what type of value is to be returned.

Description:

The **FileAttr** function returns information about a previously opened file. The file is specified by *filenumber* and the type of information to be returned is specified by *attribute*. If *attribute* is equal to 1, the **FileAttr** function returns one of the following codes:

Code	File Mode
1	Input
2	Output
4	Random
8	Append
32	Binary

If *attribute* is equal to 2, the **FileAttr** function returns the file's DOS handle.

See Also:

Open

Example:

The following program demonstrates the **FileAttr** function by displaying a previously opened file's attributes. Listing 13-46

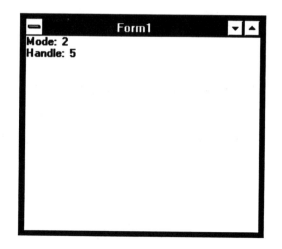

*Figure 13-46 A **FileAttr** demonstration program.*

presents the code for the program's **Form_Click** event. Figure 13-46 shows how the program's window would appear after the program has been run.

Listing 13-46:

```
Sub Form_Click ()

    Open "MAIL.DAT" For Output As 1
    Print "Mode:"; FileAttr(1, 1)
    Print "Handle:"; FileAttr(1, 2)
    Close 1

End Sub
```

Fix Function

Summary:

Fix(*expression*)

expression   is a numeric expression.

Description:

The **Fix** function truncates the fractional part of a numeric *expression*. Although **Fix** and **Int** are similar functions, **Fix** returns the next greater integer value for negative *expressions*.

See Also:

CInt and **Int**

Example:

The following program demonstrates the **Fix** function by truncating a numeric expression. Listing 13-47 presents the code for the program's **Form_Click** event. Figure 13-47 illustrates how the program's window would appear after the program has been run.

```
┌──────────────────────────────────────┐
│ ▬          Form1              ▼ ▲     │
├──────────────────────────────────────┤
│ 3.142857                             │
│ 3                                    │
│ 3                                    │
│                                      │
│                                      │
│                                      │
│                                      │
│                                      │
│                                      │
│                                      │
│                                      │
└──────────────────────────────────────┘
```

*Figure 13-47 A **Fix** demonstration program.*

Listing 13-47:

```
Sub Form_Click ()
    Dim N As Integer

    N = 22 / 7
    Print 22 / 7
    Print Fix(22 / 7)
    Print N

End Sub
```

For...Next Statement

Summary:

For *variable* **=** *start* **To** *end* [**Step** *increment*]
   statement
     .
     .
   Exit For
     .
     .
   statement
Next [*variable*[, *variable*]...]

variable	is a numeric variable.
start	is the starting value to assign to *variable*.
end	is the ending range for *variable*.
increment	is the amount to adjust *variable* by for each iteration.
statement	is a program statement.

Description:

The **For...Next** statement is an iteration structure used to implement loops in a Visual Basic program. During the first pass, Visual Basic assigns the value *start* to *variable*. Before each loop, Visual Basic compares *variable*'s value with *end*. If *variable* is still in range, Visual Basic will execute the following program statements until a corresponding **Next** statement is encountered. Once a matching **Next** statement is found, Visual Basic will adjust *variable* either by 1 or by a specified *increment*. The loop will continue with Visual Basic once again checking *variable* against *end*, and so on. A **For...Next** statement can be prematurely exited by an **Exit For** statement.

Example:

The program that follows shows how the **For...Next** statement is used by executing a pair of nested **For...Next** loops. Listing 13-48 presents the code for the program's **Form_Click** event. Figure 13-48 illustrates how the program's window would appear after the program has been run.

Listing 13-48:

```
Sub Form_Click ()
    Dim I As Integer, J As Integer

    For I = 1 To 10
        For J = 1 To 10
            Print J;
        Next J
        Print
    Next I

End Sub
```

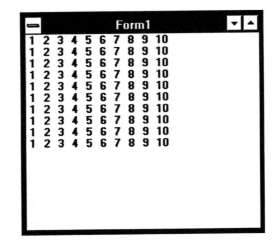

*Figure 13-48 A **For...Next** demonstration program.*

Format$ Function

Summary:

Format$(*number*[, *format*])

number	is a numeric expression.
format	is a string expression.

Description:

The **Format$** function converts a numeric expression to a string. The numeric expression is specified by *number*. The format Visual Basic is to use during the conversion is optionally specified by *format*. If *format* is omitted, Visual Basic will treat the **Format$** function call as a call to the **Str$** function. When constructing a *format* string, one or more of the below format characters may be used:

Format Character	*Description*
0	Digit. Visual Basic is to place a digit in the zero character's position. If the converted number has fewer digits than there are zero characters, Visual Basic will place a leading or trailing zero in the zero character's position.
#	Digit. Visual Basic is to place a digit in the # character's position.
%	Percentage. The numeric expression is to be multiplied by 100 and a percent character (%) is to be placed in the indicated position.
.	Decimal point. Tells Visual Basic where to insert the decimal point.
,	Commas. This tells Visual Basic to insert commas into the string before every third digit position to the left of the decimal point. If two commas are used adjacently or a comma comes right before the decimal point, Visual Basic will omit three digits from the string and round all numbers accordingly.

Format Character	Description
E-, E+, e-, or e+	Scientific notation. Tells Visual Basic to format the string using scientific notation.
/	Date separator. Used to separate the day, month, and year for date values.
-, +, $, (,), or Space	Literal character. Tells Visual Basic to insert the literal character into the string.
\	Insert next character. Used to tell Visual Basic to treat the next character as a literal character instead of a format character. A double backslash (\\) may be used to include a backslash in the converted string.
"ABC"	Insert text. Tells Visual Basic to insert the indicated text into the converted string.

When creating *format* you can use up to three separate format strings within the format string argument as follows:

Number of Strings	Description
1	The format string is used for all types of numbers.
2	The first format string is used for positive numbers and zeros and the second format string is used for negative numbers.
3	The first format string is used for positive numbers, the second format string for negative numbers, and the third format string for zeros.

You should note that multiple format strings are separated by semicolons.

The **Format$** function can also be used to convert date/time serial numbers to strings. The following table explains the various characters that the **Format$** function allows for converting date/time serial numbers:

Character	Description
d	Converts the day without a leading zero (1–31).
dd	Converts the day with a leading zero (01–31).
ddd	Converts the day as a day of the week (Sun–Sat).
dddd	Converts the day as a complete day of the week (Sunday–Saturday).
ddddd	Converts to the date serial number using the format sShortDate= specified in the WIN.INI file.
m	Convert the month without leading zeros (1–12).
mm	Converts the month with leading zeros (01–12).
mmm	Converts the month as a three-character name (Jan–Dec).
mmmm	Converts the month as a name (January–December).
yy	Converts the year as a two-digit year (00–99).
yyyy	Converts the year as a four-digit year (1900–2040).
h	Converts the hour without leading zeros (0–23).
hh	Converts the hour with leading zeros (00–23).
m	When used immediately after an h or hh, converts the minute without leading zeros (0–59).
mm	When used immediately after an h or hh, converts the minute with leading zeros (00–59).
s	Converts the second without leading zeros (0–59).
ss	Converts the second with leading zeros (00–59).
ttttt	Converts the time serial number using the format specified by sTime in the WIN.INI file. Leading zeros are used if the iTLZero= entry is set to True in the WIN.INI file.
AM/PM	Use a 12-hour clock and add AM for morning hours and PM for evening hours.
am/pm	Use a 12-hour clock and add am for morning hours and pm for evening hours.

(continued)

Character	Description
A/P	Use a 12-hour clock and add A for morning hours and P for evening hours.
a/p	Use a 12-hour clock and add a for morning hours and p for evening hours.
AMPM	Use a 12-hour clock and add the contents of the s1159 entry in the WIN.INI file for morning hours and the s2359 entry in the WIN.INI file for evening hours.

See Also:

Str$

Example:

The program that appears below demonstrates how the **Format$** function is used to display a few formatted numeric strings. Listing 13-49 presents the code for the program's **Form_Click** event. Figure 13-49 shows how the program's window would appear after the program has been run.

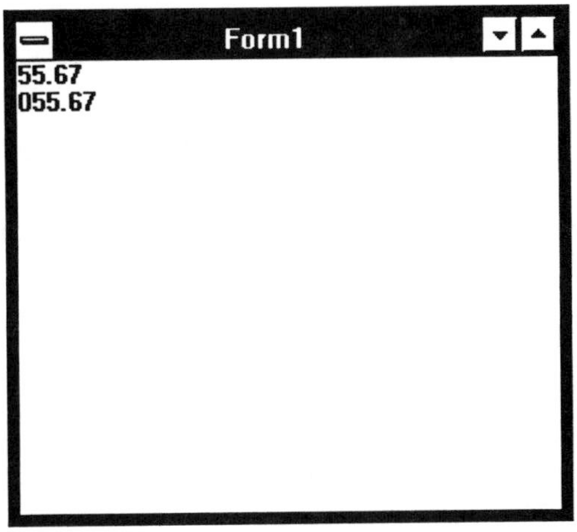

*Figure 13-49 A **Format$** demonstration program.*

Listing 13-49:

```
Sub Form_Click ()

    Print Format$(55.667, "###.##")
    Print Format$(55.667, "000.00")

End Sub
```

FreeFile Function

Summary:

`FreeFile`

Description:

The **FreeFile** function returns the next available Visual Basic file number. **FreeFile** is useful for opening files in a **Sub** or **Function** procedure.

See Also:

Open

Example:

The below program demonstrates the **FreeFile** function by displaying the next available Visual Basic file number. Listing 13-50 presents the code for the program's **Form_Click** event. Figure 13-50 illustrates how the program's window would appear after the program has been run.

Listing 13-50:

```
Sub Form_Click ()

    Print "The next available file number is:";
    FreeFile

End Sub
```

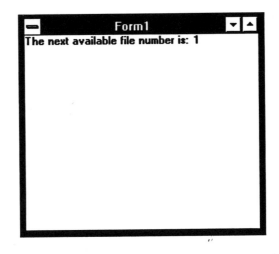

Figure 13-50 A **FreeFile** *demonstration program.*

Function Statement

Summary:

```
[Static] Function name[(parameters)] [As type]
    statement
    .
    .
    name = expression
    .
    .
    statement
End Function
```

`Static`	tells Visual Basic that the **Function** procedure's local variables are static variables and will retain their values between function calls.
`name`	is the name of the **Function** procedure.
`parameters`	is one or more parameters to be passed to the **Function** procedure.
`type`	is the return type for the **Function** procedure.

statement	is a Visual Basic statement.
expression	is an expression to be returned as the result of the **Function** procedure.

Description:

The **Function** statement defines a **Function** procedure with a name specified by *name*. Once defined, a **Function** procedure is called in a program just like any of the built-in Visual Basic functions. You simply specify the **Function** procedure's name and any optional *parameters* in an expression. A **Function** procedure returns a value by assigning the result of an *expression* to the **Function** procedure's *name*. The data type for the **Function** procedure is determined either by an optional *type* parameter or by Visual Basic's variable identifier rules as they would apply to *name*. A **Function** procedure can be prematurely exited from by an **Exit Function** statement.

See Also:

Sub

Example:

The following program demonstrates the **Function** statement by performing several calls to a sample **Function** procedure. Listing 13-51-1 presents the code for the program's **Multiply%** **Function** procedure, and Listing 13-51-2 the code for the program's **Form_Click** event. Figure 13-51 illustrates how the program's window would appear after the program has been run.

Listing 13-51-1:

```
Function Multiply% (N1%, N2%)

    Multiply% = N1% * N2%

End Function
```

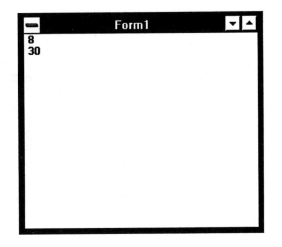

*Figure 13-51 A **Function** demonstration program.*

Listing 13-51-2:

```
Sub Form_Click ()

    Print Multiply%(2, 4)
    Print Multiply%(5, 6)

End Sub
```

Get Statement

Summary:

```
Get [#] filenumber, [position] , variable
```

filenumber	is a number of a previously opened file.
position	is the file position to read the data from.
variable	is a variable to read the data into.

Description:

The **Get** statement reads data from either a binary file or a random access file into memory. The file to read the data from is specified by *filenumber*. The **Get** statement can optionally position the file pointer before reading the data with the *position* parameter. The *position* parameter is the actual byte position the file pointer is to be moved to. If a *position* parameter isn't specified in the **Get** statement, Visual Basic will simply read the data at the present position of the file pointer. After reading the data from the disk file, Visual Basic will set *variable* to the data's value.

The **Get** statement can also be used to read data from a random access file into memory. In the case of a random access file, *position* is the record number the **Get** statement is to read, and *variable* is any variable that is less than or equal to the file's record length.

See Also:

Open and **Put**

Example:

The program that follows shows how the **Get** statement is used by reading in from disk the contents of a binary file. Listing 13-52 presents the code for the program's **Form_Click** event. Figure 13-52 illustrates how the program's window would appear after the program has been run.

Figure 13-52 A **Get** *demonstration program.*

Listing 13-52:

```
Sub Form_Click ()
    Dim I As Integer, Rec As Integer

    Print "Writing demo file....."
    Open "DEMOFILE.DAT" For Binary As 1
    For I = 1 To 10
        Put 1, , I
    Next
    Close 1
    Open "DEMOFILE.DAT" For Binary As 1
    Print "Reading demo file backwards....."
    For I = 10 To 1 Step -1
        Get 1, (I - 1) * 2 + 1, Rec
        Print Rec; "...";
        If I = 6 Then
            Print
        End If
    Next
    Print
    Close 1

End Sub
```

Global Statement

Summary:

Global *identifier*[(*subscripts*)] [**As**
type] [,*identifier*[(*subscripts*)] [**As** *type*]]...

identifier	is a variable identifier.
subscripts	is either the maximum subscript or a range of subscripts for each dimension in an array.
type	is either an elementary data type (**Integer, Long, Single, Double, Currency,** or **String**) or a previously defined record type.

Description:

The **Global** statement is used to globally declare variables in a program's global module. As with a **Dim** statement, each of the statement's variables can either be an elementary data type or a previously defined record type. Furthermore, a globally declared variable can be an array. Once a variable has been declared in a **Global** statement, it is available for use throughout all of the program's forms and modules.

See Also:

Dim, Option Base, ReDim, and **Static**

Example:

The program that appears below demonstrates the **Global** statement by globally declaring an integer array variable and a fixed-length string variable. Listing 13-53-1 presents the code for the program's global module; Listing 13-53-2 gives the code for the program's **Form_Click** event. Figure 13-53 shows how the program's window would appear after the program has been run.

Listing 13-53-1:

```
Global A(1 To 50) As Integer, FirstName As String * 10
```

Listing 13-53-2:

```
Sub Form_Click ()
    Dim I As Integer

    For I = 1 To 50
        A(I) = I
    Next
    For I = 1 To 50
        Print A(I);
        If A(I) Mod 10 = 0 Then
            Print
        End If
    Next
    FirstName = "Chrissy"
    Print FirstName

End Sub
```

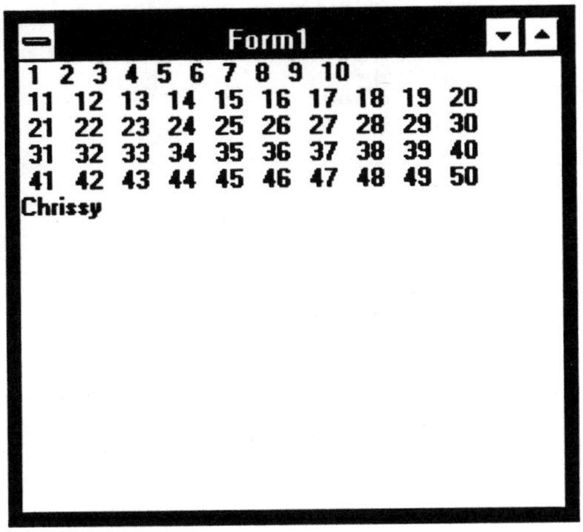

*Figure 13-53 A **Global** demonstration program.*

GoSub...Return Statement

Summary:

GoSub {*linelabel*|*linenumber*}

   .

   .

   .

Return

linelabel	is a Visual Basic line label.
linenumber	is a Visual Basic line number.

Description:

The **GoSub** statement tells Visual Basic to branch to a subroutine which starts at the location specified by either *linelabel* or *linenumber*. The subroutine will be executed until a **Return** statement is encountered. Once a **Return** statement is encountered, Visual Basic will return execution to the statement following the calling **GoSub** statement.

Figure 13-54 A **GoSub...Return** *demonstration program.*

See Also:

GoTo and **On...GoSub**

Example:

The below program demonstrates the **GoSub** and **Return** statements by performing several calls to a subroutine. Listing 13-54 presents the code for the program's **Form_Click** event. Figure 13-54 illustrates how the program's window would appear after the program has been run.

Listing 13-54:

```
Sub Form_Click ()
    Dim N1 As Integer, N2 As Integer

    N1 = 5
    N2 = 6
    GoSub Multiply
    N1 = 38
    N2 = 5
    GoSub Multiply
    Exit Sub
```

```
Multiply:
    Print N1 * N2
    Return

End Sub
```

GoTo Statement

Summary:

```
GoTo {linelabel|linenumber}
```

linelabel   is a line label.

linenumber is a line number.

Description:

The **GoTo** statement branches execution to a specified location. The desired location is specified with either a *linelabel* or a *linenumber*.

Example:

The following program shows how the **GoTo** statement is used by branching program execution around the middle of a procedure. Listing 13-55 gives the code for the program's **Form_Click** event. Figure 13-55 illustrates how the program's window would appear after the program has been run.

Listing 13-55:

```
Sub Form_Click ()

    Print "This statement is executed!"
    GoTo 10
    Print "This statement never is!"
    10 Print "This statement is executed too!"

End Sub
```

*Figure 13-55 A **GoTo** demonstration program.*

Hex$ Function

Summary:

`Hex$(expression)`

`expression`   is a numeric expression.

Description:

The **Hex$** function converts a numeric *expression* into a hexadecimal string. You should note that *expression* is rounded to either an integer or a long integer before it is converted it to a hexadecimal string.

See Also:

Oct$

Example:

The program that follows demonstrates the **Hex$** function by displaying a hexadecimal string for a variety of memory values.

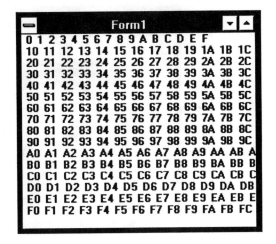

*Figure 13-56 A **Hex$** demonstration program.*

Listing 13-56 presents the code for the program's **Form_Click** event. Figure 13-56 illustrates how the program's window would appear after the program has been run.

Listing 13-56:

```
Sub Form_Click ()
    Dim I As Integer, J As Integer

    For I = 0 To 15
        For J = 0 To 15
            Print " "; Hex$(I * 16 + J);
        Next J
        Print
    Next I

End Sub
```

Hour Function

Summary:

Hour(*serialnumber*)

serialnumber   is a numeric expression.

*Figure 13-57 An **Hour** demonstration program.*

Description:

The **Hour** function returns the hour of the day that is represented by a serial number. The serial number is specified by *serialnumber*.

See Also:

Day, Minute, Month, Now, Second, Weekday, and **Year**

Example:

The program that appears below demonstrates the **Hour** function by displaying a serial number's hour of the day. Listing 13-57 presents the code for the program's **Form_Click** event. Figure 13-57 shows how the program's window would appear after the program has been run.

Listing 13-57:

```
Sub Form_Click ()

    T$ = Time$
    Serial# = TimeValue(T$)
```

```
    Print T$
    Print Hour(Serial#)

End Sub
```

If...Then...Else Statement

Summary:

If *expression* **Then** *statements* [**Else** *statements*]

or

If *expression* **Then**

.
.
.

[**ElseIf** *expression* **Then**]

.
.
.

[**Else**]

.
.
.

End If

expression	is a logical expression.
statements	is one or more program statements.

Description:

The **If...Then...Else** statement is a program control structure for conditionally branching program execution. The **If...Then...Else** statement will execute any statements following the **Then** keyword if *expression* is True. Execution will continue until the end of the line, an **End If**, an **Else**, or an **ElseIf** is encountered.

If *expression* is False and the **If...Then...Else** statement has either an **Else** or **ElseIf** clause, Visual Basic will branch execution to the statement following the **Else** or **ElseIf** keyword. If *expression* is False and the **If...Then...Else** statement does not have either an **Else** or **ElseIf** clause, Visual Basic will branch execution to either the next program line for a single line

If...Then...Else statement or to the statement following the **End If** keyword in a block **If...Then...Else** statement.

Example:

The below program demonstrates the **If...Then...Else** statement by displaying one of two conditional messages. Listing 13-58 presents the code for the program's **Form_Click** event. Figure 13-58 illustrates how the program's window would appear after the program has been run.

Listing 13-58:

```
Sub Form_Click ()

    Number = 1
    If Number = 1 Then Print "Number is equal to 1"
    Else Print "Number isn't equal to 1"
    Number = 0
    If Number = 1 Then
        Print "Number is equal to 1"
    Else
        Print "Number isn't equal to 1"
    End If

End Sub
```

Figure 13-58 An **If...Then...Else** *demonstration program.*

Input # Statement

Summary:

```
Input #filenumber, variable[, variable]...
```
filenumber   is the number of a previously opened file.

variable   is a variable to hold the input.

Description:

The **Input #** statement retrieves data from a sequential disk file. The source file is specified by *filenumber* and the data is read into one or more specified *variables*. You should note that multiple data items on the same line must be separated by commas.

See Also:

Open and **Print #**

Example:

The following program shows how the **Input #** statement is used by reading in and displaying the contents of a disk file. Listing 13-59 presents the code for the program's **Form_Click** event. Figure 13-59 illustrates how the program's window would appear after the program has been run.

Listing 13-59:

```
Sub Form_Click ()
    Dim I As Integer

    Open "TEXTDEMO.DAT" For Output As 1
    For I = 1 To 10
        Print #1, "This is data item no."; I
    Next I
    Close 1
    Open "TEXTDEMO.DAT" For Input As 1
    While Not EOF(1)
        Input #1, A$
```

```
        Print A$
    Wend
    Close 1

End Sub
```

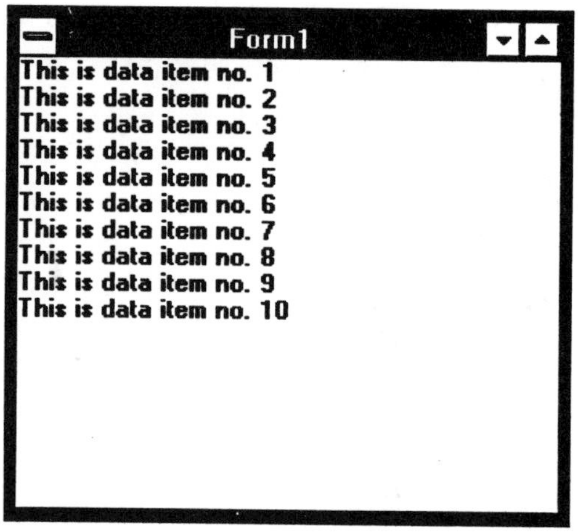

*Figure 13-59 An **Input #** demonstration program.*

Input$ Function

Summary:

Input$(*n*, [#] *filenumber*)

n   is the number of characters to be read.

filenumber is the number of a previously opened file.

Description:

The **Input$** function reads a specified number of characters from a previously opened file. The number of characters to be read from the file is specified by *n*.

See Also:

Input # and **Open**

Example:

The program that follows demonstrates the **Input$** function by reading in and displaying a text file one character at a time. Listing 13-60 presents the code for the program's **Form_Click** event. Figure 13-60 shows how the program's window would appear after the program has been run.

Listing 13-60:

```
Sub Form_Click ()
    Dim I As Integer

    Open "TEXTDEMO.DAT" For Output As 1
    For I = 1 To 10
        Print #1, "This is data item no."; I
    Next I
    Close 1
    Open "TEXTDEMO.DAT" For Input As 1
    While Not EOF(1)
        A$ = Input$(1, 1)
        Print A$;
    Wend
    Close 1

End Sub
```

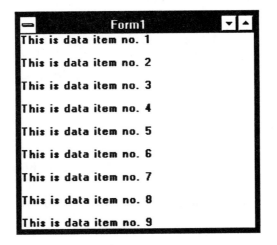

*Figure 13-60 An **Input$** demonstration program.*

InputBox$ Function

Summary:

`InputBox$(`*prompt*[, *title*[, *default*[, *x, y*]]]`)`

prompt	is a string expression that specifies the input box's prompt.
title	is a string expression that specifies the input box's title.
default	is the input box's initial contents.
x,y	is the input box's screen position.

Description:

The **InputBox$** requests the user to enter data that Visual Basic will return as a string. The input box's prompt is specified by *prompt*, its title is specified by *title*, and the box's default contents are specified by *default*. The input box's position can be specified by *x,y* and is the input box's upper left corner's position in twips from the screen's upper left corner. If *x,y* is omitted, Visual Basic will position the input box so that it is horizontally centered and one-third of the way down from the top of the screen.

See Also:

MsgBox Function and **MsgBox** Statement

Example:

The program that follows demonstrates the **InputBox$** function by requesting the user to enter his name. Listing 13-61 gives the code for the program's **Form_Click** event. Figure 13-61 illustrates how the desktop would appear after the program has been run.

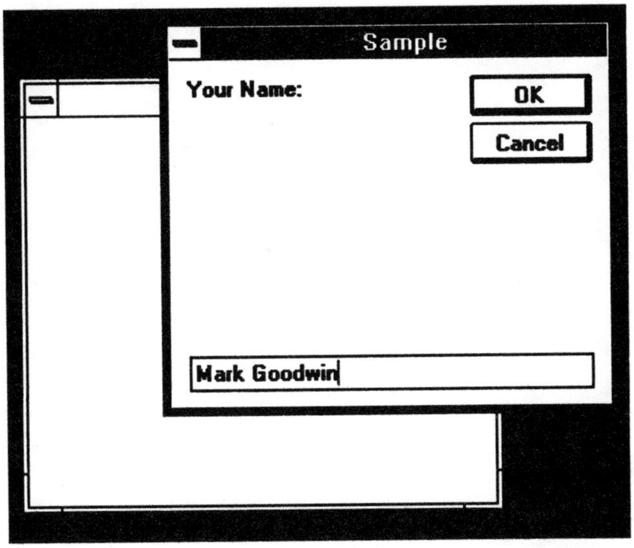

Figure 13-61 An **InputBox$** *demonstration program.*

Listing 13-61:

```
Sub Form_Click ()

    A$ = InputBox$("Your Name:", "Sample", "")
    Print A$

End Sub
```

InStr Function

Summary:

InStr([*start,*] *string1, string2*)

start	optionally specifies the position of the beginning character for the *string1* search.
string1	the string to be searched.
string2	the string to search for.

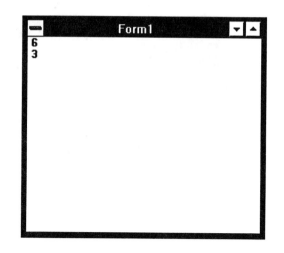

*Figure 13-62 An **InStr** demonstration program.*

Description:

The **InStr** function searches for one string (*string2*) inside of another string (*string1*). The search will begin at either *string1*'s first character or at the character specified by *start*. If a match is found, the **InStr** function returns the location in *string1* where *string2* was found. If *string2* is a null string (" "), the **InStr** function returns either *start* or 1. Otherwise, the **InStr** function returns a 0 to indicate that *string2* was not found in *string1*. You should note that the **InStr** function is case sensitive and you should use either the **LCase$** or the **UCase$** functions on both string if you do not want the search to be case sensitive.

See Also:

LCase$** and **UCase$

Example:

The following program demonstrates the **InStr** function by searching two different strings for the word **is**. Listing 13-62 presents the code for the program's **Form_Click** event. Figure 13-62 shows how the program's window would appear after the program has been run.

Listing 13-62:

```
Sub Form_Click ()

    Print InStr(5, "This is a sample InStr", "is")
    Print InStr("This is another sample InStr", "is")

End Sub
```

Int Function

Summary:

`Int(expression)`

`expression`   is a numeric expression.

Description:

The **Int** function removes the fractional part of a numeric *expression*.

See Also:

CInt and **Fix**

Example:

The following program shows how the **Int** function could be used on a numeric expression. Listing 13-63 presents the code for the program's **Form_Click** event. Figure 13-63 illustrates how the program's window would appear after the program has been run.

Listing 13-63:

```
Sub Form_Click ()
    Dim N As Integer

    N = 22 / 7
    Print 22 / 7
    Print Int(22 / 7)
    Print N

End Sub
```

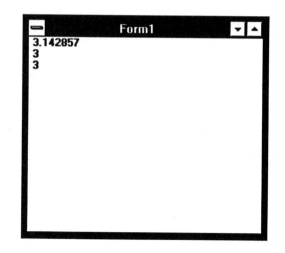

*Figure 13-63 An **Int** demonstration program.*

Kill Statement

Summary:

`Kill` *expression*

expression   is a string expression.

Description:

The **Kill** statement deletes a specified file or files from a disk. The file or files are specified by *expression*. You should note that Visual Basic allows you to use wildcard characters in *expression*. Essentially, the **Kill** statement performs the same functions as the DOS **Erase** and **Del** commands.

Example:

The program that follows demonstrates the **Kill** statement by deleting a few disk files. Listing 13-64 presents the code for the program's **Form_Click** event. Figure 13-64 illustrates how the program's window would appear after the program has been run.

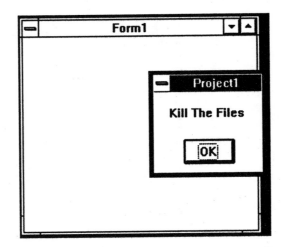

*Figure 13-64 A **Kill** demonstration program.*

Listing 13-64:

```
Sub Form_Click ()

    MsgBox "Kill The Files"
    Kill "*.DAT"

End Sub
```

LBound Function

Summary:

LBound(*array*[, *dimension*])

array　　　　　is the name of the array.

dimension　　　is the dimension.

Description:

The **LBound** function returns the smallest subscript for an *array*'s *dimension*. You should note that the *dimension* parameter is only required for multidimensional arrays. The *dimension* parameter is assumed to be 1 for arrays with only a single dimension.

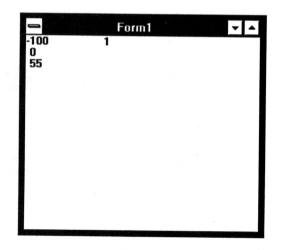

Figure 13-65 A **LBound** *demonstration program.*

See Also:

UBound

Example:

The program that appears below demonstrates the **LBound** function by returning the smallest subscript for a variety of array dimensions. Listing 13-65-1 gives the code for the form's declarations section, and Listing 13-65-2 the code for the program's **Form_Click** event. Figure 13-65 illustrates how the program's window would appear after the program has been run.

Listing 13-65-1:

```
DefInt A-Z
Dim A(-100 To 100, 1 To 5), B(56), C(55 To 60)
```

Listing 13-65-2:

```
Sub Form_Click ()

    Print LBound(A, 1), LBound(A, 2)
    Print LBound(B)
    Print LBound(C)

End Sub
```

LCase$ Function

Summary:

LCase$ (*expression*)

expression   is a string expression.

Description:

The **LCase$** function converts a string *expression* to all lower-case characters.

See Also:

UCase$

Example:

The below program demonstrates the **LCase$** function by converting and displaying a few lowercase strings. Listing 13-66 presents the code for the program's **Form_Click** event. Figure 13-66 shows how the program's window would appear after the program has been run.

Figure 13-66 A **LCase$** *demonstration program.*

Listing 13-66:

```
Sub Form_Click ()

    Print LCase$("THIS IS A LOWERCASE STRING")
    Print LCase$("This IS a LoWeRcAsE strING")

End Sub
```

Left$ Function

Summary:

Left$(*string, n*)

string   is a string expression.

n   is the number of characters to return.

Description:

The **Left$** function returns a substring from a specified *string* expression. The number of characters to be returned is specified by *n* and the substring will start with *string's* first character. If *string* has fewer characters than *n*, Visual Basic will return the whole of *string* as the result.

See Also:

Mid$** Function and **Right$

Example:

The following program demonstrates the **Left$** function by extracting and displaying a few substrings. Listing 13-67 presents the code for the program's **Form_Click** event. Figure 13-67 illustrates how the program's window would appear after the program has been run.

*Figure 13-67 A **Left$** demonstration program.*

Listing 13-67:

```
Sub Form_Click ()

    Print Left$("This is a partial string", 10)
    A$ = "Another string"
    Print Left$(A$, 3)

End Sub
```

Len Function

Summary:

Len(*string*)

or

Len(*variable*)

string	is a string expression.
variable	is a nonstring variable.

Description:

The **Len(***string***)** function returns the length of a *string* expression. The **Len(***variable***)** function returns the size of the specified nonstring *variable*.

Example:

The program that follows shows how the **Len** function is used by displaying the length of a few strings. Listing 13-68 presents the code for the program's **Form_Click** event. Figure 13-68 illustrates how the program's window would appear after the program has been run.

Listing 13-68:

```
Sub Form_Click ()

    A$ = "1234567890"
    B$ = "1234567"
    Print "A$ is "; Len(A$); "characters long"
    Print "B$ is "; Len(B$); "characters long"

End Sub
```

*Figure 13-68 A **Len** demonstration program.*

Let Statement

Summary:

```
[Let] variable = expression
```

variable   is a variable of the same data type as
                  expression.

expression   is an expression.

Description:

The **Let** statement assigns the value of an *expression* to a *variable*. The **Let** keyword is strictly optional and is rarely seen in current programs. It is included in Visual Basic to maintain compatibility with older forms of Basic.

Example:

The program that appears below demonstrates the **Let** statement by assigning expressions to variables both with and without the **Let** keyword. Listing 13-69 gives the code for the program's **Form_Click** event. Figure 13-69 illustrates how the program's window would appear after the program has been run.

Listing 13-69:

```
Sub Form_Click ()

    Let A = 55 * 60
    Let B = 66 * 50
    Print A
    Print B
    A = 55 * 60
    B = 66 * 50
    Print A
    Print B

End Sub
```

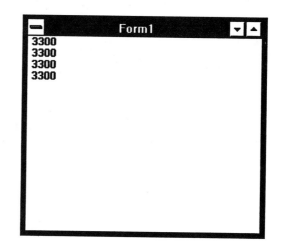

*Figure 13-69 A **Let** demonstration program.*

Line Input # Statement

Summary:

`Line Input #`*filenumber,* *variable*

filenumber	is the number of a previously opened file.
variable	is a string variable to hold the input.

Description:

The **Line Input #** statement retrieves a line of data from a sequential disk file. The source file is specified by *filenumber*. All data is read until a carriage return is encountered. Data is assigned to the specified string *variable*. The **Line Input #** statement will then set the file pointer after the line's carriage return/line feed pair.

See Also:

Input #

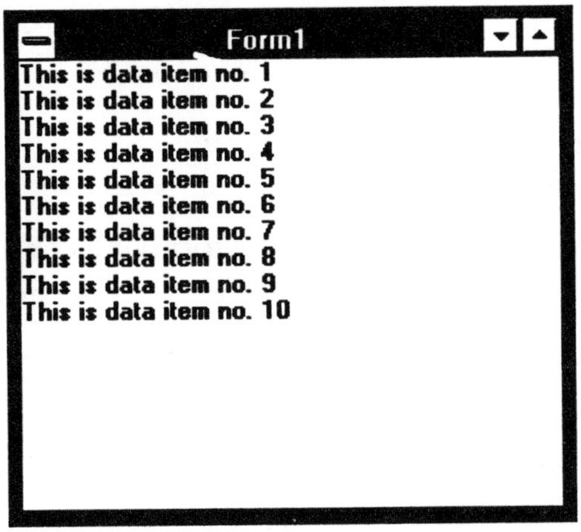

Figure 13-70 A **Line Input #** *demonstration program.*

Example:

The program below demonstrates the **Line Input #** statement by reading in a text file a line at a time. Listing 13-70 shows the code for the program's **Form_Click** event. Figure 13-70 shows how the program's window would appear after the program has been run.

Listing 13-70:

```
Sub Form_Click ()
    Dim I As Integer

    Open "TEXTDEMO.DAT" For Output As 1
    For I = 1 To 10
        Print #1, "This is data item no."; I
    Next I
    Close 1
    Open "TEXTDEMO.DAT" For Input As 1
    While Not EOF(1)
        Line Input #1, A$
        Print A$
    Wend
    Close 1

End Sub
```

Load Statement

Summary:

Load *object*

object   is a form or a control.

Description:

The **Load** statement loads either a form or a control into memory.

See Also:

Hide, Show, and **Unload**

Example:

The following program demonstrates the **Load** statement by loading a form into memory. Listing 13-71-1 presents the code for **Form1's Form_Click** event; Listing 13-71-2 gives the code for **Form2's Form_Load** event. Figure 13-71 illustrates how the desktop would appear after the program has been run.

Listing 13-71-1:

```
Sub Form_Click ()

    Load Form2

End Sub
```

Listing 13-71-2:

```
Sub Form_Load ()

    MsgBox "Form2 is now Loaded!"

End Sub
```

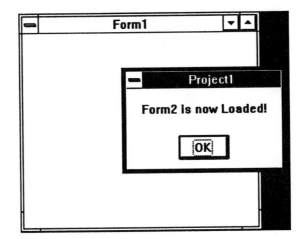

*Figure 13-71 A **Load** demonstration program.*

LoadPicture Function

Summary:

LoadPicture(*filename*)

filename   is the name of the picture to be loaded.

Description:

The **LoadPicture** function loads and returns a picture file. The picture file is specified by *filename* and can be a bitmap (.BMP), an icon (.ICO), or a Windows metafile (.WMF).

Example:

The program that follows demonstrates the **LoadPicture** function by assigning an icon to a form's **Picture** property. Listing 13-72 presents the code for the program's **Form_Click** event. Figure 13-72 illustrates how the program's window would appear after the program has been run.

*Figure 13-72 A **LoadPicture** demonstration program.*

Listing 13-72:

```
Sub Form_Click ()

    Picture =
    LoadPicture("c:\vb\icons\traffic\trffc01.ico")

End Sub
```

Loc Function

Summary:

```
Loc(filenumber)
```

filenumber   is the number of a previously opened file.

Description:

The **Loc** function returns the current location of a previously opened file. The file is specified by *filenumber*. If the file is a sequential access file, the **Loc** function returns the file pointer's current byte position divided by 128. If the file is a binary file, the **Loc** function returns the file pointer's current byte position.

See Also:

Open

Example:

The program that appears below demonstrates the **Loc** function by displaying a binary file's current byte position before each of the file's records is written to the file. Listing 13-73 presents the code for the program's **Form_Click** event. Figure 13-73 shows how the program's window would appear after the program has been run.

Listing 13-73:

```
Sub Form_Click ()
    Dim I As Integer

    Open "LOCDEMO.DAT" For Binary As 1
    For I = 1 To 10
        Print Loc(1)
        Put 1, , I
    Next I
    Close 1

End Sub
```

Figure 13-73 A **Loc** *demonstration program*

Lock...Unlock Statement

Summary:

```
Lock [#] filenumber[,{record|[start]To end}]
    .
    .
    .
Unlock [#] filenumber[,{record|[start]To end}]
```

`filenumber`	is the number of a previously opened file.
`record`	is the record number for a random access file or a byte position for a binary file.
`start`	is the first record or byte in a range of records or bytes.
`end`	is the last record or byte in a range of records or bytes.

Description:

The **Lock** and **Unlock** statements are used to lock and unlock a file in a networking or multitasking environment. By locking a part or the whole of a file, DOS will deny access to the locked portion of the file for other processes. Once a file has been unlocked, DOS will allow other processes to access the file. The file to be locked or unlocked is specified by *filenumber*. If the file is a sequential access file, the **Lock** and **Unlock** statements will apply to the entire file. If the file is a random access file, you can specify either a specific *record* that is to be locked/unlocked or a range (*start* **To** *end*) of records to be locked or unlocked. If the file is a binary file, you can specify either a specific byte (*record*) to be locked or unlocked or a range (*start* **To** *end*) of bytes to be locked/unlocked. You must be sure that your **Lock** and **Unlock** statements are identical. Moreover, you must be sure to unlock a locked file before it is closed.

See Also:

Open

Figure 13-74 A **Lock...Unlock** *demonstration program.*

Example:

The below program demonstrates the **Lock** and **Unlock** statements by locking and unlocking the records in a binary file. Listing 13-74 presents the code for the program's **Form_Click** event. Figure 13-74 illustrates how the program's window would appear after the program has been run.

Listing 13-74:

```
Sub Form_Click ()
    Dim I As Integer, Rec As Integer

    Print "Writing demo file....."
    Open "DEMOFILE.DAT" For Binary As 1
    For I = 1 To 10
        Put 1, , I
    Next I
    Close 1
    Print "Reading demo file backwards....."
    Open "DEMOFILE.DAT" For Binary Access Read Shared
    As 1
    For I = 10 To 1 Step -1
        Lock 1, (I - 1) * 2 + 1 To (I - 1) * 2 + 2
        Get 1, (I - 1) * 2 + 1, Rec
```

```
        Unlock 1, (I - 1) * 2 + 1 To (I - 1) * 2 + 2
        Print Rec; "...";
    Next
    Print
    Close 1

End Sub
```

Lof Function

Summary:

`Lof(`*filenumber*`)`

filenumber   is the number of a previously opened file.

Description:

The **Lof** function returns the length of a previously opened file. The file is specified by *filenumber* and the length is returned in bytes.

See Also:

Loc and **Open**

Example:

The following program shows how the **Lof** function is used by retrieving and displaying a file's length. Listing 13-75 presents the code for the program's **Form_Click** event. Figure 13-75 illustrates how the program's window would appear after the program has been run.

Listing 13-75:

```
Sub Form_Click ()
    Dim I As Integer

    Open "DEMOFILE.DAT" For Binary As 1
    For I = 1 To 10
        Put 1, , I
    Next I
```

```
      Close 1
      Open "DEMOFILE.DAT" For Binary As 1
      Print "The file is"; LOF(1); "bytes long"
      Close 1

End Sub
```

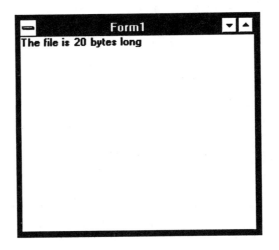

*Figure 13-75 A **Lof** demonstration program.*

Log Function

Summary:

Log(*expression*)

expression   is a numeric expression.

Description:

The **Log** function returns the natural logarithm for a numeric *expression*. You should note that *expression* must be greater than 0.

Example:

The program that follows demonstrates the **Log** function by displaying the natural logarithm for a variety of values. Listing

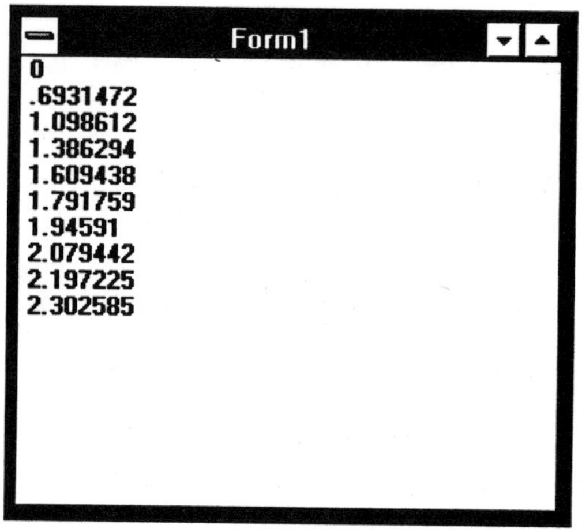

Figure 13-76   A **Log** *demonstration program.*

13-76 gives the code for the program's **Form_Click** event. Figure 13-76 illustrates how the program's window would appear after the program has been run.

Listing 13-76:

```
Sub Form_Click ()
    Dim I As Integer

    For I = 1 To 10
        Print Log(I)
    Next

End Sub
```

LSet Statement

Summary:

LSet *string* = *expression*

or

LSet *recordvariable1* = *recordvariable2*

string   is a fixed-length string variable.

`expression`	is a string expression.
`recordvariable1`	is a record variable.
`recordvariable2`	is a record variable.

Description:

The **LSet** statement left-justifies a string *expression* in a fixed-length string *variable*. If the string *expression* is shorter than the length of a *variable*, *variable* will be padded with spaces. If the string *expression* is longer than the length of *variable*, *expression* will be truncated to fit into *variable*.

Besides being able to left-justify strings, the **LSet** statement can be used to assign the contents of one record variable (*recordvariable2*) to another record variable (*recordvariable1*). You should note that the **LSet** statement can be used on record variables of differing types as long as neither contains a variable-length string.

See Also:

RSet

Example:

The following program demonstrates the **LSet** statement by left-justifying a few string expressions in a fixed-length string variable. Listing 13-77 presents the code for the program's **Form_Click** event. Figure 13-77 shows how the program's window would appear after the program has been run.

Listing 13-77:

```
Sub Form_Click ()
    Dim A As String * 5

    LSet A = "Test"
    Print A
    LSet A = "Another Test"
    Print A

End Sub
```

Figure 13-77 A **LSet** *demonstration program.*

LTrim$ Function

Summary:

`LTrim$(`*expression*`)`

expression   is a string expression.

Description:

The **LTrim$** function strips any leading spaces from a string *expression*.

See Also:

RTrim$

Example:

The program that appears below demonstrates the **LTrim$** function by stripping away the leading spaces from a few sample strings. Listing 13-78 presents the code for the program's **Form_Click** event. Figure 13-78 illustrates how the

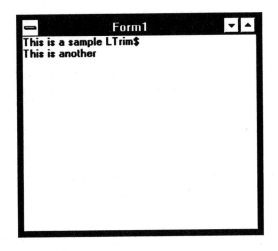

*Figure 13-78 A **LTrim$** demonstration program.*

program's window would appear after the program has been run.

Listing 13-78:

```
Sub Form_Click ()

    Print LTrim$("    This is a sample LTrim$")
    A$ = "    This is another"
    Print LTrim$(A$)

End Sub
```

Mid$ Function

Summary:

Mid$(*expression, start*[, *length*])

expression   is a string expression.

start   is the starting position of the substring.

length   is the length of the substring.

Description:

The **Mid$** function returns a substring from a string. The string source is specified by *expression* and the substring starts at the character position specified by *start*. The length of the substring is optionally specified by *length*. If *length* is not specified, or if *length* is longer than the remaining length of *expression*, Visual Basic will simply return *expression*'s remaining characters. If *start* is greater than the length of *expression*, the **Mid$** function will return a null string.

See Also:

Left$**, **Mid$ Statement, and **Right$**

Example:

The below program shows how the **Mid$** function is used by returning a few substrings from a string variable. Listing 13-79 presents the code for the program's **Form_Click** event. Figure 13-79 illustrates how the program's window would appear after the program has been run.

*Figure 13-79 A **Mid$** function demonstration program.*

Listing 13-79:

```
Sub Form_Click ()

    A$ = "1234567890"
    Print Mid$(A$, 3, 2)
    Print Mid$(A$, 5)

End Sub
```

Mid$ Statement

Summary:

Mid$(*variable*, *start*[, *length*]) = *expression*

variable	is a string variable.
start	is the starting character where the replacement is to begin.
length	is the number of characters to replace.
expression	is a string expression.

Description:

The **Mid$** statement replaces a specified number of characters in a string *variable* with a string *expression*. The starting position for the characters to be replaced is specified by *start*. If *start* is greater than *variable*'s current length, the **Mid$** statement will leave *variable* as is. The number of characters to be replaced is either *expression*'s length or specified by an optional *length* parameter. If *expression*'s length or *length* is greater than the remaining characters in *variable*, Visual Basic will only replace the remaining characters.

See Also:

Left$**, **Mid$ Function, and **Right$**

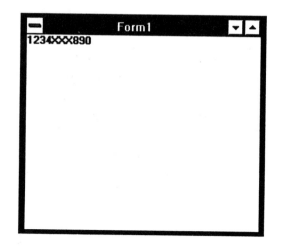

*Figure 13-80 A **Mid$** statement demonstration program*

Example:

The following program demonstrates the **Mid$** statement by replacing three characters in a string variable. Listing 13-80 presents the code for the program's **Form_Click** event. Figure 13-80 shows how the program's window would appear after the program has been run.

Listing 13-80:

```
Sub Form_Click ()

    A$ = "1234567890"
    Mid$(A$, 5) = "XXX"
    Print A$

End Sub
```

Minute Function

Summary:

Minute(*serialnumber*)

serialnumber   is a numeric expression.

Figure 13-81 A **Minute** *demonstration program.*

Description:

The **Minute** function returns the minute of the hour that is represented by a serial number. The serial number is specified by *serialnumber*.

See Also:

Day, Hour, Month, Now, Second, Weekday, and **Year**

Example:

The program that follows demonstrates the **Minute** function by displaying a serial number's minute of the hour. Listing 13-81 presents the code for the program's **Form_Click** event. Figure 13-81 illustrates how the program's window would appear after the program has been run.

Listing 13-81:

```
Sub Form_Click ()

    T$ = Time$
    Serial# = TimeValue(T$)
```

```
      Print T$
      Print Minute(Serial#)

End Sub
```

MkDir Statement

Summary:

MkDir *pathname*

pathname   is a string expression.

Description:

The **MkDir** statement creates a directory with a specified
pathname.

See Also:

ChDir, CurDir$, and **RmDir**

Example:

The program that appears below shows how the **MkDir** statement is used to create a temporary disk directory. Listing 13-82
gives the code for the program's **Form_Click** event. Figure
13-82 illustrates how the desktop would appear after the program has been run.

Listing 13-82:

```
Sub Form_Click ()

    MkDir "c:\vb\temp"
    MsgBox "Temporary directory has been created!"
    RmDir "c:\vb\temp"

End Sub
```

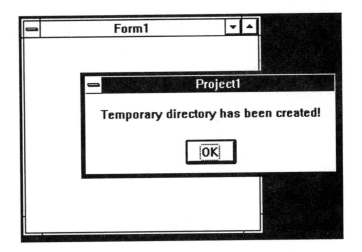

Figure 13-82 A **MkDir** *demonstration program.*

Month Function

Summary:

Month(*serialnumber*)

serialnumber   is a numeric expression.

Description:

The **Month** function returns the month of the year that is represented by a serial number. The serial number is specified by *serialnumber*.

See Also:

Day, Hour, Minute, Now, Second, Weekday, and **Hour**

Example:

The following program demonstrates the **Month** function by displaying a serial number's month of the year. Listing 13-83 presents the code for the program's **Form_Click** event.

*Figure 13-83 A **Month** demonstration program.*

Figure 13-83 illustrates how the program's window would appear after the program has been run.

Listing 13-83:

```
Sub Form_Click ()

    D$ = Date$
    Serial# = DateValue(D$)
    Print D$
    Print Month(Serial#)

End Sub
```

MsgBox Function

Summary:

MsgBox(*message*[, *type*[, *title*]])

message	is the message to be displayed in the message box.
type	is the message box's type.
title	is the message box's title.

Description:

The **MsgBox** function displays a message box and returns a value that indicates which of the message box's buttons was selected. The message box's message is specified by *message* and its title is specified by *title*. The message box type can be specified by an optional *type* parameter which is comprised of three major parts: the type of buttons to be displayed, the type of icon to be displayed, and the button that is to be used as the default button. Each of these three major parts has a unique value and the sum of all three parts is passed to the **MsgBox** function to display the appropriate message box. A list of the button types that can be selected follows:

Value	*Button(s)*
0	Display an OK button.
1	Display OK, Cancel buttons.
2	Display Abort, Retry, Ignore buttons.
3	Display Yes, No, Cancel buttons.
4	Display Yes, No buttons.
5	Display Retry, Cancel buttons.

The icon types that can be chosen appear below:

Value	*Icon*
16	Display Critical Message icon.
32	Display Warning Query icon.
48	Display Warning Message icon.
64	Display Information Message icon.

The following is a list of default button values:

Value	*Default Button*
0	First button.
256	Second button.
512	Third button.

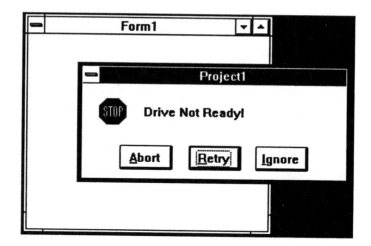

*Figure 13-84 A **MsgBox** function demonstration program (1 of 2).*

Depending on the button the user selects, the **MsgBox** function will return one of the below values:

Return Value	Button Pressed
1	OK
2	Cancel
3	Abort
4	Retry
5	Ignore
6	Yes
7	No

See Also:

InputBox$ and **MsgBox** Statement

Example:

The program that follows demonstrates the **MsgBox** function by displaying an "Abort, Retry, Ignore" message box. Listing 13-84 presents the code for the program's **Form_Click** event.

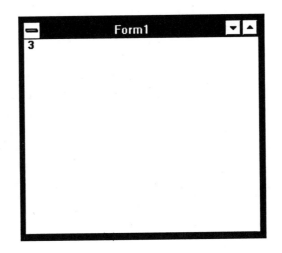

*Figure 13-85 A **MsgBox** function demonstration program (2 of 2).*

Figure 13-84 shows how the desktop would appear after the form has been clicked, and Figure 13-85 how the program's window would appear after the user has responded to the message box.

Listing 13-84:

```
Sub Form_Click ()

    Print MsgBox("Drive Not Ready!", 2 Or 16 Or 256)

End Sub
```

MsgBox Statement

Summary:

MsgBox *message*[, *type*[, *title*]]

message	is the message to be displayed in the message box.
type	is the message box's type.
title	is the message box's title.

Description:

The **MsgBox** statement displays a message box. The message box's message is specified by *message* and its title is specified by *title*. The message box type can be specified by an optional *type* parameter which is comprised of three major parts: the type of buttons to be displayed, the type of icon to be displayed, and the button that is to be used as the default button. Each of these three major parts has a unique value and the sum of all three parts is passed to the **MsgBox** statement to display the appropriate message box. The following is a list of the button types that can be selected:

Value	*Button(s)*
0	Display an OK button.
1	Display OK, Cancel buttons.
2	Display Abort, Retry, Ignore buttons.
3	Display Yes, No, Cancel buttons.
4	Display Yes, No buttons.
5	Display Retry, Cancel buttons.

A list of the icon types that can be chosen follows:

Value	*Icon*
16	Display Critical Message icon.
32	Display Warning Query icon.
48	Display Warning Message icon.
64	Display Information Message icon.

A list of default button values appears below:

Value	*Default Button*
0	First button.
256	Second button.
512	Third button.

See Also:

InputBox$ and **MsgBox** Function

Example:

The following program shows how the **MsgBox** statement is used by displaying an informational message. Listing 13-85 gives the code for the program's **Form_Click** event. Figure 13-86 illustrates how the desktop would appear after the form has been clicked.

Listing 13-85:

```
Sub Form_Click ()

    MsgBox "Drive Not Ready!", 64

End Sub
```

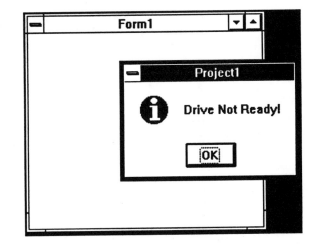

*Figure 13-86 A **MsgBox** statement demonstration program.*

Name Statement

Summary:

```
Name file1 As file2
```

file1	is a string expression.
file2	is a string expression.

Description:

The **Name** statement renames a file specified by *file1* to a new name specified by *file2*. Besides simply renaming a file, the **Name** statement can move a file to a new directory if the path in *file2* differs from the path in *file1*. In addition, the **Name** statement can rename directory names.

Example:

The program that appears below demonstrates the **Name** statement by renaming a file. Listing 13-86 presents the code for the program's **Form_Click** event. Figure 13-87 shows how the program's window would appear after the program has been run.

Figure 13-87 A **Name** *demonstration program*

Listing 13–86:

```
Sub Form_Click ()

    Name "DEMOFILE.DAT" As "TEST.DAT"
    Print "DEMOFILE.DAT has been renamed to TEST.DAT"

End Sub
```

Now Function

Summary:

Now

Description:

The **Now** function returns a date/time serial number that represents the date and time as per the setting of the computer's system clock.

See Also:

Day, Hour, Minute, Month, Second, Weekday, and **Year**

Example:

The below program shows how the **Now** function is used by displaying the current date. Listing 13-87 presents the code for the program's **Form_Click** event. Figure 13-88 illustrates how the program's window would appear after the program has been run.

Listing 13–87:

```
Sub Form_Click ()

    Serial# = Now
    Print Format$(Serial#, "mmmm dd yyyy")

End Sub
```

*Figure 13-88 A **Now** demonstration program.*

Oct$ Function

Summary:

Oct$(*expression*)

expression　　　is a numeric expression.

Description:

The **Oct$** function converts a numeric *expression* into an octal string. You should note that *expression* is rounded to either an integer or a long integer before it is converted to an octal string.

See Also:

Hex$

Example:

The following program demonstrates the **Oct$** function by displaying a series of octal numbers. Listing 13-88 presents the code for the program's **Form_Click** event. Figure 13-89

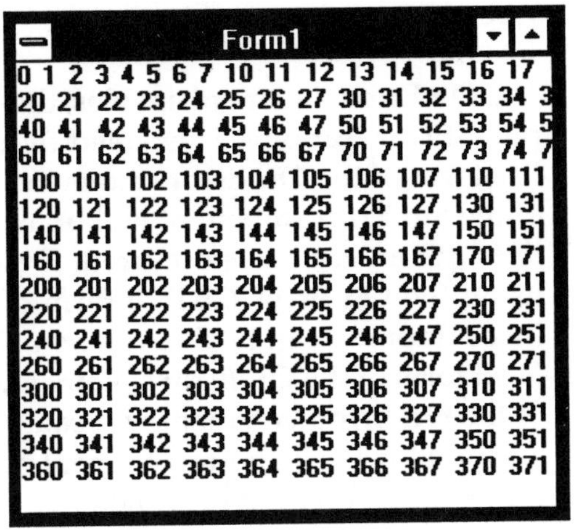

*Figure 13-89 An **Oct$** demonstration program.*

illustrates how the program's window would appear after the program is run.

Listing 13-88:

```
Sub Form_Click ()
    Dim I As Integer, J As Integer

    For I = 0 To 15
        For J = 0 To 15
            Print Oct$(I * 16 + J); " ";
        Next
        Print
    Next

End Sub
```

On Error Statement

Summary:

On [Local] Error {GoTo *line* **| Resume Next | GoTo 0}**

Local	is provided for compatibility with other forms of Basic.
line	is a line number or a line label.

Description:

The **On Error** statement enables, disables, or delays error trapping. Error trapping is enabled by using the **On Error GoTo** *line* form of the **On Error** statement. Once executed, this form of the **On Error** statement will branch execution to a specified *line* after an error has occurred. Error trapping is disabled by using the **On Error GoTo 0** form of the **On Error** statement. Error trapping can be delayed by using the **On Error Resume Next** form of the **On Error** statement. Once executed, this form of the **On Error** statement will cause Visual Basic to ignore all errors. However, the most recent error, if any, can be determined by calling the **Err** function.

See Also:

Err Function, **Err** Statement, **Error$**, and **Resume**

Example:

The program that follows demonstrates the **On Error** statement by branching execution to a specified error-handling routine. Listing 13-89 presents the code for the program's **Form_Click** event. Figure 13-90 shows how the program's window would appear after the program has been run.

Listing 13-89:

```
Sub Form_Click ()

    On Error GoTo Handler
    Error 25
    Exit Sub

Handler:
    Print "Error :"; Err; "in line:"; Erl
    Resume Next

End Sub
```

*Figure 13-90 An **On Error** demonstration program.*

On...GoSub Statement

Summary:

On *expression* **GoSub** *line*[, *line*]...

expression   is a numeric expression.

line   is a line number or a line label.

Description:

The **On...GoSub** statement branches program execution to one of a number of specified subroutines depending on the result of *expression*. The start of each subroutine is specified by a *line* parameter. After evaluating *expression*, Visual Basic will branch to the subroutine that is indicated by the result. For example, an *expression* equal to 2 would cause Visual Basic to branch to the subroutine specified by the second *line*. If *expression* is less than 1 or greater than the number of specified *lines*, Visual Basic will continue execution with the next statement.

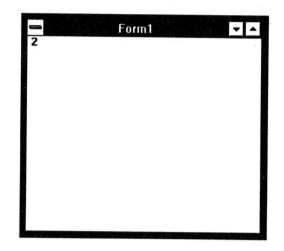

Figure 13-91 An **On...GoSub** *demonstration program.*

See Also:

On...GoTo

Example:

The program that appears below shows how the **On...GoSub** statement is used by asking the user to specify the number of the routine to be branched to. Listing 13-90 gives the code for the program's **Form_Click** event. Figure 13-91 illustrates how the program's window would appear after the program has been run.

Listing 13-90:

```
Sub Form_Click ()

    On Val(InputBox$("Enter a number between 1 and
    4")) GoSub 1, 2, 3, 4
    Exit Sub
1   Print 1
    Return

2   Print 2
    Return
```

```
3    Print 3
     Return

4    Print 4
     Return

End Sub
```

On...GoTo Statement

Summary:

On *expression* **GoTo** *line*[, *line*]...

expression	is a numeric expression.
line	is a line number or a line label.

Description:

The **On...GoTo** statement branches program execution to one of a number of specified *lines* depending on the result of *expression*. After evaluating *expression*, Visual Basic will branch to the line number that is indicated by the result. For instance, an *expression* equal to 4 would cause Visual Basic to branch to the fourth *line*. If *expression* is less than 1 or greater than the number of specified *lines*, Visual Basic will continue execution with the next statement.

See Also:

On...GoSub

Example:

The following program demonstrates the **On...GoTo** statement by asking the user to specify the number of the line to be branched to. Listing 13-91 presents the code for the program's **Form_Click** event. Figure 13-92 illustrates how the program's window would appear after the program has been run.

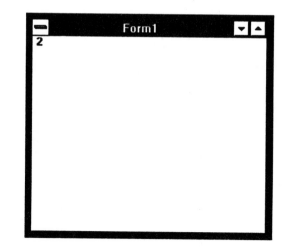

Figure 13-92 An **On...GoTo** *demonstration program.*

Listing 13-91:

```
Sub Form_Click ()
    On Val(InputBox$("Enter a number between 1 and
    4")) GoTo 1, 2, 3, 4
    Exit Sub

1   Print 1
    Exit Sub

2   Print 2
    Exit Sub

3   Print 3
    Exit Sub

4   Print 4

End Sub
```

Open Statement

Summary:

Open *file* [**For** *mode*] [**Access** *access*] [*lock*] **As**
[**#**] *number* [**Len** = *reclen*]

file   is a **string expression.**

`mode`	is the file's mode.
`access`	is the file's access.
`lock`	is the file's lock type.
`number`	is the file's number.
`reclen`	is the file's record length.

Description:

The **Open** statement will open a file specified by *file*. If the file is successfully opened, Visual Basic will assign a specified *number* to the file. This *number* is used in subsequent statements to read from the file, write to the file, and close the file. An optional record length can be specified for the file with the *reclen* parameter. The default record length is 128 for random access files and a *reclen* is only used with random access files. The other **Open** statement parameters are used as follows:

mode	Description
Output	Opens the file for output.
Input	Opens the file for input.
Append	Opens the file for output and positions the file pointer to the end of the file. Thus, the former contents of the file are preserved by the Append mode.
Random	Opens the file for random access. If an **Access** clause is not specified in the **Open** statement, Visual Basic will try to open the file as either **Read Write**, **Write**, or **Read**.
Binary	Opens the file for binary access. If an **Access** clause is not specified in the **Open** statement, Visual Basic will try to open the file for either **Read Write**, **Write**, or **Read**.

access	Description
Read	Opens the file for read only.
Write	Opens the file for write only.
Read Write	Opens the file for both reading and writing.

lock	Description
None specified	If *lock* is not specified in the **Open** statement, the file may be opened any number of times by the current process. Other processes will be denied access to the file.
Shared	Any process will be able to read from or write to the file.
Lock Read	This will deny other processes **Read** access to the file.
Lock Write	This will deny other processes **Write** access to the file.
Lock Read Write	This will deny other processes **Read** and **Write** access to the file.

See Also:

Close

Example:

The following program shows how the **Open** statement is used by opening a text file for writing and reading. Listing 13-92 presents the code for the program's **Form_Click** event. Figure 13-93 illustrates how the program's window would appear after the program has been run.

Listing 13-92:

```
Sub Form_Click ()
    Dim I As Integer

    Open "TEXTDEMO.DAT" For Output As 1
    For I = 1 To 10
        Print #1, "This is data item no."; I
    Next I
    Close 1
    Open "TEXTDEMO.DAT" For Input As 1
    While Not EOF(1)
        Input #1, A$
```

```
      Print A$
   Wend
   Close 1

End Sub
```

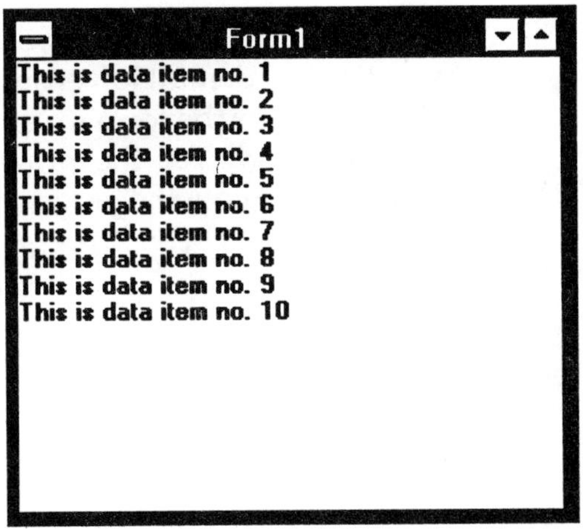

Figure 13-93 An **Open** *demonstration program.*

Option Base Statement

Summary:

Option Base *n*

n   is the new base.

Description:

The **Option Base** statement sets the default lower subscript for arrays that do not explicitly define a lower bound. The new default value is specified by *n* and can be either 0 or 1. If an **Option Base** statement isn't used in a program, Visual Basic assumes a value of 0 for the default lower subscript. You should note that the **Option Base** statement can only be used once in a form or module and must reside in the form or module's declaration section before any arrays are declared.

See Also:

Dim, LBound, ReDim, and **Static**

Example:

The program that follows demonstrates the **Option Base** statement by setting the default lower subscript to 1. Listing 13-93-1 presents the code for the form's declarations section, and Listing 13-93-2 the code for the program's **Form_Click** event. Figure 13-94 shows how the program's window would appear after the program has been run.

Listing 13-93-1:

```
Option Base 1

Dim Array(50) As Integer
```

Listing 13-93-2:

```
Sub Form_Click ()

    Print LBound(Array)

End Sub
```

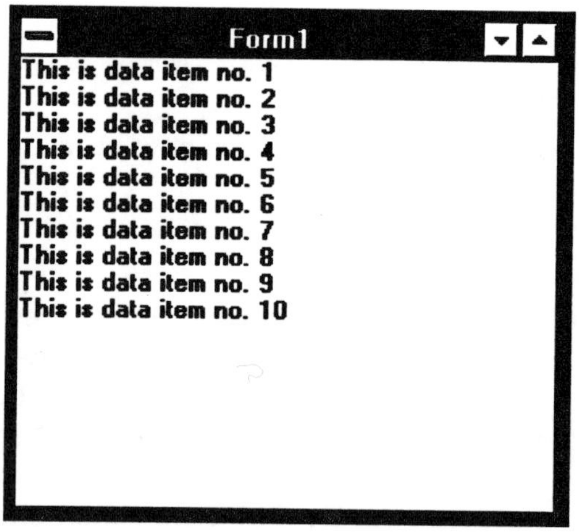

Figure 13-94 An **Option Base** *demonstration program.*

Print # Statement

Summary:

```
Print #number,[{;|,}][expression{;|,}
[expression{;|,}]...][{;|,}]
```

number   is the number of a previously opened file.

expression   is either a numeric or a string expression.

Description:

The **Print #** statement performs in the same manner as the **Print** method except that the statement's output is sent to a previously opened file. The file to send the output to is specified by number.

See Also:

Open

Example:

The program that appears below demonstrates the **Print #** statement by sending data to a disk file. Listing 13-94 presents the code for the program's **Form_Click** event. Figure 13-95 illustrates how the program's window would appear after the program has been run.

Listing 13-94:

```
Sub Form_Click ()
    Dim I As Integer

    Open "TEXTDEMO.DAT" For Output As 1
    For I = 1 To 10
        Print #1, "This is data item no."; I
    Next I
    Close 1
    Open "TEXTDEMO.DAT" For Input As 1
    While Not EOF(1)
        Input #1, A$
```

```
        Print A$
    Wend
    Close 1

End Sub
```

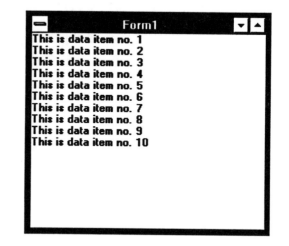

*Figure 13-95 A **Print #** demonstration program.*

Put Statement

Summary:

Put [#] *filenumber*, [*position*], *variable*

filenumber	is the number of a previously opened disk file.
position	is the file position to write the record to.
variable	is the variable to write the data from.

Description:

The **Put** statement writes data from memory to either a binary file or a random access file. The file to write the data to is specified by *filenumber*. The **Put** statement can optionally position the file pointer before writing the data with the *position* parameter. With a binary file, the *position* parameter is the actual byte position the file pointer is to be moved to. If a *position* parameter isn't specified in the **Put** statement, Visual Basic will simply write the data at the present position of the file pointer. The data to be written to the disk file is specified by *variable*.

The **Put** statement can also be used to write data to a random access file from memory. In the case of a random access file, *position* is the record number that the **Put** statement is to write and *variable* is any variable that is less than or equal to the file's record length.

See Also:

Get and **Open**

Example:

The program below demonstrates the **Put** statement by writing data to a binary disk file. Listing 13-95 presents the code for the program's **Form_Click** event. Figure 13-96 illustrates how the program's window would appear after the program has been run.

Listing 13-95:

```
Sub Form_Click ()
    Dim I As Integer, Rec As Integer

    Print "Writing demo file....."
    Open "DEMOFILE.DAT" For Binary As 1
    For I = 1 To 10
        Put 1, , I
    Next
    Close 1
    Open "DEMOFILE.DAT" For Binary As 1
    Print "Reading demo file backwards....."
    For I = 10 To 1 Step -1
        Get 1, (I - 1) * 2 + 1, Rec
        Print Rec; "...";
        If I = 6 Then
            Print
        End If
    Next
    Print
    Close 1

End Sub
```

*Figure 13-96 A **Put** demonstration program.*

QBColor Function

Summary:

`QBColor(color)`

`color`   is the color value.

Description:

The **QBColor** function returns an RGB color code for a color specified by *color*. The range of values *color* can represent is 0 to 15. Therefore, the **QBColor** function is very useful for converting QuickBasic and other color codes to equivalent RGB color codes.

See Also:

RGB

Example:

The following program demonstrates the **QBColor** function by setting a form's background color to a series of color codes.

Figure 13-97 A **QBColor** *demonstration program.*

Listing 13-96 presents the code for the program's **Form_Click** event. Figure 13-97 shows how the program's window would appear after the program has been run.

Listing 13-96:

```
Sub Form_Click ()
    Static C

    BackColor = QBColor(C)
    C = (C + 1) Mod 15

End Sub
```

Randomize Statement

Summary:

Randomize [*expression*]

expression   is a numeric expression.

Description:

The **Randomize** statement reseeds the Visual Basic random-number generator. An initial seed can be specified by *expres-*

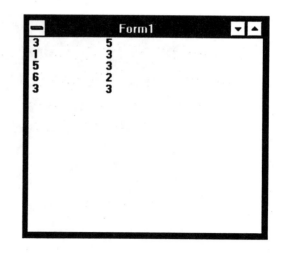

*Figure 13-98 A **Randomize** demonstration program.*

sion, which must be in the range of -32,768 to 32,767. If *expression* isn't specified, Visual Basic will use the value returned from the **Timer** function to reseed the random-number generator.

See Also:

Rnd and **Timer**

Example:

The program that follows demonstrates the **Randomize** statement by reseeding the random-number generator. Listing 13-97 presents the code for the program's **Form_Click** event. Figure 13-98 illustrates how the program's window would appear after the program has been run.

Listing 13-97:

```
Sub Form_Click ()
    Dim D1 As Integer, D2 As Integer

    Randomize
    Do
        D1 = Int(Rnd * 6) + 1
```

```
      D2 = Int(Rnd * 6) + 1
      Print D1, D2
   Loop Until D1 = D2

End Sub
```

ReDim Statement

Summary:

ReDim [**Shared**] *identifier(subscripts)* [**As** *type*] [,
identifier(subscripts) [**As** *type*]]...

Shared	is provided to maintain compatibility with older forms of Basic.
identifier	is a variable identifier.
subscripts	is either the maximum subscript or a range of subscripts for each dimension in an array.
type	is either an elementary data type (**Integer, Long, Single, Double, Currency,** or **String**) or a previously defined record type.

Description:

The **ReDim** statement is used to either declare a dynamic array variable at the procedure level or resize a previously declared dynamic array. Besides using the **ReDim** statement to declare dynamic arrays, dynamic arrays can be declared with the **Global** and **Dim** statements by specifying an array with empty parentheses. When the **ReDim** statement resizes an array, all numeric array elements are set to zero and all string array elements are set to null strings. Although the **ReDim** statement can be used to resize the number of elements in each of the array's dimensions, the **ReDim** statement cannot be used to resize the number of dimensions in an array.

See Also:

Dim and **Global**

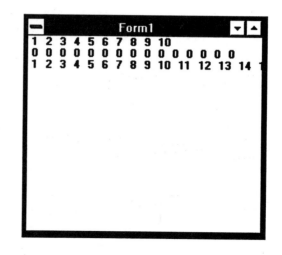

Figure 13-99 A **ReDim** *demonstration program.*

Example:

The following program demonstrates how the **ReDim** statement is used to resize an array. Listing 13-98 presents the code for the program's **Form_Click** event. Figure 13-99 illustrates how the program's window would appear after the program has been run.

Listing 13-98:

```
Sub Form_Click ()
    Dim I As Integer

    ReDim A(1 To 10) As Integer
    For I = 1 To 10
        A(I) = I
    Next I
    For I = 1 To 10
        Print A(I);
    Next
    Print

    ReDim A(1 To 15) As Integer
    For I = 1 To 15
        Print A(I);
    Next
    Print
```

```
    For I = 1 To 15
        A(I) = I
    Next
    For I = 1 To 15
        Print A(I);
    Next
    Print

End Sub
```

Rem Statement

Summary:

Rem *comment*

or

' comment

comment　　　　　is a comment.

Description:

The **Rem** statement is used to add comments to a Visual Basic program. As soon as Visual Basic encounters a **Rem** statement, it will ignore the remainder of the program line.

Example:

The below program demonstrates the **Rem** statement by adding a few comments to a program. Listing 13-99 presents the code for the program's **Form_Click** event. Figure 13-100 shows how the program's window would appear after the program has been run.

Listing 13-99:

```
Sub Form_Click ()

    Rem This is a remark
    ' This is a remark too!
    Print "This line has a remark":  'Sure enough!

End Sub
```

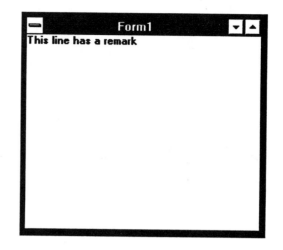

Figure 13-100 A **Rem** *demonstration program.*

Reset Statement

Summary:

```
Reset
```

Description:

The **Reset** statement closes all open files.

See Also:

Close

Example:

The following program demonstrates the **Reset** statement by closing all open disk files. Listing 13-100 presents the code for the program's **Form_Click** event. Figure 13-101 illustrates how the program's window would appear after the program has been run.

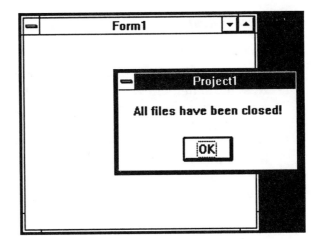

*Figure 13-101   A **Reset** demonstration program.*

Listing 13-100:

```
Sub Form_Click ()

    Open "TEST.DAT" For Output As 1
    Reset
    MsgBox "All files have been closed!"

End Sub
```

Resume Statement

Summary:

Resume [0]

or

Resume Next

or

Resume *line*

line   is either a line number or a line label.

Description:

The **Resume** statement tells Visual Basic where execution is to continue after an error-trapping routine has been called. A **Resume** statement without a parameter or a line number of 0 will continue program execution with the statement that caused the error. A **Resume** statement followed by a **Next** keyword will continue program execution with the statement that immediately follows the error. A **Resume** statement with a line parameter will continue execution at the start of the specified line.

See Also:

Err Function, **Err** Statement, **Erl**, **Error**, and **On Error**

Example:

The below program demonstrates the **Resume** statement by continuing program execution with the statements that follow program errors. Listing 13-101 gives the code for the program's **Form_Click** event. Figure 13-102 shows how the program's window would appear after the program has been run.

Listing 13-101:

```
Sub Form_Click ()

    On Error GoTo Handler
    Error 55
    Error 66
    Exit Sub

Handler:
    Print "Error:"; Err
    Resume Next

End Sub
```

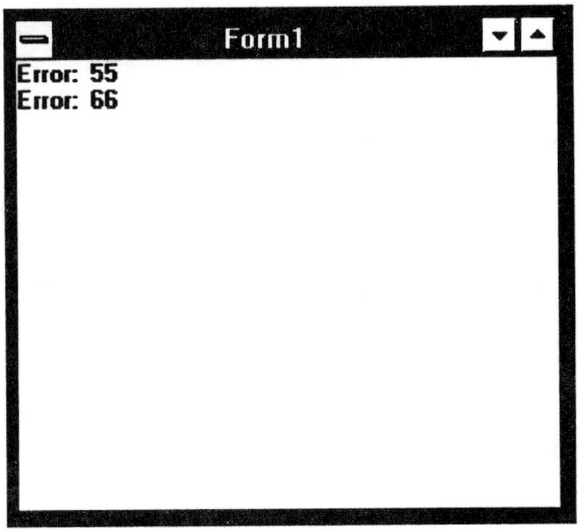

*Figure 13-102 A **Resume** demonstration program.*

Return Statement

Summary:

```
Return
```

Description:

The **Return** statement returns program execution from a called subroutine. Visual Basic will continue execution with the statement that immediately follows the subroutine's calling **GoSub** statement.

See Also:

GoSub...Return

Example:

The program that follows shows how the **Return** statement is used by returning program execution from a called subroutine.

*Figure 13-103 A **Return** demonstration program.*

Listing 13-102 presents the code for the program's **Form_Click** event. Figure 13-103 illustrates how the program's window would appear after the program has been run.

Listing 13-102:

```
Sub Form_Click ()

    N1 = 5
    N2 = 6
    GoSub Multiply
    N1 = 38
    N2 = 5
    GoSub Multiply
    Exit Sub
Multiply:
    Print N1 * N2
    Return

End Sub
```

RGB Function

Summary:

RGB(*red, green, blue*)

red	is the color's red component.
green	is the color's green component.
blue	is the color's blue component.

Description:

The **RGB** function calculates and returns an RGB color code from three separate components: *red*, *green*, and *blue*. The valid range for each of the color components is from 0 to 255.

See Also:

QBColor

Example:

The program below demonstrates the **RGB** function by changing a form's client area to white on black. Listing 13-103 presents the code for the program's **Form_Click** event. Figure 13-104 shows how the program's window would appear after the program has been run.

*Figure 13-104 An **RGB** demonstration program.*

Listing 13-103:

```
Sub Form_Click ()

    BackColor = RGB(0, 0, 0)
    ForeColor = RGB(255, 255, 255)
    Print "This is White on Black"

End Sub
```

Right$ Function

Summary:

Right$(*string*, *n*)

string   is a string expression.

n   is the number of characters to return.

Description:

The **Right$** function returns a substring from a specified *string* expression. The number of characters to be returned is specified by *n* and the substring will start with the **Len**(*string*)-*n*+1 character. If *string* has fewer characters than *n*, Visual Basic will return the whole of *string* as the result.

See Also:

Left$** and **Mid$ Function

Example:

The following program demonstrates the **Right$** function by extracting and displaying a few substrings. Listing 13-104 presents the code for the program's **Form_Click** event. Figure 13-105 illustrates how the program's window would appear after the program has been run.

*Figure 13-105   A **Right$** demonstration program.*

Listing 13-104:

```
Sub Form_Click ()

    Print Right$("This is a partial string", 10)
    A$ = "Another string"
    Print Right$(A$, 3)

End Sub
```

RmDir Statement

Summary:

RmDir *string*

string   is the directory's path.

Description:

The **RmDir** statement deletes a directory from a disk. The directory's path is specified by *string*. You should note that the directory must be empty before it can be deleted.

*Figure 13-106 A **RmDir** demonstration program.*

See Also:

ChDir and MkDir

Example:

The program that follows demonstrates the **RmDir** statement by deleting a disk directory. Listing 13-105 gives the code for the program's **Form_Click** event. Figure 13-106 shows how the program's window would appear after the program has been run.

Listing 13-105:

```
Sub Form_Click ()

    MkDir "C:\VB\TEMP"
    Print "Directory created!"
    RmDir "C:\VB\TEMP"
    Print "Directory deleted!"

End Sub
```

Rnd Function

Summary:

Rnd[(*n*)]

n   specifies a subfunction.

Description:

The **Rnd** function returns a single-precision random number between 0 and 1. If an *n* parameter is specified and *n* is less than zero, **Rnd** will always return the same number for subsequent calls with the same *n* value. If an *n* parameter is specified and *n* is equal to zero, **Rnd** will return the last number generated. If an *n* parameter is not specified or an *n* parameter is specified and *n* is greater than zero, **Rnd** will return the next random number in the random number sequence.

See Also:

Randomize

Example:

The program that appears below shows how the **Rnd** function is used by continuously displaying the value of two dice rolls until doubles come up. Listing 13-106 presents the code for the program's **Form_Click** event. Figure 13-107 illustrates how the program's window would appear after the program has been run.

Listing 13-106:

```
Sub Form_Click ()
    Dim D1 As Integer, D2 As Integer

    Randomize
    Do
        D1 = Int(Rnd * 6) + 1
```

```
         D2 = Int(Rnd * 6) + 1
         Print D1, D2
     Loop Until D1 = D2

End Sub
```

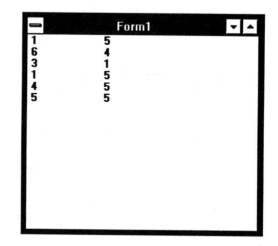

*Figure 13-107 A **Rnd** demonstration program.*

RSet Statement

Summary:

```
RSet variable = expression
```

variable   is a string variable.

expression   is a string expression.

Description:

The **RSet** statement right-justifies a string *expression* in a string *variable*. If the string *expression* is shorter than *variable*'s current length, *variable* will be padded with spaces. If the string *expression* is longer than *variable*'s current length, expression will be truncated to fit into the *variable*.

See Also:

LSet

Example:

The below program demonstrates the **RSet** statement by right-justifying a few string expressions in a string variable. Listing 13-107 presents the code for the program's **Form_Click** event. Figure 13-108 shows how the program's window would appear after the program has been run.

Listing 13-107:

```
Sub Form_Click ()
    Dim A As String * 6

    RSet A = "Test"
    Print A
    RSet A = "Another test"
    Print A

End Sub
```

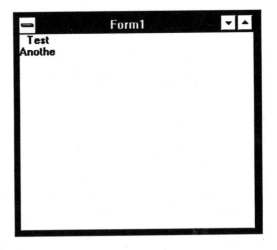

*Figure 13-108 A **RSet** demonstration program.*

RTrim$ Function

Summary:

`RTrim$(expression)`

`expression`   is a string expression.

Description:

The **RTrim$** function strips any trailing spaces from a string *expression*.

See Also:

LTrim$

Example:

The following program demonstrates the **RTrim$** function by stripping away the trailing spaces from a few strings. Listing 13-108 gives the code for the program's **Form_Click** event. Figure 13-109 illustrates how the program's window would appear after the program has been run.

Figure 13-109 A **RTrim$** *demonstration program.*

Listing 13-108:

```
Sub Form_Click ()

    Print RTrim$("This is a sample RTrim$     ");
    "****"
    Print RTrim$("This is another "); "##"

End Sub
```

SavePicture Statement

Summary:

SavePicture *pictureobject, string*

pictureobject   is the **Picture** or **Image** property to be saved.

string   is the picture file's name.

Description:

The **SavePicture** property saves either a **Picture** or an **Image** property to a disk file. If a **Picture** property was originally loaded from a disk file, the **SavePicture** statement will save the object's image using the original file format. All **Image** pictures are saved as bitmap (.BMP) files.

See Also:

LoadPicture

Example:

The program that follows demonstrates how the **SavePicture** property is used to save a form's image as a bitmap file. Listing 13-109 presents the code for the program's **Form_Click** event. Figure 13-110 shows how the program's window would appear after the program has been run.

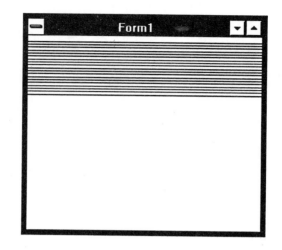

Figure 13-110 A **SavePicture** *demonstration program.*

Listing 13-109:

```
Sub Form_Click ()

    AutoRedraw = -1
    For I = 100 To 1000 Step 50
        Line (0, I)-(ScaleWidth - 1, I)
    Next
    SavePicture Image, "LINES.BMP"

End Sub
```

Second Function

Summary:

Second(*serialnumber*)

serialnumber   is a numeric expression.

Description:

The **Second** function returns the second of the minute that is represented by a serial number. The serial number is specified by *serialnumber*.

See Also:

Day, Hour, Minute, Month, Now, Weekday, and **Year**

Example:

The program that appears below demonstrates the **Second** function by displaying a serial number's second of the minute. Listing 13-110 presents the code for the program's **Form_Click** event. Figure 13-111 illustrates how the program's window would appear after the program has been run.

Listing 13-110:

```
Sub Form_Click ()

    T$ = Time$
    Serial# = TimeValue(T$)
    Print T$
    Print Second(Serial#)

End Sub
```

*Figure 13-111 A **Second** demonstration program.*

Seek Function

Summary:

Seek(*filenumber*)

filenumber   is the number of a previously opened file.

Description:

The **Seek** function returns the current position of the file pointer for a previously opened file. The file is specified by *filenumber*. If the file is a random access file, the **Seek** function returns the next record number. If the file is any other file type, the **Seek** function returns the file pointer's actual byte position.

See Also:

Get, Open, Put, and **Seek** Statement

Example:

The program below demonstrates the **Seek** function by returning the byte positions of the records in a binary file. Listing 13-111 gives the code for the program's **Form_Click** event. Figure 13-112 shows how the program's window would appear after the program has been run.

Listing 13-111:

```
Sub Form_Click ()
    Dim I As Integer, Rec As Integer

    Print "Writing demo file....."
    Open "DEMOFILE.DAT" For Binary As 1
    For I = 1 To 10
        Put 1, , I
    Next
    Close 1
    Print "Reading demo file backwards....."
    Open "DEMOFILE.DAT" For Binary As 1
    For I = 10 To 1 Step -1
        Get 1, (I - 1) * 2 + 1, Rec
```

```
        Print Rec; "..."; Seek(1)
    Next
    Print
    Close 1

End Sub
```

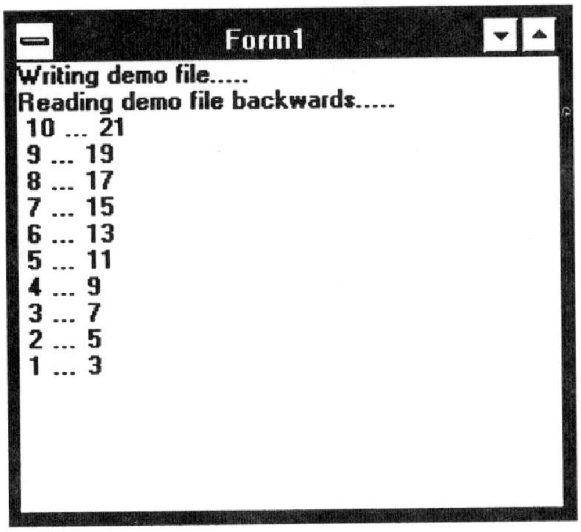

Figure 13-112 *A Seek function demonstration program.*

Seek Statement

Summary:

Seek [#] *filenumber, position*

filenumber	is the number of a previously opened file.
position	is the new file position.

Description:

The **Seek** statement moves the file pointer to a new position. The file is specified by *filenumber*. The file pointer's new position is specified by *position* and can be any value from 1 to 2,147,483,647. If the file is a random access file, *position* is the record number to move the file pointer to. If the file is any other file type, *position* is the byte number to move the file pointer to.

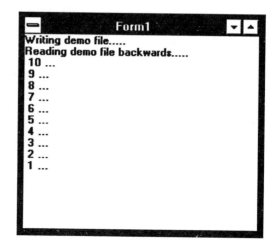

*Figure 13-113 A **Seek** statement demonstration program.*

See Also:

Get, Open, Put, and **Seek** Function.

Example:

The following program shows how the **Seek** statement is used by moving the position of the file pointer before reading a file's records. Listing 13-112 presents the code for the program's **Form_Click** event. Figure 13-113 illustrates how the program's window would appear after the program has been run.

Listing 13-112:

```
Sub Form_Click ()
    Dim I As Integer, Rec As Integer

    Print "Writing demo file....."
    Open "DEMOFILE.DAT" For Binary As 1
    For I = 1 To 10
        Put 1, , I
    Next
    Close 1
    Print "Reading demo file backwards....."
    Open "DEMOFILE.DAT" For Binary As 1
```

```
For I = 10 To 1 Step -1
    Seek 1, (I - 1) * 2 + 1
    Get 1, , Rec
    Print Rec; "..."
Next
Print
Close 1

End Sub
```

Select Case Statement

Summary:

```
Select Case expression
    Case expression list
        [statements]
    [Case expression list
        [statements]]
        .
        .
        .
    [Case Else
        [statements]]
End Select
```

expression	is either a numeric or a string expression.
expression list	is a list of expressions to check against *expression*.
statements	is one or more Visual Basic program statements.

Description:

The **Select Case** statement is used to select a routine from a variety of routines to be executed depending upon the result of an *expression*. Visual Basic checks *expression* against the individual expressions in the **Case** *expression list*. When Visual Basic finds a match, it will execute the *statements* that are associated with the selected **Case** clause. After executing the **Case** *statement*, Visual Basic will continue program execution with the program statement that immediately follows the **End**

Select statement. If Visual Basic is unable to find a matching expression in the **Case** *expression lists*, it will check for the existence of a **Case Else** clause. If a **Case Else** clause exists, Visual Basic will execute its associated *statements*. Otherwise, Visual Basic will generate an error message. Consequently, all **Select Case** statements should have a **Case Else** clause to prevent unwanted program errors.

The individual expressions in the **Case** *expression lists* can either be a single value, a range of values, or a relational check. Multiple expressions are separated by commas. A range of values uses the following syntax:

```
expression To expression
```

A relational check uses the below syntax:

```
Is operator expression
```

Where *operator* is a Visual Basic relational operator: =, <, <=, >, >=, or <>.

Example:

The program that follows demonstrates the **Select Case** statement by displaying one of a wide variety of messages depending upon the value of an expression. Listing 13-113 gives the

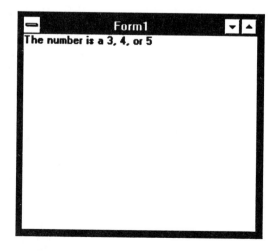

*Figure 13-114 A **Select Case** demonstration program.*

code for the program's **Form_Click** event. Figure 13-114 shows how the program's window would appear after the program has been run.

Listing 13-113:

```
Sub Form_Click ()
    Dim Number As Integer

    Number = 3
    Select Case Number
        Case Is < 1
            Print "The number is less than 1"
        Case 1
            Print "The number is a 1"
        Case 2
            Print "The number is a 2"
        Case 3 To 5
            Print "The number is a 3, 4, or 5"
        Case 7, 10
            Print "The number is a 7 or 10"
        Case 8
            Print "The number is an 8"
        Case 9
            Print "The number is a 9"
        Case Else
            Print "The number is greater than 10"
    End Select

End Sub
```

SendKeys Statement

Summary:

SendKeys *keys*[*, wait*]

keys	is a string expression.
wait	is a numeric expression.

Description:

The **SendKeys** statement sends a string of keys to the active window. Effectively, the **SendKeys** statement simulates the actual pressing of the specified keys. The keys to be sent to the active window are specified by the string expression *keys*. With a few exceptions, all keypresses to be sent are simply specified with their character representations. For example, the keypresses **v, i, s, u, a,** and **l** could be sent with the string "visual." Nondisplayable keypresses can be sent with the following codes:

Key Press	Code
BACKSPACE	{BACKSPACE}, {BS}, or {BKSP}
BREAK	{BREAK}
CAPS LOCK	{CAPSLOCK}
CLEAR	{CLEAR}
DELETE	{DELETE} or {DEL}
DOWN	{DOWN}
END	{END}
ENTER	{ENTER} or ~
ESC	{ESCAPE} or {ESC}
HELP	{HELP}
HOME	{HOME}
INSERT	{INSERT}
LEFT	{LEFT}
NUM LOCK	{NUMLOCK}
PAGE DOWN	{PG DN}
PAGE UP	{PG UP}
PRINT SCREEN	{PRTSC}
RIGHT	{RIGHT}
SCROLL LOCK	{SCROLLLOCK}
TAB	{TAB}
UP	{UP}
F1	{F1}
F2	{F2}

Key Press	Code
F3	{F3}
F4	{F4}
F5	{F5}
F6	{F6}
F7	{F7}
F8	{F8}
F9	{F9}
F10	{F10}
F11	{F11}
F12	{F12}
F13	{F13}
F14	{F14}
F15	{F15}
F16	{F16}

The shift keys can be specified with these codes:

Shift Key	Code
SHIFT	+
CONTROL	^
ALT	%

To use a shift key, you simply precede the key to be shifted with the appropriate shift-key code. Multiple shifted keys can be easily specified by enclosing them in parentheses and preceding the parentheses with the appropriate shift-key code. For instance, the keys "+A+B+C" could be more easily specified as "+(abc)."

To be able to pass the +, ^, %, {, and } keys to the active window, Visual Basic lets your specified these keys by surrounding them with braces ({}).

When the keys are to be passed to another Windows application, an optional *wait* parameter can be specified to instruct Visual Basic when it is to return after sending the keys to the active window. If the *wait* parameter is specified and it is equal to True, then Visual Basic will wait for the active window's application program to process the specified keys before control is returned to the sending application program. Otherwise, Visual Basic will return to the sending program immediately after the program has sent the keys to the active window.

Example:

The following program demonstrates the **SendKeys** statement by sending a string of six keys to the active window. Listing 13-114-1 presents the code for the program's **Form_Click** event and Listing 13-114-2 the code for the program's **Form_Key-Press** event. Figure 13-115 illustrates how the program's window would appear after the program has been run.

Listing 13-114-1:

```
Sub Form_Click ()
```

*Figure 13-115 A **SendKeys** demonstration program.*

```
    SendKeys "+abc+def"

End Sub
```

Listing 13-114-2:

```
Sub Form_KeyPress (KeyAscii As Integer)

    Print Chr$(KeyAscii);

End Sub
```

Sgn Function

Summary:

Sgn(*expression*)

expression   is a numeric expression.

Description:

The **Sgn** function returns a value that indicates the sign of a specified numeric *expression*. If *expression* is greater than zero, the **Sgn** function returns a value of 1. If *expression* is equal to zero, the **Sgn** function returns a value of 0. If *expression* is less than zero, the **Sgn** function returns a value of -1.

Example:

The program that appears below demonstrates the **Sgn** function by indicating the sign of a few numeric expressions. Listing 13-115 gives the code for the program's **Form_Click** event. Figure 13-116 shows how the program's window would appear after the program has been run.

Listing 13-115:

```
Sub Form_Click ()

    Print Sgn(0)
    Print Sgn(1)
    Print Sgn(-1)
```

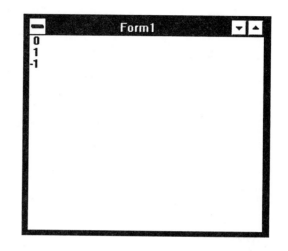

*Figure 13-116 A **Sgn** demonstration program.*

```
End Sub
```

Shell Function

Summary:

```
Shell(program[, style])
```

program   is a string expression.

style   is a numeric expression.

Description:

The **Shell** function runs a program. The program to be run is specified by *program* and must be a .COM, .EXE, .BAT, or .PIF file. An optional *style* parameter can be specified to tell Windows how the program is to be run. A list of the valid styles that can be specified with the *style* parameter follows:

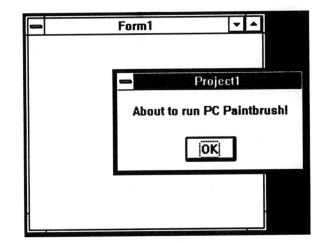

*Figure 13-117 A **Shell** demonstration program.*

Value	Style
1	Normal window with focus.
2	Minimized with focus.
3	Maximized with focus.
4	Normal window without focus.
7	Minimized without focus.

If Windows is successful in running the program, Visual Basic will return the program's task identification number. Otherwise, Visual Basic will generate an error message.

Example:

The below program shows how the **Shell** function is used to run a copy of PC Paintbrush. Listing 13-116 presents the code for the program's **Form_Click** event. Figure 13-117 illustrates how the program's window would appear after the program has been run.

Listing 13-116:

```
Sub Form_Click ()
```

```
MsgBox "About to run PC Paintbrush!"
I = Shell("PBRUSH.EXE")

End Sub
```

Sin Function

Summary:

Sin(*expression*)

expression   is a numeric expression.

Description:

The **Sin** function returns the sine of an angle. The angle is specified by *expression* and is considered to be in radians.

See Also:

Atn, Cos, and **Tan**

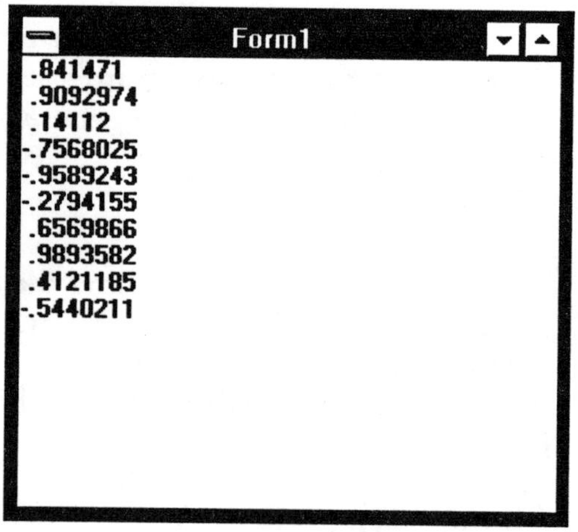

Figure 13-118 A **Sin** *demonstration program.*

Example:

The following program demonstrates the **Sin** function by displaying the sine for a series of angles. Listing 13-117 presents the code for the program's **Form_Click** event. Figure 13-118 illustrates how the program's window would appear after the program has been run.

Listing 13-117:

```
Sub Form_Click ()
    Dim I As Integer

    For I = 1 To 10
        Print Sin(I)
    Next

End Sub
```

Space$ Function

Summary:

Space$(*length*)

length   is the string's length.

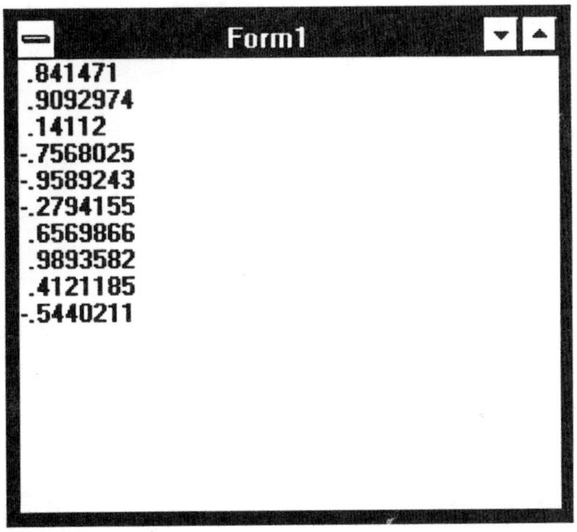

Figure 13-119 A **Space$** *demonstration program.*

Description:

The **Space$** function returns a string of spaces. The length of the string of spaces is specified by *length*.

See Also:

Spc

Example:

The program that follows demonstrates the **Space$** function by displaying a series of increasingly larger space strings. Listing 13-118 gives the code for the program's **Form_Click** event. Figure 13-119 shows how the program's window would appear after the program has been run.

Listing 13-118:

```
Sub Form_Click ()
    Dim I As Integer

    For I = 1 To 10
        Print I; "Spaces:"; Space$(I); ":"
    Next

End Sub
```

Spc Function

Summary:

Spc (*n*)

n   is the number of spaces to print.

Description:

The **Spc** function prints a specified number of spaces. The number of spaces the **Spc** function is to generate is specified by *n*. You should note that the **Spc** function can only be used with the **Print** method and the **Print #** statement.

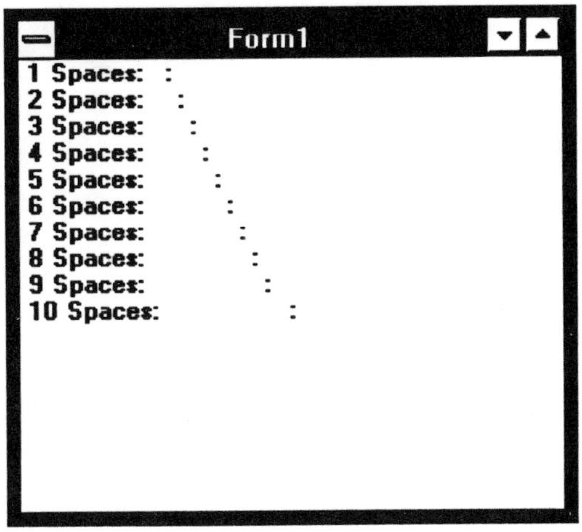

*Figure 13-120 A **Spc** demonstration program.*

See Also:

Print, Print #, and **Space$**

Example:

The program that appears below shows how the **Spc** function is used by displaying a series of messages with an increasingly larger number of spaces. Listing 13-119 presents the code for the program's **Form_Click** event. Figure 13-120 illustrates how the program's window would appear after the program has been run.

Listing 13-119:

```
Sub Form_Click ()
    Dim I As Integer

    For I = 1 To 10
        Print I; "Spaces:"; Spc(I); ":"
    Next

End Sub
```

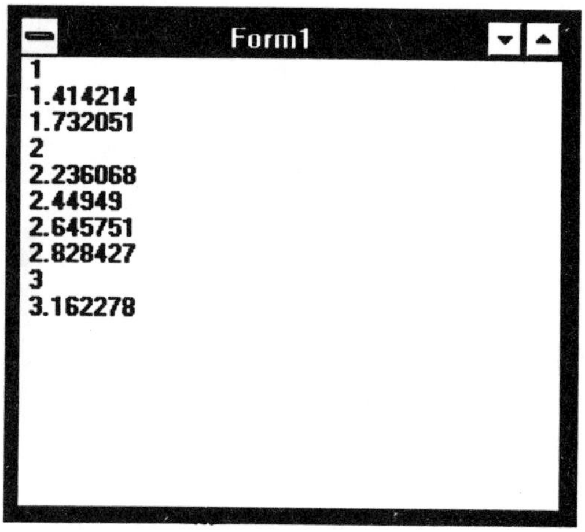

*Figure 13-121 A **Sqr** demonstration program.*

Sqr Function

Summary:

Sqr (*expression*)

expression   is a numeric expression.

Description:

The **Sqr** function returns the square root of a specified numeric *expression*. You should note that *expression* must be greater than or equal to 0.

Example:

The below program demonstrates the **Sqr** function by displaying the square root of a few values. Listing 13-120 gives the code for the program's **Form_Click** event. Figure 13-121 illustrates how the program's window would appear after the program has been run.

Listing 13-120:

```
Sub Form_Click ()
    Dim I As Integer

    For I = 1 To 10
        Print Sqr (I)
    Next

End Sub
```

Static Statement

Summary:

Static *identifier*[(*subscripts*)] [**As**
type] [,*identifier*[(*subscripts*)] [**As** *type*]]...

identifier	is a variable identifier.
subscripts	is either the maximum subscript or a range of subscripts for each dimension in an array.
type	is either an elementary data type (**Integer, Long, Single, Double, Currency,** or **String**) or a previously defined record type.

Description:

The **Static** statement is used to declare static variables at the procedure level. Each variable in a **Static** statement can either be an elementary data type or a previously defined record type. Furthermore, a variable can be declared as an array.

See Also:

Dim, Global, Option Base, and **ReDim**

Example:

The following program demonstrates the **Static** statement by declaring an integer array variable, an integer variable, and a fixed-length string variable. Listing 13-121 presents the code for the program's **Form_Click** event. Figure 13-122 shows how the program's window would appear after the program has been run.

Listing 13-121:

```
Sub Form_Click ()
    Static A(1 To 50) As Integer, I As Integer,
    FirstName As String * 10

    For I = 1 To 50
        A(I) = I
```

*Figure 13-122 A **Static** demonstration program.*

```
    Next
    For I = 1 To 50
        Print A(I);
        If A(I) Mod 10 = 0 Then
            Print
        End If
    Next
    FirstName = "Chrissy"
    Print FirstName

End Sub
```

Stop Statement

Summary:

```
stop
```

Description:

The **Stop** statement terminates program execution. Unlike an **End** statement, the **Stop** statement leaves all files open and all variables intact.

See Also:

End

Example:

The program that follows shows how the **Stop** statement is used by prematurely terminating a program halfway through a loop. Listing 13-122 presents the code for the program's

```
┌─────────────────────────────────────────────────────────┐
│ ⊐                     FORM1.FRM                          │
├─────────────────────────────────────────────────────────┤
│ Object: │Form          │ ⊻│ Proc: │Click        │     ⊻│ │
├─────────────────────────────────────────────────────────┤
│ Sub Form_Click ()                                       │
│     Dim I As Integer                                    │
│                                                         │
│     For I = 1 To 10                                     │
│         Print I                                         │
│         │If I = 5 Then Stop│                            │
│     Next                                                │
│                                                         │
│ End Sub                                                 │
│                                                         │
└─────────────────────────────────────────────────────────┘
```

*Figure 13-123 A **Stop** demonstration program.*

Form_Click event. Figure 13-123 illustrates how the desktop would appear after the program has been halted.

Listing 13-122:

```
Sub Form_Click ()
    Dim I As Integer

    For I = 1 To 10
        Print I
        If I = 5 Then Stop
    Next

End Sub
```

Str$ Function

Summary:

Str$(*expression*)

expression   is a numeric expression.

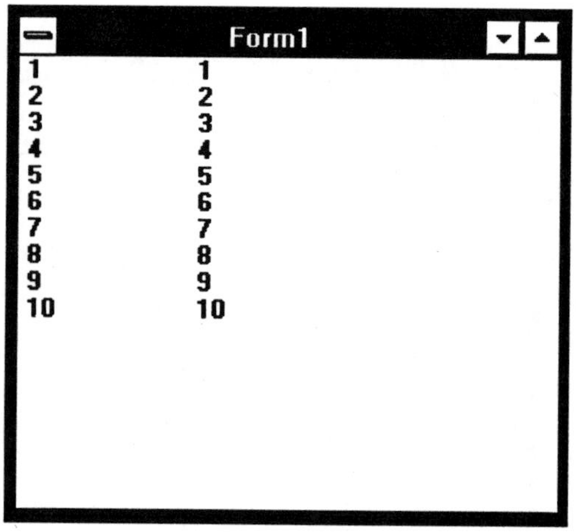

*Figure 13-124 A **Str$** demonstration program.*

Description:

The **Str$** function returns an ASCII string representation of a specified numeric expression.

See Also:

Val

Example:

The program that appears below demonstrates the **Str$** function by displaying an ASCII string for a series of numeric values. Listing 13-123 presents the code for the program's **Form_Click** event. Figure 13-124 illustrates how the program's window would appear after the program has been run.

Listing 13-123:

```
Sub Form_Click ()
    Dim I As Integer

    For I = 1 To 10
        Print I, Str$(I)
    Next

End Sub
```

String$ Function

Summary:

```
String$(length, expression)
```

length	is the string's length.
expression	is a numeric or a string expression.

Description:

The **String$** function builds a string with a specified *length*. All of the string's characters are the same and are specified by *expression*. If *expression* is numeric, it must be in the range 0 to

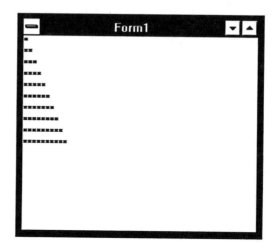

*Figure 13-125 A **String$** demonstration program.*

255 and specifies the ASCII code for the string characters. If *expression* is a string, all of the **String$** string's characters will be the same as the first character of the string *expression*.

See Also:

Space$

Example:

The below program demonstrates the **String$** function by building and displaying a series of successively longer strings. Listing 13-124 presents the code for the program's **Form_Click** event. Figure 13-125 illustrates how the program's window would appear after the program has been run.

Listing 13-124:

```
Sub Form_Click ()
    Dim I As Integer

    For I = 1 To 10
        Print String$(I, "*")
    Next
```

```
End Sub
```

Sub Statement

Summary:

```
[Static] Sub name[(parameters)]
    .
    .
    .
End Sub
```

name	is the name of the **Sub** procedure.
parameters	is one or more parameters to be passed to the **Sub** procedure.

Description:

The **Sub** statement defines a **Sub** procedure with a name specified by *name*. Once defined, a **Sub** procedure is called in a program just like any of the built-in Visual Basic statements. You simply specify the **Sub** procedure's name and any optional *parameters* in a program statement. If a **Static** keyword is used in a **Sub** statement, all of the **Sub** procedure's local variables will retain their values between procedure calls. Otherwise, all local variables are erased between calls. A **Sub** procedure can be prematurely exited by an **Exit Sub** statement.

See Also:

Function

Example:

The following program demonstrates the **Sub** statement by performing several calls to a sample **Sub** procedure. Listing 13-125-1 presents the code for the program's **Display** procedure; Listing 13-125-2 gives the code for the program's **Form_Click** event. Figure 13-126 illustrates how the program's window would appear after the program has been run.

Listing 13-125-1:

```
Sub Display (N As Integer)

    If N = 1 Then
```

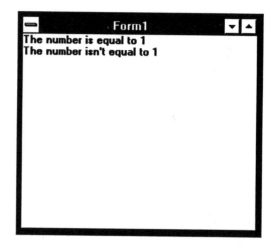

*Figure 13-126 A **Sub** demonstration program.*

```
        Print "The number is equal to 1"
    Else
        Print "The number isn't equal to 1"
    End If

End Sub
```

Listing 13-125-2:

```
Sub Form_Click ()
    Dim Number As Integer

    Number = 1
    Display Number
    Number = 0
    Display Number

End Sub
```

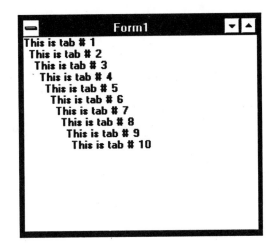

Figure 13-127 A **Tab** *demonstration program.*

Tab Function

Summary:

Tab(*position* **)**

position   is the column number.

Description:

The **Tab** function moves the text cursor to a specified column.
The column is specified by *position*. If the text cursor is already
moved beyond the specified column, Visual Basic will move
the cursor to the specified column on the next line. You should
note that the **Tab** function can only be used in conjunction with
either the **Print** method or the **Print #** statement.

See Also:

Print and **Print #**

Example:

The program that follows demonstrates the **Tab** function by displaying a message at an ever-increasing tab position. Listing 13-126 presents the code for the program's **Form_Click** event. Figure 13-127 illustrates how the program's window would appear after the program has been run.

Listing 13-126:

```
Sub Form_Click ()
    Dim I As Integer

    For I = 1 To 10
        Print Tab(I); "This is tab #"; I
    Next

End Sub
```

Tan Function

Summary:

`Tan(`*expression*`)`

expression   is a numeric expression.

Description:

The **Tan** function returns the tangent of an angle. The angle is specified by *expression* and is considered to be in radians.

See Also:

Atn, Cos, and **Sin**

Example:

The program that appears below shows how the **Tan** function is used by displaying the tangent for a series of angles. Listing 13-127 presents the code for the program's **Form_Click** statement. Figure 13-128 illustrates how the program's window would appear after the program has been run.

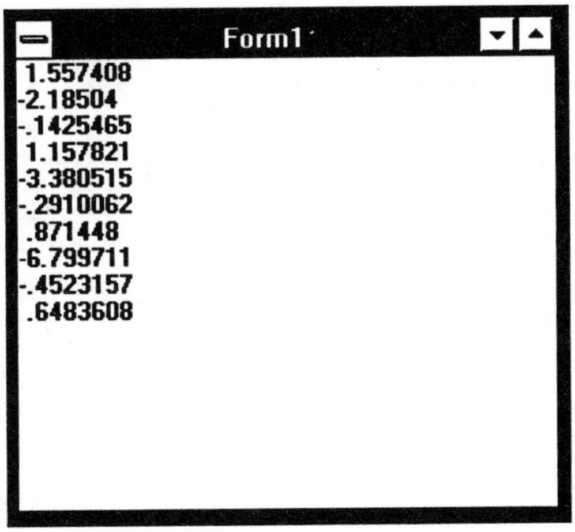

```
Form1
1.557408
-2.18504
-.1425465
 1.157821
-3.380515
-.2910062
 .871448
-6.799711
-.4523157
 .6483608
```

Figure 13-128 A **Tan** *demonstration program.*

Listing 13-127:

```
Sub Form_Click ()
    Dim I As Integer

    For I = 1 To 10
        Print Tan(I)
    Next

End Sub
```

Time$ Function

Summary:

```
Time$
```

Description:

The **Time$** function returns the current date in an eight-character string (hh:mm:ss). You should note that the result returned by **Time$** assumes a 24-hour clock.

See Also:

Time$ Statement and **Timer**

Example:

The below program demonstrates the **Time$** function by displaying the current time. Listing 13-128 gives the code for the program's **Form_Click** event. Figure 13-129 shows how the program's window would appear after the program has been run.

Listing 13-128:

```
Sub Form_Click ()

    Print Time$

End Sub
```

*Figure 13-129 A **Time$** function demonstration program.*

Time$ Statement

Summary:

Time$ = *expression*

expression   is a string expression.

Description:

The **Time$** statement sets the time for the system clock. The new time is specified by *expression* and is a string with one of the following formats:

Format	Description
hh	Specifies the hour. Visual Basic assumes 00 for both the minutes and the seconds.
hh:mm	Specifies the hour and minutes. Visual Basic assumes 00 for the seconds.
hh:mm:ss	Specifies the hour, minutes, and seconds.

You should note that the **Time$** statement uses a 24-hour clock.

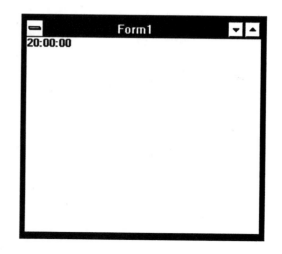

Figure 13-130 A **Time$** *statement demonstration program.*

See Also:

Time$ Function and **Timer**

Example:

The following program demonstrates the **Time$** statement by setting the system clock for 8:00 PM. Listing 13-129 presents the code for the program's **Form_Click** event. Figure 13-130 illustrates how the program's window would appear after the program has been run.

Listing 13-129:

```
Sub Form_Click ()

    Time$ = "20:00:00"
    Print Time$

End Sub
```

Timer Function

Summary:

`Timer`

Description:

The **Timer** function returns the number of seconds that have elapsed since midnight.

See Also:

Randomize, Time$** Function, and **Time$ Statement

Example:

The program that follows demonstrates the **Timer** function by displaying the number of seconds that have elapsed since midnight. Listing 13-130 gives the code for the program's **Form_Click** event. Figure 13-131 shows how the program's window would appear after the program has been run.

Listing 13-130:

```
Sub Form_Click ()

    Print Timer; "seconds have elapsed since midnight!"

End Sub
```

Figure 13-131 A **Timer** *demonstration program.*

TimeSerial Function

Summary:

```
TimeSerial(hour, minute, second)
```

hour	is a numeric expression.
month	is a numeric expression.
day	is a numeric expression.

Description:

The **TimeSerial** function returns a double-precision serial number based on a specific time. The time is specified by the function's three parameters: *hour, minute,* and *second.* The range of times the **TimeSerial** function can handle is from 00:00:00 to 23:59:59.

See Also:

Hour, Minute, Now, Second, and **TimeValue**

Example:

The program that appears below demonstrates the **TimeSerial** function by displaying a time's serial number. Listing 13-131 presents the code for the program's **Form_Click** event. Figure 13-132 illustrates how the program's window would appear after the program has been run.

Listing 13-131:

```
Sub Form_Click ()

    Print TimeSerial(12, 26, 59)

End Sub
```

*Figure 13-132 A **TimeSerial** demonstration program.*

TimeValue Function

Summary:

TimeValue(*time*)

time   is a string expression.

Description:

The **TimeValue** function returns a serial number for a specific *time*. The string argument *time* can be in one of two different formats. Below are examples of how the time 3:53 PM could be specified:

```
3:53PM
15:53
```

See Also:

Hour, Minute, Now, Second, and **TimeSerial**

Example:

The following program demonstrates the **TimeValue** function by displaying a time's serial number. Listing 13-132 presents

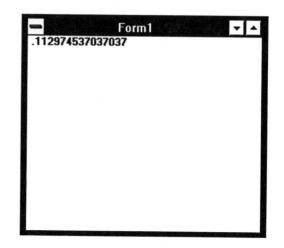

*Figure 13-133 A **TimeValue** demonstration program.*

the code for the program's **Form_Click** event. Figure 13-133 shows how the program's window would appear after the program has been run.

Listing 13-132:

```
Sub Form_Click ()

    Print TimeValue("02:42:41")

End Sub
```

Type Statement

Summary:

```
Type name
    field As type
    [field As type]
    .
    .
    .
End Type
```

name	is the user-defined type's name.
field	is a field name.
type	is the field's data type.

Description:

The **Type** statement is used to define a user-defined data type. The new data type is assigned a specified *name* and consists of one or more *fields*. A *field*'s data type is specified by *type* and can be either **Integer, Long, Single, Double, Currency, String,** or another user-defined type. You should note that the **Type** statement can only be used in the global module.

Example:

The below program demonstrates the **Type** statement by creating a record type to hold student grading data. Listing 13-133-1 presents the code for the program's global module, and Listing 13-133-2 the code for the program's **Form_Click** event. Figure 13-134 illustrates how the program's window would appear after the program has been run.

Listing 13-133-1:

```
Sub Form_Click ()
    Dim S1 As Student, S2 As Student

    S1.SName = "John Smith"
    S1.Ave = 95
    S2.SName = "Jane Doe"
    S2.Ave = 98
    Print RTrim$(S1.SName); "'s average is a"; S1.Ave
    Print RTrim$(S2.SName); "'s average is a"; S2.Ave

End Sub
```

Listing 13-133-2:

```
Sub Form_Click ()
    Dim S1 As Student, S2 As Student

    S1.SName = "John Smith"
    S1.Ave = 95
    S2.SName = "Jane Doe"
    S2.Ave = 98
    Print RTrim$(S1.SName); "'s average is a"; S1.Ave
    Print RTrim$(S2.SName); "'s average is a"; S2.Ave

End Sub
```

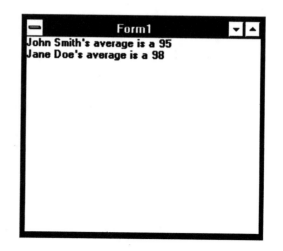

Figure 13-134 A **Type** *demonstration program.*

UBound Function

Summary:

UBound(*array*[, *dimension*])

array   is the name of the array.

dimension   is the dimension.

Description:

The **UBound** function returns the largest subscript for an *array's dimension*. You should note that the *dimension* parameter is only required for multidimensional arrays. The *dimension* parameter is assumed to be 1 for arrays with only a single dimension.

See Also:

LBound

Example:

The program that follows shows how the **UBound** function is used by returning the largest subscript for a variety of array

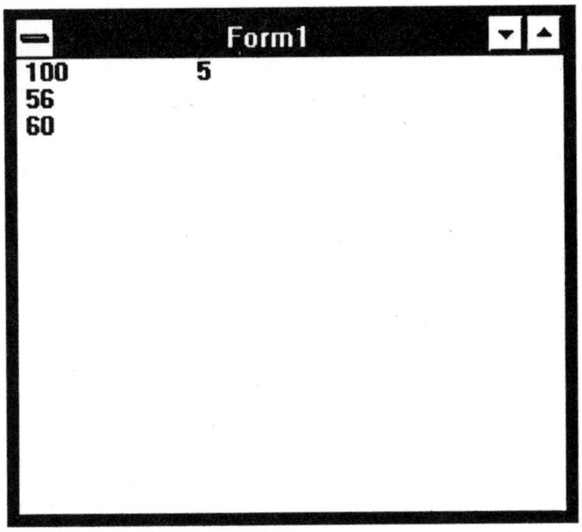

Figure 13-135 An **UBound** *demonstration program.*

dimensions. Listing 13-134 presents the code for the program's **Form_Click** event. Figure 13-135 illustrates how the program's window would appear after the program has been run.

Listing 13-134:

```
Sub Form_Click ()
    Static A(-100 To 100, 1 To 5), B(56), C(55 To 60)

    Print UBound(A, 1), UBound(A, 2)
    Print UBound(B)
    Print UBound(C)

End Sub
```

UCase$ Function

Summary:

UCase$(*expression*)

expression   is a string expression.

Description:

The **UCase$** function converts a string *expression* to all upper-case characters.

See Also:

LCase$

Example:

The program that appears below demonstrates the **UCase$** function by converting and displaying a few uppercase strings. Listing 13-135 presents the code for the program's **Form_Click** event. Figure 13-136 shows how the program's window would appear after the program has been run.

Listing 13-135:

```
Sub Form_Click ()

    Print UCase$("this is an uppercase string")
    Print UCase$("This IS an UpPeRcAsE strING")

End Sub
```

*Figure 13-136 An **UCase$** demonstration program.*

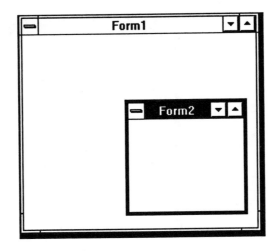

*Figure 13-137 An **Unload** demonstration program (1 of 2).*

Unload Statement

Summary:

Unload *object*

object   is a form or control.

Description:

The **Unload** statement removes a form or control from memory. The form or control to be removed is specified by *object*.

See Also:

Hide, Load, and **Show**

Example:

The below program demonstrates the **Unload** statement by unloading a form from memory. Listing 13-136 presents the code for **Form1's Form_Click** event. Figure 13-137 illustrates

Figure 13-138 An **Unload** *demonstration program (2 of 2).*

how the desktop would appear with **Form2** loaded, and Figure
13-138 how it would appear with **Form2** unloaded.

Listing 13-136:

```
Sub Form_Click ()
    Static Flag As Integer

    If Not Flag Then
        Form2.Show
    Else
        Unload Form2
    End If
    Flag = Not Flag

End Sub
```

Val Function

Summary:

Val(*expression*)

expression   is a string expression.

Description:

The **Val** function converts a string *expression* to a numeric value.

See Also:

Str$

Example:

The following program demonstrates the **Val** function by converting a few strings to numeric values. Listing 13-137 gives the code for the program's **Form_Click** event. Figure 13-139 shows how the program's window would appear after the program has been run.

Listing 13-137:

```
Sub Form_Click ()

    A$ = "33.45"
    Print Val(A$)
    Print Val("-567")

End Sub
```

*Figure 13-139 A **Val** demonstration program.*

Weekday Function

Summary:

Weekday(*serial*)

serial   is a serial number.

Description:

The **Weekday** function returns a numeric value that represents a serial number's day of the week. The serial number is specified by *serial* and the return value will be from 1 (Sunday) to 7 (Saturday).

See Also:

Day, Hour, Minute, Month, Now, Second, and **Year**

Example:

The program that follows demonstrates the **Weekday** function by displaying the current day of the week. Listing 13-138 presents the code for the program's **Form_Click** event. Figure 13-140 illustrates how the program's window would appear after the program has been run.

Listing 13-138:

```
Sub Form_Click ()

    Print "Today is ";
    Select Case Weekday(Now)
        Case 1
            Print "Sunday."
        Case 2
            Print "Monday."
        Case 3
            Print "Tuesday."
        Case 4
            Print "Wednesday."
        Case 5
            Print "Thursday."
```

```
        Case 6
            Print "Friday."
        Case 7
            Print "Saturday."
    End Select

End Sub
```

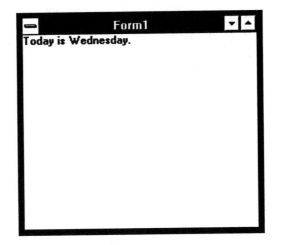

*Figure 13-140 A **Weekday** demonstration program.*

While...Wend Statements

Summary:

While *expression*

   .
   .
   .

Wend

expression   is a logical expression.

Description:

The **While...Wend** statements are an iterative control structure. Visual Basic will continuously loop between the **While** and **Wend** statements as long as *expression* is True. You should note

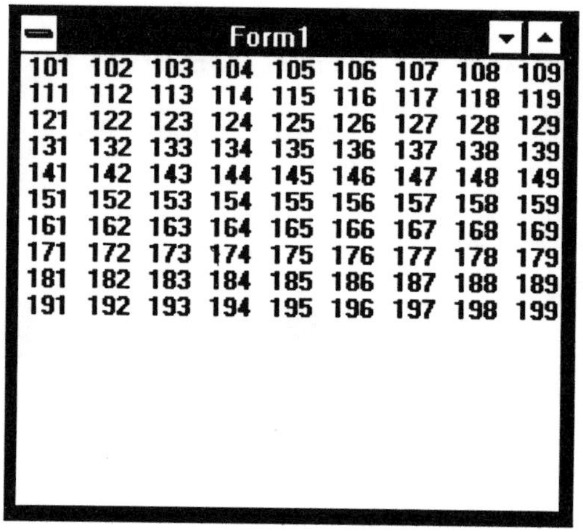

*Figure 13-141 A **While...Wend** demonstration program.*

that if *expression* is initially False, none of the statements be-tween the **While** and **Wend** statements will be executed.

See Also:

Do...Loop and **For..Next**

Example:

The program that appears below demonstrates the **While...Wend** statements by displaying all of the odd numbers between 100 and 200. Listing 13-139 presents the code for the program's **Form_Click** event. Figure 13-141 shows how the program's window would appear after the program has been run.

Listing 13-139:

```
Sub Form_Click ()
    Dim I As Integer

    I = 101
    While I < 200
        Print I;
```

```
        If I Mod 10 = 0 Then
                Print
        End If
        I = I + 1
    Wend

End Sub
```

Width # Statement

Summary:

Width #*filenumber, width*

filenumber   is the number of a previously opened file.

width   is the new line width.

Description:

The **Width #** statement sets the line width for a previously opened file. The file is specified by *filenumber* and the new line width is specified by *width*.

See Also:

Open and **Print #**

Example:

The below program shows how the **Width #** statement is used to set an output file's line width. Listing 13-140 presents the code for the program's **Form_Click** event. Figure 13-142 illustrates how the program's window would appear after the program has been run.

Listing 13-140:

```
Sub Form_Click ()
    Dim I As Integer

    Open "DEMOFILE.DAT" For Output As 1
    Width #1, 10
    For I = 1 To 10
        Print #1, "This is data item no."; I
```

```
        Next I
        Close
        Open "DEMOFILE.DAT" For Input As 1
        While Not EOF(1)
            Input #1, A$
            Print A$
        Wend
        Close

    End Sub
```

Figure 13-142 A **Width #** *demonstration program.*

Write # Statement

Summary:

```
Write #filenumber, [expression] [, expression]...
```

filenumber   is the number of a previously opened file.

expression   is either a numeric or a string expression.

Description:

The **Write #** statement writes one or more data items to a previously opened text file. The file is specified by *filenumber* and each data item is specified by an appropriate *expression*. If an *expression* is numeric, the **Write #** statement writes an ASCII representation of its value to the disk file. If an *expression* is a string, the **Write #** statement writes the string's contents surrounded by quotation marks to the disk file. Visual Basic separates multiple data items with a comma between each data item.

See Also:

Open and **Print #**

Example:

The following program demonstrates the **Write #** statement by writing data items to a disk file using both the **Write #** statement and the **Print #** statement. The differences between the two commands are clearly evident when the program reads the data items and displays them in the program's window. Listing 13-141 presents the code for the program's **Form_Click** event. Figure 13-143 illustrates how the program's window would appear after the program has been run.

Listing 13-141:

```
Sub Form_Click ()
    Dim I As Integer

    Open "DEMOFILE.DAT" For Output As 1
    I = 50
    A$ = "A String"
    Write #1, 90, 100, I, A$
    Print #1, 90, 100, I, A$
    Close
    Open "DEMOFILE.DAT" For Input As 1
    While Not EOF(1)
        Input #1, A$
        Print A$
    Wend
    Close

End Sub
```

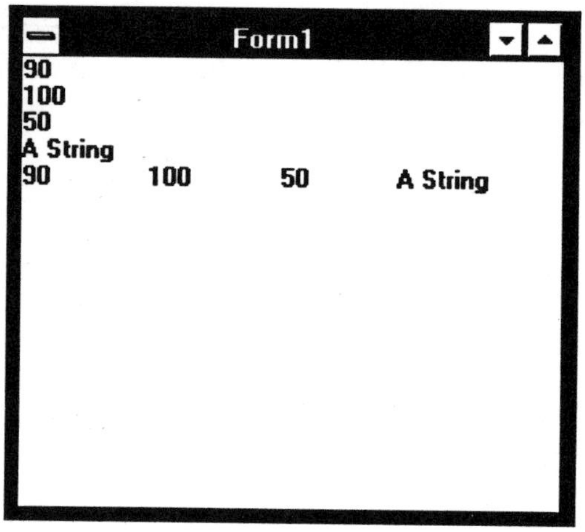

Figure 13-143 A **Write #** *demonstration program.*

Year Function

Summary:

Year(*serialnumber*)

serialnumber   is a numeric expression.

Description:

The **Year** function returns the year that is represented by a serial number. The serial number is specified by *serialnumber*.

See Also:

Day, Hour, Minute, Month, Now, Second, and **Weekday**

Example:

The program that follows demonstrates the **Year** function by displaying a serial number's year. Listing 13-142 presents the code for the program's **Form_Click** event. Figure 13-144

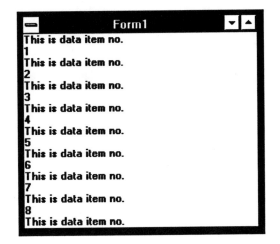

*Figure 13-144 A **Year** demonstration program.*

illustrates how the program's window would appear after the program has been run.

Listing 13-142:

```
Sub Form_Click ()

    D$ = Date$
    Serial# = DateValue(D$)
    Print D$
    Print Year(Serial#)

End Sub
```

Index

M

Max 368-369
MaxButton 369-371
Menu 226-228
Mid$ Function 581-583
Mid$ Statement 583-584
Min 371-372
MinButton 373-374
Minute 584-586
MkDir 586-587
Mod (Modulo) 50-52
Modules 12-13
Month 587-588
MouseDown 374-376
MouseMove 377-379
MousePointer 379-381
MouseUp 381-384
Move 384-386
MsgBox Function 588-591
MsgBox Statement 591-593
Multidimensional Arrays 160-166
MultiLine 386-387

N

Name 594-595
NewPage 387-388
Normal 388-390
Not (Bitwise Complement) 66-68
Not (Logical Complement) 54-55
Now 595-596

O

Oct$ 596-597
Octal Numbers 20
On Error 597-599
On...GoSub 599-601
On...GoTo 601-602
Open 199-201, 205-207, 602-605
Operator Precedence 87-91
Operators 7-8

Option Base 158, 605-606
Option Button 228-229
Or (Bitwise Or) 70-72
Or (Logical Or) 58-59

P

Page 390-391
Paint 391-392
Parent 393-394
Path 394-396
PathChange 396-397
Pattern 397-399
PatternChange 399-400
Picture 401-402
Picture Box 229-230
Point 402-403
Print # 201, 607-608
Print 403-405
Printer 231
PrintForm 405-406
Procedures 11, 131-153
Program Lines 7-9
PSet 406-407
Put 206-208, 608-610

Q

QBColor 610-611

R

Randomize 611-613
ReadOnly 408-409
Record Arrays 176-177
Records 171-178
Recursion 151-153
ReDim 24, 613-615
Refresh 409-411
Rem 10, 615-616
RemoveItem 411-413
Reset 616-617

The Program Disk

Because a Visual Basic program requires multiple source code files, this book's accompanying program disk has been set up in a rather unique manner. As with most program disks, each of the book's chapters has its own subdirectory. The following directory listing illustrates how the chapter subdirectories are set up on the program disk:

```
Volume in drive A has no label
Volume Serial Number is 0F2C-16CA
Directory of A:\


CHAP1        <DIR>      11-06-91    3:03p
CHAP2        <DIR>      11-06-91    3:06p
CHAP3        <DIR>      11-06-91    3:21p
CHAP4        <DIR>      11-06-91    3:41p
CHAP5        <DIR>      11-06-91    3:56p
CHAP6        <DIR>      11-06-91    3:57p
CHAP7        <DIR>      11-06-91    3:58p
CHAP8        <DIR>      11-06-91    3:59p
CHAP9        <DIR>      11-06-91    4:00p
CHAP10       <DIR>      11-06-91    4:01p
CHAP12       <DIR>      11-06-91    4:02p
CHAP13       <DIR>      11-06-91    4:24p
        12 file(s)            0 bytes
                         260096 bytes free
```

As it was stated above, a Visual Basic program requires multiple source code files. Accordingly, each of the book's programs has its own subdirectory in the appropriate chapter subdirectory. The following directory listing illustrates how the program subdirectories are set up for Chapter 7 in the **A:\CHAP7** subdirectory:

```
Volume in drive A has no label
Volume Serial Number is 0F2C-16CA
Directory of A:\CHAP7
```

```
   .                 <DIR>        11-06-91    3:58p
   ..                <DIR>        11-06-91    3:58p
P0701                <DIR>        11-06-91    3:58p
P0702                <DIR>        11-06-91    3:58p
P0703                <DIR>        11-06-91    3:58p
        5 file(s)                 0 bytes
                            260096 bytes free
```

The following directory listing illustrates how the source code files for Program 7-1 are set up in the **A:\CHAP7\P0701** subdirectory:

```
Volume in drive A has no label
Volume Serial Number is 0F2C-16CA
Directory of A:\CHAP7\P0701

   .                 <DIR>        11-06-91    3:58p
   ..                <DIR>        11-06-91    3:58p
P0701    MAK            35 09-25-91    3:31p
FORM1    FRM          1184 09-25-91    3:31p
        4 file(s)              1219 bytes
                            260096 bytes free
```

To use a program's source code files, you need to copy all of the files in the appropriate program's subdirectory to your Visual Basic subdirectory. For example, the source code files for Program 7-1 could be copied by simply entering **COPY A:\CHAP7\P0701*.* C:\VB**. You should note that this DOS command assumes that the program disk is in drive **A:** and your Visual Basic subdirectory is **C:\VB**.